SHAKESPEARE'S SONGS AND POEMS

SHAKESPEARE'S SONGS AND POEMS

Edward Hubler,
Princeton University

MCGRAW-HILL BOOK COMPANY, INC.
New York Toronto London 1959

30851

TO THOMAS MARC PARROTT

PREFACE

This book gathers together in one volume all of Shakespeare's poems, including those doubtfully attributed to him, all of his songs, and such passages from the plays as are of considerable interest and may be regarded as separable poems. "Songs" is taken to mean those verses which were sung in the original productions of the plays. The matter of which passages from the plays constitute separable poems is not so easily settled, and the final decisions are necessarily arbitrary. It is clear that Shakespeare considered passages in sonnet form as, in some sense, poems in themselves, and they are included in this volume. On the other hand, some passages in couplets are simply rhymed dialogue and, like some of the prologues, cannot be extracted from the plays unless they are accompanied by explanations longer than the passages themselves. It is difficult to know where scholarship ends and pedantry begins, but it is prudent for an editor to assume that when his notes are longer than the poems he is on the verge of pedantry. This is not without exception (what is to be done with a difficult couplet or quatrain?) but it serves as a rule of thumb for the exclusion or inclusion of doubtful passages. The other criterion is literary worth. An epilogue which is simply a request for applause in undistinguished verse has no place in a book such as this. Hitherto the poems in this book have been available in one volume only in complete editions of Shakespeare where the notes are necessarily at a minimum and the songs and poems from the plays have to be searched out by the reader.

This edition is intended for both the student of Shakespeare and the general reader. To that end the terminology of scholarship has been held to a minimum. The student of Shakespeare will doubtless know that the first collected edition of his plays was the Folio published in 1623, that the second was the Folio of 1632, and so on, but all readers may not have this information; the dates of all editions are therefore given each time they are referred to, as are the dates of persons mentioned in the notes. The titles of works of literature are given in full, and only the most commonplace of abbreviations are used. The spelling has been modernized, except where modernization would disturb a rhythm or alter the meaning of a word. The Elizabethans were not shackled by rules of spelling; what mattered was the sound of the word and the meaning. Within limits Shakespeare was free to spell as he would, and printers were often free to substitute their own spelling for that of the manuscript. The spelling of the original texts is useful only to scholars who would, in any case, consult the original texts or reproductions of them. The Elizabethan system of punctuation was rhetorical rather than grammatical as ours is, and it was often skillfully used to indicate rhythms and emphases, but it allowed freedoms confusing to modern readers, the interchangeability, for example, of the exclamation and the question mark. Nevertheless, the modern editor is not free to depart too far from it. The imposition of modern punctuation on Shakespeare will often break his rhythms and simplify his meanings. A phrase set off by commas in the original text, where modern punctuation would require a comma and a semicolon, was sometimes intended to glance both ways, to modify both what preceded and followed it, so that the use of modern punctuation would falsify the meaning. The punctuation in this volume therefore is a compromise between Shakespeare's usage and our own. It is loosely modern, permitting the rhythms and ambiguities Shakespeare intended.

In Shakespeare's original texts a letter is sometimes omitted and replaced by an apostrophe to indicate a rhythm. This usage has been followed and extended. For example, the "ed" ending of words was sometimes intended to be pronounced as a syllable, sometimes simply as the letter "d." When it was intended to be pronounced as a syllable, it has been spelled out; when it was not so intended, it has been printed " 'd." It is not possible to be altogether consistent in this. In some instances words ending in "ied" take on a strange resemblance to other words when the "e" is omitted. In such cases the "e" has been retained, but these instances are few in number.

Roughly half of Shakespeare's works were published in quarto texts during his lifetime, some of them more than once, and seven years after his death his plays were gathered together and published in the 1623 Folio by his friends and associates in the theatre John Heminge and Henry Condell. Othello was published in a quarto volume in 1622. These constitute the authoritative texts, although their degree of authority varies greatly. Whenever there was more than one authoritative text, the readings have been determined by a collation of them, and of course, by consulting the editions of previous editors. In a few instances I have taken readings from seventeenth-century texts later than the 1623 Folio. The 1632 Folio, for example, is a reprint of the 1623 Folio, and when it differs from it, it almost always differs for the worse, but when it corrects a manifest error, the correction, although without textual authority, has the merit of having been made by a man who was more than three centuries nearer Elizabethan English than a modern editor and an editor may prefer seventeenth-century guesses to his own. All variant readings are recorded in the notes except, in some instances, words which Shakespeare tended to use interchangeably, "then" and "than," for instance, and "band" and "bond." In almost all instances, readings in this text differing from those of other modern editions represent a return to the original texts. For example, editors have tended to hyphenate words unhyphenated in the original editions. Very often this makes no difference whatever, but when it does make a difference, the hyphens have been removed. In The Tempest, Act IV, scene 1, line 106, the 1623 Folio reading is "marriage, blessing." It has become customary to print this as "marriage-blessing," but this is a betrothal hymn and what is being besought for the young couple is both marriage and blessing and not, as the use of the hyphen makes the phrase mean, the blessing of marriage. The present editor has found it possible to resist the temptation to correct Shakespeare's grammar. The section of this book entitled "Songs and Poems from the Plays" reprints material *from twenty-six plays. All of them, except* The Two Noble Kinsmen, *were printed in the 1623 Folio. Some of them were printed in quarto. Each play presents a different textual problem. Variants between quarto and folio are indicated in the notes whenever authoritative texts differ.*

Since scholarly studies of Shakespeare are now in their third century, a responsible editor of Shakespeare will find that his book is to a considerable extent a work of assimilation, and he will bear the burden of a debt he cannot acknowledge, partly because he does not always remember from whom he has learned in years past, partly because publications about Shakespeare appear at the rate of a thousand a year and it is impossible to be aware of everything which has taken place. Emendations by other editors and sentences from other critics are acknowledged in the notes, but who is to know if a phrase on a well-worn subject is his own? But I must acknowledge a general indebtedness to the monumental variorum editions of Shakespeare's poems by the late Prof. Hyder Edward Rollins of Harvard University. There are other more particular debts which I happily acknowledge: to Profs. Moody Prior of Northwestern University and Peter Seng of Connecticut College who read the manuscript in part; to Prof. S. F. Johnson of Columbia University who read it in its entirety; and to my assistant at Princeton University, Mr. Joseph Kramer. But I have done the final revision of the manuscript myself, and the responsibility for the errors in it is mine. I want to thank my publishers for allowing me to put the notes with or opposite to the passages annotated, which is, I am convinced, where they belong, to be consulted or ignored as the reader sees fit.

The line references are to The Complete Works of Shakespeare, *one volume, edited by the late Prof. George Lyman Kittredge.*

There is an index of names, titles, and first lines of poems and well-known passages in the poems. When a title was too long to be repeated in the notes, the name of the author is given, and the reader may find the title under the author's name.

EDWARD HUBLER

INTRODUCTION

SHAKESPEARE WAS A BORN storyteller, and his career as artist began with storytelling for its own sake. His first attempt at tragedy, *Titus Andronicus,* remains a melodrama, a horror story, and so successful is it that at a recent production of the play at Stratford-on-Avon it was necessary to have a nurse in attendance to minister to the women who fainted as the play's horrors were revealed. His first comedy, *The Comedy of Errors,* is pure farce. Farce and melodrama are the same thing with different subject matter; the one entertains through laughable action, the other through horrible or pathetic action, but the primary purpose of each is entertainment. *The Comedy of Errors* is adapted from a Latin play by Plautus (254?–184 B.C.), the *Menaechmi,* a story of a pair of identical twins who are inevitably mistaken for each other. Shakespeare complicated the action of his play by having two pairs of identical twins, and he brought the whole thing off in fine style. The play is not an imitation of Plautus; it is a naturalization of him into the English comic tradition with a degree of gentleness and romance quite alien to the original. But apart from the play's display of narrative skill, there is no suggestion whatever of the excellences characteristic of Shakespeare's later work. There is nothing which invites reflection; there are no lines which sing or sear their way into the memory on first hearing; there are no brief passages which suddenly reveal character and illuminate whole areas of experience; there is no laying bare of the heart of man. All these and more were soon to be brought to Shakespeare's work, and the increasing frequency with which they appear is an index of his growth as artist. Although they are absent from his earliest plays, they emerge in the long narrative poems, *Venus and Adonis* and *The Rape of Lucrece,* and find their first striking expression in the sonnets, because, we may imagine, the young writer could more readily express his deepening understanding in the lyric than objectify it in the created characters of narrative and drama, and because the lyric is an invitation to song.

In the early poems we may observe the young Shakespeare finding himself both as craftsman and thinker, which are reciprocal processes. The effort to express experience involves a doubling back upon it so that it may be more fully understood, and the fuller understanding calls for techniques of expression of which the writer formerly had no need. As a craftsman Shakespeare is not so much the inventor as the adapter of forms. It was his way to use received forms, and then having mastered them, wrest them to his purposes, often transforming them into things hardly comparable with their originals. And this, too, is a kind of invention. In writing tragedy of the caliber of *Richard II* he had models to learn from, but he took the journey from *Richard II* to *King Lear* alone, finding the means by which the tragic vision was to be expressed as, except in the Athens of Aeschylus and Sophocles, it had never been expressed before. He was free to take usable stories and verse forms wherever he found them, but after a certain point, there was nothing available to him to suggest what he would do with them. There were no comedies, tragedies, or poems to stand with his best.

THE NEW POETRY

When Shakespeare came to London from Stratford-on-Avon, the new poetry, which was to crown the last decades of the sixteenth century and the beginning of the seventeenth, was already established. Its arrival had been announced in 1579 by the publication of Spenser's *The Shepherd's Calendar*. The book is now little read except by persons connected with English studies, but it was then recognized for what it was, the manifesto of a new movement in poetry. To the modern reader it seems pedantic in its assiduous revival of archaic English words and verse forms, its importation of continental forms, and its invention of new ones. Since much of what it offers was never assimilated into English poetry, it now has the appearance of technique for technique's sake; but what it offered was offered for use. Although Spenser himself did not achieve maturity as a poet until, a decade later, he invented yet another form, the Spenserian stanza, *The Shepherd's Calendar* was a timely demonstration of the possibilities of English poetry. There had been no English poet of the first order since Chaucer's death in 1400. He was succeeded by his imitators, now more remote than *The Shepherd's Calendar*, but in general in England the fifteenth was the century of the Latinists and the final flourishing of medieval romance in Sir Thomas Malory's *Morte d'Arthur*. It was also the century of ruinous civil wars which ended only in 1485 when Henry VII won the crown on Bosworth Field and became the first of the Tudor monarchs. Under the last of them, Elizabeth I (1533–1603), England was to gain peace and prosperity and, with the defeat of the Spanish Armada in 1588, emerge as a dominant European power. In the meantime there had been the invention of the printing press with its consequent spread of information and misinformation, the Protestant Reformation on the Continent, the break with the Church of Rome in England, the discovery of America, and the whole hodgepodge of things which, taken together, are known as the Renaissance. History is a continuum and much of the medieval survived under Elizabeth. It is easy to overemphasize both the medieval survivals and the newness of the age, as differing historians demonstrate; but for the reader of Shakespeare the inescapable fact is that he appears in his works as a man of the new era. His English history plays depict the death throes of the Middle Ages, which are already idealized in his sonnets. The cult of medievalism is not a romantic invention; the Middle Ages are already invested with an aura of romance in Shakespeare's works. The brunette beauty of the Dark Lady of the sonnets is contrasted with the true beauty of "the old age" when "black was not counted fair" (Sonnet 127), and the beauty of the young man of the sonnets is such as existed in the past. His cheek is

> *the map of days outworn*

When beauty liv'd and died as flowers do now (Sonnet 68), and he is himself the embodiment of medieval chivalry (see Sonnet 106). Shakespeare and his fellow writers were men of the new age, and they were aware of it. One of the functions of the new poetry was the celebration of the new age. Spenser dedicated *The Faerie Queene* to Queen Elizabeth "to live with the eternity of her fame."

The new poetry had been a long time in the making. Verse forms closely associated with it had been introduced into England early in the century. The Italian, or Petrarchan, sonnet, with its five rhymes and division into octave and sestet, had been imported by Sir Thomas Wyatt (1503?–1542). He varied the rhymes of the sestet, as the Italians had done before him, but he differed from them in preferring to end the sestet in a couplet. He maintained the rhyme scheme of the octave, *abbaabba*. His contemporary, Henry Howard, Earl of Surrey (1517?–1547), invented blank verse (unrhymed iambic pentameter) for his translation of two books of the *Aeneid,* and he varied Wyatt's sonnet by creating a form which placed the main pause after the twelfth line and employed seven rhymes:

abab cdcd efef gg. Because of Shakespeare's magnificent use of this form, it has come to be known as the Shakespearean sonnet. Although the indebtedness of English poetry to Wyatt and Surrey is both obvious and great, none of their surviving poems approaches the style of the first great poets writing toward the close of the century. The question here is not one of worth but of manner. The styles of Wyatt and Surrey approximate common speech; those of Spenser and Marlowe do not, and it was in a created language, anticipated in *The Shepherd's Calendar,* that Elizabethan poetry was to attain its first full flowering.

The creation of this language was a major and joint concern of the critics and poets of the Renaissance, and the creation of it in England repeated in essence what had taken place earlier in Italy and France. The first step was to win for the vernacular tongues an esteem comparable to that in which Latin was held. Although *The Divine Comedy* of Dante (1265–1321) and the sonnets of Petrarch (1304–1374) had been written in Italian, it was still held that Latin was a fitter medium for poetry. Petrarch himself regarded his Italian poems as minor accomplishments and assumed that his fame with posterity would rest upon his epic, *Africa,* and his other Latin works. But by the time of Ariosto (1474–1533) it was recognized that imitations of the Romans had been done as well as may be and that something other than re-creations of Virgilian epic and Ciceronian dialogue was in order. Ariosto wrote his *Orlando Furioso* in Italian, and the defense of the vernacular was formulated by Sperone Speroni in 1543 in his *Dialogue on Languages.* He argued that languages are created by people and can be *made* to express the conceptions of their creators, and that no language is in itself inferior to another language. In France this point of view was adopted by the poets who went by the corporate name of *La Pléiade,* of whom the chief were Ronsard (1524–1585) and du Bellay (1522–1560). The poets of the *Pléiade,* engaged in creating a new poetry for a new age, opposed themselves not so much to the Latinists as to the medievalism of their immediate predecessors. They set about to revivify French poetry by, among other things, the introduction of new words and verse forms. They reestablished the alexandrine, a six-foot line which in time became to French drama what blank verse became to the English. The sonnet was the rallying flag of their crusade. In his *Defense and Illustration of the French Language,* du Bellay repeated the arguments of Speroni and added the argument from nationalism —the nation needed a literature capable of rivaling that of other times and nations. In all the arts of the Renaissance there is something born of a boundless vigor which is not so much arrogance as a democratic assumption of equality with the best, of the felt right to look antiquity or any modern nation in the eye. In one place or another and in one way or another the assumption was justified; in the late sixteenth century in England it was justified in music and poetry.

The English poets and theoreticians of the sixteenth century did not find it necessary to oppose the medieval as the French had had to. Chaucer had been long dead, and the secret of his versification had been lost through the evolution of the language from what is now known as Middle English to modern. The greatness of Chaucer's poetry was recognized, but to the sixteenth century it had the remote beauty of the antique which constituted no threat to modernity. Spenser was free to use his medieval predecessors as he could. As E. K. put it in his introductory letter to *The Shepherd's Calendar,* Spenser had labored "to restore, as to their rightful heritage, such good and natural English words, as have been long time out of use, and almost clean disherited." It was this impoverishment of the language from its relative disuse in poetry which was the cause that "our mother tongue, which truly of itself is both full enough for prose, and stately enough for verse, hath long time been counted most bare and barren of both," and he regrets that Spenser's immediate predecessors did not "garnish and beautify it." E. K. is a partisan witness. There is more to be said for Spenser's predecessors than he suggests, or than there is space for in an introduction such as this; but it remains a truth of literary history that no sixteenth-century poet before Spenser garnished and beautified the language as he did, and such bits of his early work as survive indicate a precocious concern with the achievement of what was to be the style of *The Faerie Queene.* He had no doubt been nurtured on a concern for the English language. In England du Bellay's arguments for the use and augmentation of the mother tongue are found in many places, among them the writings of Richard Mulcaster (1530?–1611), who was the headmaster of the Merchant Taylors' school when Spenser was a scholar there. The schoolboy of the sixteenth century studied Latin, but Mulcaster argues in *The First Part of the Elementary* that the scholar should also be instructed in the reading, writing, and grammar of his mother tongue. He asserts that no language is superior to another except by the industry of the speaker who endeavors to "garnish it with eloquence, and enrich it with learning." "I love Rome," he wrote, "but London better, I favor Italy, but England more, I honor the Latin, but I worship the English." The *Elementary* was not published until 1582, long after Spenser had ceased to be Mulcaster's pupil, but who can doubt that his students were inculcated with his principles. The *Elementary* sets forth his considered opinions and matured convictions, and good schoolmasters do not rush into print with their latest notions. The introduction to "October" in *The Shepherd's Calendar* tells us that Spenser held that poetry was "a divine gift and heavenly instinct, not to be gotten by labour and learning, but adorned with both. . . ." For in the Renaissance the great poet was necessarily a learned man, and, in fact, the best poets have always been bookmen. "No man was ever yet a great poet," said Coleridge, "without being at the same time a profound philosopher. For poetry is the blossom and the fragrance of all human knowledge, human thoughts, human passions, emotions, language." Spenser's gift of poetry did not fully assimilate his learning and his labors in craftsmanship until the writing of *The Faerie Queene,* the first three books of which were published in 1590.

In the meantime the new poetry had found its way into the theater, most notably through the agency of Christopher Marlowe (1564–1593), who gave to blank verse an elevation it had not known before. He is one of a group of dramatists known as the University Wits because, profiting from their studies at the universities, they were aware of other literatures and the need for a literate theater. Marlowe's first play, *Tamburlaine,* is a conscious introduction of the new poetry into the drama. It opens with an explicit renunciation of the native English meters which had dominated dramatic writing:

> *From jigging veins of rhyming mother wits,*
> *And such conceits as clownage keeps in pay,*
> *We'll lead you to the stately tents of war,*
> *Where you shall hear the Scythian Tamburlaine,*
> *Threat'ning the world with high astounding terms. . . .*

He keeps his promise. The poetry is characterized by its elevation, its full tones, its removal from familiar speech. It is orotund without pomposity, even when it is most highly patterned, as in,

> *To ride in triumph through Persepolis!*
> *Is it not passing brave to be a king,*
> *Usumcasane and Theridimas,*
> *Is it not passing brave to be a king,*
> *And ride in triumph through Persepolis?*

This is as artfully constructed as music. The fifth line repeats the first, the fourth the second, and the two groupings are separated by a line of mouth-filling names. Yet for all its artifice, it is dramatic dialogue. It is, to borrow Cocteau's phrase, not poetry in the theater but poetry *of* the theater. The poetry is not prose statement versified, not decoration, as in the Victorian imitations of Shakespeare. The expression is appropriate, and seemingly natural, to the content. And it is a far cry from the verse of Thomas Preston's *Cambises,* a play of the late midcentury:

I feel myself a-dying now; of life bereft am I;
And death hath caught me with his dart; for want of blood I spy.
Thus, gasping, here on ground I lie; for nothing I do care.
A just reward for my misdeeds my death doth plain declare.

These verses were known as fourteeners, and were one of the "jigging veins" Marlowe renounced.

In nondramatic poetry the triumph of the new poetry over the old may be seen in Spenser's version of the Venus and Adonis story. Like Shakespeare's telling of it, it is based on part on Ovid's *Metamorphoses,* a book translated into English by Arthur Golding in 1565–1567. Golding's verses have no virtue whatever except a certain narrative pace, and it is this, perhaps, which won the book its many readers. In it the story of the wooing of a reluctant male by an ardent woman is in part as follows:

When at last the Nymph desirde most instantly but this,
As to his sister brotherly to give hir there a kisse,
And therewithall was clasping him about his Ivorie necke:
Leave off (quoth he) or I am gone, and leeve thee at a becke
With all thy trickes. Then Salmacis began to be afraide,
And to your pleasure leave I free this place my friend she sayde.
With that she turnes hir backe as though she would have gone
*   hir way:*
But evermore she looketh backe, and (closely as she may)
She hides hir in a bushie queach, where kneeling on hir knee

She always hath hır eye on him. He as a child and free,
And thinking not that any wight had watched what he did,
Romes up and downe the pleasant mede; and by and by amid
The flattring waves he dippes his feete, no more but first the sole
And to the ancles afterward both feete he plungeth whole.
And for to make the matter short, he tooke such great delight
In cooleness of the pleasant spring, that straight he stripped quight
His garments from his tender skin. When Salmacis behilde
His naked beautie, such strong pangs so ardently her hilde,
That utterly she was astraught.

Book IV, lines 411-429

And so on. In Spenser this becomes:

> *Then with what sleights and sweet allurements she*
> *Entyst the Boy, as well that art she knew,*
> *And wooed him her paramoure to bee,*
> *Now making girlands of each flowre that grew,*
> *Now leading him into a secret shade*
> *From his Beauperes, and from bright heavens vew,*
> *Where him to sleepe she gently would persuade,*
> *Or bathe him in a fountain by some covert glade:*
>
> *And whilst he slept she over him would spred*
> *Her mantle, colour'd like the starry skyes,*
> *And her soft arm lay underneath his hed,*
> *And with ambrosiall kisses bathe his eyes;*
> *And whilst he bath'd with her two crafty spyes*
> *She secretly would search each dainty lim,*
> *And throw into the well sweet Rosemaryes,*
> *And fragrant violets, and Paunces trim;*
> *And ever with sweet Nectar did she sprinkle him.*

The Faerie Queene, Book III, Canto 1, stanzas 35-36

This is the new poetry of the late sixteenth century. It represents a forsaking of much that was popular in the poetry of the time and an enrichment of what was excellent. The enrichment involved some loss, for poetry of this sort necessarily departs from the colloquial excellence of Wyatt, Surrey, and many poets of the midcentury. No one could mistake the new poetry for speech. It is characterized by its purged vocabulary, its word patterns and word play, its richness and melody. It is the school of poetry in which Shakespeare learned to write, and it is represented at its best in, for example, Sonnets 5, 29, 33, and 73. In Shakespeare we may also find demonstrations of the weaknesses inherent in the new style. When he wrote badly as a young man it was chiefly because he indulged his interest in the sound of words, as in the over-heavy alliteration of "And with old woes new wail my dear time's waste" (Sonnet 30); or because his love of word play was greater than his judgment, as in "For as you were when first your eye I eyed," (Sonnet 104); or because his interest in word patterns was such that it sometimes obscured or obliterated the sense, as in "She clepes him king of graves, and grave for kings," (*Venus and Adonis,* line 995). In contrast to this, the bad writing of his later works in general results from his making a phrase carry more meaning than it will bear, as in Edgar's "He childed as I father'd," which means "Lear was as a child to his daughters, and my father was as a child to me." But since he was a poet, he was interested in the sound and arrangement of words. He doubtless read Spenser, although it is not recorded that he did; nor is it recorded that he read Marlowe, but this second is a matter for which documentation is not necessary. His early dramatic verse, the beginning, for instance, of *Richard III,* sounds like Marlowe as the early Beethoven sounds like Haydn, and for the same reasons. The work of all artists—writers, composers, workers in the plastic arts—resembles that of the artists whose work aroused their interest in art. It could not be otherwise, for why should a young man want to become an artist at all if he did not come across some art congenial to his latent talent which he wishes to imitate and excel? "Influence," said Andre

Gide, "creates nothing, it awakens something." Shakespeare as artist was awakened by the new poetry and by Marlowe in particular.

A single style, however, was inadequate to the expression of Shakespeare's genius, and even as he was mastering the new style he was reaching out for others. In time he learned to write with both simplicity and power, using ordinary words in their prose order, as in Antony's ". . . the long day's task is done/ And we must sleep" (*Antony and Cleopatra,* Act IV, scene 14, lines 35-36). This was emergent in his early poetry. In Sonnet 8 in the midst of a patterned passage, we come across the line, "If the true concord of well-tuned sounds. . . ." This and "Time's thievish progress to eternity" (Sonnet 77) and "Give not a windy night a rainy morrow" (Sonnet 90) are promises of things to come. He learned to write with a bareness of diction commonly called "the neutral style," as in Desdemona's speech beginning "My mother had a maid call'd Barbara . . ." (*Othello,* Act IV, scene 3, line 26); and this, too, the young Shakespeare was working toward, as the couplet to Sonnet 74 demonstrates. He learned to make poetry out of ugliness, as in Hamlet's, "Nay, but to live/ In the rank sweat of an enseamed bed,/ Stew'd in corruption . . ." (*Hamlet,* Act III, scene 4, lines 90-92) where the culinary image of the last phrase is in itself, surely, as repulsive as anything one could imagine; yet it is poetry, for poetry is a transmutation of subject matter, and there is no such thing as either a poetic language or a poetic subject. Any vocabulary or any subject is appropriate to poetry. There is nothing, nothing whatever, to limit the range of a poet except the scope of his talent. The poetic transmutation of ugliness is also emergent in the early Shakespeare, as in the passage on the worms in Sonnet 146. Although in his progress as poet Shakespeare mastered new styles, he did not discard his earlier achievements. See, for instance, his uses of the new poetry in his passages on the lark in *Venus and Adonis,* lines 853-858; Sonnet 29, lines 10-12; *Cymbeline,* Act II, scene 3, lines 21-30 (page 265 in this book). And by the close of his career he could confer upon the apparent effortlessness of the neutral style as great a degree of lyricism as, earlier, he had achieved by elaborate means:

> What you do
> Still betters what is done. When you speak, sweet,
> I'd have you do it ever; when you sing,
> I'd have you buy and sell so, so give alms,
> Pray so; and for the ord'ring your affairs,
> To sing them too. When you do dance, I wish you
> A wave o' th' sea, that you might ever do
> Nothing but that; move, still, still so,
> And own no other function. Each your doing,
> So singular in each particular,
> Crowns what you are doing in the present deeds,
> That all your acts are queens.
>
> The Winter's Tale, Act IV, scene 4, lines 135-146

By 1590, when Spenser published the first three books of *The Faerie Queene,* the new poetry had come fully into its own in both dramatic and nondramatic verse. At that time Spenser was approximately thirty-eight years old and was to repeat but not surpass his achievement as a poet; Marlowe and Shakespeare, exact contemporaries, were twenty-six; Ben Jonson and John Donne were eighteen. Within a decade Jonson was to become the master of the neutral style and Donne of the metaphysical. Spenser, Jonson, and Donne are all poets' poets, each having fathered races of poets writing in styles approximating their originals; but Shakespeare is not to be associated with any one style. He contains them all.

In the summer of 1592 Robert Greene, one of the University Wits, wrote in his *Groatsworth of Wit* of a dramatist whom he regarded as an interloper presuming to compete with his betters. He called the new dramatist "an upstart crow, beautified with our feathers, that . . . supposes he is as well able to bombast out a blank verse as the best of you; and being an absolute *Johannes fac totum,* is in his own conceit the only Shake-scene in a country." The reference is to Shakespeare, although he is not specifically named. Greene died before the end of the year, and after his death his friend and editor, Henry Chettle, published an apology in which he speaks of "the only Shake-scene" as "excellent in the quality he professes," and he records that "divers of worship have reported his uprightness of dealing, which argues his honesty, and his facetious grace in writing that approves his art." All this indicates that Shakespeare was beginning to be known as a theatrical writer, but such recognition did not carry with it recognition as a man of letters, for although the theater was popular, it was not held in high esteem. The bad reputation of the theater was in part an inheritance from the early Christian era. The Church Fathers were clear in their denunciation of the stage. It bred frivolity, concupiscence, obscenity, cruelty, idolatry, impiety, and scandal. Although it was greatly modified, this attitude had not disappeared by Shakespeare's time, and in his London the residuum of it was augmented by the Puritans who disapproved of the theater on religious grounds and by the association of the theater with gaming and prostitution. The law classified actors with "rogues and vagabonds." The reputation of the theater was shortly to improve, largely through the distinction bestowed on it by Shakespeare and his fellow dramatists, but in 1593 the artistic achievement of the theater was not yet impressive enough, nor of sufficiently long standing, to redeem its bad name. So it happened that Shakespeare's life as actor and dramatist was not an altogether satisfying one to a young man of sensitivity who had been brought up in a reputable middle-class society. He recorded his mixed feelings toward his impression in his sonnets, notably Sonnets 29, 110, and 111. To gain status and win a reputation as a writer, it was necessary for him to turn to means other than the theater. Early in 1593 Shakespeare took the first step toward establishing himself as a poet.

Venus and Adonis was entered for copyright at Stationers' Hall on April 18, 1593, by Richard Field and was printed at his printing house later that year. The best evidence indicates that it was written shortly before it was copyrighted during an interval of leisure afforded Shakespeare by the closing of the theaters on account of the plague. Richard Field had been born in Stratford-on-Avon in 1561, apprenticed to a printer at the age of eighteen, and was master of his own printing house in London by 1588. He became a prominent member of the Stationers' Company. The accuracy with which the poem is printed indicates that Shakespeare provided him with a carefully prepared manuscript and, in all probability, saw the poem through the press. Field was Shakespeare's first printer, and it is reasonable to suppose that Shakespeare, less than three years his junior, had known him in Stratford, knew the excellence of his printing house (there was none better in London at the time), and took the poem to Field so that it might have the printing he desired for it. He took other means to launch his career as poet as auspiciously as possible. He dedicated the volume "To the Right Honourable Henrie Wriothesley, Earle of Shouthampton, and Baron of Titchfield," one of the most brilliant young noblemen at Elizabeth's court. Henry Wriothesley (1573–1624), third Earl of Southampton, had succeeded to his title at the age of eight, and, being in his minority, had become a royal ward. He took his M.A. at St. John's College, Cambridge, in 1589, and not long afterward was presented at court. The queen paid him kind attention, and the Earl of Essex, then her favorite, took a brotherly interest in him. Before he was twenty he was known as the handsomest and most accomplished of the young lords who frequented the royal presence, and as a patron of poets. There is a plausible tradition that he became Shakespeare's patron. The poem achieved an immediate and prolonged success. Nine editions of it were printed during Shakespeare's lifetime. Only one edition, the 1593 Quarto, was printed from the author's manuscript, and it is therefore the edition of greatest textual authority.

The story of Venus and Adonis had been alluded to or told briefly many times in English poetry from Chaucer onward, but Shakespeare was probably the first to treat the subject as a separate poem. His story derives ultimately from two stories in the *Metamorphoses* of Ovid (43 B.C.– A.D. 18?), the stories of Salmacis and Hermaphroditus (Book IV, lines 285-388) and Venus and Adonis (Book X, lines 519-739). Each is the story of a reluctant male pursued by an amorous female. Shakespeare was no doubt drawn to these stories because of his interest in Ovid, one of his favorite authors, and because at the time there was a vogue for long erotic poems in approximations of the Ovidian manner. Of these stories Marlowe's unfinished *Hero and Leander* was by far the best. Marlowe completed only two sestiads of his poem, which was later finished by George Chapman, but in a manner so different from Marlowe's that when one speaks of *Hero and Leander* one means Marlowe's sestiads.

Marlowe was supremely qualified for this undertaking, and his poem is the most nearly perfect thing he ever wrote. The Ovidian tradition is essentially literary, and Marlowe was at home in it. In his poem there is a perfect fusion of matter and manner which removes the story from the world of experience. He chose as his medium heroic couplets, mostly end-stopped. The images are artificial.

Hero's eyes are "translucent cisterns" and her tears are "liquid pearl"; this is appropriate to a poem where all is artifice. The lovers are not young people in love; their passion is all we know of them. Where there is no characterization, inconsistency does not matter. Leander at one point discourses learnedly on love and at another is innocent of the most elementary knowledge. The innocence advances the story and is the occasion of wit, and so it serves its turn. All sentiment is eschewed. There is nothing in the poem for the reader to share, since there is nothing human in it but passion, and the elaborated sensuality is kept in bounds by wit and the artifice of verse. All moral considerations of the story are irrelevant to it. It is a hard and brilliant object of pagan contemplation. Marlowe caught the Ovidian manner as it has seldom been caught in English poetry. He is indebted to his source for only the barest outline of the story; the rest is all original.

Born in the same year as Marlowe, Shakespeare matured as artist more slowly than he, and in 1593, the year of Marlowe's death, was still not craftsman enough for an Ovidian poem. In any case, this was not the direction his talent was to take. The Latin influence on him was always one of matter rather than manner.

In Ovid's story Hermaphroditus was the son of Hermes and Aphrodite who left his native mountains at fifteen to wander in unknown lands. In time he came to a clear pool where dwelt the nymph Salmacis who grew enamored of him. When she declared her love, he rebuffed her. (See the passage from Golding, page xix.) She pretended to accept his refusal but was unable to restrain her desire when she saw him bathing in the pool, and, casting off her clothes, she dived in after him, fondled and embraced him and stole reluctant kisses; but he was not to be won. She cried out to the gods asking never to be separated from him, and they were united in one being which seemed to be neither man nor woman and yet was both. The story in Ovid is brief and Shakespeare follows it up to the transformation, although there is no bathing episode. Ovid calls Hermaphroditus a boy, and Shakespeare emphasizes Adonis's youth.

In Ovid's story of Venus and Adonis, Adonis was a man. Venus, enamored of him, forsook the skies, accompanied him when he hunted, and warned him against hunting other than timorous animals such as lions and boars. Then, drawing him into a grassy shade, she laid her head on his breast, and, kissing him, told him the story of Atalanta and Hippomenes and how they were at last changed into a lioness and a lion. Venus's story takes up the greater part of the Venus and Adonis episode and was told to impress Adonis with the ferocity of beasts. Then she departed through the air, drawn by her team of swans. Adonis, ignoring her advice, followed his hounds to the hunt and was slain by a boar. Venus, seeing his death from the skies, returned, and, mourning for him, sprinkled his shed blood with nectar, and from his blood a blood-red flower sprang.

Such, in brief compass, are the events of the stories as Ovid told them. Apart from Venus's telling of the story of Hippomenes and Atalanta, of which Shakespeare made no use, they take up 368 lines. There is a minimum of characterization, the attributes of Ovid's personages being known. The backgrounds are no more than indicated. The pool in which Hermaphroditus bathes is crystal clear and bordered with fresh grass and green herbage. The stags in the Venus and Adonis story have high-branching horns, and the does are timid. The hounds and hares are simply named and have no attributes except those with which the reader endows them. There is no invitation to reflect on moral ideas. No sentiments are expressed. There is aloofness, urbanity, and the concision of the consummate teller of tales.

In Shakespeare, as Coleridge remarked, we "seem to be told nothing but to see and hear everything." This is the tale telling of a dramatist. The story is told in the present tense, as though it were happening for the first time, and it begins without preamble with the motivating event—Venus's invitation to love. In Ovid, Venus is the goddess of love exercising her function without praise or blame; in Shakespeare, her arguments are both set forth and rejected in contexts of moral ideas. The characterizations are solid, and the physical attributes of both personages are insisted upon. The animals and the countryside are those Shakespeare knew as a boy in Warwickshire. Although it is artful, the poem does not transport the reader into a world of artifice. It is of a piece with his other works, and reading it with them in mind, we see that it represents an advance along the road he was to take. He had begun his career with story for story's sake, and although he never lost his interest in action and never condescended to it, his progress to a large extent lay in his giving the stories values beyond and in addition to their values as action. The ways of doing this are infinite in number, and one of them is to adduce reasons for a proposed action.

The arguments which Venus uses in her pursuit of Adonis embody two ideas to which Shakespeare returned insistently throughout his works. One of them is the idea embodied in the parable of the talents (Matthew 25: 14-30): man is the steward and not the owner of his possessions and attributes; they were given him to use, and he may depend upon it, he will be called to an accounting. The other is the idea of plenitude, the belief in the potential goodness of all created things. The ideas, as here, often stand together in a reciprocal relationship. Venus argues that Adonis must not waste himself upon himself and that procreation is his duty, and her final comment on Adonis is "To grow unto himself was his desire" (line 1180). The modern reader may suppose that an appeal to the ideas of stewardship and plenitude is inappropriate to an invitation to love, but an Elizabethan doubtless would not have thought so. However this may be, the appeal is an instance of Shakespeare's endowing his stories with the thought characteristic of him. At one point (lines 712-713) Shakespeare seems to sense a certain unseemliness in Venus's penchant for discourse (the queen of love should command by her powers), and he has her say,

> *Unlike myself thou hear'st me moralize,*
> *Applying this to that, and so to so. . . .*

But she does not desist.

The rejection of Venus's advances is also stated in terms characteristic of Shakespeare—the distinction between love and lust. In all of Shakespeare's works there is no Platonic love relationship between man and woman. The attraction between them may be purely physical, in which case it is sooner or later recognized for what it is and labeled lust; but if to the basic physical relationship there is added, at the least, a mutual respect and liking, he is content to call it love, which may range from this to the idealized romantic passion of Romeo and Juliet. Adonis replies to Venus's arguments with the characteristic distinction between love and lust, as in lines 787-804. Her desire for him, he says, is simply lust. There is no suggestion of this in *Hero and Leander*. Shakespeare is at once a profoundly erotic and profoundly moral writer. He is not a moralist; he does not moralize, and no great poet ever observed life more dispassionately than he. But he does not observe actions in isolation. He, too, applies this to that and so to so. In his works energy and intellect stand in perilous balance, and the debate between them never ends, though energy is sometimes in better voice. No matter how dark his view of life, as in the greatest tragedies, he is never cynical; his energy keeps him sweet. The debate, absent from his earliest works, emerges in *Venus and Adonis*.

The debate is not perfectly embodied in the poem. Venus sometimes appears a little ludicrous, as in her falling down, and a male's insistent defense of his own chastity is apt at times to raise a smile. There is no reason why there should not be a comic Venus or why the presentation of Adonis should be consistently solemn. The difficulty is that, although there is wit in the poem, the reader is not always aware of the degree to which it was intended. Shakespeare was later to become the master of the blending of the comic and the serious. The alternation of them had been native to the English drama and had flourished in it from the beginning, but it remained for Shakespeare to make each a part of the other, to show the laughable aspects of the solemn and the solemn aspects of the laughable, and each is made to reinforce the other without the slightest diminution of either. The supreme instance is *Antony and Cleopatra*. But there is another aspect of his genius which is in full flower in this poem—his talent for the precise and significant observation of nature:

> Or as the snail, whose tender horns being hit,
> Shrinks backward in his shelly cave with pain,
> And there all smooth'red up in shade doth sit,
> Long after fearing to creep forth again. . . .

The snail has often been the emblem of slowness, but Shakespeare notices its antennae, so frail and seemingly gelatinous that they hardly appear to be substantial at all, and for him it becomes the image of sensitivity. He describes the movement of the hare as it flees the hounds as only an observant hunter could, and it becomes the image of misery. He had the rare ability to see what he looked at. There is little value in precise description for its own sake, but observation such as this (and the poem abounds in it) is not mere decoration. Passages like that on the lark bring a morning loveliness to the poem which no poet catches as well as Shakespeare. The description of Adonis's horse and its episode with the "breeding Gennet" convey a sense of nature's energy. And together they create an awareness of the kinship of nature and man. Venus was, of course, a goddess, and Adonis, in Greek and older mythologies, was a vegetation god, but in Shakespeare's poem they are legend naturalized into the countryside he first knew as a boy and endowed with the moral sensibility which was to become so large an element of his work. And although the created world of the poem is far from being one of artifice, it is all kept at a certain distance through wit, intellection, and the poet's mastery of the new poetry. It is, apart from Spenser, the best narrative poem of the century.

THE RAPE OF LUCRECE

The Rape of Lucrece, presumably Shakespeare's original title, was entered for copyright in the hand of the clerk at Stationers' Hall on May 9, 1594, as "a booke intituled the Ravyshement of Lucrece." It was printed in the same year by Richard Field for John Harrison. The title on the title page is *Lucrece,* but the heading at the beginning of the poem and on every page thereafter is "The Rape of Lucrece," which, with the printing of the sixth edition (1616), became the title again. The volume, like *Venus and Adonis,* is dedicated "To the Right Honourable, Henry Wriothesley, Earle of Southampton, and Baron of Titchfield." The dedication is signed "William Shakespeare." The poet's name does not appear on the title page. In the dedication to *Venus and Adonis,* published 1593, Shakespeare promises Southampton that ". . . if your Honour seem but pleased, I . . . vow to take advantage of all idle hours, till I have honoured you with some graver labour." *The Rape of Lucrece* is assuredly the graver labour. It was therefore written late in 1593 or early in 1594. The accuracy of the 1594 Quarto indicates that it was printed from Shakespeare's manuscript and that Shakespeare read the proofs. The sixth edition was published in the year of

tion. We feel, in Milton's words at the close of *Samson Agonistes*, that

> Nothing is here for tears, nothing to wail
> Or knock the breast, no weakness, no contempt,
> Dispraise or blame, nothing but well and fair,
> And what may quiet us in a death so noble.

There is nothing of this in *Richard III*. In *Richard II* and *Romeo and Juliet* the dilemma depends in part on the character of the heroes and is therefore not absolute, and the purgation exists on a lesser scale. Neither is fully realized in the plays until *Hamlet*. They are fully realized and explicit in *Othello*. The conception of them is explicit in *The Rape of Lucrece*.

The conditions imposed upon Lucrece by Tarquin constitute a dilemma. She must either submit to his advances or suffer death at his hands, but, given her view of honor, the choice offered her is not one of life or death. If she submits, she will lose her reputation, subject her husband to scorn, and perhaps bear Tarquin's child. If she resists, he will violate and murder her; then, after slaying some "rascal groom," he will bear her body to the groom's bed and swear that he killed them both because he had taken them in adultery. In either case she will be dishonored and her husband made ridiculous. The view of honor both implicit and explicit here is the view found throughout Shakespeare's later works, and it finds its first full statement in *Lucrece*. The works assume the inestimable value of reputation, which is not to be thought of as impersonal, like an attitude of the public expressed through a poll or some other indication of popularity. Shakespeare sometimes identifies reputation with honor, and he often uses the word to indicate a status with a limited group of men. In the view disclosed by Shakespeare's works a virtue cannot be said to exist until it is expressed in action, and the recognition of it on the part of a man's peers is his assurance of the reality of the virtue. And conversely, the absence of good reputation, and therefore the absence of the assurance of virtue, is associated with despair. Macbeth in his desolation knew that he "must not look to have" "honour, love, obedience, troops of friends"; and with that realization came another: "I have liv'd long enough."

The concern for honor and reputation is a basic value in Shakespeare's works. Othello, about to reassert his honor at the close of the play, asks to be spoken of "as I am," knowing that the bravery of what he is about to do will reestablish his good name. Hamlet, having at last carried out the obligation laid upon him, asks Horatio to tell his story. Antony in his failure asks to be remembered as he had been. Lucrece's concern for her good name is Shakespeare's first full statement of this attitude, and it motivates her resolve to die. Events have closed in on her, but she can rise above her fate by accepting it and asserting the greater values of the spirit:

> *For me, I am the mistress of my fate,*
> *And with my trespass never will dispense,*
> *Till life to death acquit my forc'd offence.*

Livy and Ovid were interested in the historical and political aspects of the story, but Shakespeare dispenses with them, relegating them to the argument where they are dealt with briefly. To the events of the story he devotes less than a third of the lines, and to the rape itself less than two stanzas. He concentrates on the inwardness of the story, the causes, meanings, and results of the action. He begins the story in the middle of things with Tarquin's approach to Collatine's house. Tarquin is received, entertained, and by line 120 he has gone to his bed; and then begins his debate on the nature and consequences of his proposed action. It continues until he opens the door to Lucrece's room (line 358). Brutus, in *Julius Caesar,* alone

on the night before the assassination, broods on what he
is about to do (Act II, scene 1, lines 63-69):

> Between the acting of a dreadful thing
> And the first motion, all the interim is
> Like a phantasma, or a hideous dream:
> The genius and the mortal instruments
> Are then in council; and the state of a man,
> Like to a little kingdom, suffers then
> The nature of an insurrection.

Granville-Barker has called these lines a recipe for tragedy, for the life of a tragedy lies not in the horror with
which a character is confronted but in the revelation of
the perturbation of soul as he proceeds from the "first
motion" towards the acting of a dreadful thing to the doing
of it. This revelation is perfectly dramatized in *Hamlet* and
Macbeth, and the depiction of it is the primary concern in
The Rape of Lucrece. There is first the insurrection in
Tarquin as, rejecting all other considerations, he makes
love and fortune his gods, and, backing his will with resolution, proceeds to the rape; and there is then the insurrection in Lucrece, which extends through half the poem
and culminates in her death. In her grief she raises questions which, like the speculations in *Hamlet,* generalize
the action. She asks how such injustice as has been visited
upon her can exist. She speculates on the nature of evil.
She does not speak for herself alone. Her suffering is an
instance of the suffering of mankind. The generalization
of the action is furthered in the passage on the painting
of the destruction of Troy, too often taken to be a digression used to mark the passage of time between the departure of the messenger and the return of Collatine. This is
a function which, of course, the passage serves, but its
primary purpose is that of the subplot in *King Lear.* It
repeats the main action in terms of another action, showing

the desolation wrought by the indulgence of lust, and its intention is to make Lucrece a type of national heroine, as Brutus in *Julius Caesar* is made a type of liberator. All this is imperfectly done. Much of it, like the discussion of Night, Time, and Opportunity, remains abstract, partially embodied in the action; but it is nonetheless Shakespeare's first statement of the conception of tragedy he was later to realize in *Hamlet* and *Othello,* and, so considered, the poem gains in dignity and power.

THE SONNETS

Shake-speares Sonnets, a quarto volume, was printed at London "By G. Eld for T. T. ." in 1609. In the entry of the book in the Stationers' Register, May 20, 1609, T. T. is identified as Thomas Thorpe. The scholarly consensus is that Thorpe gathered the contents of the book from manuscripts available to him and published them without Shakespeare's knowledge. The printed text is not a very good one, although it seems to rest upon an authoritative manuscript. There are enough misprints in it to make it clear that Shakespeare did not see it through the press. The sonnets end on K^1 recto and are followed by the word "Finis" in large type. At the top of the next page appears the heading, "A Louers complaint, By William Shakespeare." The poem follows. It is not a distinguished poem, and scholars have sometimes wished to deny Shakespeare's authorship of it; but while Thorpe's ascription of the poem to Shakespeare is no more conclusive than William Jaggard's ascription to him of all the poems in *The Passionate Pilgrim* (see page xliv), at least one of which is known not to be his, there is no external evidence for attributing the poem to anyone else. The poem may be his, and until the unlikely discovery of conclusive evidence for assigning it to another poet, the student of Shakespeare is not free to ignore it, although, of course, no responsible critic would depend upon it to any considerable degree in formulating his notions of Shakespeare as poet.

Although the volume of sonnets was not printed until 1609, two of them, numbers 138 and 144, were printed in *The Passionate Pilgrim,* 1599. In 1598, while listing and commenting on Shakespeare's works in his *Palladis Tamia: Wits Treasury,* Francis Meres mentioned Shakespeare's "sugred sonnets among his private friends," indicating that, according to a custom of the time, Shakespeare's sonnets were circulating in manuscript. An Elizabethan gentleman who did not wish to descend to what he took to be the vulgarity of print could gain a reputation as a poet by giving manuscript copies of his poems to his friends, who, if they liked them, could give copies to their friends, and so on. In this manner a writer's reputation could be established without publication, and this is one of the means Shakespeare took to gain the name of poet. It is not known how many of the sonnets were so circulating, and it is possible that some of the sonnets we now have were written after 1598; but the probability is that they were all written in the early 1590s. The dating of the sonnets will depend in part on the view taken of their contents.

Sonnets 1-126 are addressed to or concerned with a young man whom the poet addresses in terms of affection and esteem. Sonnets 127-152 are addressed to or concerned with a young woman, who because of her black hair and swarthy complexion, has come to be known as the Dark Lady. Sonnets 153-154 are free translations of a fifth-century A.D. Greek poem and have no connection with the sonnets of the first two groups except a common authorship. Although Elizabethan sonnet sequences are not narrative poems, the reader discerns reflections of a story in the first two groups of Shakespeare's sonnets. They tell of four people: Shakespeare, who speaks in the first person, the young man, the Dark Lady, and another poet. The young man is handsome, of good family, and, at least in the beginning, the possessor of boundless virtues. He is told that youth and beauty are brief, that fatherhood is a duty to himself and to the world (the same arguments are used in *Venus and Adonis*), and that his qualities must be preserved in the immortality which children can bestow. Shakespeare then promises to immortalize the young man in verses which will never die. After a while other poets began addressing poems to the young man, and one of them, a poet of more power than the rest, came to be regarded by Shakespeare as something of a rival. He is often referred to as the Rival Poet. Sometime after the friendship with the young man began, Shakespeare acquired a mistress, a woman younger than he, attractive with an unfashionable beauty, and with no moral principles whatsoever. The relationship between them had not a glimmer of romance, and in time the poet came to recognize it as a sexual enslavement, but not until the lady had seduced the young friend and maintained a liaison with him for some time. Finding this triangular relationship increasingly unbearable, Shakespeare resolved the problem by rejecting the lady. Such is the story reflected in the sonnets. It seems to some scholars to be purely fictitious, a mere manipulation of the conventions of the sonnet tradition. The present editor takes it to have had a basis in fact, partly because Shakespeare, if he were inventing a story, would surely have invented a better one. If the story is taken to be fictitious, we may suppose that Shakespeare added a sonnet to his sequence from time to time, perhaps up to the point of publication in 1609. If, on the other hand, the sonnets reflect events in Shakespeare's life, it is plausible to suppose that they were written while the events were in progress. One of the sonnets to the young man was clearly sent to him as a verse letter, and it is possible that others also were. The sonnets which speak of the poet's craftsmanship often express his discontent with it, and he writes of himself as an unestablished poet who will be forgotten after his death. By the end of the century he was famous. Every-thing in the sonnets suggest an early date. Sonnet 104 tells us that Shakespeare had known the young man for three years, and so it is reasonable to suppose that the sonnets were written over a period of at least three years, probably from 1592 to 1596. These dates will be acceptable to schol-ars who have no axes to grind. The 1609 Quarto is the only edition of the sonnets to be published during Shakespeare's lifetime, and all later editions derive from it. In 1640 the sonnets were reprinted by John Benson in a small octavo volume entitled *Poems: Written by Wil. Shake-speare. Gent.* The volume is a dishonest venture in publishing. Benson did not own the copyright. He scrambled the order of the sonnets, interspersing them with other poems by Shake-speare and other poets. He gave the sonnets descriptive titles which are often inept, and he changed the pronouns in some of the sonnets addressed to the young man, making them appear to be addressed to a woman. But he did cor-rect, by conjectural emendation, some of the errors in the text of the 1609 Quarto, and this edition is indebted to him for one or two readings which are indicated in the notes.

In a preface addressed to the reader Benson describes the poems as "seren, cleere amd eligantly plaine, such gentle straines as shall recreate and not perplexe your braine, no intricate or cloudy stuffe to puzzell intellect, but perfect eloquence. . . ." And ever since then there have been critics to praise the sonnets for their simplicity, although some of them are in fact among the most difficult poems in the language. Shakespeare has, of course, his simplicities. In Sonnet 66 he makes a list of the things which discourage him most, and one of them is "simple truth miscall'd simplicity." He saw things as they were, and his sophisti-cation did not compel him to condescend to the common-place. Things sometimes become clichés because they are true, and they are to be recognized as truth. Nowhere in his works is there any avoidance of this. He could be disarmingly simple where other writers would not dare to be, as in the "Good-night, sweet prince" speech in *Hamlet,* and many of the memorable passages in the sonnets are characterized by their unobtrusive melody, easy grace, and simplicity of statement. He always wrote with an unmatchable freshness on nature's morning loveliness and her plenitude, subjects to which he constantly took an unequivocal attitude, but the dominant mode of his mature work is complexity, and this first emerges fully in the sonnets. He saw all aspects of things, and they stand together in his works without canceling each other out. Spenser tends to give us the various aspects of things piecemeal. He presents one view of love in the episode of the Bower of Bliss, another in the Garden of Adonis, and still others in the stories of the Squire of Dames and of Hellenore, to mention only a few; but in Shakespeare various and sometimes conflicting aspects of things exist simultaneously. There is, for instance, virtue's potential for evil. In *Measure for Measure* it is Isabella's virtue which arouses Angelo's lust and leads him to a temptation "where prayers cross." She had no intention of tempting him, and, at the time, no awareness of having done so; yet in the end she asks mercy for him because she realizes that her innocence had been an agent of evil:

> *I partly think*
> *A due sincerity govern'd his deeds,*
> *Till he did look on me: since it is so,*
> *Let him not die.*

So it was with Lucrece who had done nothing to provoke the dilemma with which she was confronted but was nevertheless constrained to accept responsibility for what had occurred even though both husband and father assured her that there is no guilt where the mind does not consent. Here the values of innocence are themselves questioned.

Shakespeare also explores evil's potential for good; this is basic to such tragedies as *Othello* and *King Lear* in which man through error and suffering comes to self-knowledge and wisdom. This is explicit in Sonnet 119: "O benefit of ill!" After forgiving a trespass on the part of the young man, Shakespeare, in Sonnet 35, apologizes for the presumption of forgiveness. In Sonnet 111, a correction, itself justly made, must be corrected. The view of the Rival Poet is multiple. Shakespeare regards him with a mixture of admiration, envy, and resentment. Although to Shakespeare the profession of writing was "what I most enjoy," he was at times "contented least" with it (Sonnet 29), and his conflicting attitudes to both it and the profession of acting are vividly set forth in Sonnets 110 and 111. His compliments to the Dark Lady are always oblique, and at the very time when his passion for her is most uncontrollable, he views it, himself, and her with revulsion. From the beginning his protestations of admiration for the young man are touched with rebuke. In Sonnet 9 he suggests that the young man has "no love toward others." As the sonnets proceed the reproaches increase. In Sonnet 84 the friend is reproached for his vanity, and in Sonnet 69 he is told that he is growing common. In Sonnet 83 Shakespeare questions his high estimate of the friend:

> I found, or thought I found, you did exceed
> The barren tender of a poet's debt. . . .

There is no need to exhaust the reproaches here. The sonnets abound in irony and paradox, which are the manifestations of Shakespeare's awareness of his own multiplicity, an awareness he was later to confer upon Hamlet. And this is, of course, the awareness of the dramatist, for the most interesting dramatic choice is not between right and wrong but between two rights or two wrongs, or between things which are neither wholly right nor wholly wrong.

The sonnets are Shakespeare's lyric expressions of the perceptions later to find dramatic expression in the plays of his maturity—his perceptions of friendship, of love and lust, of growth through experience, of sin and expiation, of mutability, plenitude, and the knowledge of good and evil. They begin with a concern for physical beauty and exhortations to preserve it in such immortality as children can bestow, and in the promises to eternize beauty in poetry. In later sonnets mortality is found to be tainted with something more ghastly than mutability, and in this view the power of "sinful earth" to recreate itself does not console. At the close of the sonnets the body is rejected that the soul may live. At no point in the sonnets, or in the later works, is the concern for physical beauty abandoned. It is not that as Shakespeare grew older he came to love beauty less; it is rather that he had come to love other things as much, moral beauty among them. And this, too, is in the sonnets, which are a foreshadowing of the course his career as artist was to take. The best of the sonnets are in themselves perfect lyric realizations of the perceptions which were not actualized in his plays until a later time.

THE PASSIONATE PILGRIM

The Passionate Pilgrim, a small octavo volume bearing Shakespeare's name on the title page, was printed for William Jaggard in 1599. The edition was pirated, Shakespeare having no hand in the publication of it. Apparently Jaggard gathered the poems from various sources and attributed them to Shakespeare in order to take advantage of his growing reputation. To the last six poems he gave a separate title page, "Sonnets to sundry notes of Musicke," which does not give the name of the author. Poetry by Shakespeare, however, is found in both parts of the book. The first and second poems are Shakespeare's Sonnets 138 and 144, and the third, fifth, and sixteenth poems appear as Shakespeare's in *Love's Labour's Lost.* All five poems differ in detail from the texts appearing in *Shake-speares Sonnets* and in the play, and not for the better. They are therefore excluded from this edition of *The Passionate Pilgrim* and are to be found in this book at their appropriate places in the sonnets and the poems from *Love's Labour's Lost*. "Crabb'd age and youth cannot live together" has often been accepted as Shakespeare's, and he is conceivably the author of some of the others. The title of the volume is doubtless Jaggard's and is appropriate to a volume of love poems. That the pilgrim was a familiar figure in Elizabethan love literature is attested to by the dialogue between Romeo and Juliet at their first meeting when he is the "pilgrim" and she is his "saint." (See "If I profane with my unworthiest hand," page 197.)

THE PHOENIX AND THE TURTLE

In 1601 there was published a long, inconsequential poem entitled *Loves Martyr, or Rosalins Complaint.* The poem is described on the title page as "allegorically shadowing the truth of Loue, in the constant Fate of the Phoenix and Turtle. A poem enterlaced with much varietie and rarietie; now first translated out of the venerable Italian Torquato Caeliano, by Robert Chester. With the true legend of famous King Arthur, the last of the nine Worthies, being the first Essay of a new Brytish Poet: collected out of diuerse Authenticall Records." Torquato Caeliano is an invented name; the poem is doubtless Chester's. The volume is dedicated "To The Honorable, and (of me before all other) honored Knight, Sir John Salisburie. . . ." The poem would have no claim to our attention were there not appended to it poems signed "Vatum Chorus," "Ignoto," "William Shake-speare," "John Marston," "George Chapman," and "Ben Johnson." These poems are given a separate title page on which they are described as "Poeticall Essaies on the former Subject; viz: the Turtle and Phoenix. Done by the best and chiefest of our modern writers, with their names subscribed to their particular workes: never before extant. And (now first) consecrated by them all generally, to the loue and merite of the true-noble Knight, Sir John Salisburie." Shakespeare's contribution to the volume is the enigmatic and unforgettable poem known as "The Phoenix and the Turtle." It bears no title in the Chester volume.

The rambling nature of Chester's poem and his announcement of its allegorical nature have made it possible for ingenious commentators to propose a multiplicity of interpretations, some of them fantastically foolish. There is nothing approaching agreement on any one of them, nor in the present state of our knowledge is there likely to be. The volume was printed in an edition of fifty copies, only one of which, now in the British Museum, has survived. Presumably it was published for a coterie which kept its secret well. In an edition made for The New Shakespeare Society by the Rev. Alexander B. Grosart in 1878, the persons for whom the phoenix and the turtle stood were held to be Queen Elizabeth I (1533–1603) and Robert Devereux, second Earl of Essex (1566–1601). This is the reading of the poem which scholars most often discuss, if only to refute it. It has the virtue of providing a motive for the obliquity of the allegory. Essex was executed for treason on February 25, 1601, and a book written in admiration of him shortly after his execution would necessarily have had to be secretive. If this theory is to be considered at all, it must be held that the love celebrated in the book was emblematic of a wished for union which would have settled the question of the succession in the last troubled years of the Queen's reign. By far the greater number of scholars assign Shakespeare's poem to 1601, believing it to have been expressly written for Chester's volume.

The ascription of the poem to Shakespeare is accepted by most, if not all, Shakespeare scholars, and the doubts as to its authenticity usually arise from the differences between the poem and his other works. Because of its regularity the verse has sometimes been called doggerel. All but six of its sixty-seven lines are in truncated trochaic tetrameters; the other six employ the final syllable of the trochaic line. Throughout the poem the metrical beat is strong, a conformity to metrical pattern unusual in the work of Shakespeare's mature years. No other work of Shakespeare's employs so many literary conventions in comparable compass. No other poem of his is as impersonal, as abstract, as abstruse as this one, or as studiously allegorical. Generally, speaking birds in Shakespeare reflect his observation of nature; these, following the convention of the congress of birds, are austerely symbolic; their attributes are literary. But all this need not be surprising in a poem contributed to a volume compiled and published for a special public upon a special occasion. Although the occasion has been guessed at, it remains unestablished for want of definitive evidence; and until such evidence is at hand, further guesses at the historical allegory of the poem would appear to be useless. Nevertheless, it is not necessary to dismiss the poem as either a poetic exercise or an enigma, for the poem has points of likeness to, as well as difference from, Shakespeare's other works, and a consideration of them may suggest that the poem is Shakespeare's allegory of love.

The phoenix was, of course, the legendary Arabian bird, unique of its kind, which, after a life of some centuries, was consumed in fire; from its ashes arose a new phoenix to take its place. By Shakespeare's time it had become richly symbolic, the emblem of, among other things, Christian immortality; but this Shakespeare's phoenix clearly is not. There being only one phoenix, any attribution of sex to it was irrelevant; but Shakespeare's phoenix, loving and beloved, is female. The turtle dove, then as now far from unique, was a bird of no magical powers whatever. Its legendary characteristics were love and constancy, and it was thought that, having lost its mate by death, the turtle mourned its loss until the end. Shakespeare's turtle is male. In "The Phoenix and the Turtle" the titular birds are not mentioned until the sixth stanza, which states the total action of the poem. In it we learn that the phoenix and the turtle have fled. We learn in the next line that they have fled "from hence." We learn, too, that as a result of their flight by means of their flaming consummation love and constancy here in this world "is dead." The inseparableness of the two is indicated by the singular form of the verb. All the rest of the poem is preparation for this action and comment upon it.

The poem opens with an unidentified voice speaking from nowhere and commanding the bird of loudest song to summon "chaste wings" together. We learn later that the birds are to be mourners and that "the sole Arabian tree," the place from which the summons is to be issued, has been vacated by the phoenix. Only chaste birds are to be summoned, because, as we also learn later, the love to be celebrated was a chaste love. Some other birds are specifically forbidden the assembly. The "shrieking harbinger" is excluded, not because it foretells death but because it announces the end of a life to be punished in torment. It is the "foul precurrer of the fiend." All birds of prey are excluded except the eagle, which is the emblem, not of tyranny, but of royalty. The swan is summoned to fulfill a priestly function. She will not sing of her own imminent death; she will sing a requiem for the departed lovers, as in *Othello* (Act V, scene 2, lines 246-251) Emilia played the swan and sang in celebration of the chastity of her departed mistress. The crow is summoned because it was long-lived and reproduced its kind by the exchange of breath. In Shakespeare and elsewhere the association of breath with life and spirit is too commonplace to require discussion. With this, the summoning of the birds is ended. Chastity, royalty, ceremonial music, and life having no dependence upon the flesh have been assembled, and we learn in the sixth stanza of two beings embodying love and constancy who have fled in a mutual and all-consuming flame.

The next three stanzas expound the mystical concept of unity in duality, two distinct beings who are nonetheless one. All this is not allowed to pass without comment. In the tenth stanza, property, by which is meant the appropriateness of the attributes of things to the things themselves, is appalled at the violation of its essential nature. In the eleventh stanza, reason is confounded by the palpable truth of what it had not been able to conceive, and which it cannot conceive without the annihilation of its essential nature. But in the following stanza, reason, a good loser, concedes that the perception of ultimate truth is not its function but the function of love. Reason then makes the threnos which brings the poem to its close.

In the threnos the chastity of the departed lovers is made explicit for the first time. The love of the phoenix and the turtle was an ideal love existing independently of the body. The lovers were "co-supremes and stars of love," not stars in the sense of being the most eminent of their kind, but of a kind to which others can only aspire. They are "stars of love" as, in Sonnet 116, love *is* the star by which mariners steer their course but which remains in itself of an immeasurable worth unknown to mortality. Sublunary lovers' love is subject to mutability. "Rosy lips and cheeks" come within time's "bending sickle's compass," but a marriage of true minds "bears it out, even to the edge of doom." The marriage of the phoenix and the turtle was also untrammeled by sex. They died

> *Leaving no posterity:*
> *'Twas not their infirmity,*
> *It was married chastity.*

This is not Shakespeare's characteristic mode when he is

dealing with man and woman. Although his works are deeply erotic and testify throughout to the goodness of procreation, he was also aware of the ideal, and in this poem his "characters" are stripped of their natural attributes and made into symbols to be manipulated in the service of the ideal. Or they were abstractions in the first place. Everything in the poem is subjugated to thought, and although the thought may be obscured by the terseness of the expression (and this is characteristic of the mature Shakespeare), there is nothing whatever in the poem to distract the reader from its thought.

Having been the "stars of love," the phoenix and the turtle can leave nothing behind them of their own order of being. What seems to man to be truth and beauty are only therefore appearances, reflections, perhaps, of the departed reality. "Truth" is, of course, here used in the sense of constancy, and its emblem is the turtle. It is through the conjunction of beauty and truth that each finds its own identity and, at the same time, loses it in the union with the other. Beauty (the phoenix) could have existed alone on earth in a kind of sequential immortality, living to itself, from time to time renewing itself, but subject, always, in each reincarnation, to mortality. From this she could escape only by awakening a love which would make her aware of her eternal nature. Nor could either fidelity or love know its true nature until it had found something to be faithful to. It is as though one soul had been divided into two finite natures and could find completion only in reunion. This is one of the most commonplace of metaphors in Shakespeare's poetry and the poetry of the Renaissance. It may even be found in the thirty-seventh chapter of *For Whom the Bell Tolls*: "One and one is one, is one, is one. . . ." The metaphor, however, stripped of its human incarnation, ceases to be a metaphor and becomes a reality which can no longer exist in the world of phenomena. Truth and beauty, having achieved perfection by union, cannot remain in an imperfect world. What remains in the funeral urn is only "dead birds" ("The earth can have but earth, which is his due . . ."), and those who "are either true or fair" are enjoined to repair to the urn and "sigh a prayer" for what is mortal.

For the most part "The Phoenix and the Turtle" has not fared well at the hands of the scholars. Early scholars tended to ignore it and later ones to treat it as a point of departure for speculations in historical allegory, more often than not having no awareness of its greatness as a poem. The poets, however, have taken it to their hearts. In *Parnassus* (1874) Emerson found it ". . . a good example of the rule, that there is a poetry for bards proper, as well as poetry for the world of readers." And in his *William Shakespeare* (1911) John Masefield speaks of its "dark and noble verse" and finds the poem to be the work of a great mind trying to express symbolically thought too subtle to be expressed in any other way. "The poem gives to a flock of thoughts about the passing of truth and beauty the mystery and vitality of birds, who come from a far country, to fill the mind with their crying."

SONGS AND POEMS FROM THE PLAYS

It is customary for historians of music to refer to the age of Shakespeare as the golden age of English song and to assure us that song pervaded the society of the time to a degree to which we do not often realize. A lover was expected to be able to sing a serenade to his lady, and very often did. Training in music was a part of the education of a gentleman, who was expected to be able to join in a part song much as a modern man might be expected to take a hand at bridge. Henry Peacham (1576?–1643?) indicates in a familiar passage in his *Compleat Gentleman* that a "noble or gentleman" would be expected to sing his part of a part song "sure, and at first sight" and to play it

Polibius

Strabo

Ptolomeus

Aratus

VIRESCIT VVLNERE VERITAS

THE
FIRST BOOKE
of Songes or Ayres of fowre partes with Ta-
bleture for the Lute:

So made that all the partes
together, or either of them seue-
rally may be song to the Lute,
Orpherian or Viol de gambo.

Compoled by Iohn Dowland Lute-
nid and Baccler of musicke in

Astronomia

Musica

Author for two to playe vp-
on one Lute.

Nec profunt ǆomino, quæ profunt omnibus Artes.

¶ Printed by Peter Short, dwelling on
Bredstreet hill at the sign of the Starre, 1597

Tupparnus

Geometria

Arithmetica

upon an instrument. It is not to be supposed that every educated gentleman was an accomplished musician with a fine voice, but it is clear that music was regarded as an essential part of the life of the times and that a gentleman was expected to take part in it. It was Shakespeare's habitual attitude to regard his plays as representations in little of life, as his numerous comparisons of life and the stage establish, and, with some qualification, the attitude is nowhere more justified than in the use of music in his plays, which is a reflection of the musical life of his times. Madrigals and other more complex forms of polyphonic music seem to have been little used in the Elizabethan theater, except in masques, but the popular theater abounded in incidental music, folk songs, street songs, and "ayres," which we would now call art songs.

The texts of Shakespeare's plays do not record the compositions played by the musicians of the theater to the accompaniment of dramatic action. Most of the folk songs were ballads, often set in three-part harmony, or catches, that is, rounds having one melody to be sung in canon form. The catch best known today is "Three Blind Mice." Street songs were usually ballads and differed from folk songs in that the words were not conditioned by a communal tradition which had passed them on from generation to generation. They were written by a particular writer upon a particular and usually spectacular occasion. They were sold in the streets by ballad singers such as Autolycus in *The Winter's Tale.* Airs were of a higher order of music, as the art song is today. It cannot be demonstrated beyond question that any of the music for Shakespeare's songs as they were heard in the Globe Theater has survived. The authoritative texts do not give the music, and most of the music traditionally associated with the words can be traced no farther back than the eighteenth or the late seventeenth centuries. Some of the extant music, however, can be shown to have existed in Shakespeare's lifetime, and in some instances the probability that it was used in the productions of his plays approaches certainty. In this volume the notes to the songs from Shakespeare's plays mention the earliest known settings associated with them, and it will be seen that some of them were in all probability the original musical settings. Shakespeare's songs are airs, canons, catches, part songs, and songs with burdens or refrains. In subject matter they conform to the conventional types of the day. They are aubades, Bacchic songs, ballads, carols, dirges, hymns, reverdies (nature songs celebrating the coming of spring), sea chanteys, serenades, songs of the greenwood, and wedding songs.

Sometimes Shakespeare's plays indicate that a song is to be sung, although the words for it are not given in the text, as in *Love's Labour's Lost* (Act III, scene 1, line 1) and *Julius Caesar* (Act IV, scene 3, line 266). Presumably the song to be sung in these instances was determined by the exigencies of production. The dirge in *Cymbeline* (Act IV, scene 2, lines 258-281), though marked as a song in the 1623 Folio, was spoken by the boy actors, one of them remarking in character that "now our voices/ Have got the mannish crack." Words for songs appear in twenty-six plays. Some of them are fragments quoted from ballads and traditional songs, others are poems by other poets, though these are usually adapted by Shakespeare to his purposes, and still others are lyrics original with him. The notes indicate the character of each song and place it briefly in the context of the play in which it occurs. When the notes do not indicate an indebtedness to another poem, the words of the song may be presumed to be Shakespeare's. In this edition the songs and poems from the plays are printed in the order in which they appear in the plays, and the groups of songs and poems, play by play, follow in the order in which the plays were written, so that the reader may observe Shakespeare's progress as a poet from the first lyric to the last.

CONTENTS

Preface, vii
Introduction, xi

THE SONNETS

The enigmatic dedication of *Shakespeare's Sonnets,* 1609, was written by Thomas Thorpe, their publisher. Shakespeare had nothing to do with it. It has provoked prolonged and continuing controversy which centers in the identification of Mr. W. H., who is taken to be the "onlie begetter" of the sonnets, that is, the inspirer of them, the young man with whom the greater number of the sonnets are concerned. The controversy is fruitless, since there is no reputable evidence by which the issues involved in it could be settled. It is possible to avoid some of the intricacies of the argument by taking "onlie begetter" to mean the man who procured the manuscript of the sonnets for Thorpe, but by far the best thing to do is to remember that the man cannot possibly be identified on the basis of our present knowledge and dismiss the whole matter from our minds.

TO. THE. ONLIE. BEGETTER. OF.
THESE. INSVING. SONNETS.
M^R. W. H. ALL. HAPPINESSE.
AND. THAT. ETERNITIE.
PROMISED.
BY.
OVR. EVER–LIVING. POET.
WISHETH.
THE. WELL–WISHING.
ADVENTVRER. IN.
SETTING.
FORTH.
T. T.

The sonnets open with a series of seventeen poems urging a young friend of the poet's to marry and reproduce his beauty in children.

5. CONTRACTED *betrothed. There is the suggestion of Narcissus, the youth who did not love the nymphs because he loved himself.* 6. SELF-SUBSTANTIAL *the substance of one's own self.* 9. ORNAMENT *that which adorns.* 10. GAUDY *festive and showy.* 11. CONTENT *what you contain, that is, potential fatherhood.* 12. CHURL *a term of affection.* NIGGARDING *hoarding.* 14. WORLD'S DUE *The world is entitled to the propagation of the species.*

3. LIVERY *outward appearance.* 4. TOTTER'D *tattered.* 9. USE *employment, investment so as to increase the sum invested.* 11. SUM MY COUNT *pay my debt to nature.* 11. MAKE . . . EXCUSE *Justify me in my old age.*

ONE

From fairest creatures we desire increase,
That thereby beauty's rose might never die,
But as the riper should by time decease,
His tender heir might bear his memory;
5   But thou, contracted to thine own bright eyes,
Feed'st thy light's flame with self-substantial fuel,
Making a famine where abundance lies,
Thyself thy foe, to thy sweet self too cruel:
Thou that art now the world's fresh ornament
10   And only herald to the gaudy spring,
Within thine own bud buriest thy content,
And, tender churl, mak'st waste in niggarding.
        Pity the world, or else this glutton be,
        To eat the world's due, by the grave and thee.

TWO

When forty winters shall besiege thy brow
And dig deep trenches in thy beauty's field,
Thy youth's proud livery, so gaz'd on now,
Will be a totter'd weed of small worth held:
5   Then being ask'd where all thy beauty lies,
Where all the treasure of thy lusty days,
To say within thine own deep-sunken eyes
Were an all-eating shame and thriftless praise.
How much more praise deserv'd thy beauty's use,
10   If thou couldst answer, "This fair child of mine
Shall sum my count and make my old excuse,"
Proving his beauty by succession thine.
        This were to be new made when thou art old,
        And see thy blood warm when thou feel'st it cold.

3. REPAIR *condition*. 4. UNBLESS SOME MOTHER *leave some woman unblessed with motherhood.* 5. UNEAR'D *untilled.* 7. FOND *foolish.* 8. OF *because of.* 10. PRIME *springtime, youth.* 13. *but if you are living only to be forgotten.*

2. THY BEAUTY'S LEGACY *the beauty which should be the legacy of your child.* 4. FRANK *liberal.* THOSE ARE *those who are.* FREE *unrestrained, bountiful.* 8. LIVE *live fully; be remembered.* 9. TRAFFIC *commerce.* 10. DECEIVE *beguile.* 14. LIVES TH' EXECUTOR *in the person of a son.*

THREE

Look in thy glass and tell the face thou viewst
Now is the time that face should form another,
Whose fresh repair if now thou not renewest,
Thou dost beguile the world, unbless some mother.
5   For where is she so fair whose unear'd womb
Disdains the tillage of thy husbandry?
Or who is he so fond will be the tomb,
Of his self-love to stop posterity?
Thou art thy mother's glass, and she in thee
10   Calls back the lovely April of her prime;
So thou through windows of thine age shalt see,
Despite of wrinkles, this thy golden time.
    But if thou live remem'bred not to be,
    Die single, and thine image dies with thee.

FOUR

Unthrifty loveliness, why dost thou spend
Upon thyself thy beauty's legacy?
Nature's bequest gives nothing, but doth lend,
And being frank, she lends to those are free;
5   Then, beauteous niggard, why dost thou abuse
The bounteous largess given thee to give?
Profitless usurer, why dost thou use
So great a sum of sums, yet canst not live?
For, having traffic with thyself alone,
10   Thou of thyself thy sweet self dost deceive;
Then how, when nature calls thee to be gone,
What acceptable audit canst thou leave?
    Thy unus'd beauty must be tomb'd with thee,
    Which, used, lives th' executor to be.

4. UNFAIR *make unbeautiful.* FAIRLY *in beauty.* 6. CONFOUNDS *destroys.* 9. *if beauty's rose (see Sonnet 1) were not distilled into perfume.* 11. BEAUTY'S EFFECT *the perfume, or rose water, of line 9.* BEAUTY *the rose itself.* BEREFT *taken away.* 12. NOR . . . NOR *neither . . . nor.* 14. LEESE *lose.* SHOW *the physical form by which they are made manifest.* SUBSTANCE *that which constitutes the thing itself.*

In this sonnet, a continuation of the preceding one, distillation becomes the image for procreation. Shakespeare is a profoundly erotic writer, and here his eroticism is expressed with a tact and unobtrusive beauty not often enough noted.

1. RAGGED *rough.* 3. TREASURE *enrich, make precious.* 5. FORBIDDEN USURY *Taking interest on money, at whatever rate, was called usury and regarded as sinful and had been prohibited by law, but it came to be tolerated as a necessary and profitable practice. Elizabeth revived her father's statute permitting usury.* 6. HAPPIES *makes happy.* 10. REFIGUR'D *re-created as in a copy.*

FIVE

Those hours that with gentle work did frame
The lovely gaze where every eye doth dwell
Will play the tyrants to the very same
And that unfair which fairly doth excel;
5 For never-resting time leads summer on
To hideous winter and confounds him there,
Sap check'd with frost and lusty leaves quite gone,
Beauty o'ersnow'd and bareness everywhere:
Then were not summer's distillation left,
10 A liquid prisoner pent in walls of glass,
Beauty's effect with beauty were bereft,
Nor it, nor no remembrance what it was:
    But flowers distill'd, though they with winter meet,
    Leese but their show; their substance still lives sweet.

SIX

Then let not winter's ragged hand deface
In thee thy summer ere thou be distill'd;
Make sweet some vial, treasure thou some place
With beauty's treasure ere it be self-kill'd:
5 That use is not forbidden usury
Which happies those that pay the willing loan;
That's for thyself to breed another thee,
Or ten times happier, be it ten for one;
Ten times thyself were happier than thou art,
10 If ten of thine ten times refigur'd thee;
Then what could death do if thou shouldst depart,
Leaving thee living in posterity?
    Be not self-will'd, for thou art much too fair
    To be death's conquest and make worms thine heir.

1. ORIENT *east.* GRACIOUS LIGHT *the sun.* *2.* UNDER *earthly, mortal.* *5.* STEEP-UP *Compare* The Passionate Pilgrim *poem 9, line 5.* *7.* LOOKS *beholders.* *9.* CAR *the chariot of Phoebus, god of the sun.* *13.* THY-SELF . . . NOON *reaching the middle of life and passing beyond the height of physical beauty.*

Although the musical accomplishments of the average Elizabethan have doubtless been exaggerated, an educated man of Shakespeare's time could reasonably have been expected to carry a part in a multiple part song. The sonnet depends upon a knowledge of the Elizabethan mathematical notion that one is no number (see Sonnet 136, line 8) and of the lute, the strings of which, except for the highest one, were double. There is a musical setting for mezzo-soprano, flute, clarinet, and viola by Igor Stravinsky (b. 1882).

2. SWEETS *Compare Sonnets 12 (line 11), 19 (line 7), 95 (line 4), 99 (lines 2, 15), and 102 (line 12).* *4.* ANNOY *suffering. See* Venus and Adonis, *line 497 and* The Rape of Lucrece, *line 1109.* *7.* CONFOUNDS *destroys. See Sonnet 5, line 6.* *8.* PARTS *roles of husband and father.* *10. Plucking one of the double strings would make the other vibrate in sympathy with it.*

SEVEN

Lo, in the orient when the gracious light
Lifts up his burning head, each under eye
Doth homage to his new-appearing sight,
Serving with looks his sacred majesty;
5　And having climb'd the steep-up heavenly hill,
Resembling strong youth in his middle age,
Yet mortal looks adore his beauty still,
Attending on his golden pilgrimage;
But when from highmost pitch, with weary car,
10　Like feeble age, he reeleth from the day,
The eyes, 'fore duteous, now converted are
From his low tract and look another way:
　　So thou, thyself out-going in thy noon,
　　Unlook'd on diest, unless thou get a son.

EIGHT

Music to hear, why hear'st thou music sadly?
Sweets with sweets war not, joy delights in joy:
Why lov'st thou that which thou receiv'st not gladly,
Or else receiv'st with pleasure thine annoy?
5　If the true concord of well-tuned sounds,
By union married, do offend thine ear,
They do but sweetly chide thee, who confounds
In singleness the parts that thou shouldst bear:
Mark how one string, sweet husband to another,
10　Strikes each in each by mutual ordering;
Resembling sire and child and happy mother,
Who all in one, one pleasing note do sing:
　　Whose speechless song, being many, seeming one,
　　Sings this to thee: "Thou single wilt prove none."

3. ISSUELESS *childless.* 4. MAKELESS *mateless.* 5. STILL *constantly.* 7. PRIVATE *individual.* 9. LOOK WHAT *whatever.* UNTHRIFT *prodigal.* 10. HIS *its, referring to "what."* 11. *Beauty wasted on itself ceases to exist.* 14. MURD'ROUS SHAME *shameful murder.*

It was a basic notion of Shakespeare's that the existence of love can be known only through the expression of it. If hoarded, it withers away; it grows by giving. Not to return love is therefore improvident.

1. FOR SHAME *a verbal linking with the preceding sonnet.* 6. STICK'ST *hesitates.* 7. ROOF *house, that is, the body, the dwelling place of the spirit.* 9. MY MIND *my belief in your self-centeredness.* 11. PRESENCE *appearance.* GRACIOUS *handsome.* 14. STILL *always.* IN THINE *in your descendants.*

NINE

Is it for fear to wet a widow's eye
That thou consum'st thyself in single life?
Ah! if thou issueless shalt hap to die,
The world will wail thee, like a makeless wife;
5 The world will be thy widow and still weep
That thou no form of thee hast left behind,
When every private widow well may keep
By children's eyes her husband's shape in mind:
Look what an unthrift in the world doth spend
10 Shifts but his place, for still the world enjoys it;
But beauty's waste hath in the world an end,
And kept unus'd, the user so destroys it.
     No love toward others in that bosom sits
     That on himself such murd'rous shame commits.

TEN

For shame, deny that thou bear'st love to any,
Who for thyself art so unprovident:
Grant, if thou wilt, thou art belov'd of many,
But that thou none lov'st is most evident;
5 For thou art so possess'd with murd'rous hate
That 'gainst thyself thou stick'st not to conspire,
Seeking that beauteous roof to ruinate
Which to repair should be thy chief desire.
O, change thy thought, that I may change my mind:
10 Shall hate be fairer lodg'd than gentle love?
Be as thy presence is, gracious and kind,
Or to thyself at least kind-hearted prove:
     Make thee another self, for love of me,
     That beauty still may live in thine or thee.

In all of Shakespeare there is probably no idea more constantly employed, either implicitly or by direct statement, than the lesson of the parable of the talents, Matthew 25: 14–30. Man is always taken to be the steward, not the owner, of his possessions and attributes, and the obligation to put them to use is proportional to them. This is taken as true in all contexts. Procreation is taken to be the duty of those to whom nature has been bountiful.

1–2. As fast as you fade, so fast shall you, in the person of one of your children, grow toward that which you in your own person are ceasing to be. 3. YOUNGLY *early in life.* BESTOW'ST *bring into being.* 5. HEREIN *in this course of action.* 6. WITHOUT THIS *beyond this course of action.* 7. THE TIMES *the generations of men.* 9. STORE *fertility.* 11. LOOK WHOM *whomever.* 13. SEAL *engraved stamp such as used on sealing wax.*

Mutability is the constant concern of poets, especially those who celebrate youth and beauty, and it is characteristic of the poets of Elizabethan and earlier times to oppose all-conquering time with the view of love as life's instrument in its race with death. This sonnet has found a greater fame than the preceding ones because its octave states the awareness of mutability in more general terms.

1. COUNT THE CLOCK *count the strokes of the clock, watch the hours passing.* 2. BRAVE *splendid.* 3. PRIME *height of perfection.* 4. SABLE *black, dark. See* The Rape of Lucrece, *line 117, and* The Phoenix and the Turtle, *line 18.* 6. ERST *formerly.* 9. QUESTION MAKE *consider.* 11. DO THEMSELVES FORSAKE *depart from what they were.* 14. BRAVE HIM *defy time.*

ELEVEN

As fast as thou shalt wane, so fast thou grow'st,
In one of thine, from that which thou departest;
And that fresh blood which youngly thou bestow'st
Thou mayst call thine when thou from youth convertest:
5 Herein lives wisdom, beauty, and increase;
Without this, folly, age, and cold decay:
If all were minded so, the times should cease
And threescore year would make the world away.
Let those whom Nature hath not made for store,
10 Harsh, featureless, and rude, barrenly perish:
Look whom she best endow'd she gave the more,
Which bounteous gift thou shouldst in bounty cherish:
    She carv'd thee for her seal, and meant thereby
    Thou shouldst print more, not let that copy die.

TWELVE

When I do count the clock that tells the time,
And see the brave day sunk in hideous night;
When I behold the violet past prime,
And sable curls all silver'd o'er with white;
5 When lofty trees I see barren of leaves,
Which erst from heat did canopy the herd,
And summer's green all girded up in sheaves
Borne on the bier with white and bristly beard,
Then of thy beauty do I question make,
10 That thou among the wastes of time must go,
Since sweets and beauties do themselves forsake
And die as fast as they see others grow;
    And nothing 'gainst Time's scythe can make defence
    Save breed, to brave him when he takes thee hence.

2. THAN *1609 Quarto: then.* 5. IN LEASE *Again, the attribute of beauty is regarded as being in custody.* 6. DETERMINATION *limit, ending.* WERE *would be.* 9. HOUSE *See "beauteous roof," Sonnet 10, line 7.* 10. HUSBANDRY *tillage in love as in agriculture. See Sonnet 3, lines 5–6.* IN HONOUR *in marriage.* 13. UNTHRIFTS *See Sonnet 9, line 9.*

These earthly godfathers of heaven's lights
That give a name to every fixed star,
Have no more profits of their shining nights
Than those that walk and wot not what they are.
    Love's Labour's Lost, *Act I, scene 1, lines 88–91*

From women's eyes this doctrine I derive:
They sparkle still the right Promethean fire;
They are the books, the arts, the academes,
That show, contain, and nourish all the world.
    Love's Labour's Lost, *Act IV, scene 3, lines 350–353*

1. PLUCK *derive.* 2. ASTRONOMY *astrology. The word is not found in Shakespeare.* 3–4. *The lines list the traditional subjects of astrologers.* 5. MINUTES *short spaces of time.* 6. HIS *its.* 8. OFT PREDICT THAT *frequent prediction of what.* 12. STORE *fertility. Compare Sonnet 11, line 9.* 14. DATE *limit of a prescribed time.*

THIRTEEN

O that you were yourself! but, love, you are
No longer yours than you yourself here live:
Against this coming end you should prepare
And your sweet semblance to some other give:
5   So should that beauty which you hold in lease
Find no determination; then you were
Yourself again, after yourself's decease,
When your sweet issue your sweet form should bear.
Who lets so fair a house fall to decay,
10   Which husbandry in honour might uphold
Against the stormy gusts of winter's day
And barren rage of death's eternal cold?
      O, none but unthrifts! Dear my love, you know
      You had a father: let your son say so.

FOURTEEN

Not from the stars do I my judgment pluck,
And yet methinks I have astronomy,
But not to tell of good or evil luck,
Of plagues, of dearths, or seasons' quality;
5   Nor can I fortune to brief minutes tell,
Pointing to each his thunder, rain, and wind,
Or say with princes if it shall go well,
By oft predict that I in heaven find:
But from thine eyes my knowledge I derive,
10   And, constant stars, in them I read such art
As, truth and beauty shall together thrive
If from thyself to store thou wouldst convert;
      Or else of thee this I prognosticate:
      Thy end is truth's and beauty's doom and date.

This sonnet introduces a new theme: As the young man's physical beauty fades, it will blossom again in the poems Shakespeare addresses to him.

3. *The comparison of the world to a stage is a Shakespearean commonplace.* 4. COMMENT *This usage, doubtless arising from the exigencies of rhyming, is unique in Shakespeare, but it is, for him, a mild wresting of the language to his purposes. The word was used transitively to mean "devise, contrive, invent." The meaning is the astrological belief that the influence of the stars creates effects in the lives of men.* 8. WEAR *consume, wear out by degrees.* BRAVE *handsome.* OUT OF MEMORY *till it is forgotten.* 9. CONCEIT *thought.* INCONSTANT STAY *transitoriness of life.* 14. INGRAFT *graft. As a rose is made to flower more perfectly through the graft which is affixed to it, so as he grows older, the young man's beauty will flower in the poet's verses.*

6. UNSET *unplanted.* 8. LIKER *more like you.* COUNTERFEIT *portrait.* 9–12. *The basic meaning is that neither the pencil of the portraitist (whose works are subject to time) nor my pen (which is the pen of a poet who has not yet achieved his full powers) can, in their attempts to reproduce your outward beauty or your inward worth, make you live as fully in the minds of men as your descendants, should you have them, would make you live.* 9. LINES OF LIFE *lineal descendants.* LIFE REPAIR *repair life, that is, restore it in children after it has faded or died in the parent.* 13. GIVE AWAY YOURSELF *give yourself in love, cease being self-contained, beget children. The paradox of the line is only apparent. In the poet's view, life, to realize itself, must give itself away.* KEEPS *preserves.* 14. DRAWN *Shakespeare uses "draw" to mean both "to sketch" and "to write." The young man himself must supplant both artist and poet.*

FIFTEEN

When I consider every thing that grows
Holds in perfection but a little moment,
That this huge stage presenteth naught but shows
Whereon the stars in secret influence comment;
5   When I perceive that men as plants increase,
Cheer'd and check'd even by the selfsame sky,
Vaunt in their youthful sap, at height decrease,
And wear their brave state out of memory:
Then the conceit of this inconstant stay
10   Sets you most rich in youth before my sight,
Where wasteful Time debateth with Decay
To change your day of youth to sullied night;
      And all in war with Time for love of you,
      As he takes from you, I ingraft you new.

SIXTEEN

But wherefore do not you a mightier way
Make war upon this bloody tyrant, Time,
And fortify yourself in your decay
With means more blessed than my barren rhyme?
5   Now stand you on the top of happy hours,
And many maiden gardens, yet unset,
With virtuous wish would bear your living flowers,
Much liker than your painted counterfeit:
So should the lines of life that life repair,
10   Which this time's pencil, or my pupil pen,
Neither in inward worth nor outward fair,
Can make you live yourself in eyes of men.
      To give away yourself keeps yourself still;
      And you must live, drawn by your own sweet skill.

This is the last of the sonnets urging the young man to perpetuate himself through progeny.

2. DESERTS *that which merits praise or recognition. It rhymes with "parts."* 3. TOMB *Compare Sonnet 83, line 12.* 4. PARTS *that with which one is endowed. Compare Sonnet 69, line 1.* 6. NUMBERS *verses.* 8. TOUCHES *traits.* 11. RAGE *inspiration, which by its nature is suprarational and therefore irrational to the unsympathetic. Compare the Muse's fury of Sonnet 100, line 3.* 12. STRETCHED METRE *the exaggeration expected of poetry.* 13. THAT TIME *in the "time to come" of line 1.* 14. RHYME *poetry.*

None of the preceding sonnets had reached the order of poetry achieved here, and the poet seems to have taken heart from his achievement. In Sonnet 15 he had promised to embody the young man's beauty in his verse; now the verse will confer immortality upon him. This boast has been traditional with poets since, at least, the time of Horace (65–8 B.C.), and Shakespeare repeats it in Sonnets 19, 55, 60, 63, 81, 101, but with him the boast is not idle. We know nothing of the young man except what the poet tells us.

3. MAY *In the old calendar of Shakespeare's time May ran almost to the mid-June of our calendar.* 4. LEASE *allotted time. See Sonnets 107 (line 3), 124 (line 10), and 146 (line 3).* DATE *duration. Compare Sonnets 22 (line 2), 38 (line 12), and 122 (line 4).* 5. EYE OF HEAVEN *sun.* 6. DIMM'D *Compare Sonnets 33 (lines 5–8) and 35 (line 3).* 7. EVERY FAIR *every beautiful person.* FROM FAIR *from a state of being beautiful.* SOMETIME *sometimes.* 8. UNTRIMM'D *reduced from a state of perfection.* 10. FAIR *beauty.* OW'ST *own.* 12. ETERNAL LINES *these verses.*

SEVENTEEN

Who will believe my verse in time to come
If it were fill'd with your most high deserts?
Though yet, heaven knows, it is but as a tomb
Which hides your life and shows not half your parts:
5   If I could write the beauty of your eyes
And in fresh numbers number all your graces,
The age to come would say, "This poet lies;
Such heavenly touches ne'er touch'd earthly faces."
So should my papers, yellowed with their age,
10   Be scorn'd, like old men of less truth than tongue,
And your true rights be term'd a poet's rage
And stretched metre of an antique song:
        But were some child of yours alive that time,
        You should live twice, in it, and in my rhyme.

EIGHTEEN

Shall I compare thee to a summer's day?
Thou art more lovely and more temperate:
Rough winds do shake the darling buds of May,
And summer's lease hath all too short a date:
5   Sometime too hot the eye of heaven shines,
And often is his gold complexion dimm'd;
And every fair from fair sometime declines,
By chance, or nature's changing course, untrimm'd;
But thy eternal summer shall not fade
10   Nor lose possession of that fair thou ow'st,
Nor shall Death brag thou wand'rest in his shade
When in eternal lines to time thou grow'st:
        So long as men can breathe or eyes can see,
        So long lives this, and this gives life to thee.

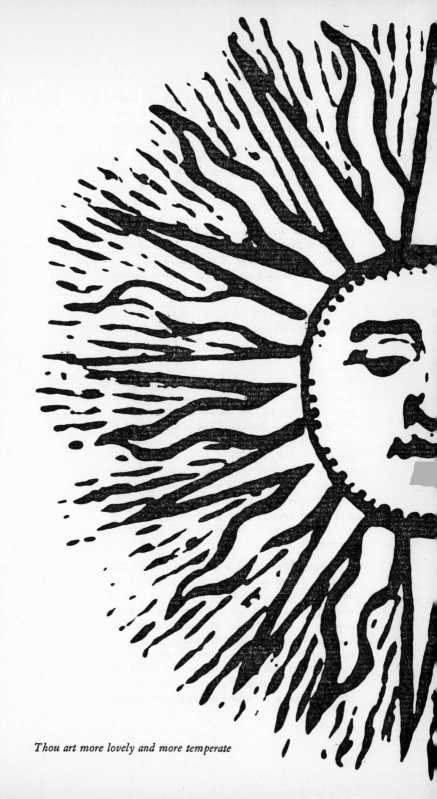

Thou art more lovely and more temperate

*The awareness of the hostility of time is found
throughout the sonnets and in the plays contemporary with them. It is also common to Elizabethan
and medieval poetry, but with a difference. In the
sonnets the hostility is not balanced with the assurance of orthodox immortality. They oppose time
with (1) the immortality conferred by progeny, (2)
the immortality conferred by art, and (3) the immortality of fame arising from virtuous action. The
first and last are Platonic (see The Symposium).
The commitment to the Christian eschatology of
Sonnet 146 is not made in relation to time. The
word "time" is used seventy-eight times in Sonnets
1–126 and not at all in the others.*

3. YAWS *jaws.* 4. PHOENIX *See page 318.* 11. UNTAINTED
untouched. "Taint" is a tilting term meaning "hit."

*This sonnet has given rise to much comment and
some indignation. Shakespeare was aware of the
possible ambiguity of his attitude toward the young
man, and he here denies any homosexual interest in
him. The young man has some feminine qualities,
but not woman's fickleness; he is less false. His
beauty is such that it seems nature, as she made him,
first intended him to be a woman, but she absent-
mindedly added male genitals, and for this reason the
young man calls forth only the poet's love (that
is, friendship) while his "love's use" is woman's
"treasure."*

1. NATURE'S *The coloring is natural.* 6. GILDING *The
eye itself was spoken of as casting beams upon the
objects of its gaze, making them visible, as the first
rays of the sun gild "pale streams with heavenly
alchemy." (Sonnet 33, line 4). See also Sonnet 28,
line 12. This conceit lies behind the commonplace
image of the eyes as suns.* 7. *"Hue" means "complexion," and "in hue," "the state in which the
humors are in a state of proper balance," so that
the young man is not dominated by any one passion.*

NINETEEN

Devouring Time, blunt thou the lion's paws,
And make the earth devour her own sweet brood;
Pluck the keen teeth from the fierce tiger's yaws,
And burn the long-liv'd phœnix in her blood;
5 Make glad and sorry seasons as thou fleet'st,
And do whate'er thou wilt, swift-footed Time,
To the wide world and all her fading sweets;
But I forbid thee one most heinous crime:
O, carve not with thy hours my love's fair brow,
10 Nor draw no lines there with thine antique pen;
Him in thy course untainted do allow
For beauty's pattern to succeeding men.
    Yet do thy worst, old Time: despite thy wrong,
    My love shall in my verse ever live young.

TWENTY

A woman's face with nature's own hand painted
Hast thou, the master mistress of my passion;
A woman's gentle heart, but not acquainted
With shifting change, as is false women's fashion;
5 An eye more bright than theirs, less false in rolling,
Gilding the object whereupon it gazeth;
A man in hue all hues in his controlling,
Which steals men's eyes and women's souls amazeth.
And for a woman wert thou first created,
10 Till Nature as she wrought thee fell a-doting,
And by addition me of the defeated
By adding one thing to my purpose nothing.
    But since she prick'd thee out for women's pleasure,
    Mine be thy love, and thy love's use their treasure.

Apart from Shakespeare there was another poet, who has come to be known as the Rival Poet, who was addressing poems to the young man. He remains unidentified. We may gather that his style was orotund. Shakespeare refers to him in an amalgam of sincerity, envy, and pique, opposing his own alleged simplicity of motive and statement to the rival's virtuosity and presumed insincerity. He makes his first appearance in this sonnet.

2. PAINTED BEAUTY *an artificial beauty as opposed to the natural beauty of Shakespeare's verse.* 3. *which uses heaven itself for ornament.* 4. EVERY FAIR *every beautiful creature or object.* REHEARSE *mention, compare.* 5. COUPLEMENT *combination.* 8. RONDURE *the dome of the skies covering the world.* 12. GOLD CANDLES *stars.*

2. OF ONE DATE *identical.* 4. EXPIATE *bring to a close because the poet is older than the young man.* 5–8. *The conceit is that since the heart of the poet dwells in the breast of the friend and the heart of the friend in the poet's breast, there is an identity of the two and there can therefore be no difference in age.* 11. CHARY *carefully.* 13. PRESUME NOT ON *do not lay claim to.*

TWENTY-ONE

So is it not with me as with that Muse,
Stirr'd by a painted beauty to his verse,
Who heaven itself for ornament doth use,
And every fair with his fair doth rehearse,
5 Making a couplement of proud compare
With sun and moon, with earth and sea's rich gems,
With April's first-born flowers, and all things rare
That heaven's air in this huge rondure hems:
O let me, true in love, but truly write,
10 And then believe me, my love is as fair
As any mother's child, though not so bright
As those gold candles fix'd in heaven's air:
      Let them say more that like of hearsay well;
      I will not praise that purpose not to sell.

TWENTY-TWO

My glass shall not persuade me I am old
So long as youth and thou are of one date;
But when in thee time's furrows I behold,
Then look I death my days should expiate.
5 For all that beauty that doth cover thee
Is but the seemly raiment of my heart,
Which in thy breast doth live, as thine in me:
How can I then be elder than thou art?
O therefore, love, be of thyself so wary
10 As I, not for myself, but for thee will,
Bearing thy heart, which I will keep so chary
As tender nurse her babe from faring ill.
      Presume not on thy heart when mine is slain:
      Thou gav'st me thine not to give back again.

1. UNPERFECT ACTOR *an actor who has not perfected his role or his craft.* 5. FOR . . . TRUST *fearing to trust myself.* 9. LOOKS *Emendation by Edward Capell (1713–1781). The point of the sonnet is that the poet has not expressed his love in words. Compare Sonnet 85. 1609 Quarto: books.* 10. DUMB PRESAGERS *silent foretellers. This suggests the dumb show in the theater and carries on the image of the imperfect actor.* 11. WHO *which.* 12. THAT TONGUE *another person, perhaps the Rival Poet. See Sonnet 21.* 14. WIT *faculty of perception.*

1. STELL'D *Emendation by Edward Capell (1713–1781). 1609 Quarto: steeld. For "stell'd" meaning "fixed" see* The Rape of Lucrece, *line 1444.* 2. TABLE *that on which something is painted or, in other instances, written.* 3. *The frame helps give the picture perspective. The line also seems to express Shakespeare's preference for Renaissance as compared to medieval painting.* 8. HIS *referring to "shop."* GLAZED *made transparent by the use of glass.* 13. CUNNING *power.* WANT *lack.*

TWENTY-THREE

As an unperfect actor on the stage,
Who with his fear is put besides his part,
Or some fierce thing replete with too much rage,
Whose strength's abundance weakens his own heart;
5   So I, for fear of trust, forget to say
The perfect ceremony of love's rite,
And in mine own love's strength seem to decay,
O'ercharg'd with burthen of mine own love's might:
O, let my looks be then the eloquence
10 And dumb presagers of my speaking breast,
Who plead for love, and look for recompense
More than that tongue that more hath more express'd.
     O learn to read what silent love hath writ:
     To hear with eyes belongs to love's fine wit.

TWENTY-FOUR

Mine eye hath play'd the painter and hath stell'd
Thy beauty's form in table of my heart;
My body is the frame wherein 'tis held,
And perspective it is best painter's art.
5   For through the painter must you see his skill
To find where your true image pictur'd lies,
Which in my bosom's shop is hanging still,
That hath his windows glazed with thine eyes.
Now see what good turns eyes for eyes have done:
10 Mine eyes have drawn thy shape, and thine for me
Are windows to my breast, wherethrough the sun
Delights to peep, to gaze therein on thee;
     Yet eyes this cunning want to grace their art;
     They draw but what they see, know not the heart.

The professions of playwriting and acting were not honored ones. The law placed actors in the same category as rogues and vagabonds, and Shakespeare, immersed in his dual profession, found consolation in the friendship of the young man. But the view of his profession reflected here is not total (see Sonnet 29).

1. IN . . . STARS *favored by fate.* 4. UNLOOK'D FOR *not sought out.* THAT *what.* 9–12. *In Shakespeare's view, good deeds are not remembered long, and virtue must continually reassert itself to maintain its identity.* 9. PAINFUL *painstaking.* FAMOUSED *famous.* WORTH *1609 Quarto. Many editors emend to "fight" for the sake of the rhyme, but Shakespeare's rhymes are sometimes imperfect.* 11. QUITE *1609 Quarto; sometimes, but unjustifiably, emended to "forth" for the sake of the rhyme.* 14. REMOVE *Compare Sonnet 116, line 4.*

Shakespeare addresses the young man as a vassal addresses his lord, using the legal terminology at which he was so adept that it has been argued that he studied law, but the jargons of all the métiers he treated are used skillfully, and he cannot have studied them all. It is more interesting to note that this is a verse letter and that the poet denies any interest in showing his virtuosity. He still feels that his technique is not adequate to his subject (see Sonnet 17).

4. WIT *power of invention.* 6. WANTING *lacking.* 7. CONCEIT *conception, image, invention.* 8. *will place my bare statement in your mind and soul, and some invention of yours, such as I have not been able to devise, will clothe my naked statement, making it worthy of my intent.* 10. ASPECT *in astrology, a star's particular influence.* 11. TOTTER'D *1609 Quarto. It was a recognized form of "tattered," the meaning of which it conveys while suggesting others.* 12. THY *Emendation by Edward Capell (1713–1781). 1609 Quarto: their. The same misreading of the manuscript occurs in Sonnet 35, line 8.*

TWENTY-FIVE

Let those who are in favour with their stars
Of public honour and proud titles boast,
Whilst I, whom fortune of such triumph bars,
Unlook'd for joy in that I honour most;
5   Great princes' favourites their fair leaves spread
But as the marigold at the sun's eye,
And in themselves their pride lies buried,
For at a frown they in their glory die.
The painful warrior famoused for worth,
10   After a thousand victories once foil'd,
Is from the book of honour rased quite,
And all the rest forgot for which he toil'd:
      Then happy I that love and am belov'd
      Where I may not remove nor be remov'd.

TWENTY-SIX

Lord of my love, to whom in vassalage
Thy merit hath my duty strongly knit,
To thee I send this written ambassage
To witness duty, not to show my wit:
5   Duty so great, which wit so poor as mine
May make seem bare, in wanting words to show it,
But that I hope some good conceit of thine
In thy soul's thought, all naked, will bestow it;
Till whatsoever star that guides my moving
10   Points on me graciously with fair aspect,
And puts apparel on my totter'd loving
To show me worthy of thy sweet respect;
      Then may I dare to boast how I do love thee,
      Till then not show my head where thou mayst prove
      me.

2. TRAVEL *1609 Quarto: trauaill; used for "travel" but carrying the meanings of both.* 4. WORK *set to work.* EXPIRED *at an end.* 6. INTEND *set out on.* 8. WHICH . . . SEE *which is all that greets the eyes of the blind.* 10. SHADOW *image.*

This is a continuation of the preceding sonnet. Poems written in absence are a commonplace of the Elizabethan sonnet sequence. None of Shakespeare's sonnets written on this theme is among his best, and at their worst they are his nearest approach to frigidity.

5. EITHER'S *each other's.* 6. SHAKE HANDS *unite.* 7. COMPLAIN *make me complain.* 9. TO PLEASE HIM *The line means both "I tell the day that you are bright in order to please him" and "In order to console the day (when it is cloudy) I tell him that you are still bright."* 12. *See the preceding sonnet where the friend's imagined image "makes black night beauteous."* TWIRE *Shakespeare invented the word for the occasion and did not use it elsewhere. This and later usages establish its meaning as "peer," but with the suggestion of "twinkle."* 14. LENGTH *Some editors, following Edward Capell (1713–1781), unnecessarily emend to "strength."*

TWENTY-SEVEN

Weary with toil, I haste me to my bed,
The dear repose for limbs with travel tired;
But then begins a journey in my head
To work my mind when body's work's expired:
5 For then my thoughts, from far where I abide,
Intend a zealous pilgrimage to thee,
And keep my drooping eyelids open wide,
Looking on darkness which the blind do see;
Save that my soul's imaginary sight
10 Presents thy shadow to my sightless view,
Which, like a jewel hung in ghastly night,
Makes black night beauteous and her old face new.
  Lo, thus, by day my limbs, by night my mind,
  For thee and for myself no quiet find.

TWENTY-EIGHT

How can I then return in happy plight
That am debarr'd the benefit of rest?
When day's oppression is not eas'd by night,
But day and night, and night by day, oppress'd;
5 And each, though enemies to either's reign,
Do in consent shake hands to torture me,
The one by toil, the other to complain
How far I toil, still farther off from thee:
I tell the day to please him thou are bright
10 And dost him grace when clouds do blot the heaven;
So flatter I the swart-complexion'd night,
When sparkling stars twire not thou gild'st the even:
  But day doth daily draw my sorrows longer,
  And night doth nightly make grief's length seem
  stronger.

The poem should be read in relation to Sonnets 25, 110, and 111. Here the poet's career in the theater, which denies him social acceptance, is, at the same time, declared to be "what I most enjoy." His discontent is in part motivated by his limitations as an artist. He aspires to the greater craftsmanship and scope of other writers whose achievement he was shortly to exceed, but here he writes as one who has not yet found fame. Born in the same year as Christopher Marlowe (1564–1593), had he died with him there would have been nothing except perhaps a few sonnets to indicate his greater genius.

1. DISGRACE *out of favor. The word is used in a less derogatory sense than in modern English, as in Sonnets 103, 126, and 127. 3.* BOOTLESS *unavailing. 12.* SULLEN *dismal, dark.*

This, one of the most celebrated of the sonnets, owes its reputation to its opening lines, which to Sir Sidney Lee "seem to illustrate the perfection of human utterance." Although the alliteration of the rest of the poem is heavy, recalling but not equaling Poe's "weary wayworn wanderer," the poem is structurally a perfect instance of a Shakespearean sonnet.

1. SESSIONS *sittings of a court of justice. This is another (compare Sonnet 26) and supreme use of legal imagery. 3.* SIGH *lament. 4.* MY . . . WASTE *the loss of my precious time; the wasting away of my time; time's destruction of things dear to me. 6.* DATELESS *endless. 7.* LOVE'S . . . WOE *the debt of grief, canceled because already paid in full. 8.* EXPENSE *loss. 9.* FOREGONE *former. 10.* TELL *count.*

TWENTY-NINE

When in disgrace with fortune and men's eyes,
I all alone beweep my outcast state,
And trouble deaf heaven with my bootless cries,
And look upon myself and curse my fate,
5 Wishing me like to one more rich in hope,
Featur'd like him, like him with friends possess'd,
Desiring this man's art, and that man's scope,
With what I most enjoy contented least;
Yet in these thoughts myself almost despising,
10 Haply I think on thee, and then my state,
Like to the lark at break of day arising
From sullen earth, sings hymns at heaven's gate;
  For thy sweet love rememb'red such wealth brings
  That then I scorn to change my state with kings.

THIRTY

When to the sessions of sweet silent thought
I summon up remembrance of things past,
I sigh the lack of many a thing I sought
And with old woes new wail my dear time's waste;
5 Then can I drown an eye unus'd to flow,
For precious friends hid in death's dateless night,
And weep afresh love's long since cancell'd woe,
And moan th' expense of many a vanish'd sight;
Then can I grieve at grievances foregone,
10 And heavily from woe to woe tell o'er
The sad account of fore-bemoaned moan,
Which I new pay as if not paid before:
  But if the while I think on thee, dear friend,
  All losses are restor'd and sorrows end.

It is necessary to remember that in Shakespeare and Elizabethan English generally the words "love" and "lover" were used, in addition to their modern meanings, to mean "friendship" and "friend," and are so used by Shakespeare in relation to the young man. When Brutus in Julius Caesar *(Act III, scene 2, line 13) addressed the crowd as "Romans, countrymen, and lovers," he meant precisely what the late President Franklin Roosevelt meant by "My friends." "Love" was the word for that which drew people together. In this poem all the dead to whom the poet had been devoted are his "lovers."*

1. ENDEARED WITH *enriched by the combined value of.* *5.* OBSEQUIOUS *appropriate to funeral rites. Hamlet is "bound/In filial obligation for some term/To do obsequious sorrow" (Act I, scene 2, lines 90–92).* *6.* RELIGIOUS LOVE *Mourning the death of a loved one is a religious duty.* *7.* INTEREST *the right. See* The Rape of Lucrece, *line 1797.* WHICH *who.* *8.* REMOV'D *absent.* THEE *Emendation by Charles Gildon (1665–1724). 1609 Quarto: there; a possible reading retained by some editors.* *11.* PARTS *shares.* *12.* DUE OF MANY *that which the many dead claimed as their right.*

The last two decades of the sixteenth century saw a flowering of poetry unmatched in England before and since. There had been nothing comparable to it since the time of Chaucer 200 years earlier. Poetry was growing better, and in this poem Shakespeare, apparently not yet assured in his heart of the degree to which he was contributing to its growth, expects to be surpassed after his death.

1. MY WELL-CONTENTED DAY *the day I shall be well-contented with.* *2.* CHURL *rude, ill-bred fellow.* **7.** RHYME *technical qualities in general.*

THIRTY-ONE

Thy bosom is endeared with all hearts,
Which I by lacking have supposed dead,
And there reigns love and all love's loving parts,
And all those friends which I thought buried.
5   How many a holy and obsequious tear
Hath dear religious love stol'n from mine eye,
As interest of the dead, which now appear
But things remov'd that hidden in thee lie!
Thou art the grave where buried love doth live,
10   Hung with the trophies of my lovers gone,
Who all their parts of me to thee did give:
That due of many now is thine alone.
      Their images I lov'd I view in thee,
      And thou, all they, hast all the all of me.

THIRTY-TWO

If thou survive my well-contented day
When that churl Death my bones with dust shall cover,
And shalt by fortune once more resurvey
These poor rude lines of thy deceased lover,
5   Compare them with the bett'ring of the time,
And though they be outstripp'd by every pen,
Reserve them for my love, not for their rhyme,
Exceeded by the height of happier men.
O, then vouchsafe me but this loving thought:
10   "Had my friend's Muse grown with this growing age,
A dearer birth than this his love had brought
To march in ranks of better equipage;
      But since he died, and poets better prove,
      Theirs for their style I'll read, his for his love."

1–2. The sun flatters the mountain tops as the sovereign flatters all he looks upon. 5. ANON *soon.* BASEST *darkest. 6.* RACK *vapor. 7.* FORLORN *unhappy because forsaken by the sun. 8.* DISGRACE *disfigurement. See note, Sonnet 29, line 1. 12.* THE REGION CLOUD *"Region" was applied to the clouds of the upper air, but the usage here is singular. There is a reference, now lost to us, to someone or something that had come between the poet and the young man. Perhaps the reference is to the Dark Lady, who in later sonnets came between them and to whom the phrase would be appropriate, but this remains a guess. 14.* STAIN *be obscured, lose color or luster.*

Since a literal reading of this poem served as a basis for Samuel Butler's misleading essay in conjectural biography, it seems necessary to remark that in many sonnets the friendship between the poet and the young man is threatened by some unnamed action on the part of the young man, or by some failure to return the friendship fully which Shakespeare represents himself as giving freely. Here the sun, as in the preceding sonnet, stands for the friend, the beauteous day for the friendship, and the cloak for the prudence which, it now appears, the poet should have shown.

3. BASE *dark. 4.* BRAV'RY *the splendor of the "beauteous day." See above. 8.* DISGRACE *See Sonnet 29, line 1, note. 9.* PHYSIC *remedy. 12.* CROSS *Emendation by Edward Capell (1713–1781). 1609 Quarto: losse. 13.* SHEEDS *So spelled to rhyme with "deeds," and in* The Rape of Lucrece, *lines 1549 and 1551.*

THIRTY-THREE

Full many a glorious morning have I seen
Flatter the mountain tops with sovereign eye,
Kissing with golden face the meadows green,
Gilding pale streams with heavenly alchemy;
5 Anon permit the basest clouds to ride
With ugly rack on his celestial face
And from the forlorn world his visage hide,
Stealing unseen to west with this disgrace:
Even so my sun one early morn did shine
10 With all triumphant splendour on my brow;
But out alack! he was but one hour mine,
The region cloud hath mask'd him from me now.
  Yet him for this my love no whit disdaineth;
  Suns of the world may stain when heaven's sun
   staineth.

THIRTY-FOUR

Why didst thou promise such a beauteous day
And make me travel forth without my cloak,
To let base clouds o'ertake me in my way,
Hiding thy brav'ry in their rotten smoke?
5 'Tis not enough that through the cloud thou break
To dry the rain on my storm-beaten face,
For no man well of such a salve can speak
That heals the wound and cures not the disgrace:
Nor can thy shame give physic to my grief;
10 Though thou repent, yet I have still the loss:
Th' offender's sorrow lends but weak relief
To him that bears the strong offence's cross.
  Ah, but those tears are pearl which thy love sheeds,
  And they are rich and ransom all ill deeds.

The poem is an instance of Shakespeare's multiple view of things. It shows an awareness of the presumption of forgiveness, because no matter how just, right, or necessary, forgiveness throws into unbalance, at least momentarily, the mutuality, the moral equality, on which true friendship must rest.

3. STAIN *obscure*. 4. CANKER *the worm that eats into the heart of a blossom*. 6. *justifying your trespass by comparing you to other men and things, all of which are imperfect*. 7-8. *My act of forgiveness exaggerates your sins, and in so doing I corrupt myself*. 8. THY . . . THY *Emendation by Edward Capell (1713-1781). 1609 Quarto: their . . . their. See Sonnet 26, line 12.* 9. SENSUAL FAULT *The most ready explanation is the sexual relationship between the friend and the Dark Lady. This is explicit in other sonnets.* IN SENSE *There is a play on "incense." "Sense" also means "understanding" and "reason."* 14. *Compare Sonnet 40, line 9.*

The sonnet takes for granted the idea of unity in division elaborated in The Phoenix and the Turtle. In spite of the particularity of the world of phenomena, there may be a unity of souls or personalities in the higher reality of the world of the spirit. The idea may have a Christian or a Neoplatonic pagan frame of reference, but in whatever context, it was available to Elizabethan poets and they availed themselves of it readily. Here the proposed separation of the friends will be apparent only in the world of phenomena.

3. BLOTS *perhaps the "corrupting" brought upon himself in the preceding sonnet*. 5. RESPECT *thought with reference to something, that is, our minds are at one*. 6. SEPARABLE *separating*. SPITE *malicious power*. 7. LOVE'S SOLE EFFECT *love's unity of spirit*. 10. GUILT *Whatever this may refer to, there is no evidence for thinking it to be anything other than the "outcast state" of Sonnet 29 or the "blots" of line 3*. 13-14. *The couplet is repeated in Sonnet 96*. 14. REPORT *reputation*.

THIRTY-FIVE

No more be griev'd at that which thou hast done:
Roses have thorns, and silver fountains mud;
Clouds and eclipses stain both moon and sun,
And loathsome canker lives in sweetest bud.
5   All men make faults, and even I in this,
Authorizing thy trespass with compare,
Myself corrupting, salving thy amiss,
Excusing thy sins more than thy sins are;
For to thy sensual fault I bring in sense—
10   Thy adverse party is thy advocate—
And 'gainst myself a lawful plea commence:
Such civil war is in my love and hate
       That I an accessary needs must be
       To that sweet thief which sourly robs from me.

THIRTY-SIX

Let me confess that we two must be twain,
Although our undivided loves are one:
So shall those blots that do with me remain,
Without thy help by me be borne alone.
5   In our two loves there is but one respect,
Though in our lives a separable spite,
Which though it alter not love's sole effect,
Yet doth it steal sweet hours from love's delight.
I may not evermore acknowledge thee,
10   Lest my bewailed guilt should do thee shame;
Nor thou with public kindness honour me,
Unless thou take that honour from thy name:
       But do not so; I love thee in such sort
       As thou being mine, mine is thy good report.

3. LAME *The reader should not be misled by the eminence of scholars who take literally Shakespeare's reference to his lameness (see also Sonnet 89). He was, after all, an actor, and could not have been seriously lame, and as a poet he speaks in metaphor.* DEAREST *most grievous.* 7. ENTITL'D IN THEIR PARTS *entitled to their places. Many editors emend "their" to "thy."* 8. ENGRAFTED *grafted and hence nourished by.* STORE *riches of all the things mentioned.* 10. SHADOW *Shakespeare often contrasts shadow and substance, and usually not in accordance with philosophical discourse. Here the shadow is the imagined union, expressed in the image of the graft, with the friend.* 13. LOOK WHAT *whatever.*

For Shakespeare and the Elizabethans generally "invention" had the primary meaning of finding, not the means of expression, but the subject matter for a composition. The sonnets which discuss invention assure us that the subject matter (the friend and the poet's relation to him) is given. What troubles the poet is the inadequacy of his technique. If we will, we may discount the adulation sometimes shown the friend, but the concern for his inadequacies as a writer (he was not yet secure in his profession) seems to be genuine.

2. THAT *who.* 3. ARGUMENT *essential subject matter, as in the argument to a poem.* 4. PAPER *anything written.* 5. IN ME *in my poems.* 6. AGAINST THY SIGHT *before your eyes.* 10. INVOCATE *invoke.* 12. NUMBERS *verses.* DATE *periods of time.* 13. CURIOUS *scrupulous, critical.*

THIRTY-SEVEN

As a decrepit father takes delight
To see his active child do deeds of youth,
So I, made lame by Fortune's dearest spite,
Take all my comfort of thy worth and truth;
5 For whether beauty, birth, or wealth, or wit,
Or any of these all, or all, or more,
Entitl'd in their parts do crowned sit,
I make my love engrafted to this store:
So then I am not lame, poor, nor despis'd
10 Whilst that this shadow doth such substance give
That I in thy abundance am suffic'd
And by a part of all thy glory live.
       Look what is best, that best I wish in thee:
       This wish I have; then ten times happy me!

THIRTY-EIGHT

How can my Muse want subject to invent
While thou dost breathe that pour'st into my verse
Thine own sweet argument, too excellent
For every vulgar paper to rehearse?
5 O, give thyself the thanks if aught in me
Worthy persual stand against thy sight;
For who's so dumb that cannot write to thee,
When thou thyself dost give invention light?
Be thou the tenth Muse, ten times more in worth
10 Than those old nine which rhymers invocate;
And he that calls on thee, let him bring forth
Eternal numbers to outlive long date.
       If my slight Muse do please these curious days,
       The pain be mine, but thine shall be the praise.

1. MANNERS *modesty.* *2.* THE . . . ME *Compare Sonnet 74, line 8: "My spirit is thine, the better part of me." 3. See Sonnet 36, comment. 6.* NAME *name as opposed to reality. 8.* THAT DUE *that which is due. 10.* WERE IT NOT *were it not that. 11.* ENTERTAIN *pass, spend. See* The Rape of Lucrece, *line 1361. 13. And were it not that you teach me how to divide into two the unity of spirit. See Sonnet 36, lines 1–2.*

We learn from other sonnets that the poet's mistress seduced the friend and became for a time, which Shakespeare found increasingly uncomfortable, the mistress of both. In this sonnet the impulse to forgive the young man is elaborately rationalized in lines capable of multiple interpretation.

3. NO LOVE *not love. 7–8. But you are to be blamed if you deceive yourself by the enjoyment of what your true self would refuse. Or perhaps it is marriage which the young man is refusing. Or if, following the quarto, we read "this selfe," the reference may be to the poet, the friend's other self. There is no wholly satisfying interpretation of the lines. 7.* THYSELF *1609 Quarto: this selfe. 8.* WILFUL *both willful and lascivious.* TASTE *enjoyment. 10.* MY POVERTY *the little I have. 12.* KNOWN *not secret. 13. The young man is both lascivious and beautiful and everything in him is becoming. Compare Sonnet 150, line 5, note.*

THIRTY-NINE

O, how thy worth with manners may I sing
When thou art all the better part of me?
What can mine own praise to mine own self bring?
And what is't but mine own when I praise thee?
5   Even for this let us divided live,
And our dear love lose name of single one,
That by this separation I may give
That due to thee which thou deserv'st alone.
O absence, what a torment wouldst thou prove,
10   Were it not thy sour leisure gave sweet leave
To entertain the time with thoughts of love,
Which time and thoughts so sweetly doth deceive,
        And that thou teachest how to make one twain,
        By praising him here who doth hence remain!

FORTY

Take all my loves, my love, yea, take them all;
What hast thou then more than thou hadst before?
No love, my love, that thou mayst true love call;
All mine was thine before thou hadst this more.
5   Then if for my love thou my love receivest,
I cannot blame thee for my love thou usest;
But yet be blam'd if thou thyself deceivest
By wilful taste of what thyself refusest.
I do forgive thy robb'ry, gentle thief,
10   Although thou steal thee all my poverty;
And yet love knows it is a greater grief
To bear love's wrong than hate's known injury.
        Lascivious grace, in whom all ill well shows,
        Kill me with spites; yet we must not be foes.

1. PRETTY *pleasing. They are attractive because in the young man "all ill well shows." Sonnet 40, line 13.* 2. SOMETIME *sometimes, for some time.* 4. STILL *always.* 8. SHE *Emendation by Edmund Malone (1741–1812). 1609 Quarto: he.* 9. SEAT *place.* 11. WHO *which.*

3. OF MY WAILING CHIEF *the chief cause of my sorrow.* 4. NEARLY *closely.* 8. APPROVE *prove, experience in a sexual sense.* 11. BOTH TWAIN *the one as well as the other.*

FORTY-ONE

Those pretty wrongs that liberty commits
When I am sometime absent from thy heart,
Thy beauty and thy years full well befits,
For still temptation follows where thou art.
5   Gentle thou art, and therefore to be won;
Beauteous thou art, therefore to be assailed;
And when a woman woos, what womans' son
Will sourly leave her till she have prevailed?
Ay me, but yet thou mightst my seat forbear,
10 And chide thy beauty and thy straying youth,
Who lead thee in their riot even there
Where thou art forc'd to break a twofold truth:
    Hers, by thy beauty tempting her to thee,
    Thine, by thy beauty being false to me.

FORTY-TWO

That thou hast her, it is not all my grief,
And yet it may be said I lov'd her dearly;
That she hath thee is of my wailing chief,
A loss in love that touches me more nearly.
5   Loving offenders, thus I will excuse ye:
Thou dost love her because thou know'st I love her;
And for my sake even so doth she abuse me,
Suff'ring my friend for my sake to approve her.
If I lose thee, my loss is my love's gain,
10 And losing her, my friend hath found that loss;
Both find each other, and I lose both twain,
And both for my sake lay on me this cross.
    But here's the joy: my friend and I are one;
    Sweet flattery! then she loves but me alone.

1. WINK *close my eyes in sleep.* 2. UNRESPECTED *un-noticed and unworthy of notice. 4. And bright, although closed, are clearly directed in the darkness.* 5. SHADOW *image.* SHADOWS *darkness.* 6. THY SHADOW'S FORM *your physical presence.* SHOW *display.* 11. THY *Emendation by Edmund Malone (1741–1812). 1609 Quarto: their. 13.* ARE NIGHTS TO SEE *look like nights.*

This and the following sonnet take for granted a knowledge of the common belief that the constituents of life are the four elements: earth, water, fire, and air. The body is composed of the first two, the heavier elements, and is subject to gravity and the confines of space. Thought is air and is free to move as it will. Tears are, of course, water. Sonnets on thought's triumph over space are common in Renaissance poetry.

4. LIMITS *places.* WHERE *to where.* 8. HE *it.* 9. THOUGHT . . . THOUGHT *The realization that I cannot transcend space, as thought can, kills me.* 12. ATTEND *wait for.*

FORTY-THREE

When most I wink, then do mine eyes best see,
For all the day they view things unrespected;
But when I sleep, in dreams they look on thee,
And, darkly bright, are bright in dark directed.
5 Then thou, whose shadow shadows doth make bright,
How would thy shadow's form form happy show
To the clear day with thy much clearer light,
When to unseeing eyes thy shade shines so!
How would, I say, mine eyes be blessed made
10 By looking on thee in the living day,
When in dead night thy fair imperfect shade
Through heavy sleep on sightless eyes doth stay!
    All days are nights to see till I see thee,
    And nights bright days when dreams do show thee
    me.

FORTY-FOUR

If the dull substance of my flesh were thought,
Injurious distance should not stop my way;
For then, despite of space, I would be brought,
From limits far remote, where thou dost stay.
5 No matter then although my foot did stand
Upon the farthest earth remov'd from thee,
For nimble thought can jump both sea and land
As soon as think the place where he would be.
But ah, thought kills me that I am not thought,
10 To leap large lengths of miles when thou art gone,
But that, so much of earth and water wrought,
I must attend time's leisure with my moan,
    Receiving naught by elements so slow
    But heavy tears, badges of either's woe.

1. SLIGHT *unsubstantial.* *4.* PRESENT-ABSENT *Hyphen-ated by Edmund Malone (1741–1812); now here, now there.* *8.* MELANCHOLY *one of the four hu-mours. It was associated with earth anl death.* *9.* LIFE'S *1609 Quarto: lines.* RECUR'D *restored.* *12.* THY *Emendation by Charles Gildon (1665–1724). 1609 Quarto: their.*

The basic matter of this sonnet is a legal action between the poet's eye and his heart to determine their respective shares in the young friend. The poem is a fanciful presentation of an action for partition. The legal terminology is used precisely, but the poem remains a tour de force. In the following sonnet the mind and the heart come to terms.

2. THY SIGHT *the view of you which is one of the spoils of the war.* *3, 8, 13, 14.* THY *Emendation by Edward Capell (1713–1781). 1609 Quarto: their.* *4.* THE . . . RIGHT *the right of that freedom.* *9.* 'CIDE *decide. 1609 Quarto: side.* *10.* QUEST *inquest or jury.* *12.* MOIETY *share.*

FORTY-FIVE

The other two, slight air and purging fire,
Are both with thee, wherever I abide;
The first my thought, the other my desire,
These present-absent with swift motion slide.
5   For when these quicker elements are gone
In tender embassy of love to thee,
My life, being made of four, with two alone
Sinks down to death, oppress'd with melancholy;
Until life's composition be recur'd
10   By those swift messengers return'd from thee,
Who even but now come back again, assur'd
Of thy fair health, recounting it to me:
      This told, I joy; but then no longer glad,
      I send them back again and straight grow sad.

FORTY-SIX

Mine eye and heart are at a mortal war
How to divide the conquest of thy sight;
Mine eye my heart thy picture's sight would bar,
My heart mine eye the freedom of that right.
5   My heart doth plead that thou in him dost lie
(A closet never pierc'd with crystal eyes);
But the defendant doth that plea deny
And says in him thy fair appearance lies.
To 'cide this title is impanneled
10   A quest of thoughts, all tenants to the heart,
And by their verdict is determined
The clear eye's moiety and the dear heart's part:
      As thus: mine eye's due is thy outward part,
      And my heart's right thy inward love of heart.

1. LEAGUE *agreement.* *8.* HIS *the heart's.* *10.* ARE *1609 Quarto. Editors usually emend to "art," but there is no reason for correcting Shakespeare's grammar.* *11.* NOT *1609 Quarto: nor. Another possible emendation is "no."*

2. TRIFLE *thing of value which is a trifle as compared to the friend.* TRUEST *used in the sense of not deviating from its condition or nature. The truest bars are the strongest, the most barring bars.* *4.* HANDS OF FALSE-HOOD *thieves.* *5.* TO *in comparison with.* *6.* NOW . . . GRIEF *because he is absent.* *8.* VULGAR *common.* *11. Compare* Venus and Adonis, *line 782.* *14.* TRUTH *Compare* Venus and Adonis, *line 724: "Rich preys make true men thieves."*

FORTY-SEVEN

Betwixt mine eye and heart a league is took,
And each doth good turns now unto the other:
When that mine eye is famish'd for a look,
Or heart in love with sighs himself doth smother,
5   With my love's picture then my eye doth feast
And to the painted banquet bids my heart;
Another time mine eye is my heart's guest
And in his thoughts of love doth share a part:
So, either by thy picture or my love,
10 Thyself away are present still with me;
For thou not farther than my thoughts canst move,
And I am still with them and they with thee;
        Or, if they sleep, thy picture in my sight
        Awakes my heart to heart's and eye's delight.

FORTY-EIGHT

How careful was I when I took my way,
Each trifle under truest bars to thrust,
That to my use it might unused stay
From hands of falsehood, in sure wards of trust!
5   But thou, to whom my jewels trifles are,
Most worthy comfort, now my greatest grief,
Thou, best of dearest and mine only care,
Art left the prey of every vulgar thief.
Thee have I not lock'd up in any chest,
10 Save where thou art not, though I feel thou art,
Within the gentle closure of my breast,
From whence at pleasure thou mayst come and part;
        And even thence thou wilt be stol'n, I fear,
        For truth proves thievish for a prize so dear.

1. AGAINST *denoting a provision made in preparation for an expected event.* *3.* WHEN AS *when.* CAST *computed, calculated.* HIS *its.* UTMOST *last. The account is now closed.* *4.* ADVIS'D RESPECTS *deliberate and prudent considerations.* *5.* STRANGELY *like a stranger.* *6.* THAT . . . EYE *Compare Sonnet 33.* *8.* *shall, by a process of rationalization, find impressive reasons for leaving me.* *9.* ENSCONCE ME *fortify myself. See Sonnet 63, line 9.* *10.* DESART *desert; that which is due to a person, his merit, his worth.* *11–14. The poet will swear to the validity of the friend's rationalized reasons for leaving him; it would be idle to do anything else since love does not spring from rational cause and is not subject to persuasion.* *11.* MY . . . UPREAR *the gesture accompanying the swearing of an oath.*

1. HEAVY *sorrowfully.* *3.* THAT EASE . . . REPOSE *the ease and repose he will find at his travel's end.* *6.* DULLY *Emendation by Edmund Malone (1741–1812). 1609 Quarto: duly.* TO BEAR *bearing. Compare "heavy," line 1.*

FORTY-NINE

Against that time (if ever that time come)
When I shall see thee frown on my defects,
When as thy love hath cast his utmost sum,
Call'd to that audit by advis'd respects;
5   Against that time when thou shalt strangely pass
And scarcely greet me with that sun, thine eye,
When love, converted from the thing it was,
Shall reasons find of settled gravity;
Against that time do I ensconce me here
10   Within the knowledge of mine own desart,
And this my hand against myself uprear,
To guard the lawful reasons on thy part:
     To leave poor me thou hast the strength of laws,
     Since why to love I can allege no cause.

FIFTY

How heavy do I journey on the way,
When what I seek (my weary travel's end)
Doth teach that ease and that repose to say,
"Thus far the miles are measur'd from thy friend!"
5   The beast that bears me, tired with my woe,
Plods dully on, to bear that weight in me,
As if by some instinct the wretch did know
His rider lov'd not speed, being made from thee:
The bloody spur cannot provoke him on
10   That sometimes anger thrusts into his hide,
Which heavily he answers with a groan,
More sharp to me than spurring to his side;
     For that same groan doth put this in my mind:
     My grief lies onward and my joy behind.

This is a continuation of the preceding sonnet.

1. SLOW OFFENCE *offense of slowness.* 2. DULL BEARER
See Sonnet 50, lines 5–6. SPEED *travel.* 4. POSTING
going fast. 6. SWIFT EXTREMITY *extreme swiftness.*
8. MOTION *progression.* 10–11. *I take these lines to
mean that desire, which is fire (see Sonnet 45, lines
1–3) and not flesh (see Sonnet 44), will race like the
lighter elements to the friend, neighing like a spirited
horse; but no one will suppose this to be worthy of
the poem. It may be that "neigh" ("naigh" in the
quarto) is a printer's error.* 10. PERFECT'ST *1609
Quarto: perfects.* 12. FOR *for the sake of, in return
for.* 14. GO *walk.*

1. KEY *The word was pronounced to rhyme with
"survey."* 4. FOR *for fear of.* SELDOM *Shakespeare
sometimes uses adverbs as adjectives.* 8. CAPTAIN *chief.*
CARCANET *collar of jewels.* 9. *Compare Sonnet 65,
line 10.* 12. HIS *its.* 13–14. *Blessed are you whose
worthiness is such that in your presence I triumph
and in your absence I hope for your return.*

FIFTY-ONE

Thus can my love excuse the slow offence
Of my dull bearer when from thee I speed;
From where thou art, why should I haste me thence?
Till I return, of posting is no need.
5　O, what excuse will my poor beast then find,
When swift extremity can seem but slow?
Then should I spur, though mounted on the wind,
In winged speed no motion shall I know:
Then can no horse with my desire keep pace;
10　Therefore desire, of perfect'st love being made,
Shall neigh—no dull flesh—in his fiery race;
But love, for love, thus shall excuse my jade:
　　　Since from thee going he went wilful slow,
　　　Towards thee I'll run and give him leave to go.

FIFTY-TWO

So am I as the rich whose blessed key
Can bring him to his sweet up-locked treasure,
The which he will not ev'ry hour survey,
For blunting the fine point of seldom pleasure.
5　Therefore are feasts so solemn and so rare,
Since, seldom coming, in the long year set,
Like stones of worth they thinly placed are,
Or captain jewels in the carcanet.
So is the time that keeps you as my chest,
10　Or as the wardrobe which the robe doth hide,
To make some special instant special blest
By new unfolding his imprison'd pride.
　　　Blessed are you, whose worthiness gives scope,
　　　Being had, to triumph, being lack'd, to hope.

It was a common notion in Petrarchan love poetry that beautiful aspects of persons, creatures, or things had been borrowed from the poet's beloved. Here and elsewhere (see, for instance, Sonnets 99 and 113) Shakespeare employs this idea in addressing his friend. He also assumes an awareness of the Platonic idea that everything in the world of phenomena is only a pale reflection of the idea of it existing in the mind of God, and he suggests that the friend's perfection is such that his "substance" is divine.

2. STRANGE *not your own.* SHADOWS *images. They are referred to later: Adonis, Helen, etc.* TEND *wait on. See Sonnet 57, line 1.* 3–4. *Everyone has only one shadow, but you who are only one person can cast many reflections of yourself.* 3. SHADE *shadow.* 5. COUNTERFEIT *description.* 8. TIRES *attire.* NEW *anew.* 9. FOISON *harvest and therefore autumn.*

2. TRUTH *honesty, genuineness, fidelity.* 5. CANKER-BLOOMS *perhaps the wild dog rose, but more probably the blossoms into which cankerworms have eaten. Compare Sonnets 35, 70, 95, and 99.* DYE *color.* 6. TINCTURE *color.* 7. WANTONLY *capriciously.* 8. DISCLOSES *opens.* 9. FOR *because.* VIRTUE ONLY *only merit.* SHOW *visual beauty.* 10. UNRESPECTED *unlooked at, neglected.* 11. TO THEMSELVES *Compare Sonnet 94, lines 9–10.* 12. ARE . . . MADE *are distilled into perfume.* 14. THAT *your beauty.* VADE *depart, decay.* BY . . . TRUTH *Your truth perpetuates itself by means of poetry. In the sonnets distillation (see Sonnet 6, lines 1–4) is sometimes the metaphor for procreation. Taken literally, "distils" would mean "falls drop by drop."* BY *1609 Quarto. Edmund Malone (1741–1812), followed by many editors, emends to "my."*

FIFTY-THREE

What is your substance, whereof are you made,
That millions of strange shadows on you tend?
Since every one hath, every one, one shade,
And you, but one, can every shadow lend:
5   Describe Adonis, and the counterfeit
Is poorly imitated after you;
On Helen's cheek all art of beauty set,
And you in Grecian tires are painted new:
Speak of the spring and foison of the year,
10   The one doth shadow of your beauty show,
The other as your bounty doth appear;
And you in every blessed shape we know.
      In all external grace you have some part,
      But you like none, none you, for constant heart.

FIFTY-FOUR

O, how much more doth beauty beauteous seem
By that sweet ornament which truth doth give!
The rose looks fair, but fairer we it deem
For that sweet odour which doth in it live:
5   The canker-blooms have full as deep a dye
As the perfumed tincture of the roses,
Hang on such thorns, and play as wantonly
When summer's breath their masked buds discloses:
But for their virtue only is their show,
10   They live unwoo'd and unrespected fade;
Die to themselves. Sweet roses do not so;
Of their sweet deaths are sweetest odours made:
      And so of you, beauteous and lovely youth,
      When that shall vade, by verse distills your truth.

Of their sweet deaths
are sweetest odours made

1. MONUMENTS *Emendation by Edmund Malone (1741–1812). 1609 Quarto: monument.* 3. THESE CONTENTS *the content of these poems.* 4. UNSWEPT STONE *memorial inscriptions in the floors of churches.* SLUTTISH *slatternly.* 9. ALL OBLIVIOUS ENMITY *all enmity which brings oblivion. Many editors, following Malone, hyphenate "all oblivious."* 10. PACE FORTH *continue, go on.* 12. WEAR THIS WORLD OUT *outlast this world.* 13. THAT *when you.* 14. THIS *this poem.* LOVERS' *admirers'.*

1. LOVE *love itself, not the person loved.* 2. EDGE *keenness.* 6. WINK *close in sleep. See Sonnet 43, line 1.* 9–12. *The basic image is that of a pair of newly betrothed lovers who, separated by a body of water, come daily to the shores to look toward the place where the other is.* 9. SAD INT'RIM *sad interim. Perhaps a period of apathy in the friendship, but more probably a period of absence, as in the sonnet following.* 13. OR *Emendation by Edward Capell (1713–1781). 1609 Quarto: As.* IT *the sad interim.* WINTER *Compare Sonnets 97 (line 1) and 98 (line 13).*

FIFTY-FIVE

Not marble nor the gilded monuments
Of princes shall outlive this pow'rful rhyme,
But you shall shine more bright in these contents
Than unswept stone, besmear'd with sluttish time.
5 When wasteful war shall statues overturn,
And broils root out the work of masonry,
Nor Mars his sword nor war's quick fire shall burn
The living record of your memory.
'Gainst death and all oblivious enmity
10 Shall you pace forth, your praise shall still find room
Even in the eyes of all posterity
That wear this world out to the ending doom.
       So, till the judgment that yourself arise,
       You live in this, and dwell in lovers' eyes.

FIFTY-SIX

Sweet love, renew thy force; be it not said
Thy edge should blunter be than appetite,
Which but to-day by feeding is allay'd,
To-morrow sharpen'd in his former might:
5 So, love, be thou; although to-day thou fill
Thy hungry eyes even till they wink with fulness,
To-morrow see again, and do not kill
The spirit of love with a perpetual dulness:
Let this sad int'rim like the ocean be
10 Which parts the shore, where two contracted new
Come daily to the banks, that, when they see
Return of love, more blest may be the view;
       Or call it winter, which, being full of care,
       Makes summer's welcome thrice more wish'd, more
          rare.

1. TEND *wait.* *5.* WORLD-WITHOUT-END *seemingly end-less.* *6.* WATCH THE CLOCK *wait through the passing hours. Compare Sonnet 12, line 1.* *7.* NOR THINK *nor dare I think.* *10.* SUPPOSE *guess at.* *12.* THOSE *those who are with you.* *13.* WILL *(1) the poet, Will Shakespeare, and (2) desire. If the word is read with a capital letter, as in the 1609 Quarto, the lines mean that love makes me such a fool that I think no ill of you whatever you may do. If the word is read in the second sense, the lines mean that love is such a fool that he thinks no ill of you no matter what you do in the pursuance of your desire.*

1–2. May that god who first made me your slave forbid that I should think of controlling your pleasures. *3.* ACCOUNT *computation.* *4.* STAY *wait upon.* *5.* BECK *summons.* *7. And let tame patience endure each rebuff to the point of torment. 1609 Quarto: tame,. Many editions, plausibly but unnecessarily, print "patience, tame to sufferance . . ."* *8.* INJURY *injustice, insult.* *10.* PRIVILEGE *authorize, license.* *10–11.* TIME/TO *1609 Quarto. Many editions unnecessarily emend to "time:/Do."* *12.* SELF-DOING *both by one's self and to one's self.*

FIFTY-SEVEN

Being your slave, what should I do but tend
Upon the hours and times of your desire?
I have no precious time at all to spend,
Nor services to do, till you require.
5   Nor dare I chide the world-without-end hour
Whilst I, my sovereign, watch the clock for you,
Nor think the bitterness of absence sour
When you have bid your servant once adieu.
Nor dare I question with my jealous thought
10   Where you may be, or your affairs suppose,
But, like a sad slave, stay and think of nought
Save where you are how happy you make those.
    So true a fool is love that in your Will,
    Though you do anything, he thinks no ill,

FIFTY-EIGHT

That god forbid that made me first your slave,
I should in thought control your times of pleasure,
Or at your hand th' account of hours to crave,
Being your vassal, bound to stay your leisure!
5   O, let me suffer, being at your beck,
Th' imprison'd absence of your liberty;
And patience tame to sufferance bide each check,
Without accusing you of injury.
Be where you list, your charter is so strong
10   That you yourself may privilege your time
To what you will; to you it doth belong
Yourself to pardon of self-doing crime.
    I am to wait, though waiting so be hell,
    Not blame your pleasure, be it ill or well.

In this sonnet Shakespeare speculates on the cyclic theory of history, a concept available to him from many sources, the most ready of which was Ecclesiastes 1:9: "The thing that hath been, it is that which shall be; and that which is done is that which shall be done: and there is no new thing under the sun." Compare Sonnet 123 in which, for the purposes of the poem, the theory is accepted.

3. LABOURING FOR INVENTION *searching for subject matter.* AMISS *wrongly, futilely.* 3–4. BEAR . . . CHILD *produce something which had been in existence before.* 5. RECORD *memory, the faculty by which things are recorded.* 6. COURSES . . . SUN *years.* 8. CHARACTER *letters, writing.* 10. COMPOSED WONDER *wonderful composition.* 11. MENDED *made better.* WHE'R *whether.* 1609 *Quarto: where.* 12. *or whether the new cycle is the same as the old.*

1. LIKE AS *just as. See Sonnet 118, line 1.* PIBBLED *pebbled.* 4. SEQUENT *successive.* 5. NATIVITY *newborn baby.* MAIN *ocean.* 7. CROOKED *malignant, thwarting.* 8. CONFOUND *destroy.* 9. TRANSFIX *pierce through, destroy.* FLOURISH *outward embellishment.* 10. PARALLELS *wrinkles. Compare Sonnet 19, line 9.* 11. RARITIES . . . TRUTH *the rare, true things created by nature.* 13. TIMES IN HOPE *future times.*

FIFTY NINE

If there be nothing new, but that which is
Hath been before, how are our brains beguil'd,
Which, labouring for invention, bear amiss
The second burthen of a former child!
5   O, that record could with a backward look,
Even of five hundred courses of the sun,
Show me your image in some antique book,
Since mind at first in character was done.
That I might see what the old world could say
10   To this composed wonder of your frame;
Whether we are mended, or whe'r better they,
Or whether revolution be the same.
      O, sure I am, the wits of former days
      To subjects worse have given admiring praise.

SIXTY

Like as the waves make towards the pibbled shore,
So do our minutes hasten to their end,
Each changing place with that which goes before,
In sequent toil all forwards do contend.
5   Nativity, once in the main of light,
Crawls to maturity, wherewith being crown'd,
Crooked eclipses 'gainst his glory fight,
And Time that gave doth now his gift confound.
Time doth transfix the flourish set on youth
10   And delves the parallels in beauty's brow,
Feeds on the rarities of nature's truth,
And nothing stands but for his scythe to mow:
      And yet to times in hope my verse shall stand,
      Praising thy worth, despite his cruel hand.

4. SHADOWS *images. See Sonnet 27, line 10.* 8. TENURE *meaning. The "tenour" of some editions is an emendation by Edward Capell (1713–1781).* 11. DEFEAT *destroy.* 13. WAKE *revel at night.* 14. *Compare Sonnet 143, line 11.*

The poem is a compliment stated in terms of the poet's assumed vanity. It turns upon the conceit of identity, or unity in division. Compare Sonnets 22 and 36. It also employs the convention of the assumption of age. Shakespeare was probably about thirty when the poem was written, but he was older than his friend and the Dark Lady, and no doubt he sometimes felt old.

5. GRACIOUS *handsome. See Sonnet 10, line 11.* 6. TRUTH *fidelity, genuineness.* 8. AS *in such a way that.* OTHER *an old plural form of the word. See also Sonnet 85, line 5.* 10. BEATED *"Beated" and "beaten," two past participial forms of "beat," were available to Shakespeare.* CHOPT *creased. See* The Rape of Lucrece, *line 1452.* ANTIQUITY *old age.* 12. SELF-LOVING *loving what I see in the glass.* 13. THEE (MYSELF) *you, my second self.* 14. DAYS *youth.*

SIXTY-ONE

Is it thy will thy image should keep open
My heavy eyelids to the weary night?
Dost thou desire my slumbers should be broken
While shadows like to thee do mock my sight?
5 Is it thy spirit that thou send'st from thee
So far from home into my deeds to pry,
To find out shames and idle hours in me,
The scope and tenure of thy jealousy?
O no, thy love, though much, is not so great:
10 It is my love that keeps mine eye awake;
Mine own true love that doth my rest defeat,
To play the watchman ever for thy sake:
　　For thee watch I whilst thou dost wake elsewhere,
　　From me far off, with others all too near.

SIXTY-TWO

Sin of self-love possesseth all mine eye
And all my soul and all my every part;
And for this sin there is no remedy,
It is so grounded inward in my heart:
5 Methinks no face so gracious is as mine,
No shape so true, no truth of such account,
And for myself mine own worth do define
As I all other in all worths surmount.
But when my glass shows me myself indeed,
10 Beated and chopt with tann'd antiquity,
Mine own self-love quite contrary I read;
Self so self-loving were iniquity.
　　'Tis thee (myself) that for myself I praise,
　　Painting my age with beauty of thy days.

1. AGAINST *in anticipation of that time when.* 2. CRUSH'D AND O'ERWORN *overwhelmed and despoiled.* 5. AGE'S STEEPY NIGHT *the precipitous descent into old age.* 10. CONFOUNDING *destroying.* See Sonnet 5, line 6. KNIFE *time's scythe.* See Sonnet 100, line 14. 13. BLACK LINES *Compare Sonnet 65, line 14.*

The quatrains of this sonnet present images of triumphant mutability: the architectural ruins of ages past, the shifting dominions of earth and sea, the decay of greatness. Although they defy paraphrase, they could not be more eloquent.

1. FELL *fierce, cruel.* 2. COST *splendor, that on which large sums of money are spent.* AGE *time or times past.* 3. SOMETIME LOFTY TOWERS *towers which were once lofty.* 4. BRASS ETERNAL *To Shakespeare brass was the emblem of durability.* See Sonnets 65, 107, and 120. *Here the allusion is probably to commemorative tablets.* MORTAL RAGE *the rage of mortality.* 8. STORE *abundance. The land's abundance becomes less as the sea wears it away; the worn-away land becomes the sea's abundance; the sea's loss becomes the earth's abundance as the sea deposits sand and builds up the land.* 9. STATE *condition.* 10. STATE *greatness.* CONFOUNDED *disrupted.* 14. TO HAVE *because it has.*

SIXTY-THREE

Against my love shall be as I am now
With Time's injurious hand crush'd and o'erworn,
When hours have drain'd his blood and fill'd his brow
With lines and wrinkles, when his youthful morn
5   Hath travell'd on to age's steepy night,
And all those beauties whereof now he's king
Are vanishing, or vanish'd out of sight,
Stealing away the treasure of his spring;
For such a time do I now fortify
10   Against confounding age's cruel knife,
That he shall never cut from memory
My sweet love's beauty, though my lover's life:
    His beauty shall in these black lines be seen,
    And they shall live, and he in them still green.

SIXTY-FOUR

When I have seen by Time's fell hand defaced
The rich proud cost of outworn buried age,
When sometime lofty towers I see down rased,
And brass eternal slave to mortal rage;
5   When I have seen the hungry ocean gain
Advantage on the kingdom of the shore,
And the firm soil win of the wat'ry main,
Increasing store with loss and loss with store;
When I have seen such interchange of state,
10   Or state itself confounded to decay,
Ruin hath taught me thus to ruminate
That Time will come and take my love away.
    This thought is as a death, which cannot choose
    But weep to have that which it fears to lose.

A continuation of the preceding sonnet.

1. SINCE *since there is neither. 3.* THIS RAGE *the rage of mortality. See Sonnet 64, line 4. 4.* ACTION *vigor. 5.* HONEY *For the adjectival use of "honey" see* Venus and Adonis, *lines 16, 452, and 538. 6.* WRACKFUL *destructive.* BATT'RING *This, taken in connection with "gates of steel," suggests the battering ram used against a beseiged city. 8.* DECAYS *causes them to decay. 10.* TIME'S CHEST *The image of a receptacle in which Time stores his conquests is a familiar one in Shakespeare. The "wallet," for instance, in* Troilus and Cressida *(Act III, scene 3, line 145) in which "he puts alms for oblivion." 12.* SPOIL *impairment, destruction. 14.* MY LOVE *my friend.*

This sonnet, like Sonnet 129, is not written in quatrains, although the rhyme scheme characteristic of the Shakespearean sonnet is retained. The poet enumerates some of the things which discourage him most, and they are in accord with the impression of him we receive from his works.

1. THESE *the evils listed below. 2.* DESERT *a deserving person. 3.* NOTHING *the undeserving; they are "needy" because they lack merit.* TRIMM'D IN JOLLITY *magnificently arrayed. 4.* UNHAPPILY *miserably. 5.* GILDED *golden.* HONOUR . . . MISPLAC'D *honor bestowed upon those unworthy of it. 6.* STRUMPETED *made into a strumpet. 7.* DISGRAC'D *disfigured. 8.* power dissipated *by weakness which enjoys a position of authority. 9.* ART *all learning including the arts.* AUTHORITY *censorship among other things. 10.* DOCTOR-LIKE *with the air of a learned man. 11.* SIMPLICITY *silliness, stupidity.*

SIXTY-FIVE

Since brass, nor stone, nor earth, nor boundless sea,
But sad mortality o'er-sways their power,
How with this rage shall beauty hold a plea,
Whose action is no stronger than a flower?
5   O how shall summer's honey breath hold out
Against the wrackful siege of batt'ring days,
When rocks impregnable are not so stout,
Nor gates of steel so strong, but Time decays?
O fearful meditation! where, alack,
10   Shall Time's best jewel from Time's chest lie hid?
Or what strong hand can hold his swift foot back,
Or who his spoil of beauty can forbid?
    O none, unless this miracle have might,
    That in black ink my love may still shine bright.

SIXTY-SIX

Tir'd with all these, for restful death I cry:
As to behold desert a beggar born,
And needy nothing trimm'd in jollity,
And purest faith unhappily forsworn,
5   And gilded honour shamefully misplac'd,
And maiden virtue rudely strumpeted,
And right perfection wrongfully disgrac'd,
And strength by limping sway disabled,
And art made tongue-tied by authority,
10   And folly, doctor-like, controlling skill,
And simple truth miscall'd simplicity,
And captive good attending captain ill:
    Tir'd with all these, from these would I be gone,
    Save that to die, I leave my love alone.

1. INFECTION *the state of being tainted or corrupted; the unhappy state of affairs set forth in the preceding sonnet, that is, the state of the contemporary world.* 2. IMPIETY *wickedness, corruption.* 4. LACE *adorn, embellish.* 5. FALSE PAINTING *the use of cosmetics, the art of portraiture.* 6. DEAD SEEING *lifeless appearance. Compare Sonnet 5 where the friend's beauty is "the lovely gaze." Because Shakespeare does not elsewhere use "seeing" to mean appearance, some editors emend to "seeming."* 7. POOR BEAUTY *This corresponds to "false painting."* INDIRECTLY *at second hand.* SEEK *seek out in order to paint.* 8. OF SHADOW *of second hand or of false beauty.* 9. BANKROUT *bankrupt.* 10. *Bankrupt nature no longer has the blood needed to produce blushes through the use of living veins; that is, blushes are now produced by cosmetics.* 11–14. *Nature, proud of the many beautiful persons she had "in days long since," has now no real treasure of beauty but him, and she keeps him to show what wealth she had in former days.*

The sonnet is a continuation of the preceding one. In both poems the young man's beauty stands in contrast to the beauty produced by cosmetics, the use of which Shakespeare, unlike John Donne, deplores. The ideal female beauty was gold and white and red—golden tresses, skin like lilies, cheeks like roses—and Elizabethan ladies stopped at nothing to achieve it. Ceruse, a popular cosmetic used to achieve whiteness, was a mixture of white lead and vinegar. Fucus, the strongest cosmetic used to produce the red, was made from red crystalline mercuric sulphide.

1. MAP *representation.* DAYS OUTWORN *the olden times.* 3. BASTARD SIGNS *cosmetics, wigs, etc.* FAIR *beauty.* BORN *produced.* *1609 Quarto: borne.* 6. THE RIGHT OF SEPULCHRES *The meaning is that the dead had a right to keep their tresses.* 11. GREEN *foliage.* 13–14. *The couplet returns to the first two lines of the poem.*

SIXTY-SEVEN

Ah, wherefore with infection should he live
And with his presence grace impiety,
That sin by him advantage should achieve
And lace itself with his society?
5 Why should false painting imitate his cheek,
And steal dead seeing of his living hue?
Why should poor beauty indirectly seek
Roses of shadow, since his rose is true?
Why should he live, now Nature bankrout is,
10 Beggar'd of blood to blush through lively veins?
For she hath no exchequer now but his,
And, proud of many, lives upon his gains.
    O, him she stores to show that wealth she had
    In days long since, before these last so bad.

SIXTY-EIGHT

Thus is his cheek the map of days outworn,
When beauty liv'd and died as flowers do now,
Before these bastard signs of fair were born
Or durst inhabit on a living brow;
5 Before the golden tresses of the dead,
The right of sepulchres, were shorn away
To live a second life on second head;
Ere beauty's dead fleece made another gay:
In him those holy antique hours are seen,
10 Without all ornament, itself and true,
Making no summer of another's green,
Robbing no old to dress his beauty new;
    And him as for a map doth Nature store,
    To show false Art what beauty was of yore.

The poet continues to praise the friend's physical beauty, but it is now contrasted to a deficiency of inward beauty.

1. *your outward parts.* 2. WANT *lack.* THOUGHT OF HEARTS *hearts' desire.* 4. BARE *unadorned.* EVEN . . . COMMEND *truthfully, without flattery.* 5. THY *Emendation by Edmund Malone (1741–1812). 1609 Quarto: Their.* OUTWARD PRAISE *praise from the unprejudiced outsider.* 6. THINE OWN *your due.* 7. CONFOUND *destroy.* 8. SHOWN *seen.* 14. SOIL *(1) the soil from which this springs, and (2) blemish.*

The sonnet as it stands is inconsistent with the sonnet which precedes it, but we should remember that the precise order in which the sonnets were written has never been established and the poem may have been written before Shakespeare was aware of anything in the young friend deserving reproof. We should also remember that a series of poems written over a number of years is not likely to be free of inconsistency.

1. ARE *1609 Quarto. Many editors emend to "art," but see Sonnet 47, line 10, note.* 3. SUSPECT *suspicion.* 5. SO *if only, provided that.* 6. THY *Emendation by Edmund Malone (1741–1812). 1609 Quarto: Their.* BEING WOO'D OF TIME *If the subject of the phrase is taken to be "Thy worth," the meaning is that the friend's worth will be cherished through the course of time; if either "thou" or "slander" is taken to be the subject, the phrase means "the favorite of the age." In any case, this is an instance of careless writing.* 7. CANKER VICE *vice preying like the canker, a worm which feeds on blossoms.* 8. PRIME *youth.* 9. AMBUSH OF YOUNG DAYS *the temptations to which youth is subject.* 11–12. *The virtue for which you are praised cannot protect you from envious criticism, for envy, if imprisoned, is always set free.* 13. SUSPECT *suspicion.* THY SHOW *what you are taken to be.* 14. OWE *own.*

SIXTY-NINE

Those parts of thee that the world's eye doth view
Want nothing that the thought of hearts can mend;
All tongues, the voice of souls, give thee that due,
Uttering bare truth, even so as foes commend.
5 Thy outward thus with outward praise is crown'd;
But those same tongues, that give thee so thine own,
In other accents do this praise confound
By seeing farther than the eye hath shown.
They look into the beauty of thy mind,
10 And that, in guess, they measure by thy deeds;
Then, churls, their thoughts (although their eyes were kind)
To thy fair flower add the rank smell of weeds:
     But why thy odour matcheth not thy show,
     The soil is this, that thou dost common grow.

SEVENTY

That thou are blam'd shall not be thy defect,
For slander's mark was ever yet the fair;
The ornament of beauty is suspect,
A crow that flies in heaven's sweetest air.
5 So thou be good, slander doth but approve
Thy worth the greater, being woo'd of time;
For canker vice the sweetest buds doth love,
And thou present'st a pure unstained prime.
Thou hast pass'd by the ambush of young days,
10 Either not assail'd, or victor being charg'd;
Yet this thy praise cannot be so thy praise
To tie up envy, evermore enlarg'd:
     If some suspect of ill mask'd not thy show,
     Then thou alone kingdoms of hearts shouldst owe.

This and the following sonnet comprise one poem urging the friend to forget him, as unworthy of remembrance, after his death. They reflect the emergent poet's discouragement with his growth as an artist. Although he was sometimes confident that his poems would be remembered, he is not always confident that he will be, and in his discouragement he sometimes hopes that he will not. He expected "the wise world" to be aware of the shortcomings of his poems. No doubt the conflict of the second sonnet also refers to the obloquy arising from his life in the theater, on which, in a few years, he was to confer a growing dignity.

2. THAN *1609 Quarto: Then.* 4. VILDEST *vilest.*

1. RECITE *tell.* 4. PROVE *find. See* The Rape of Lucrece, *line 613.* 6. DESERT *that which a person deserves. It is pronounced to rhyme with "impart."* 8. *Compare* Sonnet 69, *line 4.* 10. UNTRUE *contrary to truth.* *11.* MY NAME BE *let my name be.* 12. NOR . . . NOR *neither . . . nor.*

SEVENTY-ONE

No longer mourn for me when I am dead
Than you shall hear the surly sullen bell
Give warning to the world that I am fled
From this vile world, with vildest worms to dwell:
5   Nay, if you read this line, remember not
The hand that writ it; for I love you so,
That I in your sweet thoughts would be forgot,
If thinking on me then should make you woe.
O if, I say, you look upon this verse
10   When I, perhaps, compounded am with clay,
Do not so much as my poor name rehearse,
But let your love even with my life decay;
      Lest the wise world should look into your moan,
      And mock you with me after I am gone.

SEVENTY-TWO

O, lest the world should task you to recite
What merit liv'd in me that you should love
After my death, dear love, forget me quite,
For you in me can nothing worthy prove;
5   Unless you would devise some virtuous lie,
To do more for me than mine own desert,
And hang more praise upon deceased I
Than niggard truth would willingly impart:
O, lest your true love may seem false in this,
10   That you for love speak well of me untrue,
My name be buried where my body is,
And live no more to shame nor me nor you.
      For I am sham'd by that which I bring forth,
      And so should you, to love things nothing worth.

*This is a perfect instance of the Shakespearean sonnet.
There is a pause at the close of each quatrain, the
greatest pause coming after the third. Each quatrain
presents a visual image of approaching age—autumn,
twilight, dying embers—and they unite to create an
awareness of imminent death. The couplet, two
adagio lines, comments on what has gone before
without the slightest suggestion of the epigrammatic
which so often mars the conclusion of Shakespeare's
sonnets.*

2. OR NONE, OR FEW *either none or few, that is, few
if any.* 4. BARE RUIN'D CHOIRS *1640 edition: Bare ruin'd
quires. 1609 Quarto: Bare rn'wd quires. The image
is that of churches fallen into ruins of which, perhaps,
only the choir, the part of the church in which the
services were sung, remains standing.* 7. BY AND BY
shortly, immediately. 8. DEATH'S SECOND SELF *sleep.*

*The theme and mood of the preceding sonnet are
continued in this one, but by the use of different
means. The conventional and beautiful images for
death of the preceding sonnet give way to the homely
one of the officer who comes to make an arrest for
a crime for which there is no release on bail. There
is an appropriate homeliness, an ugliness even, in
the diction. The sonnet ends in a couplet barren of
connotation which achieves its power by its perfect
articulation with what has gone before.*

3. THIS LINE *this verse, as in Sonnet 71, line 5.*
INTEREST *part, share; that is, that part of my life
which is embodied in my verses.* 4. STILL *always.*
6. CONSECRATE *older form of "consecrated."* 7. WHICH
IS HIS DUE *"All go unto one place; all are of the dust,
and all turn to dust again" (Ecclesiastes 3:20).* 11.
CONQUEST *Compare Sonnet 6, line 14.* A WRETCH'S
KNIFE *the mortal instrument of Time. Compare
Sonnet 63, line 10.* 12. REMEMBERED *1609 Quarto:
remembred.* 13. OF THAT *of anything.* 14. AND THAT
IS THIS *And the contents of my body is my spirit
which is embodied in this poem.*

SEVENTY-THREE

That time of year thou mayst in me behold
When yellow leaves, or none, or few, do hang
Upon those boughs which shake against the cold,
Bare ruin'd choirs, where late the sweet birds sang:
5 In me thou see'st the twilight of such day
As after sunset fadeth in the west;
Which by and by black night doth take away,
Death's second self, that seals up all in rest:
In me thou see'st the glowing of such fire,
10 That on the ashes of his youth doth lie,
As the death-bed whereon it must expire,
Consum'd with that which it was nourish'd by.
    This thou perceiv'st, which makes thy love more
      strong,
    To love that well which thou must leave ere long.

SEVENTY-FOUR

But be contented: when that fell arrest
Without all bail shall carry me away,
My life hath in this line some interest,
Which for memorial still with thee shall stay.
5 When thou reviewest this, thou dost review
The very part was consecrate to thee:
The earth can have but earth, which is his due;
My spirit is thine, the better part of me:
So then thou hast but lost the dregs of life,
10 The prey of worms, my body being dead;
The coward conquest of a wretch's knife,
Too base of thee to be remembered.
    The worth of that is that which it contains,
    And that is this, and this with thee remains.

2. SWEET SEASON'D *gentle, sweet and seasonable, as in April.* 3. THE PEACE OF YOU *the peace that comes from association with you.* 4. *Compare Sonnet 51, lines 1–4.* 5. ENJOYER *possessor, proprietor.* 6. DOUBTING *fearing.* 8. *Made happier by the world's seeing the pleasure I take in knowing you.* 10. BY AND BY *immediately afterward.* CLEAN *wholly.* 12. TOOK *a strong form of the participle. Compare Sonnet 17, line 1.* 14. OR . . . OR *either . . . or.* ON ALL *on everything.* OR ALL AWAY *or having nothing to feed on...*

A compliment to the friend takes the form of a discussion of the poet's style which, he asserts, remains the same because it is both personal to him and appropriate to an unchanging friendship. He therefore has no need of such diction as, say, the young John Donne was beginning to use. Although it will be granted that some of the sonnets are repetitious enough, the assertion is only partly true. Shakespeare's growing virtuosity is nowhere better illustrated than in his sonnets (see, for instance, Sonnets 73 and 74).

1. PRIDE *ornament, manner of writing.* 3. WITH THE TIME *with the passing of time, or after the new fashion.* 4. COMPOUNDS *compound words.* 6. KEEP . . . WEED *keep writing on the same subject in the, by now, familiar manner.* 7. THAT *so that.* TELL *Emendation by Edward Capell (1713–1781). 1609 Quarto: fel.* 8. WHERE *whence.* 10. ARGUMENT *theme, subject.* 11–12. *Compare Sonnet 59, lines 1–4.* 11. DRESSING . . . NEW *arranging familiar terms in a new order.*

SEVENTY-FIVE

So are you to my thoughts as food to life,
Or as sweet season'd showers are to the ground;
And for the peace of you I hold such strife
As 'twixt a miser and his wealth is found;
5   Now proud as an enjoyer, and anon
Doubting the filching age will steal his treasure;
Now counting best to be with you alone,
Then better'd that the world may see my pleasure:
Sometime all full with feasting on your sight,
10   And by and by clean starved for a look;
Possessing or pursuing no delight,
Save what is had or must from you be took.
        Thus do I pine and surfeit day by day,
        Or gluttoning on all, or all away.

SEVENTY-SIX

Why is my verse so barren of new pride,
So far from variation or quick change?
Why with the time do I not glance aside
To new found methods and to compounds strange?
5   Why write I still all one, ever the same,
And keep invention in a noted weed,
That every word doth almost tell my name,
Showing their birth and where they did proceed?
O, know, sweet love, I always write of you,
10   And you and love are still my argument;
So all my best is dressing old words new,
Spending again what is already spent:
        For as the sun is daily new and old,
        So is my love still telling what is told.

The sonnet accompanied a gift of "tables," a book of blank leaves on which to record one's thoughts and observations. It discloses one of the functions of writing, which is "To take a new acquaintance of thy mind." In Sonnet 122 the poet writes of a gift of tables received from the friend.

2. DIAL *pocket sundial.* 4. THIS LEARNING *the decline into age reflected in the glass and recorded in the book.* 6. MOUTHED *devouring. Compare* Venus and Adonis, *line 757.* 7. SHADY STEALTH *the imperceptible movement of the shadow.* 9. LOOK WHAT *whatever.* 10. BLANKS *Emendation by Lewis Theobald (1688–1744). 1609 Quarto: blacks.* 13. OFFICES *the duties of recording in the book and reading what has been recorded.*

With the exception of Sonnet 81, Sonnets 78 to 86 are concerned with other poets who were addressing poems to the young friend. One of them, singled out in Sonnets 79, 80, 83, and 85, has come to be known as the Rival Poet. In the present state of our knowledge there is no knowing who he was.

2. ASSISTANCE *inspiration which comes both from the muse and the subject of the poems, or assuming that the young man was the Earl of Southampton to whom* Venus and Adonis *and* The Rape of Lucrece *were dedicated, aid from a patron.* 3. AS *that.* EVERY ALIEN PEN *other poets who are strangers to the young man or less closely associated with him than Shakespeare was.* GOT MY USE *have taken on my custom of addressing verses to you.* 4. UNDER THEE *with your patronage, or with your, at least, tacit permission.* 5. ON HIGH *aloud.* 6. HEAVY IGNORANCE *The same phrase is used in* Othello *(Act II, scene 1, line 144). Here the phrase may mean Shakespeare himself as opposed to the learned poet of the following line.* 7. ADDED FEATHERS *Broken feathers in a falcon's wing were replaced or mended by splicing.* 8. GRACE *excellence.* 9. COMPILE *compose.* 10. INFLUENCE *inspiration.*

SEVENTY-SEVEN

Thy glass will show thee how thy beauties wear,
Thy dial how thy precious minutes waste;
The vacant leaves thy mind's imprint will bear,
And of this book this learning mayst thou taste.
5   The wrinkles which thy glass will truly show
Of mouthed graves will give thee memory;
Thou by thy dial's shady stealth mayst know
Time's thievish progress to eternity.
Look what thy memory cannot contain
10   Commit to these waste blanks, and thou shalt find
Those children nurs'd, deliver'd from thy brain,
To take a new acquaintance of thy mind.
        These offices, so oft as thou wilt look,
        Shall profit thee and much enrich thy book.

SEVENTY-EIGHT

So oft have I invok'd thee for my Muse
And found such fair assistance in my verse
As every alien pen hath got my use
And under thee their poesy disperse.
5   Thine eyes, that taught the dumb on high to sing
And heavy ignorance aloft to fly,
Have added feathers to the learned's wing
And given grace a double majesty.
Yet be most proud of that which I compile,
10   Whose influence is thine, and born of thee:
In others' works thou dost but mend the style,
And arts with thy sweet graces graced be;
        But thou art all my art and dost advance
        As high as learning my rude ignorance.

3. GRACIOUS *attractive.* NUMBERS *verses.* 4. GIVE AN-
OTHER PLACE *give place to another.* 5. THY LOVELY
ARGUMENT *the theme of your loveliness. See Sonnet
38, lines 2–4.* 7. THY POET *the poet writing of you.*
8. HE ROBS THEE OF *because (see Sonnet 84) in you
is stored up the sum of all excellence.* 11. AFFORD
offer. 14. OWES *Laudatory poems are thought of as
a debt owed to such a friend or patron. See Sonnet 85, line 4.*

Here and in Sonnet 86 the poetry of the rival is
characterized by its stateliness. The recurrent image
for it is that of a tall ship in full sail moving majestic-
ally on.

1. FAINT *feel discouraged.* 2. BETTER SPIRIT *poet of
greater talent, that is, the man who has come to be
known as the Rival Poet.* 5–6. *Since your worth is
as wide as the ocean it bears the humblest as well as
the proudest sail. The "est" is not used with
"humble" for the sake of euphony.* 7. SAUCY *im-
pudent, insolent.* 8. WILFULLY *at will.* 10. SOUNDLESS
unfathomable. 12. TALL BUILDING *stout, sturdy, and
large construction.* PRIDE *splendor.*

SEVENTY-NINE

Whilst I alone did call upon thy aid,
My verse alone had all thy gentle grace;
But now my gracious numbers are decay'd,
And my sick Muse doth give another place.
5 I grant, sweet love, thy lovely argument
Deserves the travail of a worthier pen;
Yet what of thee thy poet doth invent
He robs thee of, and pays it thee again.
He lends thee virtue, and he stole that word
10 From thy behaviour; beauty doth he give,
And found it in thy cheek: he can afford
No praise to thee but what in thee doth live.
    Then thank him not for that which he doth say,
    Since what he owes thee thou thyself dost pay.

EIGHTY

O, how I faint when I of you do write,
Knowing a better spirit doth use your name,
And in the praise thereof spends all his might,
To make me tongue-tied, speaking of your fame.
5 But since your worth, wide as the ocean is,
The humble as the proudest sail doth bear,
My saucy bark, inferior far to his,
On your broad main doth wilfully appear.
Your shallowest help will hold me up afloat,
10 Whilst he upon your soundless deep doth ride;
Or, being wreck'd, I am a worthless boat,
He of tall building and of goodly pride:
    Then if he thrive and I be cast away,
    The worst was this: my love was my decay.

The sonnets in which Shakespeare says that his poetry will live although he himself will be forgotten are not to be discounted. There was an abundance of precedent for this. He knew of the "makers" of the Middle Ages whose poems survived anonymously. At the time when he was writing the sonnets he was moving into artistic maturity, but his reputation was not yet secure.

1. OR *whether.* *3.* FROM HENCE *from the earth.* *4.* EACH PART *all that I am.* *5.* FROM HENCE *from these poems.* *11.* REHEARSE *re-create.* *12.* BREATHERS *men now living.* *14.* Shakespeare's meanings often depend upon the close association of breath and life, of breathing and living. Sometimes the terms are synonymous.

2. ATTAINT *dishonor.* O'ERLOOK *look over, peruse.* *3.* DEDICATED *devoted.* *4.* BLESSING EVERY BOOK *The friend's perusal of the books blesses them; or the devotion expressed in the books blesses them.* *6.* FINDING *The subject of "Finding" is "Thou."* LIMIT *extent, reach.* *8.* STAMP *imprint.* TIME BETTERING DAYS *See comment on Sonnet 32.* *10.* STRAINED *exaggerated.* *11.* TRULY FAIR *true to the ideal of beauty.* TRULY SYMPATHIZ'D *truthfully represented.* Compare *The Rape of Lucrece*, *line 1113.* *14.* IN . . . ABUS'D *When used in relation to you, it is an abuse.*

EIGHTY-ONE

Or I shall live your epitaph to make,
Or you survive when I in earth am rotten;
From hence your memory death cannot take,
Although in me each part will be forgotten.
5   Your name from hence immortal life shall have,
Though I, once gone, to all the world must die;
The earth can yield me but a common grave,
When you entombed in men's eyes shall lie.
Your monument shall be my gentle verse,
10   Which eyes not yet created shall o'er-read,
And tongues to be your being shall rehearse,
When all the breathers of this world are dead;
> You still shall live (such virtue hath my pen)
> Where breath most breathes, even in the mouths of
> men.

EIGHTY-TWO

I grant thou wert not married to my Muse,
And therefore mayst without attaint o'erlook
The dedicated words which writers use
Of their fair subject, blessing every book.
5   Thou art as fair in knowledge as in hue,
Finding thy worth a limit past my praise,
And therefore art enforc'd to seek anew
Some fresher stamp of the time bettering days.
And do so, love; yet when they have devis'd
10   What strained touches rhetoric can lend,
Thou truly fair wert truly sympathiz'd
In true plain words by thy true telling friend;
> And their gross painting might be better us'd
> Where cheeks need blood; in thee it is abus'd.

Readers should notice that Shakespeare's adulation of the young man is not unmixed with rebuke. His self-love is commented on in the opening sonnets. Here there is a touch of irony in line 3, and in the following sonnet he is seen to have grown vain.

1. PAINTING *beautifying.* 2. FAIR *beauty.* 4. BARREN TENDER *fruitless proffer.* POET'S DEBT *the debt a poet owes to beauty.* 5. SLEPT . . . REPORT *refrained from reporting your beauty.* 7. MODERN *commonplace.* 7–8. DOTH COME . . . DOTH GROW *falls too short when, speaking of worth, it attempts to do justice to your worth.* 9–10. *You took this silence to be a wrong on my part, but it is rather my glory, because I recognized you did not need praise.* 12. *When others, meaning to celebrate you, do you injustice by the inadequacy of their poetry.* BRING A TOMB *Compare Sonnet 17, lines 1–4.*

1. MOST? *1609 Quarto: most,.* WHICH *which of the poets praising you.* 3–4. *you, in whom is stored up the beauty which would have to be drawn on to create your equal. Compare Sonnet 67: "beauty . . . hath no exchequer now but his. . . ."* 6. HIS *its.* 8. SO *thereby.* 10. CLEAR *glorious.* 11. COUNTERPART *copy.* FAME *make famous.* 14. ON *of.* WHICH *your being found of praise.* MAKES . . . WORSE *because, as stated above, your excellence should be merely described; or the praise expended on you is bad because it encourages your vanity; or both; take it as you will.*

EIGHTY-THREE

I never saw that you did painting need,
And therefore to your fair no painting set:
I found (or thought I found) you did exceed
The barren tender of a poet's debt:
5 And therefore have I slept in your report,
That you yourself, being extant, well might show
How far a modern quill doth come too short,
Speaking of worth, what worth in you doth grow:
This silence for my sin you did impute,
10 Which shall be most my glory, being dumb,
For I impair not beauty being mute,
When others would give life and bring a tomb.
    There lives more life in one of your fair eyes
    Than both your poets can in praise devise.

EIGHTY-FOUR

Who is it that says most? which can say more
Than this rich praise, that you alone are you
In whose confine immured is the store
Which should example where your equal grew?
5 Lean penury within that pen doth dwell
That to his subject lends not some small glory;
But he that writes of you, if he can tell
That you are you, so dignifies his story.
Let him but copy what in you is writ,
10 Not making worse what nature made so clear,
And such a counterpart shall fame his wit,
Making his style admired every where.
    You to your beauteous blessings add a curse,
    Being fond on praise, which makes your praises worse.

1. IN MANNERS *politely.* HOLDS HER STILL *is silent.*
2. COMPIL'D *composed. 3.* RESERVE *preserve.* CHARACTER
*writing. The meaning of this obscure line seems to
be that the comments preserve their writing for
eternity with eloquent pen. The text may be corrupt.
None of the many interpretations is altogether satis-
factory. 5.* OTHER *others. 6.* STILL *always. 7.* AFFORDS
*offers. See Sonnets 79 (line 11) and 105 (line 12).
10.* MOST *height. 13.* BREATH OF WORDS *Compare* Hamlet (*Act III, scene 4, line 197*), "if words be made of
breath." RESPECT *"Respect" has two objects, "others"
and "me." 14.* SPEAKING IN EFFECT *having the effect of
speech.*

1. HIS *the Rival Poet's. 3.* INHEARSE *confine as in a
coffin. 4. Making the womb wherein they grew their
tomb. 5–10. On the assumption that Shakespeare
meant these lines to be taken seriously, scholars have
speculated on the identity of the poet who was said
to have written by spirit aid, but on the basis of our
present knowledge all such speculation is idle. Whatever the specific references may be, the passage assumes the validity of the theory of poetic inspiration,
and the suggestion that the poet's muse plays him
false is unmistakable. 6.* DEAD *silent. 7.* COMPEERS *associates. 8.* ASTONISHED *amazed, stunned. See* The
Rape of Lucrece, *line 1730. 10.* GULLS *tricks. 13.*
COUNTENANCE *authority, credit, patronage; physical
beauty.*

EIGHTY-FIVE

My tongue-tied Muse in manners holds her still,
While comments of your praise, richly compil'd,
Reserve their character with golden quill
And precious phrase by all the Muses fil'd.
5 I think good thoughts whilst other write good words,
And, like unlettered clerk, still cry "Amen"
To every hymn that able spirit affords
In polish'd form of well-refined pen.
Hearing you prais'd, I say, " 'Tis so, 'tis true,"
10 And to the most of praise add something more;
But that is in my thought, whose love to you,
Though words come hindmost, holds his rank before.
    Then others for the breath of words respect;
    Me for my dumb thoughts, speaking in effect.

EIGHTY-SIX

Was it the proud full sail of his great verse,
Bound for the prize of all too precious you,
That did my ripe thoughts in my brain inhearse,
Making their tomb the womb wherein they grew?
5 Was it his spirit, by spirits taught to write
Above a mortal pitch, that struck me dead?
No, neither he nor his compeers by night
Giving him aid, my verse astonished.
He, nor that affable familiar ghost
10 Which nightly gulls him with intelligence,
As victors, of my silence cannot boast;
I was not sick of any fear from thence:
    But when your countenance fill'd up his line,
    Then lack'd I matter; that enfeebled mine.

*This sonnet seems to be the last of a series, begin-
ning with 78 and excepting 81, in which the poet
becomes increasingly aware of the friend's vanity,
and at last offers to bring the friendship to an end.
The rhymes are all double, and excepting lines 2
and 4 which have thereby an added force, the endings are feminine.*

2. ESTIMATE *value.* 3. CHARTER *privilege.* OF *deriving from.* 4. BONDS *Compare Sonnet 117, line
4.* DETERMINATE *ended. Compare Sonnet 13, line
6.* 6. RICHES *The word, deriving from the French*
richesse, *was originally singular, as here.* 7. WANT-
ING *lacking.* 8. PATENT *privilege.* BACK . . . SWERVING
returns to you, as in line 12. 11. UPON MISPRISION
GROWING *arising from an error.*

1. SET *value. 2. And view my merit with a scornful
eye.* 7. CONCEAL'D *unknown to the world.* ATTAINTED
infected. Compare Sonnet 82, line 2. 8. THAT *so that.*
LOSING *1609 Quarto:* loosing, *a variant spelling of
"losing."* 11–12. *The injuries that I do to myself in
doing good to you do me a double good because (1)
a good done to you is also done to me, and (2) it
is good to bear the wrongs of another. 12.* VANTAGE
advantage.

EIGHTY-SEVEN

Farewell! thou art too dear for my possessing,
And like enough thou know'st thy estimate:
The charter of thy worth gives thee releasing;
My bonds in thee are all determinate.
5   For how do I hold thee but by thy granting,
And for that riches where is my deserving?
The cause of this fair gift in me is wanting,
And so my patent back again is swerving.
Thyself thou gav'st, thy own worth then not knowing,
10   Or me, to whom thou gav'st it, else mistaking;
So thy great gift, upon misprision growing,
Comes home again, on better judgment making.
     Thus have I had thee as a dream doth flatter,
     In sleep a king, but waking no such matter.

EIGHTY-EIGHT

When thou shalt be dispos'd to set me light,
And place my merit in the eye of scorn,
Upon thy side against myself I'll fight,
And prove thee virtuous, though thou art forsworn.
5   With mine own weakness being best acquainted,
Upon thy part I can set down a story
Of faults conceal'd, wherein I am attainted,
That thou in losing me shalt win much glory:
And I by this will be a gainer too;
10   For bending all my loving thoughts on thee,
The injuries that to myself I do,
Doing thee vantage, double vantage me.
     Such is my love, to thee I so belong,
     That for thy right myself will bear all wrong.

1. SAY *if it is assumed.* *2.* COMMENT *discourse.* *3. If you attribute some fault to me, I shall assume, or pretend, that I have it. To think, as some commentators do, that Shakespeare was actually lame is to misread the line.* *5.* DISGRACE *discredit.* *6. To give the appearance of the change you desire.* *8.* I . . . STRANGLE *I will end our familiarity.* LOOK STRANGE *appear to be a stranger.* *11.* PROFANE *irreverent.* *12.* HAPLY *by chance.* *13.* DEBATE *warfare.*

Whatever the unknown events motivating the writing of this sonnet may have been, they have brought about a peerless expression of one of the most common of experiences, the sense of injured love. It was the awareness of such experience which did so much to make Hamlet the best loved of all tragic heroes. The sonnet is an instance of Shakespeare's growing ability to write powerfully without the ornamentation which graced his earlier verse.

4. FOR AN AFTER LOSS *to cause still more grief.* *10.* OTHER PETTY GRIEFS *other griefs which are petty in comparison to loss of you.* *11.* SHALL *1609 Quarto: stall.* *13.* STRAINS *kinds.*

EIGHTY-NINE

Say that thou didst forsake me for some fault,
And I will comment upon that offence;
Speak of my lameness, and I straight will halt,
Against thy reasons making no defence.
5 Thou canst not, love, disgrace me half so ill,
To set a form upon desired change,
As I'll myself disgrace; knowing thy will,
I will acquaintance strangle and look strange,
Be absent from thy walks, and in my tongue
10 Thy sweet beloved name no more shall dwell,
Lest I, too much profane, should do it wrong,
And haply of our old acquaintance tell.
    For thee, against myself I'll vow debate,
    For I must ne'er love him whom thou dost hate.

NINETY

Then hate me when thou wilt; if ever, now;
Now, while the world is bent my deeds to cross,
Join with the spite of fortune, make me bow,
And do not drop in for an after loss.
5 Ah, do not, when my heart hath 'scap'd this sorrow,
Come in the rearward of a conquer'd woe;
Give not a windy night a rainy morrow,
To linger out a purpos'd overthrow.
If thou wilt leave me, do not leave me last,
10 When other petty griefs have done their spite,
But in the onset come: so shall I taste
At first the very worst of fortune's might;
    And other strains of woe, which now seem woe,
    Compar'd with loss of thee will not seem so.

Throughout the sonnets to the young man Shakespeare writes that although he may seem to cultivate the young man for prudential reasons such is not the case. There are some who glory in birth, skill, wealth, strength, possessions, and outward show, but "these particulars are not my measure." This is consistent with the point of view disclosed throughout his works. He nowhere either says or implies that birth and wealth are unimportant. They are admired for certain values, but they are never admired for themselves alone. What is most important in the sonnets is the young man's truth and worth.

3. NEW-FANGLED ILL *fashionable and ugly.* 5. HUMOUR *disposition.* ADJUNCT *attendant.* 7. MEASURE *standard of judgment.* 9. BETTER THAN 1609 *Quarto: bitter then.* 12. *The friendship is declared to be of more value than all the things other men take pride in. Compare Sonnet 29.*

Unless we assume that the poet had in mind the concept of unity in division (see Sonnet 36 and the comment on it), this is an extravagant proclamation of the poet's devotion to and dependence on the friend, yet it ends with a gentle rebuke for an apprehended flaw in the friend, and it thus introduces a series of sonnets (93 to 96) in which the rebukes continue with varying intensity.

2. TERM *time, that is, my lifetime.* 3. THAN 1609 *Quarto: then.* 5. THE WORST OF WRONGS *to lose the friend.* 6. LEAST OF THEM *the least sign of change in the friend.* 8. HUMOUR *caprice.* 10. *Since I would die should you desert me.* 11. HAPPY TITLE *title to happiness.* 13–14. *Note the contrast to the ending of Sonnet 25.*

NINETY-ONE

Some glory in their birth, some in their skill,
Some in their wealth, some in their bodies' force;
Some in their garments, though new-fangled ill;
Some in their hawks and hounds, some in their horse;
5   And every humour hath his adjunct pleasure,
Wherein it finds a joy above the rest:
But these particulars are not my measure;
All these I better in one general best.
Thy love is better than high birth to me,
10   Richer than wealth, prouder than garments' cost,
Of more delight than hawks or horses be;
And having thee, of all men's pride I boast:
     Wretched in this alone, that thou mayst take
     All this away and me most wretched make.

NINETY-TWO

But do thy worst to steal thyself away,
For term of life thou art assured mine,
And life no longer than thy love will stay,
For it depends upon that love of thine.
5   Then need I not to fear the worst of wrongs,
When in the least of them my life hath end;
I see a better state to me belongs
Than that which on thy humour doth depend:
Thou canst not vex me with inconstant mind,
10   Since that my life on thy revolt doth lie.
O, what a happy title do I find,
Happy to have thy love, happy to die!
     But what's so blessed fair that fears no blot?
     Thou mayst be false, and yet I know it not.

At no point in Shakespeare's career did he abandon his concern with physical beauty, yet as he matured the concept of beauty expanded to include a greater concern with inward beauty or the lack of it. In this series he writes of the discrepancy between appearance and reality.

2. LOVE'S FACE *the appearance of love as opposed to the reality.* 8. MOODS *external appearances expressive of disposition.*

The octave of the sonnet is ironic. The poet states as true that which throughout his works he declares to be false: those men whose appearance does not square with reality, whose deeds do not fulfill their promise, are proclaimed the heirs to heaven's graces. They are the owners of themselves, whereas throughout Shakespeare's works self-possession in the sense of living without regard for others is intolerable. There is no moral idea to which he returns more insistently than that of man's stewardship as set forth in the parable of the talents, Matthew 25:14–30. The sestet abandons the irony and turns to the most familiar image of the young man, the flower blooming for itself alone. In the opening sonnets he had asked that the young man reproduce his beauty. Later, as here, his concern is for moral beauty.

1. POW'R TO HURT *Those who have the power to inspire affection have the power to hurt by withdrawing or refusing it.* WILL DO NONE *will not return the love they inspire. See lines 3–4.* 11. BASE INFECTION *There is no knowing what the young man's "infection" was, for it is referred to conditionally and may have been apprehended rather than actual, but it is clear that the poet had in mind a denial of something he held essential to human decency.*

NINETY-THREE

So shall I live, supposing thou art true,
Like a deceived husband; so love's face
May still seem love to me, though alter'd new;
Thy looks with me, thy heart in other place:
5 For there can live no hatred in thine eye,
Therefore in that I cannot know thy change;
In many's looks the false heart's history
Is writ in moods and frowns and wrinkles strange:
But heaven in thy creation did decree
10 That in thy face sweet love should ever dwell;
Whate'er thy thoughts or thy heart's workings be,
Thy looks should nothing thence but sweetness tell.
  How like Eve's apple doth thy beauty grow,
  If thy sweet virtue answer not thy show!

NINETY-FOUR

They that have pow'r to hurt and will do none,
That do not do the thing they most do show,
Who moving others, are themselves as stone,
Unmoved, cold and to temptation slow;
5 They rightly do inherit heaven's graces
And husband nature's riches from expense;
They are the lords and owners of their faces,
Others but stewards of their excellence.
The summer's flow'r is to the summer sweet,
10 Though to itself it only live and die,
But if that flow'r with base infection meet,
The basest weed outbraves his dignity:
  For sweetest things turn sourest by their deeds;
  Lilies that fester smell far worse than weeds.

The Neoplatonic notion of the coincidence of inward and outward beauty is one of the most widely spread commonplaces of Elizabethan poetry, yet it is highly uncharacteristic of Shakespeare. He was much too sensible not to know that it had been demonstrably false since the time of Helen of Troy. Here the young man's beauty graces his vices, but only, it is suggested, temporarily.

2. CANKER *the worm which feeds on blossoms.* 3. NAME *reputation.* 6. SPORT *doubtless sexual indulgence.* 9. MANSION *dwelling place. Compare Sonnets 10 (line 7) and 146 (line 6).*

This sonnet concludes the series introduced in Sonnet 92.

1. WANTONNESS *lasciviousness.* 3. OF MORE AND LESS *by people of all ranks.* 8. TRANSLATED *transformed.* 10. *If he could assume the appearance of a lamb.* 12. STATE *both state of being (attractiveness) and status (position in society).* 13–14. *The couplet is repeated from Sonnet 36. Here it repeats a rhyme from the first couplet.*

NINETY-FIVE

How sweet and lovely dost thou make the shame
Which, like a canker in the fragrant rose,
Doth spot the beauty of thy budding name!
O, in what sweets dost thou thy sins enclose!
5   That tongue that tells the story of thy days,
(Making lascivious comments on thy sport)
Cannot dispraise but in a kind of praise;
Naming thy name blesses an ill report.
O, what a mansion have those vices got
10   Which for their habitation chose out thee,
Where beauty's veil doth cover every blot
And all things turns to fair that eyes can see!
    Take heed, dear heart, of this large privilege;
    The hardest knife ill us'd doth lose his edge.

NINETY-SIX

Some say, thy fault is youth, some wantonness;
Some say, thy grace is youth and gentle sport;
Both grace and faults are lov'd of more and less:
Thou mak'st faults graces that to thee resort:
5   As on the finger of a throned queen
The basest jewel will be well esteem'd,
So are those errors that in thee are seen
To truths translated and for true things deem'd.
How many lambs might the stern wolf betray,
10   If like a lamb he could his looks translate!
How many gazers mightst thou lead away,
If thou wouldst use the strength of all thy state!
    But do not so; I love thee in such sort,
    As thou being mine, mine is thy good report.

*Various editors find that this sonnet, the first of
two on the theme of absence, is hastily written, that
its images are blurred beyond recognition, and that
it is in part logically absurd. Yet it makes its impact
and is, in part at least, unforgettable. It represents
the triumph of poetic genius over the craft of
analysis.*

2. THE PLEASURE . . . YEAR *the friend who makes any
part of the year pleasurable.* 5. TIME REMOV'D *time of
absence.* SUMMER'S TIME *summer and early autumn.*
6. TEEMING *burgeoning, pregnant.* 7. WANTON *play-
ful, luxuriant.* PRIME *the young manhood of the
year, the season of fertilization.* 10. HOPE OF OR-
PHANS *such hope as orphans have.*

2. PROUD PIED *splendidly dappled.* TRIM *ornamentation.* 4. THAT *so that.* SATURN *Saturn, the god who
reigned before Jupiter, was thought to have a
morose temperament.* 5. LAYS *songs.* 6. DIFFERENT
FLOWERS *flowers different.* 7. SUMMER'S STORY *a story
suitable for summer as opposed to "a sad tale" which
is "best for winter." (A Winter's Tale, Act II, scene
1, line 25).* 11. WERE *1609 Quarto: weare. 1640
edition: were.* BUT SWEET *The flowers were delightful only in so far as they resembled the friend.*
FIGURES *forms.* 12. *You are the pattern after which
the flowers were drawn.* 14. SHADOW *This refers
back to line 12 and looks forward to the continuation of the conceit in the next sonnet.*

NINETY-SEVEN

How like a winter hath my absence been
From thee, the pleasure of the fleeting year!
What freezings have I felt, what dark days seen,
What old December's bareness every where!
5 And yet this time remov'd was summer's time;
The teeming autumn, big with rich increase,
Bearing the wanton burthen of the prime,
Like widowed wombs after their lord's decease:
Yet this abundant issue seem'd to me
10 But hope of orphans and unfather'd fruit;
For summer and his pleasures wait on thee,
And, thou away, the very birds are mute;
      Or, if they sing, 'tis with so dull a cheer
      That leaves look pale, dreading the winter's near.

NINETY-EIGHT

From you have I been absent in the spring,
When proud pied April, dress'd in all his trim,
Hath put a spirit of youth in everything,
That heavy Saturn laugh'd and leapt with him.
5 Yet nor the lays of birds, nor the sweet smell
Of different flowers in odour and in hue,
Could make me any summer's story tell,
Or from their proud lap pluck them where they grew;
Nor did I wonder at the lily's white,
10 Nor praise the deep vermilion in the rose;
They were but sweet, but figures of delight
Drawn after you, you pattern of all those.
      Yet seem'd it winter still, and you away,
      As with your shadow I with these did play.

. . . but figures of delight
Drawn after you

The poem has fifteen lines, the first standing as introduction to a structurally regular Shakespearean sonnet. It is the last of a series of three.

1. FORWARD *early. 3.* PURPLE *In poetry "purple" is used vaguely but generally to mean red.* PRIDE *display of beauty. 5.* GROSSLY *obviously. 6. I blamed the lily for stealing the whiteness of your hand. 7. This probably means that the hair was golden. 9.* ONE *Emendation by George Sewell (d. 1726). 1609 Quarto: Our. 12.* IN . . . GROWTH *when it was in full bloom. 13.* EAT *the imperfect tense. 15.* SWEET *It is possible that "sweet" is the printer's misreading of "scent."*

1–2. Compare Sonnet 85, line 1. 3. FURY *the "fine frenzy" of* A Midsummer Night's Dream *(Act V, scene 1, line 12). 6.* GENTLE *noble.* NUMBERS *verses. 7.* LAYS *poems. 8.* ARGUMENT *subject matter. 9.* RESTY *lazy. 10.* IF *to see if. 11.* BE . . . DECAY *satirize decay. 14.* PREVENT'ST *frustrate.*

NINETY-NINE

The forward violet thus did I chide:
Sweet thief, whence didst thou steal thy sweet that smells,
If not from my love's breath? The purple pride
Which on thy soft cheek for complexion dwells
5   In my love's veins thou hast too grossly dy'd.
The lily I condemned for thy hand,
And buds of marjoram had stol'n thy hair;
The roses fearfully on thorns did stand,
One blushing shame, another white despair;
10   A third, nor red nor white, had stol'n of both,
And to his robb'ry had annex'd thy breath;
But, for his theft, in pride of all his growth
A vengeful canker eat him up to death.
     More flowers I noted, yet I none could see
     But sweet or colour it had stol'n from thee.

Where art thou, Muse, that thou forget'st so long
To speak of that which gives thee all thy might?
Spend'st thou thy fury on some worthless song,
Dark'ning thy power to lend base subjects light?
5   Return, forgetful Muse, and straight redeem
In gentle numbers time so idly spent;
Sing to the ear that doth thy lays esteem
And gives thy pen both skill and argument.
Rise, resty Muse, my love's sweet face survey,
10   If Time have any wrinkle graven there;
If any, be a satire to decay,
And make Time's spoils despised every where.
     Give my love fame faster than Time wastes life;
     So thou prevent'st his scythe and crooked knife.

Truth, as in this sonnet, may be taken to include value, worth, and genuineness. True beauty, too, is genuine; one of its opposites is artificiality. The friend's beauty, like Olivia's, is "in grain, sir; 'twill endure wind and weather." (Twelfth Night, Act I, scene 5, line 256.) Shakespeare never says that beauty is truth, truth beauty, but in the friend the two are inseparable.

2. TRUTH . . . DY'D value embodied in beauty. 3. MY LOVE the friend, not the poet's emotion. 4. DIGNIFIED be dignified. 5. HAPLY perhaps. 6. Given in him the natural embodiment of value in beauty, value needs no embellishment. 7. TO LAY to set forth, spread out, as in laying a carpet. 8. Perfect truth and perfect beauty are best without embellishment. 9–12. Although he needs no praise now, he must be celebrated in poetry so that he will be known and praised in future ages after his tomb has fallen into decay.

2. SHOW manifestation of my love. 3. MERCHANDIZ'D treated as something which can be bought and sold. ESTEEMING worth. 4. Compare Sonnet 21, line 14. 7. As the nightingale which sings in early summer. 8. HIS 1609 Quarto. Many editors emend to "her" to make the reference consistent with lines 10 and 13. But Shakespeare may have known that it is the cock nightingale which sings, and in any case he is capable of inconsistencies. 10. HUSH make silent. 11. BURTHENS EVERY BOUGH is sung by every poet. Compare Sonnet 85, line 5.

O truant Muse, what shall be thy amends
For thy neglect of truth in beauty dy'd?
Both truth and beauty on my love depends;
So dost thou too, and therein dignified:
5   Make answer, Muse: wilt thou not haply say,
"Truth needs no colour, with his colour fix'd;
Beauty no pencil, beauty's truth to lay;
But best is best, if never intermix'd"?
Because he needs no praise, wilt thou be dumb?
10   Excuse not silence so; for't lies in thee
To make him much outlive a gilded tomb
And to be prais'd of ages yet to be.
        Then do thy office, Muse; I teach thee how
        To make him seem, long hence, as he shows now.

My love is strengthen'd, though more weak in seeming;
I love not less, though less the show appear:
That love is merchandiz'd whose rich esteeming
The owner's tongue doth publish every where.
5   Our love was new, and then but in the spring,
When I was wont to greet it with my lays;
As Philomel in summer's front doth sing,
And stops his pipe in growth of riper days:
Not that the summer is less pleasant now
10   Than when her mournful hymns did hush the night,
But that wild music burthens every bough,
And sweets grown common lose their dear delight:
        Therefore, like her, I sometime hold my tongue,
        Because I would not dull you with my song.

1. POVERTY *poor or inferior matter.* 2. THAT HAVING *while she has.* SCOPE *See Sonnet 105, lines 12–14.* 3. THE ARGUMENT *the subject matter of my poems, that is, you.* ALL BARE *in yourself.* 7. OVER-GOES *exceeds.* MY BLUNT INVENTION *the clumsy craftsmanship which I bring to my subject matter.* 8. DULLING *making dull.* DISGRACE *discredit.* 9. MEND *enhance.* 11. PASS *purpose.*

We may conclude from this sonnet that it was written three years after Shakespeare first saw the young friend and was impressed by his beauty, and that the friendship celebrated in the sonnets lasted at least three years. In Elizabethan poetry the pun was taken seriously as a figure of speech, and Shakespeare achieves some of his best as well as some of his worst effects through the use of it. No doubt he wrote the three-way pun which ends the second line and found it good.

2. WHEN . . . EY'D *when I first saw you.* 4. PRIDE *splendor.* 6. PROCESS *the passing.* 7. BURN'D *dissipated.* 9–10. *Beauty departs from his figure imperceptibly, as the hand of the clock moves away from the figure on the dial.* 11. HUE *complexion, coloring.* METHINKS *it seems to me.* STILL (*1*) *motionless,* (*2*) *forever.* 14. BEAUTY'S SUMMER *full flowering of beauty.*

Alack, what poverty my Muse brings forth,
That, having such a scope to show her pride.
The argument, all bare, is of more worth
Than when it hath my added praise beside.
5   O blame me not, if I no more can write!
Look in your glass, and there appears a face
That over-goes my blunt invention quite,
Dulling my lines and doing me disgrace.
Were it not sinful then, striving to mend,
10   To mar the subject that before was well?
For to no other pass my verses tend
Than of your graces and your gifts to tell;
      And more, much more, than in my verse can sit,
      Your own glass shows you when you look in it.

To me, fair friend, you never can be old,
For as you were when first your eye I ey'd,
Such seems your beauty still. Three winters cold
Have from the forests shook three summers' pride,
5   Three beauteous springs to yellow autumn turn'd
In process of the seasons have I seen,
Three April perfumes in three hot Junes burn'd,
Since first I saw you fresh, which yet are green.
Ah, yet doth beauty, like a dial hand
10   Steal from his figure, and no pace perceiv'd;
So your sweet hue, which methinks still doth stand,
Hath motion, and mine eye may be deceiv'd:
      For fear of which, hear this, thou age unbred;
      Ere you were born was beauty's summer dead.

2. SHOW *appear.* 3. *Compare Sonnet 76.* 8. DIFFER-
ENCE *variety.* 9. FAIR *beautiful.* KIND *Shakespeare
uses "kind" to mean natural, benevolent, tender,
and such as a person ought to be, that is, not de-
parting from the ideal. All these meanings are suggested here.* 11. CHANGE *the changes rung on the
repeated themes.* 12. WONDROUS SCOPE *Their scope
is "wondrous" because they are the good, the beautiful, and the true.* 14. KEPT . . . ONE *united in one
man.*

1. WASTED TIME *times past.* 2. FAIREST WIGHTS *most
beautiful persons.* 3. MAKING . . . RHYME *making old
rhyme beautiful.* 4. LOVELY *charming, attractive.* 5.
BLAZON *showing forth.* 11-12. *And because they
had only their intuition of you, not knowing you in
actuality, what they knew, even though it was
splendid, was still not enough to enable them to
celebrate such worth as yours. Many editors emend
the "still" of line 12 to "skill," but the meaning is
that the poets of olden times lacked the subject
matter. The couplet goes on to say that as for us,
the poets of the present time, we, beholding you,
have the subject matter but lack the skill needed
to celebrate the worth before us. Shakespeare says
elsewhere that he as artist is not adequate to the
subject before him. See Sonnet 103.*

Let not my love be call'd idolatry,
Nor my beloved as an idol show,
Since all alike my songs and praises be
To one, of one, still such, and ever so.
5   Kind is my love to-day, to-morrow kind,
Still constant in a wondrous excellence;
Therefore my verse to constancy confin'd,
One thing expressing, leaves out difference.
"Fair, kind, and true," is all my argument,
10   "Fair, kind, and true," varying to other words;
And in this change is my invention spent,
Three themes in one, which wondrous scope affords.
     "Fair, kind, and true," have often liv'd alone,
        Which three till now never kept seat in one.

When in the chronicle of wasted time
I see descriptions of the fairest wights,
And beauty making beautiful old rhyme
In praise of ladies dead and lovely knights,
5   Then in the blazon of sweet beauty's best,
Of hand, of foot, of lip, of eye, of brow,
I see their antique pen would have express'd
Even such a beauty as you master now.
So all their praises are but prophecies
10   Of this our time, all you prefiguring;
And, for they look'd but with divining eyes,
They had not still enough your worth to sing:
     For we which now behold these present days
        Have eyes to wonder, but lack tongues to praise.

The many scholars who have attempted to date this sonnet through the references of the second quatrain have succeeded only in documenting their own predispositions.

1. PROPHETIC SOUL *the soul which by intuition has intimations of things to come. The phrase is used in the same sense in Hamlet (Act I, scene 5, line 40). 3.* LEASE *allotted time, lifetime. 4.* CONFIN'D DOOM *a limited or early doom, that is, mortality. 5–8. There is no agreement on the meaning of the references in these lines. The mortal moon is generally taken to be Queen Elizabeth, but the eclipse which she endured (that is, the impending catastrophe which she survived) remains unidentified. In any case, those who sadly predicted disaster now mock their own predictions, uncertainties are ended, and there is an assured prospect of long peace. 10.* SUBSCRIBES *submits. 12.* INSULTS *exults insultingly.* DULL . . . TRIBES *those whose verse has not made them immortal. 13.* THIS *this poem.*

1. THAT . . . CHARACTER *that may be expressed in writing. 2.* FIGUR'D *revealed. 3–4. What new thing is there to say that, as I now take up my pen to write, may express my love or your merit. 3.* WHAT NOW *Editors sometimes needlessly emend to "what new." 7–8. thinking of even old expressions of love as fresh, since we are to each other as we were when I addressed my first poem to you. The poem does not regard as impious the use of language from the Lord's Prayer. 9.* IN . . . CASE *in my poems which are fresh though their manner is familiar, or in the friend's youthful appearance. 10.* WEIGHS NOT *attaches no importance to. 12.* MAKES . . . PAGE *makes old age his perpetual servant. 13. finding the first conception of love rooted there.*

Not mine own fears, nor the prophetic soul
Of the wide world dreaming on things to come,
Can yet the lease of my true love control,
Suppos'd as forfeit to a confin'd doom.
5   The mortal moon hath her eclipse endur'd,
And the sad augurs mock their own presage;
Incertainties now crown themselves assur'd,
And peace proclaims olives of endless age.
Now with the drops of this most balmy time
10   My love looks fresh, and Death to me subscribes,
Since, spite of him, I'll live in this poor rhyme,
While he insults o'er dull and speechless tribes:
       And thou in this shalt find thy monument,
       When tyrants' crests and tombs of brass are spent.

What's in the brain that ink may character,
Which hath not figur'd to thee my true spirit?
What's new to speak, what now to register,
That may express my love, or thy dear merit?
5   Nothing, sweet boy, but yet, like prayers divine,
I must each day say o'er the very same,
Counting no old thing old, thou mine, I thine,
Even as when first I hallow'd thy fair name.
So that eternal love in love's fresh case
10   Weighs not the dust and injury of age,
Nor gives to necessary wrinkles place,
But makes antiquity for aye his page;
       Finding the first conceit of love there bred,
       Where time and outward form would show it dead.

There is no knowing what the occasion of the absence referred to in this sonnet was, or of that referred to in other sonnets, and all statements about these occasions are pure speculation.

2. FLAME *Compare Sonnet 115, line 4.* QUALIFY *moderate or mitigate.* 4. *For recurrences of the same conceit see Sonnets 22, 24, 113, and Venus and Adonis, lines 580–582.* 5. MY . . . LOVE *the home of my love.* RANG'D *strayed.* 6. HIM *one.* 7. JUST *punctual.* EXCHANG'D *changed.* 8. *so that my return washes away the offence of my absence.* 10. BLOOD *temperament. Blood is the emblem of the carnal and mortal nature of man.* 11. PREPOSTEROUSLY BE STAIN'D *This refers back to the stain, or offence, of line 8. Absence is an offence; desertion would be a preposterous offence.* 13–14. FOR . . . THOU *You excepted, I count this wide universe as nothing.* 14. ROSE *See Sonnet 1, lines 1–2.*

This and the following sonnet, which disclose Shakespeare's discontent with his life as actor and theatrical writer, should be read in relation to Sonnets 25 and 29. The discontent seems to have arisen in part from the feeling that the craft of writing involves a writer in an essential indecency, that of exposing his inmost thoughts and feelings to the public view.

2. MOTLEY . . . VIEW *public jester. Motley was the traditional dress of the fool.* 3. GOR'D *ripped out and exposed to public view.* WHAT . . . DEAR *my emotions and innermost convictions and allegiances.* 4. *offended old friends by neglecting them for new ones.* 5. TRUTH *fidelity. See Sonnet 54, line 2.* 6. ASKANCE *1609 Quarto: Asconce—a variant spelling.* STRANGELY *as a stranger. See Sonnet 49, line 5.* 7. BLENCHES *side glances.* 8. WORSE ESSAYS *trials of less worthy friendships.* 9. WHAT . . . END *my constant friendship.* 10. GRIND *whet.* 11. PROOF *experiment.* TRY *examine or test by comparison.* 12. GOD IN LOVE *This may be reminiscent of Sonnet 105.* CONFIN'D *bound.*

O never say that I was false of heart,
Though absence seem'd my flame to qualify;
As easy might I from myself depart
As from my soul, which in thy breast doth lie:
5 That is my home of love: if I have rang'd,
Like him that travels, I return again;
Just to the time, not with the time exchang'd,
So that myself bring water for my stain.
Never believe, though in my nature reign'd
10 All frailties that besiege all kinds of blood,
That it could so preposterously be stain'd,
To leave for nothing all thy sum of good;
     For nothing this wide universe I call,
     Save thou, my rose; in it thou art my all.

Alas, 'tis true I have gone here and there,
And made myself a motley to the view,
Gor'd mine own thoughts, sold cheap what is most dear,
Made old offences of affections new;
5 Most true it is that I have look'd on truth
Askance and strangely: but, by all above,
These blenches gave my heart another youth,
And worse essays prov'd thee my best of love.
Now all is done, have what shall have no end:
10 Mine appetite I never more will grind
On newer proof, to try an older friend,
A god in love, to whom I am confin'd.
     Then give me welcome, next my heaven the best,
     Even to thy pure and most most loving breast.

1. WITH *Emendation by Charles Gildon (1665–1724).*
1609 Quarto: wish. 2. THE GUILTY GODDESS *the goddess who is guilty. 3.* THAT *who. 4.* PUBLIC MEANS *a
profession depending on public approval.* PUBLIC MAN-
NERS *vulgar manners. 6–7.* SUBDU'D/TO *colored by.
8.* RENEW'D *cured. 10.* EISEL *vinegar, which was
thought to prevent the spreading of contagious
diseases. 11.* BITTERNESS *bitter medicine. 12. Shakespeare was aware of the other sides of things. While
assuring the friend that he will do anything to remove the stains deriving from his life as theatrical
performer and writer, he is also aware that his life
as artist is, as in Sonnet 29, "what I most enjoy,"
and so the cleansing itself will be a kind of stain.
There will have to be a "double penance," to remove the stain and to "correct correction."*

*This sonnet continues both the themes and the ironic
self-consciousness of the preceding one. Declaring
that no opinion but that of the friend matters to
him, he is aware that this is a denial of the honor
and reputation he cherishes and seeks and that the
devotion to the friend is at the same time a great good
and a "profound abysm."*

1. DOTH . . . FILL *remove the scar. 2.* VULGAR *public.*
STAMP'D *The allusion is to the old custom of brand-
ing a felon. 4.* O'ER-GREEN *to cover with verdure in
order to conceal a defect.* ALLOW *approve. 7–8. You
are the only living person who can make me change
my fixed sense of what is right or what is wrong.
10.* MY ADDER'S SENSE *my ears. The adder was thought
to be deaf. 12. Mark how I excuse my neglect of the
opinion of others. 13. You are so strongly centered
in my bent of mind. For this use of "bred" compare
Sonnet 108, line 13. 14.* ALL . . . BESIDES *everyone
else.* METHINKS *it seems to me.* ARE *1609 Quarto:
y'are.*

O, for my sake do you with Fortune chide,
The guilty goddess of my harmful deeds,
That did not better for my life provide
Than public means which public manners breeds.
5 Thence comes it that my name receives a brand,
And almost thence my nature is subdu'd
To what it works in, like the dyer's hand:
Pity me then and wish I were renew'd;
Whilst, like a willing patient, I will drink
10 Potions of eisel 'gainst my strong infection;
No bitterness that I will bitter think,
Nor double penance, to correct correction.
    Pity me then, dear friend, and I assure ye
    Even that your pity is enough to cure me.

Your love and pity doth the impression fill
Which vulgar scandal stamp'd upon my brow;
For what care I who calls me well or ill,
So you o'er-green my bad, my good allow?
5 You are my all the world, and I must strive
To know my shames and praises from your tongue;
None else to me, nor I to none alive,
That my steel'd sense or changes right or wrong.
In so profound abysm I throw all care
10 Of others' voices, that my adder's sense
To critic and to flatterer stopped are.
Mark how with my neglect I do dispense:
    You are so strongly in my purpose bred
    That all the world besides methinks are dead.

1. MINE . . . MIND *I see you with my mind.* Compare *The Rape of Lucrece, line 1426,* and *Hamlet's* "*my mind's eye.*" *2.* THAT . . . ABOUT *his eyes, which direct his steps. 3.* PART *divide.* HIS *its. Probably the line means that the eye perceives images but does not convey them to the mind, which is dominated by the image of the friend. 4.* SEEMS SEEING *seems to be seeing.* EFFECTUALLY *in reality. 6.* LATCH *Emendation by Edmund Malone (1741–1812), who explains that latch formerly signified "lay hold of."* 1609 *Quarto: lack. 7.* QUICK OBJECTS *object presented quickly. See Sonnet 114, line 8. 10.* SWEET-FAVOUR *delightful figure or countenance. 12.* IT . . . FEATURE *It transforms them into the image of you. 13.* INCAPABLE *unable to take in. 14.* TRUE *faithful.* MAKETH MINE UNTRUE *1609 Quarto. Many editors emend to* "mak'th mine eye untrue." UNTRUE *untruth. Shakespeare here, as elsewhere, uses an adjective as a noun.*

1. OR WHETHER *can it be that.* BEING CROWN'D WITH *being exalted and made kinglike by the possession of. 2.* FLATTERY *making over objects into the image of you. See Sonnet 113, lines 9–12. 3–4. Or can it be that my eyes see truly and that your love gave it this power actually to transform? "Alchemy" was usually used to mean the process by which base metal was transmuted into gold. 5.* INDIGEST *formless. 7.* CREATING EVERY BAD *transforming every bad object into. 8. The belief was that the eye actually cast beams which made the object visible. Compare Sonnet 20, line 6. 11.* WHAT . . . 'GREEING *what is pleasing to the taste of the mind. 12. And prepares a drink pleasing to the taste of the mind. 13–14. If the drink is poisoned, the preparation of the drink is not as great a wrong as it might seem to be, for the eye is as fond of seeing things in a flattering way as the mind is, and it will drink first. The allusion here is to the taster who first partook of the king's food and drink to determine if it had been poisoned.*

Since I left you mine eye is in my mind,
And that which governs me to go about
Doth part his function and is partly blind,
Seems seeing, but effectually is out;
5   For it no form delivers to the heart
Of bird, of flower, or shape, which it doth latch;
Of his quick objects hath the mind no part,
Nor his own vision holds what it doth catch;
For if it see the rud'st or gentlest sight,
10 The most sweet-favour or deformed'st creature,
The mountain or the sea, the day or night,
The crow or dove, it shapes them to your feature:
      Incapable of more, replete with you,
      My most true mind thus maketh mine untrue.

Or whether doth my mind, being crown'd with you,
Drink up the monarch's plague, this flattery?
Or whether shall I say mine eye saith true,
And that your love taught it this alchemy,
5   To make of monsters and things indigest
Such cherubins as your sweet self resemble,
Creating every bad a perfect best
As fast as objects to his beams assemble?
O, 'tis the first; 'tis flatt'ry in my seeing,
10 And my great mind most kingly drinks it up:
Mine eye well knows what with his gust is 'greeing,
And to his palate doth prepare the cup:
      If it be poison'd, 'tis the lesser sin
      That mine eye loves it and doth first begin.

2. EVEN THOSE *Such lines as Sonnet 31, line 14. 5. but when I consider Time who calls everything to an accounting, Time whose casualties are numbered by the millions.* 7. TAN *deprive of the freshness of youth.* 8. ALT'RING THINGS *things as they change. The sentence, which begins with line 5, is here left incomplete, but its sense is picked up in the following line with "Time's tyranny," which is time's power to alter all things for the worse, as set forth in the preceding quatrain.* 11–12. *When I, in the full awareness of my love, having no consciousness of mutability (compare Sonnet 107, line 7), glorified the present moment and hesitated to believe in the reality of times to come.* 13–14. *Love is a baby and will grow, and that is why I should not have said I could not love you more, for saying so denied the principle of growth to growing things.*

This sonnet, often taken to be a love poem, has doubtless helped many a courtship on its way, but for the more careful reader it remains a celebration of perfect friendship, the union of faithful minds being, for Shakespeare, an incomplete description of the union of man and woman. A variant version of this sonnet was set to music by Henry Lawes (1596–1662).

2. IMPEDIMENTS *The reference is to the marriage service in the Book of Common Prayer: "If any of you know cause or just impediment. . . ."* 3. ALTERATION *change in the loved one.* 4. THE REMOVER TO REMOVE *machinations of a third person. Compare Sonnet 25, line 14.* 5. MARK *An object, such as a beacon, serving to guide mariners.* 7. THE STAR *the North Star by which mariners guide their course.* 8. *The star's value is inestimable although its position in the sky may be calculated for purposes of navigation.* 9. TIME'S FOOL *the plaything of time.* 10. BENDING SICKLE'S *Compare Sonnets 100 (line 14) and 12 (line 13).* 12. BEARS IT OUT *survives.* EDGE OF DOOM *Last Judgment.* 13. UPON ME *against me.*

Those lines that I before have writ do lie,
Even those that said I could not love you dearer:
Yet then my judgment knew no reason why
My most full flame should afterwards burn clearer.
5 But reckoning Time, whose million'd accidents
Creep in 'twixt vows, and change decrees of kings,
Tan sacred beauty, blunt the sharp'st intents,
Divert strong minds to th' course of alt'ring things;
Alas, why, fearing of Time's tyranny,
10 Might I not then say "Now I love you best,"
When I was certain o'er incertainty,
Crowning the present, doubting of the rest?
    Love is a babe; then might I not say so,
    To give full growth to that which still doth grow.

Let me not to the marriage of true minds
Admit impediments. Love is not love
Which alters when it alteration finds,
Or bends with the remover to remove:
5 O no! it is an ever fixed mark,
That looks on tempests and is never shaken;
It is the star to every wandering bark,
Whose worth's unknown, although his height be taken.
Love's not Time's fool, though rosy lips and cheeks
10 Within his bending sickle's compass come;
Love alters not with his brief hours and weeks,
But bears it out even to the edge of doom:
    If this be error and upon me proved,
    I never writ, nor no man ever loved.

1–2. THAT . . . REPAY *that I have done sparingly all the things which your great worth required of me.* 3. FORGOT *that I have forgot.* 4. BONDS *moral ties, obligations of friendship.* 5. FREQUENT . . . MINDS *been intimate with nonentities, or with strangers.* 6. GIVEN TO TIME *squandered.* YOUR . . . RIGHT *the time or considerations owing to you by the rights of our friendship.* 9. BOOK *register.* 10. *And add what you may guess at to what you may justly prove.* 11. LEVEL *range, aim.* 13–14. *Compare Sonnet 110, lines 7–12.*

1. LIKE AS *just as. See Sonnet 60, line 1.* 2. EAGER COMPOUNDS *sharp or sour sauces.* URGE *stimulate.* 3. PREVENT *anticipate, forestall.* 4. PURGE *take a cathartic.* 6. *See Sonnet 117, line 5.* 7. SICK OF WELFARE *surfeited with well-being.* MEETNESS *fitness.* 9. POLICY *prudence.* 10. ILLS . . . NOT *anticipated satiety which never eventuated.* ASSUR'D *actual.* 11. *Submitted a healthy condition to medical treatment.* 12. RANK OF *replete with.*

Accuse me thus: that I have scanted all
Wherein I should your great deserts repay,
Forgot upon your dearest love to call,
Whereto all bonds do tie me day by day;
5   That I have frequent been with unknown minds,
And given to time your own dear purchas'd right;
That I have hoisted sail to all the winds
Which should transport me farthest from your sight.
Book both my wilfulness and errors down,
10   And on just proof surmise accumulate;
Bring me within the level of your frown,
But shoot not at me in your waken'd hate;
      Since my appeal says I did strive to prove
      The constancy and virtue of your love.

Like as to make our appetites more keen,
With eager compounds we our palate urge;
As, to prevent our maladies unseen,
We sicken to shun sickness when we purge;
5   Even so, being full of your ne'er-cloying sweetness,
To bitter sauces did I frame my feeding;
And sick of welfare found a kind of meetness
To be diseas'd ere that there was true needing.
Thus policy in love to anticipate
10   The ills that were not, grew to faults assur'd,
And brought to medicine a healthful state,
Which, rank of goodness, would by ill be cur'd:
      But thence I learn, and find the lesson true,
      Drugs poison him that so fell sick of you.

It is orthodox doctrine that nothing, not even evil, is entirely evil, for good may grow out of it. This is the "benefit of ill" (line 9). The poet, like his tragic heroes, grows in wisdom and self-knowledge through error and suffering.

1. SIREN *doubtless the lady of sonnets 127 to 152.* 2. LIMBECKS *alembics.* 3. APPLYING *This is a continuation of the medical terminology.* 4. STILL *always.* LOSING . . . WIN *Gaining the love of others than his friend was in reality a loss.* 7–8. *Spheres, here used figuratively, were the orbits in which the stars moved. The fits of maddening sexual passion have deflected the poet from his true course. The contrast between the inner reality and what the eyes see is a constant theme in the sonnets to the Dark Lady.*

1–3. *The wrong you once did to me now stands me in good stead, for the remembrance of what I suffered then teaches me the weight of my wrong to you and makes me bow under it.* 1. ONCE UNKIND *This probably refers to the episode of the Dark Lady, but it is not possible to know with certainty.* 6. HELL *Compare* The Rape of Lucrece, *line 1287.* 7. HAVE . . . TAKEN *have not taken the time.* 8. CRIME *the unkind act of line 1.* 9. NIGHT OF WOE *the estrangement resulting from the offences committed by each.* REMEMB'RED *reminded.* 10. MY DEEPEST SENSE *my most profound awareness.* 11. SOON *as soon.* 12. HUMBLE SALVE *balm of humility. Compare Sonnet 34, line 7.* 13–14. *Your former transgression against me becomes the fee with which I can buy back my transgression against you.*

What potions have I drunk of Siren tears,
Distill'd from limbecks foul as hell within,
Applying fears to hopes and hopes to fears,
Still losing when I saw myself to win?
5 What wretched errors hath my heart committed
Whilst it hath thought itself so blessed never?
How have mine eyes out of their spheres been fitted
In the distraction of this madding fever?
O benefit of ill! Now I find true
10 That better is by evil still made better,
And ruin'd love, when it is built anew,
Grows fairer than at first, more strong, far greater.
    So I return rebuk'd to my content,
    And gain by ills thrice more than I have spent.

That you were once unkind befriends me now,
And for that sorrow which I then did feel
Needs must I under my transgression bow,
Unless my nerves were brass or hammer'd steel.
5 For if you were by my unkindness shaken,
As I by yours, y'have pass'd a hell of time;
And I, a tyrant, have no leisure taken
To weigh how once I suffer'd in your crime.
O that our night of woe might have rememb'red
10 My deepest sense, how hard true sorrow hits,
And soon to you, as you to me then, tend'red
The humble salve which wounded bosoms fits!
    But that your trespass now becomes a fee;
    Mine ransoms yours, and yours must ransom me.

1–4. It is better to be vile than not to be vile and have the reputation for being so, and in addition, lose the pleasure which we do not feel to be wrong but which is taken to be wrong in the judgment of others. 5. ADULTERATE *unchaste, lewd. 6. Treat my amorous nature as akin to their own. 7. This is another case of the mote and the beam.* SPIES *Compare Sonnet 125, line 13. 8.* WILLS *Such judgments as it is their pleasure to make. 9.* THAT *who.* LEVEL *aim. See Sonnet 117, line 11. 11.* BEVEL *slanting, not upright.*

Sonnet 77 was written to accompany a gift of a journal to the friend. Here Shakespeare explains why he has given away a journal which the friend had given him.

1. TABLES *memorandum book, a journal. 2.* CHARACTER'D *inscribed. 3.* IDLE RANK *useless series of leaves. 4.* DATE *time. 7.* RAZ'D OBLIVION *oblivion which destroys everything. 9.* POOR RETENTION *the tables, which could not contain as much as the poet's mind. 10.* TALLIES *sticks on which notches are cut to keep accounts by. 13.* ADJUNCT *anything, such as tables and tallies, to assist the memory.*

'Tis better to be vile than vile esteemed
When not to be receives reproach of being,
And the just pleasure lost, which is so deemed
Not by our feeling but by others' seeing.
5   For why should others' false adulterate eyes
Give salutation to my sportive blood?
Or on my frailties why are frailer spies,
Which in their wills count bad what I think good?
No, I am that I am, and they that level
10 At my abuses reckon up their own:
I may be straight though they themselves be bevel;
By their rank thoughts my deeds must not be shown,
       Unless this general evil they maintain,
       All men are bad and in their badness reign.

Thy gift, thy tables, are within my brain
Full character'd with lasting memory,
Which shall above that idle rank remain
Beyond all date, even to eternity;
5   Or at the least, so long as brain and heart
Have faculty by nature to subsist,
Till each to raz'd oblivion yield his part
Of thee, thy record never can be miss'd.
That poor retention could not so much hold,
10 Nor need I tallies thy dear love to score;
Therefore to give them from me was I bold,
To trust those tables that receive thee more:
       To keep an adjunct to remember thee
       Were to import forgetfulness in me.

1–4. Shakespeare asserts that he is so far from chang-ing that he does not believe in change, that even new constructions strike him not as novelties but as re-creations of things which have existed before. 2. PYRAMIDS *any impressive constructions, as in "palaces and pyramids" (Macbeth, Act IV, scene 1, line 57). 5.* DATES *allotted times of life.* ADMIRE *re-gard with wonder. 6. the old things you try to pass off on us as new. 7.* MAKE . . . DESIRE *accept them as the new things we desire. "Them" refers back to "What thou dost foist." 9.* THY REGISTERS *your records, manifestations of you. 12–14. Although I swear that all things are made to change by the passage of time, my devotion shall remain changeless.*

The preceding sonnet contrasts constancy to the muta-bility brought about by time; here the contrast is to public life.

1. MY DEAR LOVE *my love for you.* STATE *circumstance of nature or fortune, station, rank, greatness, power. All meanings are possible. 2–3. If fortune is thought of as the father, the love ("Fortune" now having taken on the additional meaning of wealth) would be subject to the ravages of time. Or the lines may mean that the poet's love would be revealed as the by-blow of fortune having no true father and hence subject to time. The possible meanings are many. 6–7. It is not effected by prosperity deriving from the great or by the actions of those who are discontented because they are oppressed. 8. The line may mean that both our times and our nature invite us to discon-tent (see* The Rape of Lucrece, *line 1319). 9.* POLICY *intriguing, stratagem arising from self-interest.* HERETIC *Policy is so called because it has no place in true love. 11.* POLITIC *Professor Dowden (1843–1913) explains: Love itself is infinitely prudent, prudent for eternity. 12.* NOR . . . NOR *neither . . . nor. 13.* FOOLS OF TIME *timeservers. 14. The line may mean people who make deathbed repentances after living criminal lives.*

No, Time, thou shalt not boast that I do change:
Thy pyramids build up with newer might
To me are nothing novel, nothing strange;
They are but dressings of a former sight:
5   Our dates are brief, and therefore we admire
What thou dost foist upon us that is old,
And rather make them born to our desire
Than think that we before have heard them told:
Thy registers and thee I both defy,
10   Not wond'ring at the present nor the past,
For thy records and what we see doth lie,
Made more or less by thy continual haste:
        This I do vow and this shall ever be;
        I will be true, despite thy scythe and thee.

If my dear love were but the child of state,
It might for Fortune's bastard be unfather'd,
As subject to Time's love or to Time's hate,
Weeds among weeds, or flowers with flowers gather'd.
5   No, it was builded far from accident;
It suffers not in smiling pomp, nor falls
Under the blow of thralled discontent,
Whereto th' inviting time our fashion calls:
It fears not policy, that heretic,
10   Which works on leases of short-numb'red hours,
But all alone stands hugely politic,
That it nor grows with heat nor drowns with show'rs.
        To this I witness call the fools of time,
        Which die for goodness, who have liv'd for crime.

Having said in the preceding sonnet that his love was not subject to the adversities of public life, Shakespeare goes on to say that he wants neither prominence nor profit.

1. WERE'T *would it be. 1 if I.* CANOPY *such a canopy as is borne over distinguished personages in ceremonial processions. 2. By my external actions honoring the attributes of a man, either you or anyone else, which are not inherent in him as a person. 3. The line may refer to the sonnets promising to eternize the young man's beauty in verse. 5.* DWELLERS . . . FAVOUR *those who set store on external appearance and patronage. 6. forfeit their patrons favor by their obsequiousness. 7. For the compound sweet of external appearance and success forgo the taste of more satisfying simple things. 8. pitiable people, like courtiers waiting for preferment, who, in their eager watchfulness, come to nothing. 9.* OBSEQUIOUS *humbly devoted. 11.* SECONDS *baser matter.* ART *artifice. 12.* MUTUAL RENDER *each gives himself in return for the other. 13.* SUBORN'D INFORMER *witness who has been induced to commit perjury. The person who brought the charges of opportunism denied in lines 1–8.*

This, the last of the poems addressed to the young friend, consists of six couplets.

1–2. In his edition of the Sonnets (1936), Tucker Brooke explains that time has three objects which the young man holds in his power: "a glass or mirror, in which young faces are with fickleness turned to old ones; a scythe or sickle; an hour-glass." 3. BY WANING GROWN *become more beautiful by growing older. Compare Sonnet 11, line 1. 5.* WRACK *ruin. 6.* GOEST ONWARDS *advance in years.* PLUCK THEE BACK *that is, by keeping your beauty unimpaired. 7–8.* THAT . . . KILL *in order that her skill in preserving the young man's beauty may discredit Time, kill Time's wretched minutes. 9.* MINION *favorite. 10.* STILL *always. 11.* AUDIT *final accounting. 12.* QUIETUS *final settling of accounts.* RENDER *surrender.*

Were't aught to me I bore the canopy,
With my extern the outward honouring,
Or laid great bases for eternity,
Which proves more short than waste or ruining?
5 Have I not seen dwellers on form and favour
Lose all and more by paying too much rent,
For compound sweet forgoing simple savour,
Pitiful thrivers in their gazing spent?
No, let me be obsequious in thy heart,
10 And take thou my oblation, poor but free,
Which is not mix'd with seconds, knows no art,
But mutual render, only me for thee.
    Hence, thou suborn'd informer! a true soul
    When most impeach'd stands least in thy control.

O thou, my lovely boy, who in thy power
Dost hold Time's fickle glass, his sickle, hour;
Who hast by waning grown, and therein show'st
Thy lovers withering as thy sweet self grow'st;
5 If Nature, sovereign mistress over wrack,
As thou goest onwards, still will pluck thee back,
She keeps thee to this purpose, that her skill
May Time disgrace and wretched minutes kill.
Yet fear her, O thou minion of her pleasure!
10 She may detain, but not still keep, her treasure;
Her audit, though delay'd, answer'd must be,
And her quietus is to render thee.

*This is the first of the series of sonnets addressed to
or concerned with the poet's mistress, who, because
she was a swarthy, dark-eyed brunette, has come to
be known as the Dark Lady. In all significant respects she is the opposite of the ladies of most Renaissance sonnet sequences. The Elizabethan ideal of
feminine beauty, following that of the chivalric ro-
mances and the Petrarchan tradition, was blonde, and
in their efforts to appear fair and fragile, Elizabethan
women applied make-up thickly. One of the pro-
cedures was to cover the face, neck, and breasts with
a white paint. It was often made with an egg-white
base and was applied like tempera. When this had
dried, rouge and other cosmetics were put on.*

1. THE OLD AGE *the age of chivalry.* FAIR *beautiful.*
*3–4. But now what is not beautiful is painted to
appear beautiful, and it thus becomes the successor
to true beauty, which it slanders by appearing to be
its bastard. 6.* FAIRING *making beautiful. 7–8. True
beauty has lost its identity and place of abode. It is
discredited, because the widespread use of cosmetics
will cause it to be thought artificial. 9.* BROWS *Emendation by Howard Staunton (1810–1874). 1609
Quarto: eyes. 10–12. The eyes seem to be in mourning for those who, not having been born beautiful,
achieve an artificial beauty and thus appear to be
what they are not. 10.* SO SUITED *matching the brows.
13.* BECOMING OF *adorned by.*

1. THOU, MY MUSIC *you who enchant me as music
does. 2.* BLESSED *blessed because they are touched by
her fingers.* WOOD *the wooden keys of the spinet or
virginal. 3.* SWAY'ST *evoke. 4.* CONCORD *the "concord of
sweet sounds," as in* The Merchant of Venice, *Act V,
scene 1, line 84.* CONFOUNDS *amazes with delight.
5.* JACKS *keys. Shakespeare's usage here is not precise. The jack is that part of the action which holds
the quill which plucks the string. 10.* CHIPS *keys.
11, 14.* THY FINGERS *Emendation by Charles Gildon
(1665–1724). 1609 Quarto: their fingers.*

In the old age black was not counted fair,
Or if it were, it bore not beauty's name;
But now is black beauty's successive heir,
And beauty slander'd with a bastard shame:
5 For since each hand hath put on nature's power,
Fairing the foul with art's false borrow'd face,
Sweet beauty hath no name, no holy bower,
But is profan'd, if not lives in disgrace.
Therefore my mistress' brows are raven black,
10 Her eyes so suited, and they mourners seem
At such who, not born fair, no beauty lack,
Sland'ring creation with a false esteem:
   Yet so they mourn, becoming of their woe,
   That every tongue says beauty should look so.

How oft when thou, my music, music play'st,
Upon that blessed wood whose motion sounds
With thy sweet fingers, when thou gently sway'st
The wiry concord that mine ear confounds,
5 Do I envy those jacks that nimble leap
To kiss the tender inward of thy hand,
Whilst my poor lips, which should that harvest reap,
At the woods's boldness by thee blushing stand.
To be so tickled, they would change their state
10 And situation with those dancing chips,
O'er whom thy fingers walk with gentle gait,
Making dead wood more blest than living lips.
   Since saucy jacks so happy are in this,
   Give them thy fingers, me thy lips to kiss.

1. EXPENSE *expenditure, loss.* SPIRIT *vital power. It was a misbelief of Elizabethan physiology that an artery carried the impregnating fluid directly from the heart to the male genitals.* 2. TILL ACTION *until expressed in action.* 4. RUDE *brutal.* NOT TO TRUST *not to be trusted.* 7–8. *Compare Sonnet 147.* 9. MAD *Correction by Edmund Malone (1741–1812). 1609 Quarto: Made.* 10. EXTREME *excessive, violent.* 11. IN PROOF *during the act of gratification.* PROV'D, A *Malone's emendation. 1609 Quarto: proud and.* 12. DREAM *illusion. See* The Rape of Lucrece, *line 212.*

Taken in itself, this sonnet is an instance of pure comedy, embodying the spirit in which the host of Shakespeare's comic ne'er-do-wells, from Bottom to Autolycus, were conceived. One is aware of their faults, but no reader in his senses ever wished any of them to be better than he is. Here the poet is aware of the lady's faults and he loves her, not in spite of them, but faults and all. On the other hand, if the poem is considered in relation to other sonnet sequences, it becomes a satire on the ladies of the Petrarchan sonnet tradition who were blonde, pale, and aloof. They were described in accordance with the celebrated descending description. The poet began with the lady's golden hair, her ivory forehead, her ruby lips, and proceeded downward.

2. CORAL *1609 Quarto: Currall.* 3. DUN *dark.* 5. DAMASK'D *mingled.* 11. GO *walk. For the way a goddess walks, see* Venus and Adonis, *line 1028.* 14. ANY SHE *any woman who is.*

Th' expense of spirit in a waste of shame
Is lust in action; and till action, lust
Is perjur'd, murd'rous, bloody, full of blame,
Savage, extreme, rude, cruel, not to trust;
5   Enjoy'd no sooner, but despised straight;
Past reason hunted; and no sooner had,
Past reason hated as a swallow'd bait
On purpose laid to make the taker mad:
Mad in pursuit, and in possession so;
10 Had, having, and in quest to have, extreme;
A bliss in proof, and prov'd, a very woe;
Before, a joy propos'd; behind, a dream.
　　All this the world well knows; yet none knows well
　　To shun the heaven that leads men to this hell.

My mistress' eyes are nothing like the sun;
Coral is far more red than her lips' red;
If snow be white, why then her breasts are dun;
If hairs be wires, black wires grow on her head:
5   I have seen roses damask'd red and white,
But no such roses see I in her cheeks;
And in some perfumes is there more delight
Than in the breath that from my mistress reeks:
I love to hear her speak, yet well I know
10 That music hath a far more pleasing sound:
I grant I never saw a goddess go,
My mistress, when she walks, treads on the ground.
　　And yet, by heaven, I think my love as rare
　　As any she belied with false compare.

I love to hear her speak, yet well I know
That music hath a far more pleasing sound

The ladies of the sonnet tradition were tyrannous by virtue of the subjection in which they held the men who offered them their love. They were held to be cruel because of their chaste refusal to return the love proffered them. In Shakespeare's sonnets the tyranny arises from the sexual enslavement in which the lady held the poet, and her cruelty consisted chiefly in her infidelity to him. This is the first sonnet to hint at her infidelity.

1. SO . . . ART *being as you are, dark not fair.* 2. *as those who, through pride in their beauty, become cruel to their lovers.* 3. DEAR *fond, loving.* 7. TO SAY *to assert formally or publicly.* 9. THAT . . . FALSE *that which I swear to myself is not false.* 10. BUT THINKING ON *when I but think of.* 13–14. *See Sonnet 147, lines 13–14.* 14. SLANDER *This may refer to what some say in line 7 above, but it more probably refers to some gossip arising from the lady's promiscuity (see Sonnet 137, line 6) and her seduction of Shakespeare's young friend. See Sonnet 134.*

In an invitation to love the poet returns to his oblique compliments on the lady's unconventional beauty.

2. TORMENTS *1640 edition. 1609 Quarto: torment.* 3. *Compare Sonnet 127, line 10.* 4. RUTH *pity.* 5–8. *These comparisons, traditional in the sonnet literature of the Renaissance, are the kind Shakespeare declined to make in Sonnet 130.* 5. MORNING *with a punning play on "mourning," line 9.* 9. MOURNING *1609 Quarto: morning. But since the word is a morning-mourning pun, it does not matter which word is printed.* 12. *Let every part wear mourning for me and pity me.*

Thou art as tyrannous, so as thou art,
As those whose beauties proudly make them cruel;
For well thou know'st to my dear doting heart
Thou art the fairest and most precious jewel.
5 Yet in good faith some say that thee behold,
Thy face hath not the power to make love groan:
To say they err I dare not be so bold,
Although I swear it to myself alone.
And to be sure that is not false I swear,
10 A thousand groans, but thinking on thy face,
One on another's neck, do witness bear
Thy black is fairest in my judgment's place.
    In nothing art thou black save in thy deeds,
    And thence this slander, as I think, proceeds.

Thine eyes I love, and they as pitying me,
Knowing thy heart torments me with disdain,
Have put on black and loving mourners be,
Looking with pretty ruth upon my pain.
5 And truly not the morning sun of heaven
Better becomes the grey cheeks of th' east,
Nor that full star that ushers in the even
Doth half that glory to the sober west,
As those two mourning eyes become thy face:
10 O, let it then as well beseem thy heart
To mourn for me, since mourning doth thee grace,
And suit thy pity like in every part.
    Then will I swear beauty herself is black,
    And all they foul that thy complexion lack.

1. Compare Sonnet 131, lines 6–14. BESHREW *woe to.
It is a very mild form of imprecation. 4.* SLAVE TO
SLAVERY *bound by a sexual enslavement. 5. You have
put me beside myself. Or you have made me depart
from my better self. 6.* MY NEXT SELF *my other self,
my young friend.* ENGROSS'D *To engross was to
acquire a monopoly of something, leaving no share
of it to others. 8.* CROSS'D *thwarted. Compare Sonnet
90, line 2. 9.* WARD *prison cell. 10.* BAIL *go bail for.
11.* WHOE'ER KEEPS ME *whoever may be my jailer.*
HIS GUARD *the protector of my friend. Or my friend's
guardhouse. 12.* USE . . . JAIL *make my imprison-
ment seem rigorous. 13.* PENT *imprisoned.*

A continuation of the preceding sonnet.
2. WILL *both carnal desire and intention. 3.* SO *provided that.* OTHER MINE *the "my next self" of Sonnet
133, line 6. 4.* STILL *in the future. 5.* WILT NOT *will
not restore him to me.* NOR HE WILL NOT *In Elizabethan English the double negative emphasizes the
negativeness. 6.* KIND *affectionately natural. 7.* SURETY-
LIKE *like a sponsor or guarantor. The notion in this
and the following lines is that the friend went to
woo the lady for Shakespeare, as in* Twelfth Night
*Viola in the guise of Cesario urged Orsino's suit,
and that the lady fell in love with the messenger.*
WRITE FOR ME *endorse my bond. 9.* STATUTE *security
for money. 10.* USURER *one who takes interest on
money.* TO USE *for advantage, for profit or gain.
11.* CAME *who became. 12.* MY UNKIND ABUSE *your
unkind abuse of me, and my abuse of him in allowing him to be a substitute wooer. 14. Although he
has paid the debt, you refuse to release me from it.*

Beshrew that heart that makes my heart to groan
For that deep wound it gives my friend and me!
Is't not enough to torture me alone,
But slave to slavery my sweet'st friend must be?
5   Me from myself thy cruel eye hath taken,
And my next self thou harder hast engross'd:
Of him, myself, and thee, I am forsaken;
A torment thrice threefold thus to be cross'd.
Prison my heart in thy steel bosom's ward,
10   But then my friend's heart let my poor heart bail;
Whoe'er keeps me, let my heart be his guard;
Thou canst not then use rigour in my jail:
     And yet thou wilt; for I being pent in thee,
     Perforce am thine, and all that is in me.

So, now I have confess'd that he is thine,
And I myself am mortgag'd to thy will,
Myself I'll forfeit, so that other mine
Thou wilt restore to be my comfort still:
5   But thou wilt not, nor he will not be free,
For thou art covetous and he is kind;
He learn'd but surety-like to write for me
Under that bond that him as fast doth bind.
The statute of thy beauty thou wilt take,
10   Thou usurer that put's forth all to use,
And sue a friend came debtor for my sake;
So him I lose through my unkind abuse.
     Him have I lost; thou hast both him and me:
     He pays the whole, and yet am I not free.

Shakespeare's propensity for punning is well known, and in this and the following sonnet it is given full rein. In his time the pun was a legitimate figure of speech. It had not yet fallen into the disrepute from which it now suffers. These poems are clusters of four-way puns on the word "will" The word meant, then as now, volition or intention; it also meant carnal desire. Will was the poet's name and the name, or pet name, of the young man. Still another meaning is possible. Will may have been the name of the lady's husband. Each usage of the word carries some or all of these significations. The poems, though now held in low esteem, are bravura pieces in an outmoded manner, and their manner is consistent with their matter—a laughing invitation to love. In this and the following sonnet the capitalizations and italics are from the 1609 Quarto.

4. MAKING ADDITION THUS *by adding myself.* 5, 7. *The rhyming words,* spacious *and* gracious, *are here trisyllabic.* 13. UNKIND *unkindness.*

1. CHECK *rebuke.* COME SO NEAR *that is, in addressing myself to you in the preceding sonnet.* 2. BLIND SOUL *The lady's soul, the guardian of her bedchamber, may be thought to be blind, or she may pretend that it is.* THY "WILL" *your husband.* 6. AY *1609 Quarto: I. "Ay" is probably the primary meaning, but the word is a pun.* 7. THINGS . . . RECEIPT *things which receive freely.* 8. *There was an Elizabethan saying that one is no number. Compare Sonnet 8 and comment.* 10. STORE'S ACCOUNT *reckoning, the inventory, as it were, of your lovers.* 13. STILL *always.*

Whoever hath her wish, thou hast thy *Will,*
And *Will* to boot, and *Will* in overplus;
More than enough am I that vex thee still,
To thy sweet will making addition thus.
5 Wilt thou, whose will is large and spacious,
Not once vouchsafe to hide my will in thine?
Shall will in others seem right gracious,
And in my will no fair acceptance shine?
The sea, all water, yet receives rain still
10 And in abundance addeth to his store;
So thou, being rich in *Will,* add to thy *Will*
One will of mine to make thy large *Will* more.
      Let no unkind, no fair beseechers kill;
      Think all but one, and me in that one *Will.*

If thy soul check thee that I come so near,
Swear to thy blind soul that I was thy *Will,*
And will, thy soul knows, is admitted there;
Thus far for love, my love-suit, sweet, fulfil.
5 *Will* will fulfil the treasure of thy love,
Ay, fill it full with wills, and my will one.
In things of great receipt with ease we prove
Among a number one is reckon'd none:
Then in the number let me pass untold,
10 Though in thy store's account I one must be;
For nothing hold me, so it please thee hold
That nothing me, a something sweet to thee.
      Make but my name thy love and love that still,
      And then thou lov'st me, for my name is *Will.*

4. *Consider the lady to be beautiful and true.*
5. LOOKS *acts of looking.* 7. EYES' FALSEHOOD *the false-hood I have been led to accept as truth.* 9. THAT *that place, that woman.* SEVERAL *private.* 10. COMMON *belonging equally to all.* 12. TO PUT *so as to put.* 14. FALSE PLAGUE *the plague of falseness. Here, as in Sonnet 147, the poet's love for the lady is recognized as a disease.*

A version of this sonnet was printed in The Passionate Pilgrim, *1599.*

1. TRUTH *fidelity.* 3. THAT *so that.* 7. SIMPLY *in the simplicity I assume for the occasion.* 9. UNJUST *un-faithful.* 11. HABIT *dress, appearance.* 12. TO HAVE *The Passionate Pilgrim.* 1609 Quarto: t'have. *With this exception, the text is that of the 1609 Quarto.* TOLD *counted.*
The other variant readings in The Passionate Pilgrim *are as follows:* 4. UNLEARNED *unskillful.* SUB-TILTIES *forgeries.* 6. DAYS ARE *years be.* 7. SIMPLY *I smiling.* 8. *outfacing faults in love, with love's ill rest.* 9. *But wherefore says my love that she is young?* 11. HABIT . . . TRUST *habit's in a soothing tongue.* 13. I . . . SHE *I'll lie with Love, and love.* 14. *Since that our faults in love thus smother'd be.*

Thou blind fool, Love, what dost thou to mine eyes,
That they behold and see not what they see?
They know what beauty is, see where it lies,
Yet what the best is take the worst to be.
5   If eyes, corrupt by over-partial looks,
Be anchor'd in the bay where all men ride,
Why of eyes' falsehood hast thou forged hooks,
Whereto the judgment of my heart is tied?
Why should my heart think that a several plot
10   Which my heart knows the wide world's common place?
Or mine eyes seeing this, say this is not,
To put fair truth upon so foul a face?
        In things right true my heart and eyes have erred,
        And to this false plague are they now transferred.

When my love swears that she is made of truth,
I do believe her, though I know she lies,
That she might think me some untutor'd youth
Unlearned in the world's false subtilties.
5   Thus vainly thinking that she thinks me young,
Although she knows my days are past the best,
Simply I credit her false-speaking tongue;
On both sides thus is simple truth suppress'd.
But wherefore says she not she is unjust?
10   And wherefore say not I that I am old?
O, love's best habit is in seeming trust,
And age in love loves not to have years told.
        Therefore I lie with her and she with me,
        And in our faults by lies we flatter'd be.

In this poem Shakespeare attempts to excuse the fickleness of the Dark Lady as he had excused the young man in Sonnet 41, and both the man and the lady in Sonnet 42.

2. UNKINDNESS *lack of love and tenderness. See* Venus and Adonis, *line 478.* 4. USE POWER WITH POWER *Use energetically the power and authority you have over me.* BY ART *by your wiles and pretenses.* 5. IN MY SIGHT *when you are with me.* 7. WHAT *why.* 8. O'ER-PRESS'D DEFENCE *overwhelmed forces.* BIDE *resist.* 11. MY FOES *her eyes.* 14. RID *dispatch.*

4. MANNER *sort, nature.* PITY-WANTING *unpitied.* 5. WIT *wisdom. See line 1.* 6. *to tell me you love me even though you do not.* 7. TESTY *fretful.* 11. ILL-WRESTING *putting an unfavorable interpretation on everything.* 12. MAD EARS *the ears of persons not astute enough to recognize that I am slandering you.* 13. BE SO *be believed.* 14. PROUD *self-indulgent, unkind.* GO WIDE *wander.*

O call not me to justify the wrong
That thy unkindness lays upon my heart;
Wound me not with thine eye, but with thy tongue;
Use power with power, and slay me not by art.
5 Tell me thou lov'st elsewhere; but in my sight,
Dear heart, forbear to glance thine eye aside:
What need'st thou wound with cunning when thy might
Is more than my o'er-press'd defence can bide?
Let me excuse thee: ah, my love well knows
10 Her pretty looks have been mine enemies,
And therefore from my face she turns my foes,
That they elsewhere might dart their injuries:
    Yet do not so; but since I am near slain,
    Kill me outright with looks, and rid my pain.

Be wise as thou art cruel: do not press
My tongue-tied patience with too much disdain,
Lest sorrow lend me words, and words express
The manner of my pity-wanting pain.
5 If I might teach thee wit, better it were,
Though not to love, yet, love, to tell me so;
As testy sick men, when their deaths be near,
No news but health from their physicians know.
For if I should despair, I should grow mad,
10 And in my madness might speak ill of thee:
Now this ill-wresting world is grown so bad
Mad sland'rers by mad ears believed be.
    That I may not be so, nor thou belied,
    Bear thine eyes straight, though thy proud heart go
        wide.

4, 11. WHO *which, that is, my heart.* 4. IN DESPITE OF
VIEW *in spite of what my eyes see.* 5. THY TONGUE'S
TUNE *the sound of your voice. See Sonnet 130, lines
9–10.* 6. *nor my acute sense of feeling which is
prone to amorous embraces.* 9. FIVE WITS *the mental
faculties in general.* 10. SERVING *loving.* 11. UNSWAY'D
ungoverned except by the heart. LIKENESS *mere
semblance.* 13. ONLY . . . FAR *my plague only thus
far, or but my plague thus far.* PLAGUE *Compare
Sonnet 137, line 14.* 14. PAIN *suffering, punishment
for my sin.*

1. DEAR *most characteristic.* 2. ON SINFUL LOVING *on
the sinful nature of my love, or on your sinful
affairs with others.* 4. IT *my state.* 6. SCARLET ORNA-
MENTS *The phrase refers to the wax seals on the
bonds of the following line.* 8. *The line refers to the
lady's affairs with other married men. She was herself married. See Sonnet 152, line 3.* 9. BE IT LAWFUL
let it be lawful that. 11–12. *Let pity grow in your
heart so that you may deserve to be pitied.* 13. WHAT
THOU DOST HIDE *pity which you refuse to extend to
me.*

In faith, I do not love thee with mine eyes,
For they in thee a thousand errors note;
But 'tis my heart that loves what they despise,
Who in despite of view is pleas'd to dote;
5   Nor are mine ears with thy tongue's tune delighted,
Nor tender feeling to base touches prone,
Nor taste, nor smell, desire to be invited
To any sensual feast with thee alone;
But my five wits nor my five senses can
10   Dissuade one foolish heart from serving thee,
Who leaves unsway'd the likeness of a man,
Thy proud heart's slave and vassal wretch to be:
        Only my plague thus far I count my gain,
        That she that makes me sin awards me pain.

Love is my sin, and thy dear virtue hate,
Hate of my sin, grounded on sinful loving:
O, but with mine compare thou thine own state,
And thou shalt find it merits not reproving;
5   Or if it do, not from those lips of thine,
That have profan'd their scarlet ornaments
And seal'd false bonds of love as oft as mine,
Robb'd others' beds' revenues of their rents.
Be it lawful I love thee as thou lov'st those
10   Whom thine eyes woo as mine importune thee:
Root pity in thy heart, that, when it grows,
Thy pity may deserve to pitied be.
        If thou dost seek to have what thou dost hide,
        By self-example mayst thou be denied!

*In a sonnet of extraordinary homeliness Shakespeare
declares that his subjugation to the lady is such that
he is willing to be just one of her lovers. The poem
is not comic, as many commentators have supposed.
It is simply that Shakespeare's view of life is free
from both bravado and apology. He comes to con-
clusions about life, but first he observes it and this
poem is an observation of himself, a kind of self-
observation few men are both able and willing to
make.*

1. CAREFUL *provident.* HOUSEWIFE *1609 Quarto: hus-
wife.* *2.* FEATHER'D CREATURES *The phrase, meaning
chickens or other domestic fowl, suggests, in contrast to the poet himself, a certain modish elegance
in the lady's other lovers.* *5.* HOLDS . . . CHASE *chases
her.* *8.* NOT PRIZING *not taking any account of.*
13. "WILL" *The word is capitalized and italicized in
the 1609 Quarto, doubtless to suggest the identity of
the man being pursued. We do not know who he
was, but see the comment on Sonnet 135.*

A version of this sonnet was printed in The Passionate Pilgrim, *1599.*

2. SUGGEST *trouble, disturb, haunt.* STILL *always.*
6. SIDE *The Passionate Pilgrim, 1609 Quarto: sight.*
8. PRIDE *wantonness.* *9.* FIEND *The Passionate Pilgrim: feend. 1609 Quarto: finde.* *10.* DIRECTLY
clearly, with certainty. *11.* FROM *away from.* BOTH . . .
FRIEND *both friendly to each other.* *12.* HELL *This is
probably a reference to the story of Rusticus and Ali-
bech in Boccaccio's* Decameron, *Book 3, 10, although
the word was often used for any place both dark and
out of sight.*
The variant readings in The Passionate Pilgrim, *not
given above, are as follows:* *2.* WHICH *That.* *3, 4.* THE
My. *8.* FOUL *fair.* *11.* BUT *For.* FROM ME *to me.* *13.* YET
. . . NE'ER *The truth I shall not.*

Lo, as a careful housewife runs to catch
One of her feather'd creatures broke away,
Sets down her babe, and makes all swift dispatch
In pursuit of the thing she would have stay,
5   Whilst her neglected child holds her in chase,
Cries to catch her whose busy care is bent
To follow that which flies before her face,
Not prizing her poor infant's discontent;
So runn'st thou after that which flies from thee,
10 Whilst I thy babe chase thee afar behind,
But if thou catch thy hope, turn back to me,
And play the mother's part, kiss me, be kind:
     So will I pray that thou mayst have thy *Will,*
     If thou turn back and my loud crying still.

Two loves I have of comfort and despair,
Which like two spirits do suggest me still:
The better angel is a man right fair,
The worser spirit a woman colour'd ill.
5   To win me soon to hell, my female evil
Tempteth my better angel from my side,
And would corrupt my saint to be a devil,
Wooing his purity with her foul pride.
And whether that my angel be turn'd fiend
10 Suspect I may, yet not directly tell;
But being both from me, both to each friend,
I guess one angel in another's hell:
     Yet this shall I ne'er know, but live in doubt,
     Till my bad angel fire my good one out.

Because this sonnet is written in tetrameter verses and depicts a lady more gracious than the Dark Lady is commonly represented as being, scholars have sometimes denied Shakespeare's authorship of the poem or suggested that it is not an integral part of the sequence, but we need not suppose that the Dark Lady was always unkind. Some of the sonnets celebrate Shakespeare's satisfaction in his love, and we may take it that in this sonnet she grants the pity he pleads for in Sonnets 140 and 142.

7. *was accustomed to giving kindly judgments.* 9. END *ending.* 11–12. *References to night as the child of hell are common in the literatures of Elizabethan and other times. See* The Rape of Lucrece, *lines 1081–1083.* 13. FROM . . . THREW *She took away their meaning of hatred.*

1. SINFUL EARTH *body.* 2. FOOL'D BY *Emendation suggested by Edmund Malone (1741–1812). The compositor of the 1609 Quarto inadvertently repeated the last three words of the first line at the beginning of the second. Another widely accepted emendation is "Thrall to."* REBEL POW'RS *The flesh which is in revolt against the dictates of the soul.* ARRAY *clothe.* 4. PAINTING . . . WALLS *adorning the body.* 5. COST *expense.* 7. EXCESS *The body which in contrast to the immortal soul is merely impedimenta.* 8. CHARGE *The body which is entrusted to the care of the soul, or the body on which so much is spent.* 9. SERVANT'S *body's.* 10. THAT *the body.* AGGRAVATE *increase.* STORE *riches.* 11. TERMS DIVINE *ages of salvation.* 13–14. *The meaning is precisely that of I Corinthians 15: 54–56: "So when this corruptible shall have put on incorruption, and this mortal shall have put on immortality, then shall be brought to pass the saying that is written, Death is swallowed up in victory. O death, where is thy sting? O grave, where is thy victory? The sting of death is sin. . . ."*

Those lips that Love's own hand did make
Breath'd forth the sound that said "I hate,"
To me that languish'd for her sake:
But when she saw my woeful state,
5   Straight in her heart did mercy come,
Chiding that tongue that ever sweet
Was used in giving gentle doom;
And taught it thus anew to greet;
"I hate" she alter'd with an end,
10   That follow'd it as gentle day
Doth follow night, who, like a fiend,
From heaven to hell is flown away;
    "I hate" from hate away she threw,
      And sav'd my life, saying "not you."

Poor soul, the centre of my sinful earth,
Fool'd by these rebel pow'rs that thee array,
Why dost thou pine within and suffer dearth,
Painting thy outward walls so costly gay?
5   Why so large cost, having so short a lease,
Dost thou upon thy fading mansion spend?
Shall worms, inheritors of this excess,
Eat up thy charge? Is this thy body's end?
Then, soul, live thou upon thy servant's loss,
10   And let that pine to aggravate thy store;
Buy terms divine in selling hours of dross;
Within be fed, without be rich no more:
    So shalt thou feed on Death that feeds on men,
      And Death once dead, there's no more dying them.

1. STILL *always.* 3. PRESERVE THE ILL *prolong the illness. See "nurseth the disease," line 2.* 7-8. 1 . . . EXCEPT *I, in my desperation, now learn through experience that desire, to which reason had objected, is death. But if "physic" is taken to be the object of "except" the meaning would be that desire had rejected reason.* 12. RANDON *the old spelling of "random."* 13-14. *Compare Sonnet 152, lines 13-14.*

In the couplet of the preceding sonnet and in this, the first of a series of three sonnets, Shakespeare returns to the theme of the discrepancy between appearance and reality, between what the eyes take to be truth and what the heart knows to be truth. Compare Sonnets 127, 131, 132, and 141.

2. WHICH *The word refers to the eyes.* 4. CENSURES *judges, estimates.* 9. HOW CAN IT? *How can it be true?* 10. WATCHING *watchfulness.* 11. MISTAKE MY VIEW *err in seeing.* 13. LOVE *The reference is to both love personified and to the lady.*

My love is as a fever, longing still
For that which longer nurseth the disease,
Feeding on that which doth preserve the ill,
Th' uncertain sickly appetite to please:
5 My reason, the physician to my love,
Angry that his prescriptions are not kept,
Hath left me, and I desperate now approve
Desire is death, which physic did except.
Past cure I am, now reason is past care,
10 And frantic-mad with evermore unrest,
My thoughts and my discourse as madmen's are,
At randon from the truth vainly express'd;
    For I have sworn thee fair, and thought thee bright,
    Who art as black as hell, as dark as night.

O me, what eyes hath Love put in my head,
Which have no correspondence with true sight;
Or if they have, where is my judgment fled,
That censures falsely what they see aright?
5 If that be fair whereon my false eyes dote,
What means the world to say it is not so?
If it be not, then love doth well denote
Love's eye is not so true as all men's: no,
How can it? O, how can Love's eye be true,
10 That is so vex'd with watching and with tears?
No marvel then though I mistake my view:
The sun itself sees not till heaven clears.
    O cunning Love! with tears thou keep'st me blind,
    Lest eyes well-seeing thy foul faults should find.

This poem continues the theme of the preceding sonnet.

2. *when I take your part, arguing against myself.*
3–4. DO . . . MYSELF *See Sonnet 143 in which Shakespeare, casting his pride to the winds, accepts his subjection to her tyranny.* 4. ALL . . . SAKE *For your sake I am tyrannical over myself.* 5. *Compare Sonnet 89, line 14.* 7. IF THOU LOW'R'ST *if you frown.* 9. RESPECT *value.* 10. TO DESPISE *proud enough to despise you.* 11. DEFECT *lack of true beauty or merit, the insufficiency of Sonnet 150, line 2.* 12. MOTION *proposal, request.* 14. THOSE . . . LOV'ST *you love those who can see.*

2. INSUFFICIENCY *lack of true beauty or merit. See Sonnet 149, line 11.* 5. BECOMING . . . ILL *power to make everything seem beautiful and attractive. Compare Sonnet 40, line 13, and* Antony and Cleopatra, *Act I, scene 1, lines 48–51:*
Fie wrangling queen!
Whom everything becomes, to chide, to laugh,
To weep: how every passion fully strives
To make itself, in thee, fair and admir'd.
6. REFUSE *that which is thrown away as worthless or worse.* 7. WARRANTISE OF SKILL *power to sanction or justify.* 14. *My unworthiness makes me the more worthy of your love.*

Canst thou, O cruel! say I love thee not
When I against myself with thee partake?
Do I not think on thee when I forgot
Am of myself, all tyrant for thy sake?
5 Who hateth thee that I do call my friend?
On whom frown'st thou that I do fawn upon?
Nay, if thou low'r'st on me, do I not spend
Revenge upon myself with present moan?
What merit do I in myself respect
10 That is so proud thy service to despise,
When all my best doth worship thy defect,
Commanded by the motion of thine eyes?
    But, love, hate on, for now I know thy mind;
    Those that can see thou lov'st, and I am blind.

O, from what pow'r hast thou this pow'rful might
With insufficiency my heart to sway,
To make me give the lie to my true sight
And swear that brightness doth not grace the day?
5 Whence hast thou this becoming of things ill,
That in the very refuse of thy deeds
There is such strength and warrantise of skill
That in my mind thy worst all best exceeds?
Who taught thee how to make me love thee more,
10 The more I hear and see just cause of hate?
O, though I love what others do abhor,
With others thou shouldst not abhor my state:
    If thy unworthiness rais'd love in me,
    More worthy I to be belov'd of thee.

Shakespeare's treatment of the bodily aspects of sex ranges from the tact and grace of Sonnet 6, lines 1–4, to the bluntness of this poem. In all instances there is an acceptance of the body and its functions which precludes both sniggering and insistence.

1–2. Love is too young to have awareness and understanding (conscience in the sense of consciousness), yet everyone knows that the awareness of guilt arises from the indulgence of passion. 3. CHEATER *She has betrayed him and others.* URGE *stress.* AMISS *wrongdoing. 6.* NOBLER PART *reason, knowledge of right and wrong. 8.* FLESH *the penis.* STAYS *waits for.* REASON *debate, discourse. 10.* TRIUMPHANT PRIZE *the prize of his triumph.* PRIDE *See* The Rape of Lucrece, *lines 427–432. Shakespeare uses "in pride" to mean in heat. 13.* WANT OF CONSCIENCE *lack of understanding.*

1. I AM FORSWORN *I have broken an oath, that is, his marriage vows. 3.* BED-VOW *marriage vows. This is an indication that the lady was married.* NEW FAITH *new pledges of love, that is, pledges made to Shakespeare. 6.* TWENTY *all the vows Shakespeare had made concerning her. 7.* MISUSE *misrepresent, for example, his calling her beautiful. 8.* ALL . . . LOST *A secondary meaning is "all my integrity is lost through knowing you." 9.* DEEP *solemn. 11.* TO ENLIGHTEN THEE *to make thee bright.* GAVE EYES TO BLINDNESS *The reference is to his own blindness. Being blind, he spoke as though he had seen, or he gave up his power of sight to blindness. 13.* PERJUR'D I *Emendation by George Sewell (d. 1726). 1609 Quarto: eye. 14. Compare Sonnet 147, lines 13–14.*

Love is too young to know what conscience is;
Yet who knows not conscience is born of love?
Then, gentle cheater, urge not my amiss,
Lest guilty of my faults thy sweet self prove:
5   For thou betraying me, I do betray
My nobler part to my gross body's treason;
My soul doth tell my body that he may
Triumph in love; flesh stays no farther reason,
But, rising at thy name, doth point out thee
10 As his triumphant prize: proud of this pride,
He is contented thy poor drudge to be,
To stand in thy affairs, fall by thy side.
        No want of conscience hold it that I call
          Her "love" for whose dear love I rise and fall.

In loving thee thou know'st I am forsworn,
But thou art twice forsworn, to me love swearing;
In act thy bed-vow broke, and new faith torn
In vowing new hate after new love bearing.
5   But why of two oaths' breach do I accuse thee
When I break twenty? I am perjur'd most;
For all my vows are oaths but to misuse thee,
And all my honest faith in thee is lost:
For I have sworn deep oaths of thy deep kindness,
10 Oaths of thy love, thy truth, thy constancy;
And, to enlighten thee, gave eyes to blindness,
Or made them swear against the thing they see;
        For I have sworn thee fair; more perjur'd I,
          To swear against the truth so foul a lie!

Sonnets 153 and 154 are free translations of a fifth-century Greek epigram by Marianus Scholasticus. We do not know if Shakespeare worked with the original Greek or with some translation of it. In Marianus' poem the waters are not said to have curative powers. Presumably Shakespeare wrote the poems to give to a lady who was going to Bath. Since the poems are in no way concerned with either the young man or the Dark Lady, Shakespeare's authorship has sometimes been questioned, but they were printed as his in the 1609 Quarto and there is no evidence for attributing them to anyone else.

1. BRAND *flaming torch.* 2. DIAN'S *Diana, the goddess of chastity, required vows of chastity from the nymphs who were her attendants.* ADVANTAGE *favorable opportunity.* 6. DATELESS *endless. See Sonnet 30, line 6.* LIVELY *living.* STILL *always.* 7. SEETHING *boiling.* PROVE *find through experience.* 8. SOVEREIGN *supremely effective. See* Venus and Adonis, *line 916.* 9. NEW FIRED *caught fire again.* 10. THE BOY *Cupid.* 11. BATH *a reference to the city of Bath, celebrated for its thermal springs.* 12. DISTEMPER'D *sick in mind or body.* 14. EYES *1640 edition. 1609 Quarto: eye. The rhyme requires the plural.*

1. LOVE-GOD *Cupid.* 2. BRAND *flaming torch.* 5. VOTARY *nymph who has taken a vow to chastity.* 7. GENERAL *leader, commander.* 9. BY *nearby.* 12. THRALL *slave.* 13. PROVE *learn through experience.*

Cupid laid by his brand and fell asleep:
A maid of Dian's this advantage found
And his love-kindling fire did quickly steep
In a cold valley-fountain of that ground;
5   Which borrow'd from this holy fire of Love
A dateless lively heat, still to endure,
And grew a seething bath, which yet men prove
Against strange maladies a sovereign cure.
But at my mistress' eye Love's brand new fired,
10 The boy for trial needs would touch my breast;
I, sick withal, the help of bath desired
And thither hied, a sad distemper'd guest,
    But found no cure: the bath for my help lies
    Where Cupid got new fire, my mistress' eyes.

The little Love-god, lying once asleep,
Laid by his side his heart-inflaming brand,
Whilst many nymphs that vow'd chaste life to keep
Came tripping by; but in her maiden hand
5   The fairest votary took up that fire
Which many legions of true hearts had warm'd;
And so the general of hot desire
Was, sleeping, by a virgin hand disarm'd.
This brand she quenched in a cool well by,
10 Which from Love's fire took heat perpetual,
Growing a bath and healthful remedy
For men diseas'd; but I, my mistress' thrall,
    Came there for cure, and this by that I prove:
    Love's fire heats water, water cools not love.

SONGS AND POEMS
FROM THE PLAYS

The letter to Silvia is a metrical experiment. Struc-
turally it is a sonnet reduced to ten lines by the omis-
sion of the third quatrain. The first eight lines have
feminine endings and double rhymes.

2. THAT *who.* 4. SENSELESS *without sensation, being*
bodiless. 5. THEM *themselves.* 6. IMPORTUNE *urge.*
8. WANT MY SERVANTS' FORTUNE *lack my thoughts'*
good fortune. Compare Sonnet 44. 10. WOULD *1623*
Folio: should. Corrected in later folios.

This charming and somewhat conventional song
from one of Shakespeare's earliest plays is perhaps the
first song he ever wrote. The earliest musical setting
by Richard Leveridge, about 1725, sometimes errone-
ously attributed to Dr. T. A. Arne, is to be found in
Caulfield. Since the eighteenth century it has been
a favorite with composers, but the superb setting by
Franz Schubert (1797–1828), "An Sylvia," Opus 106,
No. 4, overshadows all the others. There is a modern
setting by Roger Quilter (1877–1953).

My thoughts do harbour with my Silvia nightly,
    And slaves they are to me, that send them flying:
O, could their master come and go as lightly,
    Himself would lodge where, senseless, they are lying!
5 My herald thoughts in thy pure bosom rest them,
    While I, their king, that thither them importune,
Do curse the grace that with such grace hath blest them,
    Because myself do want my servants' fortune,
I curse myself, for they are sent by me,
10 That they should harbour where their lord would be.

Act III, scene 1, lines 140–149

Who is Silvia? what is she,
    That all our swains commend her?
Holy, fair, and wise is she;
    The heaven such grace did lend her,
5 That she might admired be.

Is she kind as she is fair?
    For beauty lives with kindness:
Love doth to her eyes repair
    To help him of his blindness;
10 And being help'd, inhabits there.

Then to Silvia let us sing
    That Silvia is excelling;
She excels each mortal thing
    Upon the dull earth dwelling.
15 To her let us garlands bring.

Act IV, scene 2, lines 39–53

Armado speaks with his page, Moth, about his love, who is, he says, of complexion "most immaculate white and red." Moth replies that the most impure thoughts are "masked under such colours," since blushes indicate faults and a white countenance, fears. "White" and "red" may also indicate cosmetics, spanish white and vermillion.

3. BLUSHING *1632 Folio. 1623 Folio and Quartos: blush-in.* 8. OWE *own.*

Armado has just explained that an envoy is an explanatory postscript to some statement, and the game is for Moth to add an extemporary envoy to the statement Armado makes. Love's Labour's Lost *abounds in personal and topical allusions, some of them lost to us, and scholars do not agree on what is being glanced at here. In* The School of Night, *Muriel Bradbrook takes the three animals to represent aspects of Sir Walter Raleigh: "the Fox his Machiavellianism, the Ape court flattery, the Humble Bee court amours." All three of these activities were brought to an end by his intrigue and subsequent marriage with Elizabeth Throckmorton. The interpretation is plausible if not inevitable.*

2. AT ODDS *not of an even number.* 7. GOOSE *slang for prostitute.* 13. STAYING THE ODDS *This may be a phallic joke. Compare the poem on the humble-bee, page 249.*

If she be made of white and red,
 Her faults will ne'er be known,
For blushing cheeks by faults are bred,
 And fears by pale white shown:

5 Then if she fear, or be to blame,
 By this you shall not know,
For still her cheeks possess the same
 Which native she doth owe.

Act I, scene 2, lines 104–111

 The fox, the ape, and the humble-bee
 Were still at odds, being but three.

There's the moral. Now the *l'envoy*.
 MOTH:
 I will add the *l'envoy*. Say the moral again.

 ARMADO:
5 The fox, the ape, and the humble-bee
 Were still at odds, being but three.
 MOTH:
 Until the goose came out of door,
 And stay'd the odds by adding four.

Now will I begin your moral, and do you follow with my *l'envoy*.

10 The fox, the ape, and the humble-bee
 Were still at odds, being but three.
 ARMADO:
 Until the goose came out of door,
 Staying the odds by adding four.

Act III, scene 1, lines 85–99

SONGS AND POEMS FROM THE PLAYS / *171*

The verses are appended to Armado's boastful proposal to Jacquenetta, a country wench. He was a man of "high-born words," and could do no better. The Nemean lion is the beast slain by Hercules in the first of his labors.

The lines are from a passage elaborately equivocating a hunter's remark into off-color jest. The first line of the exchange is proverbial. The tune for this is printed in Chappell.

3. AN *if. Emendation by Lewis Theobald (1688–1744). 1598 Quarto: And. Not in 1623 Folio. 4.* AN *Theobald's emendation. 1598 Quarto and 1623 Folio: And.*

Holofernes, the pedantic schoolmaster, composed these verses as "an extemporal epitaph on the death of a deer." He was probably not aware of the indecencies which Pandarus insisted upon in his song. See page 247.

1. PRICKET *a buck in its second year. 2.* SORE *a buck in its fourth year. 3.* EL *"L" is thought of as both a letter and a Roman numeral.* SOREL *a buck in its third year.*

In Love's Labour's Lost *the King of Navarre and three courtiers, Berowne, Dumain, and Longaville, set up a "little academe" and swear to study there*

Thus dost thou hear the Nemean lion roar
    'Gainst thee, thou lamb, that standest as his prey;
Submissive fall his princely feet before,
    And he from forage will incline to play.
5   But if thou strive, poor soul, what art thou then?
Food for his rage, repasture for his den.

Act IV, scene 1, lines 90–95

ROSALIND:
Thou canst not hit it, hit it, hit it,
Thou canst not hit it, my good man.

BOYET:
An I cannot, cannot, cannot,
An I cannot, another can.

Act IV, scene 1, lines 127–130

The preyful princess pierc'd and prick'd a pretty pleasing
    pricket;
        Some say a sore; but not a sore till now made sore with
            shooting.
The dogs did yell; put el to sore, then sorel jumps from
    thicket,
        Or pricket sore, or else sorel; the people fall a-hoot-
            ing.
5   If sore be sore, then L to sore makes fifty sores one sorel.
Of one sore I an hundred make by adding but one more L.

Act IV, scene 2, lines 58–63

If love make me forsworn, how shall I swear to love?
Ah! never faith could hold, if not to beauty vow'd;

for three years, during which time they will sleep only three hours a night, eat one meal a day, fast one day in seven, and see no women. When the Princess of France and her ladies enter upon the scene, the men fall in love and break their vows, as this and the three following poems attest. The play is, among other things, Shakespeare's comedy on education, and it views as pedantry all humane studies which are unrelated to experience. In the end the young men resolve to "lose our oaths to find ourselves,/Or else we lose ourselves to keep our oaths." This poem was printed in The Passionate Pilgrim, *1599. It is a Shakespearean sonnet in hexameter lines.*

1. FORSWORN *perjured.* 4. OSIERS *willows.* 5. BIAS *tendency.*

In both subject matter and technique Love's Labour's Lost *is Shakespeare's most artificial play. It abounds in end-stopped lines, rhymes, formal experiments, and satirical uses of the doggerel verses of the age just past. The best evidence indicates that it was first written when he was writing the sonnets,* Venus and Adonis, *and* The Rape of Lucrece. *It teems with echoes of them. It indulges the poet's budding virtuosity. This poem is a sonnet with an additional couplet.*

1. KISS THE GOLDEN SUN *Compare Sonnet 33.* 4. NIGHT OF DEW *tears shed during the night.* 5–8. *Compare* Venus and Adonis, *lines 491–492.* 14. GLASSES *mirrors.*

Though to myself forsworn, to thee I'll faithful prove:
Those thoughts to me were oaks, to thee like osiers bow'd.
5 Study his bias leaves and makes his book thine eyes,
Where all those pleasures live that art would comprehend.
If knowledge be the mark, to know thee shall suffice;
Well learned is that tongue that well can thee commend;
All ignorant is that soul that sees thee without wonder;
10 Which is to me some praise that I thy parts admire.
Thy eye Jove's lightning bears, thy voice his dreadful
    thunder,
Which, not to anger bent, is music and sweet fire.
        Celestial as thou art, O! pardon love this wrong,
        That sings heaven's praise with such an earthly
            tongue.

Act IV, scene 2, lines 109–122

So sweet a kiss the golden sun gives not
To those fresh morning drops upon the rose
As thy eyebeams when their fresh rays have smot
The night of dew that on my cheeks down flows;
5 Nor shines the silver moon one half so bright
Through the transparent bosom of the deep
As doth thy face through tears of mine give light;
Thou shin'st in every tear that I do weep:
No drop but as a coach doth carry thee;
10 So ridest thou triumphing in my woe.
Do but behold the tears that swell in me,
And they thy glory through my grief will show:
        But do not love thyself; then thou wilt keep
        My tears for glasses, and still make me weep.
15   O queen of queens, how far dost thou excel
        No thought can think nor tongue of mortal tell.

Act IV, scene 3, lines 26–41

This sonnet was also printed in The Passionate Pilgrim, *1599.*

3. FALSE PERJURY *breaking his oath to study and see no women. See comment, page 174.* 7. THOU A *thou art a.* 9. VOWS . . . BREATH *It is often remarked in Shakespeare that a word is but air.* 11. EXHAL'ST *draws out, absorbs.*

This, the last of the poems from Love's Labour's Lost *in which the young courtiers renounce study for love, was printed in* The Passionate Pilgrim, *1599, and in* England's Helicon, *1600.*

6. CAN *Quartos and 1623 Folio. The Passionate Pilgrim and England's Helicon:* gan. 16. FORSWORN *perjured.*

Did not the heavenly rhetoric of thine eye,
'Gainst whom the world cannot hold argument,
Persuade my heart to this false perjury?
Vows for thee broke deserve not punishment.
5 A woman I forswore; but I will prove,
Thou being a goddess, I forswore not thee:
My vow was earthly, thou a heavenly love;
Thy grace being gain'd cures all disgrace in me.
Vows are but breath, and breath a vapour is:
10 Then thou, fair sun, which on my earth dost shine,
Exhal'st this vapour-vow; in thee it is;
If broken then, it is no fault of mine:
    If by me broke, what fool is not so wise
    To lose an oath to win a paradise?

Act IV, scene 3, lines 60–73

On a day, alack the day!
Love, whose month is ever May,
Spied a blossom passing fair
Playing in the wanton air:
5 Through the velvet leaves the wind,
All unseen can passage find;
That the lover, sick to death,
Wish'd himself the heaven's breath.
Air, quoth he, thy cheeks may blow;
10 Air, would I might triumph so!
But alack! my hand is sworn
Ne'er to pluck thee from thy thorn:
Vow, alack! for youth unmeet,
Youth so apt to pluck a sweet.
15 Do not call it sin in me,
That I am forsworn for thee;
Thou for whom Jove would swear

Love, whose month is ever May

18. ETHIOP *blackamoor. The Elizabethan ideal beauty was blonde. 19.* DENY . . . JOVE *deny his divine nature.*

The songs of Spring and Winter bring Love's Labour's Lost to its close. One song is "maintained" by the owl, the emblem of sobriety; the other by the cuckoo, the emblem of a certain insouciance. The cuckoo mates but does not keep house. She lays her eggs in other birds' nests, leaving her young to be cared for by the unwilling foster parents. The species is named in imitation of the call of the male during mating season, and the call was used to indicate, or to taunt, a cuckold, that is, a man whose wife was known to be unfaithful to him. The jest is ancient. Both "cuckold" and "cuckoo" derive from the Latin name of the bird, cuculus. *The earliest known setting for "When daisies pied" is by Richard Leveridge, about 1725. Igor Stravinsky (b. 1882) has a setting for mezzo-soprano, flute, clarinet, and viola. The best-known settings for both songs are by Dr. T. A. Arne (1710–1778) and may be found in Caulfield. "When icicles hang" has been set to music by Roger Quilter (1877–1953).*

1. PIED *variegated. The reference is to the yellow, white, and red English daisy. 1, 2. The lines appear in reverse order in both the 1598 Quarto and the 1623 Folio. They were transposed by Lewis Theobald (1688–1744) to make the metrical structure of the first stanza conform to that of the others. 2.* LADY-SMOCKS *cuckooflower; perhaps a corruption of "Our Lady's smock." 3.* CUCKOO-BUDS *spring-blooming buttercups. 10.* OATEN STRAWS *musical instruments of the country folk. 11.* ARE PLOUGHMEN'S CLOCKS *awaken the ploughmen. "Up with the lark" is still a common phrase. 12.* TURTLES *turtledoves.* TREAD *mate.*

Juno but an Ethiop were;
And deny himself for Jove,
20 Turning mortal for thy love.

Act IV, scene 3, lines 101–120

Songs of Spring and Winter

ARMADO:

This side is *Hiems,* Winter; this *Ver,* the Spring; the one maintained
by the owl, th' other by the cuckoo. *Ver,* begin.

Spring

When daisies pied and violets blue
    And lady-smocks all silver-white
And cuckoo-buds of yellow hue
    Do paint the meadows with delight,
5 The cuckoo then, on every tree,
Mocks married men; for thus sings he,
        Cuckoo,
Cuckoo, cuckoo! O word of fear
Unpleasing to a married ear!

10 When shepherds pipe on oaten straws,
    And merry larks are ploughmen's clocks,
When turtles tread, and rooks, and daws,
    And maidens bleach their summer smocks,
The cuckoo then, on every tree,
15 Mocks married men; for thus sings he,
        Cuckoo,
Cuckoo, cuckoo! O word of fear,
Unpleasing to a married ear!

HIS NAIL *used widely to mean waiting patiently, or impatiently, while one has nothing to do. Here it also means "warming the fingers by blowing on them."* 23. FOUL *1598 Quarto: full. 1623 Folio: fowle.* 27. KEEL THE POT *cool the pot, keep it from boiling over by stirring; skim.* 29. SAW *moral saying, maxim.* 32. CRABS *crab apples.*

Bottom practices speaking "a part to tear a cat in." 5. PHIBBUS' CAR *Phoebus', the sun's, chariot.*

Winter

When icicles hang by the wall,
20   And Dick the shepherd blows his nail,
And Tom bears logs into the hall,
    And milk comes frozen home in pail,
When blood is nipp'd, and ways be foul,
Then nightly sings the staring owl,
25   Tu-whit, to-who,
        A merry note,
While greasy Joan doth keel the pot.

When all aloud the wind doth blow,
    And coughing drowns the parson's saw,
30 And birds sit brooding in the snow,
    And Marian's nose looks red and raw,
When roasted crabs hiss in the bowl,
Then nightly sings the staring owl,
        Tu-whit, to-who,
35   A merry note,
While greasy Joan doth keel the pot.

Act V, scene 2, lines 901–939

A MIDSUMMER NIGHT'S DREAM

The raging rocks
And shivering shocks
Shall break the locks
    Of prison gates;
5 And Phibbus' car
Shall shine from far
And make and mar
    The foolish Fates.

Act I, scene 1, lines 33–40

The poem is our introduction to the fairies in the play. Coleridge remarked on the meter that it "had been invented and employed by Shakespeare for the sake of its appropriateness to the rapid and airy motion of the fairy by whom the speech is delivered." The poem was first set to music by William Jackson (1730–1803), English organist and composer.

2. THOROUGH *through.* 3. PALE *an enclosed space.* 6. SPHERE *In the Ptolemaic astronomy the earth was thought to be at the center of nine or ten concentric crystal spheres to which the moon, planets, and fixed stars were affixed. These spheres were moved around the earth daily by the force of the top sphere or* primum mobile. 8. ORBS *fairy rings, a circular fungus growth thought to mark the place where the fairies had danced.* 9. PENSIONERS *gentlemen in the personal service of the king or queen.*

The fairies sing their queen, Titania, to sleep. The earliest known setting of these lines was made by John Christopher Smith for The Fairies, *1754, his opera based upon the play. The incidental music for the play by Felix Mendelssohn (1809–1847) includes a setting of these lines for two sopranos and a chorus of sopranos and altos.*

2. HEDGE-HOGS *any of the Old World nocturnal, insectivorous mammals with both hair and spines; in America, the porcupine.* 3. BLIND-WORMS *burrowing, snakelike lizards which, because of the smallness of their eyes, were thought to be blind.* 5. PHILOMELE *the nightingale, whose song became the emblem of melancholy and suffering for the Elizabethan poets. In Greek mythology as told by Ovid in* Metamorphoses, *Book VI, line 413ff, Philomel, or Philomela, was turned into a nightingale because she avenged herself on the man who ravished her.* 6. OUR *Quartos. 1623 Folio:* your.

Over hill, over dale,
Thorough bush, thorough brier,
Over park, over pale,
Thorough flood, thorough fire,
I do wander everywhere,
Swifter than the moones sphere;
And I serve the Fairy Queen,
To dew her orbs upon the green:
The cowslips tall her pensioners be;
In their gold coats spots you see;
Those be rubies, fairy favours;
In those freckles live their savours:
I must go seek some dewdrops here,
And hang a pearl in every cowslip's ear.

Act II, scene 1, lines 2–15

You spotted snakes with double tongue,
Thorny hedge-hogs, be not seen;
Newts and blind-worms, do no wrong,
Come not near our Fairy Queen.

Philomele with melody,
Sing in our sweet lullaby;
Lulla, lulla, lullaby; lulla, lulla, lullaby.
Never harm
Nor spell nor charm,
Come our lovely lady nigh;
So good-night, with lullaby.

Weaving spiders, come not here;
Hence you long-legg'd spinners, hence!
Beetles black, approach not near;
Worm nor snail, do no offence.

Oberon puts a charm upon Titania as she sleeps which will make her "madly dote" upon the next creature she sees.

4. OUNCE *an animal somewhat resembling the leopard.*
5. PARD *leopard.*

Bottom, left alone in the woods, sings to keep his courage up. It is a mark of his amiable stupidity that he does not understand the joke in his own song. For a comment on the song of the cuckoo, see page 180. An anonymous musical setting, which is the earliest known, is reprinted in Caulfield. There is a setting by Dr. Charles Burney, 1762.

1. WOOSEL COCK *Bottom's pronunciation of "ouzel-cock," the male blackbird.* 4. QUILL *strong wing feather.* 6. PLAIN-SONG *a simple melody. The song of the cuckoo is without variation.*

Oberon, having sent for Demetrius's true love, places a charm upon him to make him fall in love with her again. The lines were set to music in John Christopher Smith's The Fairies, *1754.*
1. DYE *color. The flower from which the elixir is*

Be as thou wast wont to be;
See as thou wast wont to see:
Dian's bud o'er Cupid's flower
Hath such force and blessed power.

Act IV, scene 1, lines 74–77

PYRAMUS:
But stay, O spite!
But mark, poor knight,
What dreadful dole is here!
Eyes, do you see?
5   How can it be?
O dainty duck! O dear!
Thy mantle good,
What, stain'd with blood!
Approach, ye Furies fell!
10   O Fates, come, come
Cut thread and thrum;
Quail, crush, conclude, and quell! . . .
O wherefore, Nature, didst thou lions frame?
Since lion vile hath here deflow'r'd my dear,
15   Which is . . . no, no . . . which was the fairest dame
That liv'd, that lov'd, that lik'd, that look'd with cheer.
Come, tears, confound;
Out, sword, and wound
The pap of Pyramus;
20   Ay, that left pap,
Where heart doth hop.
Thus die I, thus, thus, thus.   (*Stabs himself.*)
Now am I dead,
Now am I fled;

The play within the play continues as Thisby returns to the rendezvous.

13. SISTERS THREE *the Furies of line 9 in the preceding set of verses.* 17. SHORE *severed.* 21. IMBRUE *shed the blood of.*

25 My soul is in the sky.
  Tongue, lose thy light;
  Moon, take thy flight.
Now die, die, die, die, die!

Act V, scene 1, lines 281–311

THISBY:
  Asleep, my love?
  What, dead, my dove?
O Pyramus, arise!
  Speak, speak! Quite dumb?
5 Dead, dead? A tomb
Must cover thy sweet eyes.
  These lily lips,
  This cherry nose,
These yellow cowslip cheeks,
10   Are gone, are gone;
  Lovers, make moan!
His eyes were green as leeks.
  O Sisters Three,
  Come, come to me,
15 With hands as pale as milk;
  Lay them in gore,
  Since you have shore
With shears his thread of silk.
  Tongue, not a word:
20   Come, trusty sword:
Come, blade, my breast imbrue!
  And farewell, friends;   (*Stabs herself.*)
  Thus Thisby ends:
Adieu, adieu, adieu!

Act V, scene 1, lines 331–354

The play within the play is ended. The lovers have departed to meet again in a fortnight at the wedding of Theseus and Hippolyta. It is midnight. Puck enters and addresses the audience. His lines have been set to music by Felix Mendelssohn (1809–1847) for soprano solo and a chorus of sopranos and altos.

2. BEHOWLS *Emendation in Lewis Theobald's edition, 1734. Quartos and 1623 Folio: beholds.* 4 FORDONE *exhausted.* 14. TRIPLE HECATE'S TEAM *Hecate's chariot was drawn by two horses, one black and one white. She was the goddess of sorcery and the underworld. A threefold character, she was Luna in heaven, Diana on earth, and Hecate in the underworld. The fairies, who frolicked at night, followed her in her capacity as Luna, the moon.* 17. FROLIC *gay, merry.* 20. *to sweep away the dust which lies behind the door.*

The sonnet, spoken by a single actor at the beginning of Romeo and Juliet, *serves as forthright if not technically skillful exposition. It announces the place, the nature, and the outcome of the story, and it indicates the approximate acting time of a Shakespearean play. The sonnet, printed in all the quartos, was omitted from the folios.*

5. FATAL *instrumental to destiny.* 6. STAR-CROSS'D *fated.* TAKE THEIR LIFE *are born.* 7. MISADVENTUR'D *unfortunate.*

Now the hungry lion roars,
    And the wolf behowls the moon;
Whilst the heavy ploughman snores,
    All with weary task fordone.
5   Now the wasted brands do glow,
    Whilst the screech owl, screeching loud,
Puts the wretch that lies in woe
    In remembrance of a shroud.
Now it is the time of night
10   That the graves, all gaping wide,
Every one lets forth his sprite,
    In the churchway paths to glide;
And we fairies, that do run
    By the triple Hecate's team
15   From the presence of the sun,
    Following darkness like a dream,
Now are frolic. Not a mouse
Shall disturb this hallow'd house.
I am sent, with broom, before,
20   To sweep the dust behind the door.

Act V, scene 1, lines 378–397

ROMEO AND JULIET

Two households, both alike in dignity,
In fair Verona, where we lay our scene,
From ancient grudge break to new mutiny,
Where civil blood makes civil hands unclean.
5   From forth the fatal loins of these two foes
A pair of star-cross'd lovers take their life;
Whose misadventur'd piteous overthrows
Doth with their death bury their parent's strife.

Romeo, seeing Juliet at Capulet's ball, falls in love with her and resolves to "make blessed my rude hand" by "touching hers." He addresses her as a pilgrim approaching a shrine. Since he was one of the "maskers" at the ball, it may be that he was wearing the costume of a pilgrim. Their first conversation takes the form of a sonnet with six rather than the usual seven rhymes. The form, not noticeable in the theater, lends their speech a shy and youthful gravity.

2. FINE *conclusion; an emendation by John Warburton (1682–1759). The original texts read "sin" and "sinne" using, in all cases, a long "s."* 3. READY *1597 Quarto. 1623 Folio: did ready.*

The fearful passage of their death-mark'd love,

10   And the continuance of their parents' rage,

Which, but their children's end, naught could remove,

Is now the two hours' traffic of our stage;

    The which if you with patient ears attend,

    What here shall miss, our toil shall strive to mend.

Act I, Prologue

ROMEO:

If I profane with my unworthiest hand

This holy shrine, the gentle fine is this:

My lips, two blushing pilgrims, ready stand

To smooth that rough touch with a tender kiss.

JULIET:

5   Good pilgrim, you do wrong your hand too much,

Which mannerly devotion shows in this;

For saints have hands that pilgrims' hands do touch,

And palm to palm is holy palmers' kiss.

ROMEO:

Have not saints lips, and holy palmers too?

JULIET:

10   Ay, pilgrim, lips that they must use in pray'r.

ROMEO:

O, then, dear saint, let lips do what hands do;

They pray; grant thou, lest faith turn to despair.

JULIET:

Saints do not move, though grant for prayers' sake.

ROMEO:

Then move not while my prayer's effect I take.

(Kisses her.)
Act I, scene 5, lines 95–108

The sonnet, also addressed to the audience by a single actor, follows immediately after the scene in which the lovers meet. It characterizes Romeo's former love for Rosaline as desire and the new love as affection, which includes desire but is not confined by it. In Shakespeare true love is never perverted either toward the sensual or the platonic. Here, consummation is simply taken for granted. This is a marriage ready-made.

2. GAPES *The image is that of a newborn infant.* 3. FAIR *fair person. The usage is analogous to the modern use of "beauty."* 6. ALIKE BEWITCHED *Both are bewitched.* 11. HER MEANS MUCH LESS *She has many fewer means.*

The stage direction of the 1597 Quarto indicates that Mercutio sang this punning bit of bawdry, but the original music for it has been lost and later composers have understandably ignored it.

1. HARE *slang for prostitute or light wench.* HOAR *moldy, with a pun on "whore."* 3. MEAT *any food, a whore or wanton.* 6. SPENT *consumed, expended sexually.*

In the brief comic scene which follows the discovery of Juliet's supposedly dead body, Peter, the servant, asks the musicians who were to play at her wedding for music to relieve the general grief. The lines, with some alterations, are from a poem by Richard Edwards printed in The Paradyse of Daynty Devises, *1576.*

2. DUMPS *low spirits, melancholy.*

Now old desire doth in his deathbed lie
And young affection gapes to be his heir;
That fair for which love groan'd for and would die,
With tender Juliet match'd, is now not fair.
5 Now Romeo is belov'd, and loves again,
Alike bewitched by the charm of looks;
But to his foe suppos'd he must complain,
And she steal love's sweet bait from fearful hooks.
Being held a foe, he may not have access
10 To breathe such vows as lovers use to swear,
And she as much in love, her means much less
To meet her new beloved anywhere;
        But passion lends them power, time means, to meet,
        Temp'ring extremities with extreme sweet.

Act II, Prologue

        An old hare hoar,
        And an old hare hoar,
Is very good meat in Lent;
        But a hare that is hoar
5   Is too much for a score
When it hoars ere it be spent.

Act II, scene 4, lines 141–146

When griping griefs the heart doth wound,
        And doleful dumps the mind oppress,
Then music with her silver sound . . .
Then music with her silver sound,
5   With speedy help doth lend redress.

Act IV, scene 5, lines 128–130, 145–146

By the terms of her father's will Portia will be given
in marriage to the suitor who chooses the right one
of three caskets—one of gold, one of silver, and one
of lead. The Prince of Morocco chooses the golden
casket and finds a scroll with these verses.

1. *a common saying.* 5. TOMBS *Emendation by Dr.
Johnson (1709–1784). Quartos and 1623 Folio: tim-
ber.* 8. *Such an answer as this would not have been
written.*

The Prince of Arragon chooses the silver casket and
finds "the portrait of a blinking idiot," "a fool's
head," and these verses.

1. THIS *the maxims which follow.* 4. SHADOWS *reflections or images of the reality, not the reality itself.*
6. IWIS *certainly.* 7. SILVER'D O'ER *with silvered hair,
that is, old.* 9. I *the idiot portrayed in the casket.*
10. SPED *dispatched, sent away.*

The song is sung while Bassanio, about to choose the
casket which will win him Portia's hand, "comments
on the casket to himself." It is probable that Portia,
who favored Bassanio over the other suitors, devised
the song so that the rhyme of the first three lines
would suggest the leaden casket. The earliest known
setting is by Dr. T. A. Arne (1710–1778), who wrote
it to be sung by Olivia when the song was interpolated
into a production of Twelfth Night, and he omitted
the last four lines as inappropriate to her. There is a
complete setting by Roger Quilter (1877–1953).

1. FANCY *love.* 2. OR . . . OR *either . . . or.*

All that glisters is not gold,
Often have you heard that told;
Many a man his life hath sold
But my outside to behold;
5 Gilded tombs do worms infold:
Had you been as wise as bold,
Young in limbs, in judgment old,
Your answer had not been inscroll'd:
Fare you well; your suit is cold.

Act II, scene 7, lines 65–73

The fire seven times tri'd this:
Seven times tri'd that judgment is
That did never choose amiss;
Some there be that shadows kiss,
5 Such have but a shadow's bliss;
There be fools alive, iwis,
Silver'd o'er; and so was this:
Take what wife you will to bed,
I will ever be your head:
10 So be gone; you are sped.

Act II, scene 9, lines 63–72

Tell me where is fancy bred,
Or in the heart or in the head?
How begot, how nourished?
    ALL: Reply, reply.
5 It is engend'red in the eyes,
With gazing fed; and fancy dies
In the cradle where it lies.
        Let us all ring fancy's knell:
        I'll begin it—Ding, dong, bell.
        ALL: Ding, dong, bell.

Act III, scene 2, lines 63–72

Bassanio chooses the leaden casket and finds Portia's portrait and the scroll awarding him her hand in marriage.

Falstaff sings the opening words of a song, "Lancelot du Lake," which was sung to the tune "Flying Fame" or "Chevy Chace." The music is reprinted in Chappell.

2. JORDAN *chamber pot.*

Justice Shallow, who had been a student at Clement's Inn fifty-five years earlier, entertains Justice Silence and Sir John Falstaff, friends of his youth. Silence, in his cups, keeps breaking into song. What may be the earliest music for lines 1–6 and 7–11 is reprinted in Caulfield. Later settings for lines 12–14, 15–16, and 17–19 are also to be found in Caulfield. A four-part setting of lines 17–19 by Orlandus Lassus (1530–1594), which may be the original music, is reprinted by Eleanor Brougham. Line 20 is a recollection of an old ballad. The names are to be found in this order in "Robin Hood and the Pinder of Wakefield," but of course they occur together elsewhere.

2. GOD *1598 Quarto. 1623 Folio:* heauen. 6. EVER AMONG *all the while.* 10. SHROVETIDE *Shrovetide carols celebrated the merriment of the festivities of the days immediately preceding Lent.*

You that choose not by the view
Chance as fair and choose as true:
Since this fortune falls to you,
Be content and seek no new.
5   If you be well pleas'd with this,
And hold your fortune for your bliss,
Turn you where your lady is
And claim her with a loving kiss.

Act III, scene 2, lines 131–138

SECOND PART OF KING HENRY THE FOURTH

When Arthur first in court . . .
Empty the jordan.
And was a worthy king. . . .

Act II, scene 4, lines 36–38

Do nothing but eat and make good cheer
And praise God for the merry year,
When flesh is cheap and females dear,
And lusty lads roam here and there
5   So merrily,
And ever among so merrily.

Act V, scene 3, lines 18–23

Be merry, be merry, my wife has all,
For women are shrews, both short and tall:
'Tis merry in hall when beards wag all,
10   And welcome merry Shrovetide.
Be merry, be merry.

Act V, scene 3, lines 35–39

13. LEMAN *Originally
the word meant "sweetheart," but in Shakespeare it
means an illicit sexual partner.* 17. DO ME *pledge me,
drink to me.* 19. SAMINGO *Shortly after this song,
Silence was carried to bed. This is his drunken recollection of Sir Mingo, a character who, as the song
has it, "for quaffing doth surpasse."*

*Hortensio, disguised as a music teacher, gives Bianca
a lesson in Elizabethan solfeggio by singing the scale
in the modern key of G. The names of the musical
notes are the beginning syllables of phrases in a
Latin hymn for St. John the Baptist's Day. Toward
the end of the seventeenth century "Si" came to be
accepted for "B" and "Ut" was changed to "Do."*

1. GAMOUTH *gamut.* 5. CLIFF *clef.*

*"Why, that's all one," Baptista had replied when in-
formed that Petruchio's "horse comes with him on
his back." The verses are the servant's rejoinder.*

A cup of wine that's brisk and fine,
And drink unto the leman mine;
    And a merry heart lives long-a.

Act V, scene 3, lines 48–50

15   Fill the cup and let it come;
    I'll pledge you a mile to the bottom.

Act V, scene 3, lines 56–57

        Do me right,
    And dub me knight:
        Samingo!

Act V, scene 3, lines 77–79

20   And Robin Hood, Scarlet, and John. . . .

Act V, scene 3, line 107

THE TAMING OF THE SHREW

Gamouth I am, the ground of all accord,
    A re, to plead Hortensio's passion;
B mi, Bianca, take him for thy lord,
    C fa ut, that loves with all affection:
5 *D sol re,* one cliff, two notes have I;
    E la mi, show pity, or I die.

Act III, scene 1, lines 73–78

Nay, by Saint Jamy,
I hold you a penny,
    A horse and a man
    Is more than one,
5 And yet not many.

Act III, scene 2, lines 84–88

This is the beginning of a popular ballad, now lost. It is sung by Petruchio as he waits for the supper he will not allow Kate to share. The fragment was expanded into a lyric in Kiss Me, Kate, *1948. Both lyric and music are by Cole Porter. The first line is repeated in* The Second Part of King Henry the Fourth, *Act V, scene 3, line 146.*

A fragment of a lost ballad.

1. ORDERS GREY *a Franciscan.*

The function of the song in the scene is to foreshadow the perfidy of Don John and Borachio and the jealousy of Claudio. An allegedly sixteenth-century setting of these verses to the tune of "Heart's-ease" and another setting by Thomas Ford (d. 1648) are reprinted by Long. A setting by Dr. T. A. Arne (1710–1778) is reprinted in Caulfield. It was set by many composers in the eighteenth and nineteenth centuries and has been given modern settings by Roger Quilter (1877–1953) and Peter Warlock, pseudonym of Philip Haseltine (1894–1930).

10. MOE *1600 Quarto. 1623 Folio: more. 11.* DUMPS *low spirits. It was formerly a word of greater dignity. 12.* WAS *1600 Quarto. 1623 Folio: were. 13.* LEAVY *full of leaves.*

Where is the life that late I led?
Where are those. . . .

Act IV, scene 1, lines 143–144

It was a friar of orders grey,
As he forth walked on his way. . . .

Act IV, scene 1, lines 148–149

MUCH ADO ABOUT NOTHING

Sigh no more, ladies, sigh no more,
    Men were deceivers ever;
One foot in sea, and one on shore,
    To one thing constant never.
5   Then sigh not so,
        But let them go,
    And be you blithe and bonny,
Converting all your sounds of woe
        Into Hey nonny, nonny.

10 Sing no more ditties, sing no moe,
    Of dumps so dull and heavy;
The fraud of men was ever so,
    Since summer first was leavy.
        Then sigh not so,
15   But let them go,
    And be you blithe and bonny,
Converting all your sounds of woe
        Into Hey nonny, nonny.

Act II, scene 3, lines 64–76

Benedick, who "was not born under a rhyming planet," can manage only the beginning of a love song. The lines are taken, with minimal changes, from a ballad written by William Elderton in the 1560s. The only musical setting is the anonymous one in Caulfield.

4. How much I am deserving of pity.

Claudio, now convinced of Hero's fidelity and believing that his jealous fury had caused her death, reads her epitaph from a scroll, hangs the scroll upon her tomb, and calls for the funeral hymn. The earliest known setting of the hymn, by Dr. T. A. Arne (1710–1778), is reprinted in Caulfield.

3. GUERDON reward. 10. GODDESS OF THE NIGHT Diana, the protectress of virgins.

The Bishop of Ely reminds King Henry of "a saying very old and true."

The god of love,
That sits above,
And knows me, and knows me,
How pitiful I deserve. . . .

Act V, scene 2, lines 26–29

Done to death by sland'rous tongues
    Was the Hero that here lies:
Death, in guerdon of her wrongs,
    Gives her fame which never dies.
5 So the life that died with shame
    Lives in death with glorious fame.

Hang thou here upon the tomb,
Praising her when I am dumb.
Now music sound, and sing your solemn hymn

Song

10 Pardon, goddess of the night,
Those that slew thy virgin knight;
For the which, with songs of woe,
Round about her tomb they go.
    Midnight, assist our moan;
15   Help us to sigh and groan,
        Heavily, heavily.
Graves, yawn and yield your dead,
    Till death be uttered,
        Heavily, heavily.

20 Now, unto thy bones good night!
Yearly will I do this rite.

Act V, scene 3, lines 3–23

KING HENRY THE FIFTH

If that you will France win,
Then with Scotland first begin.

Act I, scene 2, lines 167–168

These verses follow King Henry's exhortation to his troops at the battle of Harfleur, "Once more unto the breach, dear friends, once more," and represent the unheroic view of battle. Pistol refers to his verses as plain song, and it is possible that they were taken from a popular song, but there is no reason to suppose that they were intended to be sung in the performance of the play. There is no record of a musical setting for the lines.

In Richard II *Shakespeare had written of the deposition which led to the civil wars of* Henry IV, *1 and 2. In the latter plays Prince Hal had emerged as a hero, and here in* Henry V *he is the hero king who subdues France, marries the French princess, and brings dissension at home and abroad to an end. It is a fine play with England as its theme, and it crowns the tetralogy, yet here and elsewhere in the play Shakespeare apologizes for the inadequacy of the theater in portraying the military exploits of his mighty men of action. He was on the point of turning to another kind of play in which pageantry is of lesser importance and what matters most is the inner action. His next two heroes were to be Brutus and Hamlet.*

2. BENDING *"stooping to your clemency."* See page 239. 7. WORLD'S BEST GARDEN *England, as contrasted to* Richard II *(Act III, scene 4, lines 43–44) where ". . . our sea-walled garden, the whole land,/Is full of weeds. . . ."*

PISTOL:

Knocks go and come; God's vassals drop and die;
    And sword and shield
    In bloody field
    Doth win immortal fame.

BOY:

Would I were in an ale house in London! I would give all my fame for a
pot of ale, and safety.

PISTOL:

And I:

If wishes would prevail with me,
My purpose should not fail with me,
    But thither would I hie.

BOY:

        As duly,
    But not as truly,
As bird doth sing on bough.

Act III, scene 2, lines 8–20

Thus far, with rough and all-unable pen,
Our bending author hath pursu'd the story,
In little room confining mighty men,
Mangling by starts the full course of their glory.
Small time, but in that small most greatly liv'd
This star of England: Fortune made his sword,
By which the world's best garden he achiev'd,
And of it left his son imperial lord.
Henry the Sixth, in infant bands crown'd King
Of France and England, did this king succeed;
Whose state so many had the managing
That they lost France and made his England bleed;
    Which oft our stage hath shown; and for their sake
    In your fair minds let this acceptance take.

Epilogue

*The names of Page and Ford are transposed in the
1623 Folio, a manifest error. The 1602 Quarto, a corrupt text, preserves the proper order. The text otherwise follows the folio.*

2. EKE *also.* 3. VARLET *rascal.* 4. DOVE *wife.* PROVE *bring
to the test.*

*These verses comprise the conclusion of Falstaff's
letter to Mistress Page. In it he speaks as a military
man and hopeful lover. A gentleman was expected to
be able to write verses.*

*The verses, spoken by Master Ford to Falstaff, appear
in the text as a quotation. They are adapted from
Whitney's emblem, "Mulier umbra viri," in* The
Choice of Emblems, *1586.*

1. SUBSTANCE *material means.* LOVE PURSUES *pursues
love.* 2. THAT THAT *that which.*

*While awaiting his opponent at the dueling place,
Sir Hugh Evans, the Welsh parson, sings to keep his
courage up and confuses Marlowe's "Come live with
me" (see page 309) with Psalm 137. He imposes his
Welsh accent on both. The version of the Psalter he
quotes from is by Thomas Sternhold (d. 1549) and
John Hopkins (d. 1570):*
    *"When as we sat in Babylon, the rivers round
        about,*
        *And in remembrance of Sion, the tears for grief
        burst out."*
*The version was ridiculed by Dryden in "Absolom
and Achitophel."*

8. *1623 Folio. The 1602 Quarto prints a line from
an old ballad: "There dwelt a man in Babylon."* 9.
VAGRAM *an illiterate alteration of "vagrant" which
Sir Hugh confuses with "fragrant."*

NYM:
I will discuss the humour of this love to Page.
    PISTOL:
And I to Ford shall eke unfold,
    How Falstaff, varlet vile,
His dove will prove, his gold will hold,
5   And his soft couch defile.

                    Act I, scene 3, lines 104–108

Thine own true knight,
By day or night,
Or any kind of light,
With all his might
5 For thee to fight,
            John Falstaff.

                    Act II, scene 1, lines 15–19

Love like a shadow flies when substance love pursues,
Pursuing that that flies, and flying what pursues.

                    Act II, scene 2, lines 215–216

To shallow rivers, to whose falls
Melodious birds sing madrigals;
There will we make our peds of roses
And a thousand fragrant posies.
5   To shallow—
Mercy on me! I have a great dispositions to cry.
Melodious birds sing madrigals—
When as I sat in Pabylon—
And a thousand vagram posies.
10   To shallow &c.

                    Act III, scene 1, lines 17–26

SONGS AND POEMS FROM THE PLAYS / 213

*Quoted by Falstaff to Mistress Ford from the "Son-
nets of Variable Verse" in Sir Philip Sidney's* Astro-
phel and Stella, *1591.*

1. THEE *1623 Folio. Not in 1602 Quarto or Sidney.*

*This is the "scornful rhyme" sung by the fairies in
the scene in which Falstaff's lecherous ambitions are
disclosed to all. During the singing of the song children disguised as fairies pinch him. It was one of the
functions of fairies to punish erring mortals by pinch-
ing them black and blue.*

1. FANTASY *erotic fantasies. 2.* LUXURY *lechery. 3.*
BLOODY FIRE *fire in the blood. 7.* MUTUALLY *all together.*

*Songs of the greenwood tree are ancient in England
and were very popular in the sixteenth and seventeenth centuries. Shakespeare uses his, the first song
in the play, to establish the mood of pastoral romance
as contrasted to the world of the court. But the mature
Shakespeare sees the other sides of things, and the
song is followed by Jaques's mocking of the pastoral
life. What may be the original tune to which Shakespeare fitted his words is printed by John H. Long.
The musical setting by Dr. T. A. Arne is reprinted
in Caulfield. There is also a setting by Roger Quilter
(1877–1953).*

*3–4. sing his song in accompaniment, or in counter-
point, to the song of the birds.*

Have I caught thee, my heavenly jewel?

Act III, scene 3, line 45

Fie on sinful fantasy!
Fie on lust and luxury!
Lust is but a bloody fire,
Kindled with unchaste desire,
5   Fed in heart, whose flames aspire
As thoughts do blow them, higher and higher.
Pinch him, fairies, mutually;
Pinch him for his villany!
Pinch him and burn him and turn him about
10   Till candles and starlight and moonshine be out.

Act V, scene 5, lines 97–106

AS YOU LIKE IT

AMIENS:
Under the greenwood tree
Who loves to lie with me,
And turn his merry note
Unto the sweet bird's throat,
5   Come hither, come hither, come hither:
Here shall he see
No enemy
But winter and rough weather. . . .

Who doth ambition shun
10   And loves to live i' th' sun,
Seeking the food he eats,
And pleas'd with what he gets,

21. DUCDAME *The scholarly explanations of this word are learned but not sensible. The best is still Jaques's: " 'Tis a Greek invocation to call fools into a circle."*

Songs of the holly were popular in England long before the time of Shakespeare. They were sung by men (as opposed to songs sung by women in praise of the ivy) and were emblematic of Christmas and the warmth and cheer of the hall while the winter weather raged outside. Here the song suggests the solidarity of the banished duke and his men in the forest of Arden. The earliest known setting by Dr. T. A. Arne (1710–1778) is reprinted in Caulfield. It omits the refrain, the music for which was supplied by William Linley and printed in his Shakespeare's Dramatic Songs, 1816. *There is also a setting by Roger Quilter (1877–1953).*

2. UNKIND *unnatural.* 9. THEN *Emendation by Nicholas Rowe (1674–1718). 1623 Folio: The.* 12. NIGH *near, close to the heart.*

Come hither, come hither, come hither:
      Here shall he see
15   No enemy
But winter and rough weather.

Act II, scene 5, lines 1–8, 40–47

JACQUES:
If it do come to pass
That any man turn ass,
Leaving his wealth and ease
A stubborn will to please,
20 Ducdame, ducdame, ducdame!
      Here shall he see
      Gross fools as he,
An if he will come to me.

Act II, scene 5, lines 52–59

Blow, blow, thou winter wind,
Thou art not so unkind
     As man's ingratitude;
Thy tooth is not so keen
5 Because thou art not seen,
     Although thy breath be rude.
Heigh-ho! sing heigh-ho, unto the green holly:
Most friendship is feigning, most loving mere folly:
     Then heigh-ho! the holly!
10   This life is most jolly.

Freeze, freeze, thou bitter sky
That dost not bite so nigh

14. WARP *drive furiously about. Rosalind reads the verses written to her and Touchstone comments on their monotony: "I'll rhyme you so eight years together, dinners and suppers and sleeping hours excepted. . . . This is the very false gallop of verses." In the poem which follows he improvises a parody of them.*

5. FAIREST LIN'D *most finely drawn.*

1. HART *stag.* HIND *female red deer.* 3. WILL AFTER KIND *will behave according to its nature.* 5 WINTRED *made ready for winter.* 8. CART *Shakespeare elsewhere puns on "cart" and "court."*

   As benefits forgot:
   Though thou the waters warp,
15   Thy sting is not so sharp
    As friend remember'd not.
Heigh-ho! sing heigh-ho, unto the green holly:
Most friendship is feigning, most loving mere folly:
   Then heigh-ho! the holly!
20   This life is most jolly.

        Act II, scene 7, lines 174–190

From the east to western Ind,
No jewel is like Rosalinde;
Her worth, being mounted on the wind,
Through all the world bears Rosalinde.
5 All the pictures fairest lin'd
Are but black to Rosalinde;
Let no face be kept in mind,
But the fair of Rosalinde.

        Act III, scene 2, lines 93–100

If a hart do lack a hind,
Let him seek out Rosalinde:
If the cat will after kind,
So be sure will Rosalinde:
5 Wintred garments must be lin'd,
So must slender Rosalinde:
They that reap must sheaf and bind,
Then to cart with Rosalinde.
Sweetest nut hath sourest rind,
10 Such a nut is Rosalinde.

In the forest of Arden Celia reads the verses Orlando had written about Rosalind and hung upon a tree.

1. DESERT *uninhabited tract of land.* 2. FOR *because.* 4. CIVIL SAYINGS *the grave sayings which follow.* 6. ERRING *wandering.* 7. SPAN *Psalm 39: "Behold thou hast made my days as it were a span long."* 14–16. *Heaven wanted to embody in one person the quintessence of all souls.* 19. WIDE ENLARG'D *widely spread abroad.* 20. PRESENTLY *at once.* 23. ATALANTA'S BETTER PART *Atalanta's beauty and chastity rather than her disdainful treatment of her suitors.* 24. LUCRETIA'S *Lucrece's. See* The Rape of Lucrece. 28. TOUCHES DEAREST PRIZ'D *most dearly prized traits.*

He that sweetest rose will find
Must find love's prick, and Rosalinde.

Act III, scene 2, lines 107–118

Why should this a desert be,
    For it is unpeopl'd? No;
Tongues I'll hang on every tree,
    That shall civil sayings show:
5 Some how brief the life of man
    Runs his erring pilgrimage,
That the stretching of a span
    Buckles in his sum of age;
Some of violated vows
10   'Twixt the souls of friend and friend:
But upon the fairest boughs,
    Or at every sentence end,
Will I Rosalinda write,
    Teaching all that read to know
15 The quintessence of every sprite
    Heaven would in little show.
Therefore Heaven Nature charg'd
    That one body should be fill'd
With all graces wide enlarg'd:
20   Nature presently distill'd
Helen's cheek, but not her heart,
    Cleopatra's majesty,
Atalanta's better part,
    Sad Lucretia's modesty.
25 Thus Rosalind of many parts
    By heavenly synod was devis'd;
Of many faces, eyes and hearts,
    To have the touches dearest priz'd.
Heaven would that she these gifts should have,
30   And I to live and die her slave.

Act III, scene 2, lines 133–162

The marriage of Touchstone and Audrey, about to take place with Sir Oliver Martext, a vicar, officiating, is postponed, appropriately enough in a comedy, until the end of the play. The first three verses are a scrap of an old song.

The song, to be sung by hunters and others on convivial occasions, is in all probability a traditional one adapted by Shakespeare to his purposes. Although the ancient jests based on the horn as the emblem of the cuckold are still current in Western Europe, they are obsolete in America. An early, though not the original, musical setting was published, though not composed, by John Hilton in Catch that Catch Can, *1652, and is printed in modern transcription in Long.*

4. BURTHEN *chorus. The first three lines are solo, the rest a chorus in which the other gentlemen join.*

This is a song for the marriage of Audrey, "a country wench," and Touchstone, a clown who found the song "foolish." It has, nevertheless, enjoyed a

4. RING-TIME *Emendation by Nicholas Rowe (1674– 1718). 1623 Folio:* rang time—*a manifest error. Ringtime is the season for exchanging rings, for courtship.*

TOUCHSTONE:
Come, sweet Audrey,
We must be married, or we must live in bawdry. Farewell, good Master
Oliver: not—

    O sweet Oliver,
5   O brave Oliver,
Leave me not behind thee:
but,
    Wind away,
    Be gone, I say,
10 I will not to wedding with thee.

Act III, scene 3, lines 98–107

What shall he have that kill'd the deer?
His leather skin and horns to wear:

Then sing him home.
The rest shall bear this burthen.

5 Take thou no scorn to wear the horn;
It was a crest ere thou wast born:
    Thy father's father wore it,
      And thy father bore it:
The horn, the horn, the lusty horn
10 Is not a thing to laugh to scorn.

Act IV, scene 2, lines 11–19

It was a lover and his lass,
    With a hey, and a ho, and a hey nonino,
That o'er the green cornfield did pass
    In springtime, the only pretty ring-time,
5 When birds do sing, hey ding a ding, ding;
Sweet lovers love the spring.

Between the acres of the rye,
    With a hey, and a ho, and a hey nonino,

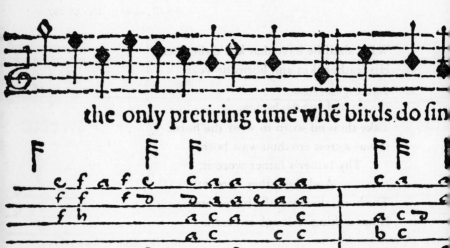

the only pretiring time whē birds do sin

ing ading ading ij.   ij.   ſweete

long if intermittent popularity. What is doubtless the original music was composed by Thomas Morley (1557–1603?) and published in his First Book of Ayres, *1600. The music, reprinted by Sir Frederick Bridge, is that from which the swing version of recent memory takes off. The poem has been set to music by Roger Quilter (1877–1953).*

Hymen, the god of marriage, appears in order to preside over the marriages which bring the play to a close. He speaks the lines to an accompaniment of soft music. The earliest known musical settings for these lines and the song which follows are by Thomas Chilcot and were printed in his Twelve English Songs with their Symphonies, *1745.*

3. ATONE *accord, are at one. 8.* HER *Emendation by Edmund Malone (1741–1812). Folio: his.*

1. JUNO'S *Juno represented the great element of motherhood in the natural order of things.*

These pretty country folks would lie
10   In springtime, &c.

This carol they began that hour,
          With a hey, and a ho, and a hey nonino,
How that a life was but a flower
          In springtime, &c.

15   And therefore take the present time,
          With a hey, and a ho, and a hey nonino,
For love is crowned with the prime
          In springtime, the only pretty ring-time,
When birds do sing, hey ding a ding, ding;
20   Sweet lovers love the spring.

Act V, scene 3, lines 17–34

Then is there mirth in heaven
When earthly things made even
          Atone together.
Good Duke, receive thy daughter;
5   Hymen from heaven brought her,
          Yea, brought her hether,
That thou might join her hand with his
Whose heart within her bosom is.

Act V, scene 4, lines 114–121

Song

Wedding is great Juno's crown:
          O blessed bond of board and bed!
'Tis Hymen peoples every town;
          High wedlock then be honoured:
5   Honour, high honour and renown,
          To Hymen, God of every town!

Act V, scene 4, lines 147–152

Feste, the clown, offers Sir Andrew and Sir Toby the choice of a love song "or a song of good life." They choose the love song. There are two contemporary versions of the music for it. It was printed in Thomas Morley's The First Book of Consort Lessons, *1599, and it was arranged as a set of six variations by William Byrd (1543–1623). Neither composer gives the words. Shakespeare and Morley were neighbors in Bishopsgate and it is possible that Shakespeare commissioned him to set the words to music. It is equally possible that both composers independently set down the music of a popular song to which Shakespeare, also independently, fitted the words. Both Morley's and Byrd's music are reprinted by Sir Frederick Bridge. There is a late setting by Roger Quilter (1877–1953).*

The revelers, having finished singing a catch, "Hold thy peace, thou knave," and being in their cups, are reminded of song by everything they hear. Sir Toby quotes from some old songs, "Three merry men be we" and "Peg-a-Ramsey," and having heard the word "lady," is reminded of a song with the refrain "Lady, lady." He quotes from it and begins another song. At this point Malvolio enters to put an end to the revel. As he leaves, his last word, "farewell," starts Sir Toby on still another song, "Farewell, dear love, since thou wilt needs be gone." He sings the line, changing it to his own purposes. Feste continues in the same manner, and together they work a good part of the song into the play. The music and words were first printed in Robert Jones's The First Book of Ayres, *1600. The music is reprinted by Naylor, 1931.*
2. The refrain is also sung by Mercutio with another repetition of "lady" in Romeo and Juliet, *Act II, scene 4, line 151.*

O mistress mine, where are you roaming?
O, stay and hear; your true-love's coming,
    That can sing both high and low.
Trip no further, pretty sweeting;
5 Journeys end in lovers meeting,
    Every wise man's son doth know. . . .

What is love? 'tis not hereafter;
Present mirth hath present laughter;
    What's to come is still unsure:
10 In delay there lies no plenty;
Then come kiss me, sweet and twenty!
    Youth's a stuff will not endure.

Act II, scene 3, lines 40–53

SIR TOBY:
There dwelt a man in Babylon,
    Lady, lady. . . .
O, the twelf day of December. . . .
Farewell, dear heart, since I must needs be gone . . .
FESTE:
5 His eyes do show his days are almost done. . . .
SIR TOBY:
But I will never die . . .
FESTE:
Sir Toby, there you lie . . .
SIR TOBY:
Shall I bid him go?
FESTE:
What an if you do?
SIR TOBY:

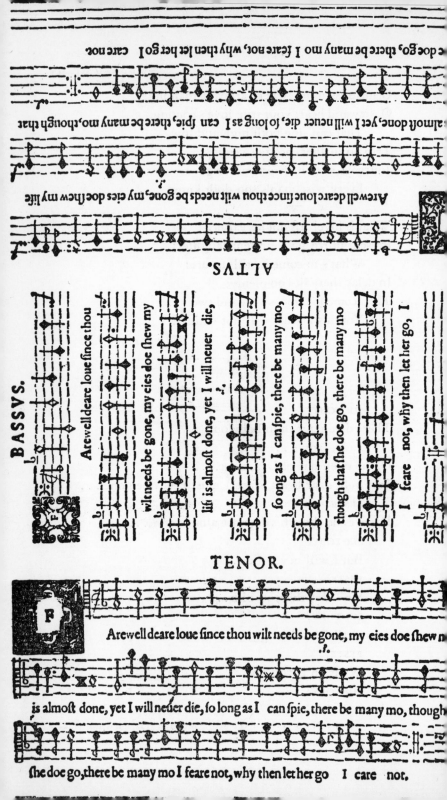

Orsino, sentimentally in love and wishing to feed his melancholy, calls for a song which "dallies with the innocence of love, / Like the old age," and Shakespeare provides one, sung by Feste, the fool, on the theme of "Come, sweet death." Like Orsino's grief, it is gently extravagant. The earliest known musical setting by Dr. T. A. Arne (1710–1778) is reprinted by Caulfield. The song was also set by Brahms (1833–1897) for a women's chorus, two horns, and a harp (Opus 17). Long provides a setting based on the Elizabethan tune, "Heart's-ease."

1. COME AWAY *come here, come to me.* 2. CYPRESS *The cypress was the emblem of mourning.* 3. FLY AWAY, FLY *Emendation by Nicholas Rowe (1674–1718). 1623 Folio: Fye away, fie.* 5. YEW *The yew tree, planted in churchyards, became the emblem of death.* 7. MY PART OF DEATH *the death allotted to me.*

Malvolio, the steward, reads from the letter Maria has written to gull him into thinking that the lady of the house is in love with him.

6. LUCRECE KNIFE *See* The Rape of Lucrece, *lines 1721–1724.* 8. M, O, A, I *Malvolio in his vanity takes the letters to indicate himself, but he is, as Sir Toby remarks, "at a cold scent," as have been all the scholars who tried to make more of them.*

10 Shall I bid him go, and spare not?
       FESTE:
    O no, no, no, no, you dare not!

Act II, scene 3, lines 84–121

    Come away, come away, death,
         And in sad cypress let me be laid;
    Fly away, fly away, breath;
         I am slain by a fair cruel maid.
5   My shroud of white, stuck all with yew,
              O, prepare it:
    My part of death, no one so true
              Did share it.

    Not a flower, not a flower sweet,
10   On my black coffin let there be strown;
    Not a friend, not a friend greet
         My poor corpse, where my bones shall be thrown.
    A thousand thousand sighs to save,
              Lay me, O where
15 Sad true lover never find my grave,
              To weep there.

Act II, scene 4, lines 52–67

         Jove knows I love;
              But who?
         Lips, do not move;
              No man must know. . . .

5   I may command where I adore;
         But silence, like a Lucrece knife,
         With bloodless stroke my heart doth gore:
         M, O, A, I, doth sway my life.

Act II, scene 5, lines 107–110, 115–118

In his baiting of Malvolio, Feste quotes, with some changes, the opening lines of a poem, "A, Robin, jolly Robin," by Sir Thomas Wyatt (1503?–1542). The lines were set as a trio for strings and voices by William Cornishe (1465?–1524?), a composer who enjoyed the patronage of Henry VIII. A modern transcription of the music is printed by Naylor, 1912.

4. PERDIE *by God, in sooth.*

Feste leaves Malvolio, who is confined incommunicado in the dark as a madman, promising to bring him "light and paper and ink." He is aware of the similarity of the stage fool to the old Vice, a rowdy character and satirical commentator in the Tudor morality plays. In the older plays the Vice was a member of the Devil's retinue, but he became the antagonist of the Devil, belaboring him with his wooden sword or dagger. The Devil was thought to keep his nails unpared.

Alone on the stage, Feste sings the song which closes the comedy and enforces our awareness of its underlying truth and sadness. The world will indulge "a

1. TINY *The 1623 Folio reads "tine," meaning "vat" or "tub," that is, a little tub of a lad. Shakespeare nowhere uses the modern spelling. But both the rhythm of the line and the traditional music require a dissyllable and so the modern spelling, an emendation by Nicholas Rowe (1674–1718), is retained.* 15. TOSSPOTS *topers.*

FESTE:

Hey, Robin, jolly Robin,
Tell me how thy lady does.

MALVOLIO:
Fool!

FESTE:

5 My lady is unkind, perdie!

MALVOLIO:
Fool!

FESTE:

Alas, why is she so?

MALVOLIO:
Fool, I say!

FESTE:

She loves another.

Act IV, scene 2, lines 78–85

I am gone sir,
        And anon sir,
I'll be with you again,
        In a trice,
5   Like to the old Vice,
Your need to sustain;

Who with dagger of lath,
In his rage and his wrath,
Cries Ah ha! to the divel:
10   Like a mad lad,
        Pare thy nails, dad;
Adieu, goodman divel.

Act IV, scene 2, lines 130–141

When that I was and a little tiny boy,
        With hey, ho, the wind and the rain,

little tiny boy" who delights in idle toys, but when he comes to "man's estate," it will not tolerate knavery or thievery, nor can he thrive in marriage by blustering, nor avoid the cost of overindulgence. The world is very old; it has always been this way; it is not likely to change, "for the rain it raineth every day." Shakespeare adapted part of this song to his purpose in King Lear (See page 257). The original music for this song has been lost. The traditional music, by a composer whose identity may be guessed at but not known, is reprinted by Elson and Long. There are other settings by Robert Schumann (1810–1856) in German translation, Opus 127, No. 5, and by Roger Quilter (1877–1953).

The letter which Ophelia, in obedience to her father, turned over to him.

7. NUMBERS *verses.* 9. MACHINE *body.*

A foolish thing was but a toy,
>> For the rain it raineth every day.

5   But when I came to man's estate,
>> With hey, ho, the wind and the rain,
'Gainst knaves and thieves men shut their gate,
>> For the rain it raineth every day.

But when I came, alas! to wive,
10 >> With hey, ho, the wind and the rain,
By swaggering could I never thrive,
>> For the rain it raineth every day.

But when I came unto my beds,
>> With hey, ho, the wind and the rain,
15 With tosspots still had drunken heads,
>> For the rain it raineth every day.

A great while ago the world begun,
>> With hey, ho, the wind and the rain;
But that's all one, our play is done,
20 >> And we'll strive to please you every day.

Act V, scene 1, lines 398–417

HAMLET

To the celestial, and my soul's idol, the most beautified Ophelia. . . .
In her excellent white bosom, these &c. . . .
>> Doubt thou the stars are fire,
>> Doubt that the sun doth move,
5 >> Doubt truth to be a liar,
>> But never doubt I love.

O dear Ophelia, I am ill at these numbers, I have not the art to reckon
my groans; but that I love thee best, O most best, believe it. Adieu.
Thine evermore, most dear lady, whilst this machine is to him, Hamlet.

Act II, scene 2, lines 109–124

In his baiting of Polonius Hamlet quotes from a ballad, "Jephta, Judge of Israel."

13. PIOUS *scriptural*.

The prologue to the play within the play. Hamlet's comment on it is: "Is this a prologue or the posy of a ring?"

Hamlet's exultant cry when the play causes the king to disclose his guilt.

1. STRUCKEN *struck by an arrow*. 2. UNGALLED *uninjured*. 4. SO *1623 Folio. 1604 Quarto: Thus*.

2–3. THIS . . . HIMSELF *The kingdom was robbed of a king who had the majesty of Jove*.

HAMLET:

O Jephta, judge of Israel, what a treasure hadst thou!

POLONIUS:

What a treasure had he, my lord?

HAMLET:

Why,

> **One fair daughter and no more,**
> **The which he loved passing well . . .**

POLONIUS:

If you call me Jephta, my lord, I have a daughter that I love passing **well.**

HAMLET:

Nay, that follows not.

POLONIUS:

What follows then, my lord?

HAMLET:

Why,

> **As by lot, Got wot,**

and then, you know,

> **It came to pass, as most like it was—**

the first row of the pious chanson will show you more.

Act II, scene 2, lines 422–439

For us and for our tragedy,
Here stooping to your clemency,
We beg your hearing patiently.

Act III, scene 2, lines 159–161

Why, let the strucken deer go weep,
> **The hart ungalled play;**
For some must watch, while some must sleep;
> **So runs the world away.**

Act III, scene 2, lines 282–285

HAMLET:

For thou dost know, O Damon dear,
> **This realm dismantled was**

4. PAJOCK *perhaps peacock; the word is not found elsewhere in Shakespeare. Doubtless Hamlet intended to say "A very, very ass," but he hesitated and substituted "pajock."*

Ophelia's songs, broken into fragments interspersed in the dialogue, consist of original lines by Shakespeare and fragments and adaptations of ballads and popular song. In her grief-stricken madness the inhibitions of her normal life are dissipated, and the bits of song welling up from her unconscious, she sings of bawdry, her dominant father, and love. It was conventional in Elizabethan drama to have maddened innocence speak bawdry, but there is more than convention here. This is another of Shakespeare's anticipations of modern psychology, but with him such anticipations are only an aspect of his view of the scene, and to turn his characters into case histories is to oversimplify them and impoverish the story.

3. COCKLE *mussel or scallop. The cockle shell worn in the hat was the emblem of the pilgrim who had journeyed to shrines overseas. The association of the pilgrim and the lover was common (See page 196).* 4. SHOON *shoes.* 9. WHITE *the customary color of shrouds.* 10. ALL *1604 Quarto. Not in 1623 Folio.* 11. GRAVE *1623 Folio. 1604 Quarto: ground.*

1–4. *The notion was that a man would become the true love of the first girl he saw on Saint Valentine's Day.* 6. DUPP'D *opened, did up.* 9. GIS *a corruption of Jesus.* SAINT CHARITY *holy charity.*

Of Jove himself; and now reigns here
    A very, very—pajock.

HORATIO:
5   You might have rhym'd.

Act III, scene 2, lines 292–295

How should I your true love know
    From another one?
By his cockle hat and staff
    And his sandal shoon. ...

5   He is dead and gone, lady,
    He is dead and gone;
At his head a grass-green turf,
    At his heels a stone. ...

White his shroud as the mountain snow.
10   Larded all with sweet flowers,
Which bewept to the grave did not go
    With true love showers.

Act IV, scene 5 lines 23–39

To-morrow is Saint Valentine's day,
    All in the morning betime,
And I a maid at your window,
    To be your valentine.
5   Then up he rose and donn'd his clothes
    And dupp'd the chamber door,
Let in the maid that out a maid
    Never departed more. ...

By Gis and by Saint Charity,
10   Alack and fie for shame!

disguise of the name of God. 17. AND *The "an"*
of many editions is an emendation by Sir Thomas
Hanmer (1677–1746).

Early in the nineteenth century the traditional music
for Ophelia's mad songs was set down by William
Linley as he remembered them from performances
in the Drury Lane Theatre. They are reprinted by
Naylor, 1931, and Chappell. Doubtless it was the
blending of the tender and the grotesque in the
verses which attracted Richard Strauss to them. He
set them to music in German translation, Opus 67,
1919.

2. 1623 Folio. Not in Quartos. This has suggested to
some scholars that the line is an actor's interpolation,
but the line accords well enough with the sudden
and startling juxtapositions to which Shakespeare's
greatest works owe so much of their power. 4. DOWN
A-DOWN *a refrain of popular song. 5. "Bonny sweet*
Robin" and "My Robin is to the green wood gone"
were alternate titles of a ballad. The tune for the
ballad is reprinted in Chappell but the words have
not survived. 6–15. The seventeenth century variants
of this song are probably adapted from Shakespeare.
12. POLL *head. 15.* GOD A MERCY *1604 Quarto. 1623*
Folio: Gramercy.

The gravedigger's song is a garbled version of parts
of a poem by Thomas Lord Vaux, "The aged lover

Young men will do't if they come to't;
    By Cock, they are to blame.
Quoth she, before you tumbled me,
    You promis'd me to wed:

15   HE ANSWERS:
So would I ha' done, by yonder sun,
And thou hadst not come to my bed.

Act IV, scene 5, lines 48–66

They bore him barefac'd on the bier;
Hey non nonny, nonny, hey nonny;
And in his grave rain'd many a tear....

Down a-down, and you call him a-down-a....

5   For bonny sweet Robin is all my joy....

And will he not come again?
And will he not come again?
    No, no, he is dead,
    Go to thy death-bed,
10 He never will come again.

His beard was as white as snow,
All flaxen was his poll;
    He is gone, he is gone,
    And we cast away moan:
15 God a mercy on his soul!

Act IV, scene 5, lines 164–199

In youth when I did love, did love,
    Methought it was very sweet,

renounceth love," first published in Richard Tottel's
Songs and Sonnets, *1557. The two traditional tunes
to which these verses are sung are reprinted by
Chappell.*

3. BEHOVE *behoof, advantage.* 4. MEET *fitting.* 7. INTIL
into. 10. FOR AND *and.*

*Lavatch's comment on the verses is: "If men could
be contented to be what they are, there were no
fear in marriage."*

4. CUCKOO *See comment page 180.* KIND *nature.*

*Lavatch, the clown, is a "calumnious knave" whose
jokes lack the good nature of those of Feste and
Touchstone. The mention of his countess's gentle-
woman, Helen, suggests Helen of Troy to him. At
the conclusion of the verses on her, the countess*

3. *The line, referring to the sacking of Troy for
as worthless a woman as Helen, probably means
"foolishly done, done foolishly."*

To contract, *Oh!* the time for, *Ah!* my behove,
    O, methought there was nothing meet. . . .

5 But age with his stealing steps
    Hath claw'd me in his clutch,
And hath shipp'd me intil the land,
    As if I had never been such. . . .

(*He digs up a skull.*)
A pickaxe and a spade, a spade,
10   For and a shrouding sheet;
O, a pit of clay for to be made
    For such a guest is meet. . . .

(*He digs up another skull.*)
O, a pit of clay for to be made
    For such a guest is meet.

Act V, scene 1, lines 69–105

ALL'S WELL THAT ENDS WELL

For I the ballad will repeat,
    Which men full true shall find;
Your marriage comes by destiny,
    Your cuckoo sings by kind.

Act I, scene 3, lines 64–67

Was this fair face the cause, quoth she,
    Why the Grecians sacked Troy?
Fond done, done fond,
    Was this King Priam's joy?
5 With that she sighed as she stood,

remarks, "You corrupt the song." Perhaps the reference is to some song then well known and now lost. It is not likely that the lines were intended to be sung. The only musical setting was made by William Linley, 1816.

8. AMONG *in the midst of.*

A letter in sonnet form from Helena to the Countess of Rousillon to whose son Bertram she has been married by the King of France as a reward for restoring him to health. Bertram, however, does not return her love and prefers leaving for the wars to fulfilling his marital duties. To win his love, Helena follows him in the guise of a pilgrim, and they are ultimately united.

2. AMBITIOUS LOVE *She has married above her station.* 9. TAKEN LABOURS *voluntary military service.*

In a play which takes a grimly comic view of "war and lechery," Pandarus, who has given his name to a trade, sings of love to Paris and Helen, neither of whom, as Shakespeare sees them, is a romantic figure, although they have a decadent charm.

1. STILL LOVE *Quartos. Not in 1623 Folio.* 4. CONFOUNDS *mingles with, amazes, perplexes, destroys.* 5. NOT THAT IT *The meanings here are multiple: the shaft does not destroy that which it wounds; it perplexes because it does not wound, etc.* 6. SORE *a wound, a buck in its fourth year, the vulva. The same pun is found in Holofernes's verses (See page 173).* 7. DIE *the climax of the sexual act.*

With that she sighed as she stood,
  And gave this sentence then:
Among nine bad if one be good,
Among nine bad if one be good,
  There's yet one good in ten.

10

Act I, scene 3, lines 74–83

I am Saint Jacques' pilgrim, thither gone:
Ambitious love hath so in me offended,
That bare-foot plod I the cold ground upon
With sainted vow my faults to have amended.
Write, write that from the bloody course of war
My dearest master, your dear son, may hie:
Bless him at home in peace, whilst I from far
His name with zealous fervour sanctify:
His taken labours bid him me forgive;
I, his despiteful Juno, sent him forth
From courtly friends with camping foes to live,
Where death and danger dogs the heels of worth:
  He is too good and fair for death and me;
  Whom I myself embrace to set him free.

5

10

Act III, scene 4, lines 4–17

TROILUS AND CRESSIDA

Love, love, nothing but love, still love, still more!
      For, oh! love's bow
      Shoots buck and doe;
      The shaft confounds
      Not that it wounds,
    But tickles still the sore.
These lovers cry, O ho! they die!

5

Compare The Passionate Pilgrim, *poem 9, lines 12–14.* KILL *aggravate.*

Pandarus speaks these lines as Troilus and Cressida lament their enforced separation. In his view the only "ease" of love is physical union. Although the lines have been set to music, there is no reason to think that they were intended to be sung.

Pandarus' verses to explain why the work of bawds is at last ill-requited. The humble-bee was an emblem of the philanderer. Compare "The Fox, the ape, and the humble-bee," page 171.

The song is sung by a boy servant to the forsaken Mariana. It also appears, with an additional stanza, in John Fletcher's The Bloody Brother, *where the new and anticlimactic matter changes the false lover to a woman. The new material is doubtless Fletcher's, but it was attributed to Shakespeare in the 1640 edition of his poems and the attribution continues, erroneously, from time to time. The earliest known setting is by John Wilson (1595–1673) and was published in John Playford's* Select Airs and Dialogues, *1659. It is printed in modern transcription by Sir Frederick Bridge. There are modern settings by Roger Quilter (1877–1953) and Peter Warlock, pseudonym of Philip Haseltine (1894–1930).*

Yet that which seems the wound to kill
     Doth turn O ho! to ha! ha! he!
10   So dying love lives still.
     O ho! awhile, but ha! ha! ha!
O ho! groans out for ha! ha! ha!—Hey ho!

Act III, scene 1, lines 125–136

"O heart," as the goodly saying is,
          O heart, heavy heart,
          Why sigh'st thou without breaking?
when he answers again,
5   Because thou canst not ease thy smart
          By friendship nor by speaking.

Act IV, scene 4, lines 17–21

Full merrily the humble-bee doth sing
Till he hath lost his honey and his sting,
And being once subdu'd in armed tail,
Sweet honey and sweet notes together fail.

Act V, scene 10, lines 42–45

MEASURE FOR MEASURE

Take, O take those lips away,
     That so sweetly were forsworn;
And those eyes, the break of day,
     Lights that do mislead the morn:
5 But my kisses bring again,
          Bring again,
Seals of love, but seal'd in vain,
     Seal'd in vain.

Act IV, scene 1, lines 1–8

Iago uses this song to induce Cassio to drink. The tune for it is reprinted in Caulfield.

1. CANAKIN *little can.* 4. O, MAN'S LIFE'S *1623 Folio. 1622 Quarto: A life's.*

Iago sings a popular song which has survived in several versions. Elson reprints a version of the tune, "Tak your auld cloak about ye," to which it was sung.

1. KING STEPHEN *Stephen, King of England (1135–1154), had a popular reputation for stinginess.* AND-A *1623 Folio. "and" not in 1622 Quarto.* 3. 'EM *1622 Quarto. 1623 Folio: them.* 4. LOWN *lout, base fellow.* 8. THEN *1622 Quarto. 1623 Folio: And.* THINE *1622 Quarto. 1623 Folio: thy.*

The willow tree was the emblem of unhappy love, and willow songs were traditional and very popular. A song, "All a greene wyllow . . . is my garland," was written by John Heywood, perhaps as early as 1530. A ballad on the theme was printed by Bishop Percy (1729–1811) in his Reliques of Ancient English Poetry. *Shakespeare is here adapting traditional material to his purposes. The earliest known music for the traditional song is found in Thomas Dallis's manuscript "Lute-book," 1583, and is printed in modern transcription by Sir Frederick Bridge. Shakespeare's poem was set to music by Sir Arthur Sullivan (1842–1900). The setting by Giuseppe Verdi (1813–1901) for his opera* OTELLO *is the best-known.*

13. MOE *more.*

And let me the canakin clink, clink,
And let me the canakin clink:
    A soldier's a man,
    O, man's life's but a span,
5 Why then, let a soldier drink.

Act II, scene 3, lines 71–75

King Stephen was and-a worthy peer,
    His breeches cost him but a crown;
He held 'em sixpence all too dear,
    With that he call'd the tailor lown.

5 He was a wight of high renown,
    And thou art but of low degree:
'Tis pride that pulls the country down;
    Then take thine auld cloak about thee.

Act II, scene 3, lines 92–99

The poor soul sat sighing by a sycamore tree,
    Sing all a green willow;
Her hand on her bosom, her head on her knee,
    Sing willow, willow, willow:

5 The fresh streams ran by her, and murmur'd her moans;
    Sing willow, willow, willow;
Her salt tears fell from her, and soft'ned the stones;
    Sing willow, willow, willow:
Sing all a green willow must be my garland.

10 Let nobody blame him; his scorn I approve. . . .
I call'd my love false love, but what said he then?
    Sing willow, willow, willow:
If I court moe women, you'll couch with moe men.

Act IV, scene 3, lines 41–57

The Fool gives Lear a gnomic lesson in prudence.

1. Don't display all you have. 2. Don't say everything you know. 3. OWEST *own. 4.* GOEST *walk. 5.* TROWEST *believe. 6. In the game of dice wager less than you throw for. 9–10. For each score you shall have more than twenty.*

The Fool, having been called "a bitter Fool," explains to Lear the difference between a bitter fool and a sweet one.

6. PRESENTLY *at once. 7.* MOTLEY *the garb of the fool and jester. 8. He points to Lear as the bitter fool.*

Dr. Johnson (1709–1784) explains the Fool's verses: "There never was a time when fools were less in favour; and the reason is, that they were never so little wanted, for wise men now supply their place."

1. GRACE *1623 Folio. 1608 Quarto: wit. 2.* FOPPISH *foolish. 3.* AND *1623 Folio. 1608 Quarto: They.* TO *1623 Folio. 1608 Quarto: do. 4.* APISH *imitative, like an ape.*

The first two lines of the Fool's song are adapted from a ballad by John Careless (d. 1556). Caulfield prints a tune for it. The original music has been lost.

1. THEY *the daughters to whom Lear had subjugated himself. 3.* PLAY BO-PEEP *refuse to see, like a child playing a game. 4.* FOOLS *1608 Quarto. 1623 Folio: Foole. The Folio reading is possible if we take "among" to mean "in the meantime," as it sometimes did.*

Have more than thou showest,
Speak less than thou knowest,
Lend less than thou owest,
Ride more than thou goest,
5 Learn more than thou trowest,
Set less than thou throwest;
Leave thy drink and thy whore,
And keep in-a-door,
And thou shalt have more
10 Than two tens to a score.

Act I, scene 4, lines 131–140

That lord that counsell'd thee
      To give away thy land,
Come place him here by me,
      Do thou for him stand:
5 The sweet and bitter fool
      Will presently appear;
The one in motley here,
      The other found out there.

Act I, scene 4, lines 154–161

Fools had ne'er less grace in a year,
      For wise men are grown foppish,
And know not how their wits to wear,
      Their manners are so apish.

Act I, scene 4, lines 181–184

Then they for sudden joy did weep,
      And I for sorrow sung,
That such a king should play bo-peep
      And go the fools among.

Act I, scene 4, lines 191–194

A comment by the Fool on Lear's division of his kingdom.

2. NOR ... NOR *1623 Folio. 1608 Quarto: neither ... nor.*

This and the two following verses are oblique comments by the Fool on Lear's relation to his villainous daughters.

1. CUCKOO *For a comment on the domestic habits of the cuckoo, see page 180.* 2. *that it had its head bit off by its young.*

King Lear leaves Goneril in anger to seek refuge with Regan. Goneril commands the Fool to follow him, and he speaks these verses as he exits.

2. SUCH A DAUGHTER *such a daughter as Goneril.*

These verses are the Fool's comment in the scene of Lear's indignation on his discovery that Goneril and her husband have put Kent in the stocks.

2. BLIND *blind to the neediness of the fathers.* 3. BAGS *moneybags.*

The Fool asserts his fidelity.

1. WHICH *1623 Folio. 1608 Quarto: that.* 3. PACK *desert his master.* 8. PERDY *in truth, by God.*

Mum, mum,
He that keeps nor crust nor crumb,
Weary of all, shall want some.

Act I, scene 4, lines 216–218

The hedge-sparrow fed the cuckoo so long
That it had it head bit off by it young.

Act I, scene 4, lines 235–236

A fox, when one has caught her,
    And such a daughter,
Should sure to the slaughter,
If my cap would buy a halter:
5   So the fool follows after.

Act I, scene 4, lines 340–344

Fathers that wear rags
    Do make their children blind,
But fathers that bear bags
    Shall see their children kind.
5   Fortune, that arrant whore,
Ne'er turns the key to th' poor.

Act II, scene 4, lines 48–53

That sir which serves and seeks for gain,
    And follows but for form,
Will pack when it begins to rain
    And leave thee in the storm.
5   But I will tarry; the fool will stay,
    And let the wise man fly.
The knave turns fool that runs away;
    The fool no knave, perdy.

Act II, scene 4, lines 79–86

In the oblique manner which his position as fool imposes on him, the Fool asserts that the man who begets children before providing shelter for himself shall suffer the pains of poverty, that beggars propagate promiscuously, and that the man who inverts his basic human functions shall come to grief.

1. CODPIECE *penis.* *3.* LOUSE *become lousy.* *5.* TOE *any mean or unworthy part of the body.* *7.* OF *1623 Folio. 1608 Quarto:* have.

For the Fool's verses when he is with the king on the heath in the storm, Shakespeare adapts part of the poem he had used to close Twelfth Night (*see page 237*).

1. AND *1623 Folio. Not in 1608 Quarto.* *4.* THOUGH *1623 Folio. 1608 Quarto:* for.

In these and the following verses from King Lear, Edgar, in the guise of Tom o' Bedlam, pretends madness. The verses are essentially part of the pretense; they do not have the perspicacity of the Fool's.

1. SWITHOLD *Saint Withold.* 'OLD *wold, treeless plain.* *2.* NIGHT-MARE *an evil spirit.* NINE FOLD *nine familiar spirits.* *4.* TROTH PLIGHT *pledge herself to do no harm.* *5.* AROINT *be gone.*

With conscious incongruity Edgar, pretending to be mad, associates "Fie, foh, and fum" with the heroic Child Rowland.

1. TOWER CAME *1623 Folio. 1608 Quarto:* towne come.

Edgar addresses Goneril, whom Lear has imagined to be present, in the words of an old song now lost and the Fool interrupts with an indecent improvisation. The storm-tossed ship in The Tempest *is "as leaky as an unstanched wench."*

1. BOURN *Emendation by Edward Capell (1713–1781). 1608 Quarto:* broome. *Not in 1623 Folio. A bourn is a brook.* *2. She is in her menstrual period.*

The codpiece that will house
 Before the head has any,
The head and he shall louse;
 So beggars marry many.
5 The man that makes his toe
 What he his heart should make,
Shall of a corn cry woe,
 And turn his sleep to wake.

Act III, scene 2, lines 27–34

He that has and a little tiny wit,
 With hey, ho, the wind and the rain,
Must make content with his fortunes fit,
 Though the rain it raineth every day.

Act III, scene 2, lines 74–77

Swithold footed thrice the 'old;
He met the night-mare and her nine fold;
 Bid her alight
 And her troth plight,
5 And aroint thee, witch, aroint thee.

Act III, scene 4, lines 125–129

Child Rowland to the dark tower came;
His word was still: Fie, foh, and fum!
I smell the blood of a British man.

Act III, scene 4, lines 187–189

 EDGAR:
Come o'er the bourn, Bessy, to me—
 FOOL:
 Her boat hath a leak,
 And she must not speak
Why she dares not come over to thee.

Act III, scene 6, lines 27–30

Edgar's lines are, perhaps, adapted from a popular song. They glance at the absence of responsible leadership in Lear's kingdom.

3. FOR ONE BLAST *in the time it takes to blow one blast.* MINIKIN *shrill.*

The mad Lear imagines that dogs are barking at him, and Edgar, in the guise of Poor Tom, scares them away.

2. OR . . . OR *either . . . or.* 5. BRACH *bitch.* HIM *Many editors, following Sir Thomas Hanmer (1677–1746), improve the grammar by emending to "lym," a species of bloodhound. It may be correct.* 6. OR *1623 Folio. Not in 1608 Quarto.* TIKE *1608 Quarto. 1623 Folio: tight.* TRUNDLE-TAIL *1608 Quarto. 1623 Folio: troudle taile. A trundle tail was a dog whose long drooping tail seemed to trundle after him.* 7. THEM *1608 Quarto. 1623 Folio: him.* 9. LEAP *1608 Quarto. 1623 Folio: leapt. To leap the hatch means to make a hurried exit. A hatch is the lower half of a divided door.*

Apemantus offers grace, as, a guest at Timon's feast, he sits aside and watches Timon's parasitical friends abuse his hospitality.

1. PELF *money, gain.* 3. FOND *foolish.*

Sleepest or wakest thou, jolly shepherd?
    Thy sheep be in the corn;
And for one blast of thy minikin mouth
    Thy sheep shall take no harm.

Act III, scene 6, lines 43–46

Tom will throw his head at them. Avaunt, you curs!
    Be thy mouth or black or white,
    Tooth that poisons if it bite;
    Mastiff, greyhound, mongrel grim,
5   Hound or spaniel, brach or him;
    Or bobtail tike or trundle-tail;
    Tom will make them weep and wail:
    For with throwing thus my head
    Dogs leap the hatch, and all are fled.

Act III, scene 6, lines 69–76

TIMON OF ATHENS

Immortal gods, I crave no pelf;
I pray for no man but myself:
Grant I may never prove so fond
To trust man on his oath or bond,
5 Or a harlot for her weeping,
Or a dog that seems a-sleeping,
Or a keeper with my freedom,
Or my friends, if I should need 'em.
Amen. So fall to't:
10 Rich men sin, and I eat root.

Act I, scene 2, lines 63–72

Shakespeare found two alternate epitaphs for Timon in North's translation of Plutarch's "Life of Mark Antony" and combined them, changing only "wretches" to its synonym "caitiffs." He would doubtless have noticed the incompatibility of the epitaphs had he given the play the revision it needs.

The song was sung "as loud as . . . sides can volley" by the rulers of the Roman world as they danced in a ring aboard Pompey's galley. The text calls for an accompaniment of drums, trumpets, and flutes, but the original music has been lost. The earliest known setting by Thomas Chilcot (d. 1766) is reprinted in Caulfield.

2. BACCHUS *the god of wine and revelry.* PINK EYNE *eyes which are small like the pink, a flower.* 3. FATS *vats.*

An epitaph for Marina, written to persuade her father, Pericles, that she is dead. The play was first published with Shakespeare's name on the title page in 1609. Although there were three more editions of the play before 1623, it was not included in the First Folio. The text is very corrupt, and it is certain that as it stands the play cannot all be by one man. The epitaph may be by Shakespeare, or it may not, or it may be only partly his.

3. TYRUS *Tyre.* 6. THETIS *a confusion of Thetis, a sea nymph and later the mother of Achilles, and Tethys, wife of Oceanus. She is taken to represent the sea, in whose domain Marina was born. The conceit is that the sea, in pride of Marina, overflowed part of the earth, and the earth, fearing inundation, sent Marina to heaven, while the sea, in return, beats the rocky shores.*

Here lies a wretched corse, of wretched soul bereft:
Seek not my name: a plague consume you wicked caitiffs
    left!
Here lie I, Timon, who, alive, all living men did hate:
Pass by and curse thy fill; but pass, and stay not here thy
    gait.

Act V, scene 4, lines 70–73

Come, thou monarch of the vine,
Plumpy Bacchus with pink eyne!
In thy fats our cares be drown'd,
With thy grapes our hairs be crown'd:
5   Cup us till the world go round,
        Cup us till the world go round!

Act II, scene 7, lines 118–123

The fairest, sweet'st, and best lies here,
Who wither'd in her spring of year:
She was of Tyrus the King's daughter,
On whom foul death hath made this slaughter;
5   Marina was she call'd, and at her birth,
Thetis, being proud, swallow'd some part o' th' earth:
Therefore the earth, fearing to be o'erflow'd,
Hath Thetis' birth-child on the heavens bestow'd;
Wherefore she does, and swears she'll never stint,
10 Make raging batt'ry upon shores of flint.

Act IV, scene 4, lines 34–43

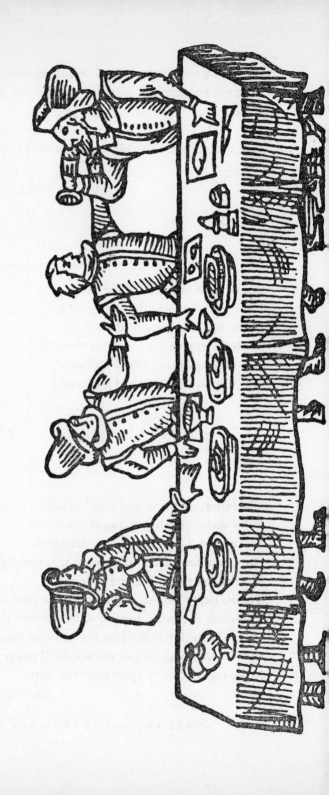

With thy grapes our hairs be crown'd:
Cup us till the world go round

Both this song and "Who is Slyvia" (see page 169) are sung by a singer engaged by a man who wishes to win a lady from her true love. Both songs have been set to music by Franz Schubert (1797–1828). An extant anonymous musical setting of the early seventeenth-century school of composition cannot have been the one used in performance since it omits the third and fourth lines of the poem. The earliest known setting of Shakespeare's complete poem is by Dr. T. A. Arne (1710–1778). There is a modern setting by Roger Quilter (1877–1953).

2. PHOEBUS *the sun.* 3. THOSE SPRINGS *the dew.* 4. CHALIC'D FLOWERS *cup-shaped flowers.* 5. MARY-BUDS *marigolds.*

Because their voices "have got the mannish crack," the two young princes speak, rather than sing, these lines over the body of Imogen, supposed dead. The tone of the poem is that of Shakespeare's last plays. There is an acceptance quite unlike the attitudes toward death in the sonnets. Death here is a release, but there is no renunciation of the world's values. A. E. Housman's "golden lads" owe much to this poem, and his treatment of them is an instructive contrast to Shakespeare. The earliest known musical setting is by Dr. T. A. Arne (1710–1778). There is a recent setting by Roger Quilter (1877–1953).

11. PHYSIC *the art of healing, and by extension, all science.* 14. THUNDER-STONE *thunderbolt.*

Hark, hark! the lark at heaven's gate sings,
    And Phoebus gins arise,
His steeds to water at those springs
    On chalic'd flowers that lies;
5 And winking Mary-buds begin
    To ope their golden eyes.
With every thing that pretty is,
    My lady sweet, arise:
        Arise, arise!

Act II, scene 3, lines 22–30

GUIDERIUS:
Fear no more the heat o' th' sun
    Nor the furious winter's rages;
Thou thy worldly task hast done,
    Home art gone, and ta'en thy wages;
5 Golden lads and girls all must,
As chimney-sweepers, come to dust.
ARVIRAGUS:
Fear no more the frown o' th' great,
    Thou art past the tyrant's stroke;
Care no more to clothe and eat,
10   To thee the reed is as the oak:
The scepter, learning, physic, must
All follow this and come to dust.
GUIDERIUS:
Fear no more the lightning flash,
ARVIRAGUS:
    Nor the all-dreaded thunder-stone;
GUIDERIUS:
15 Fear not slander, censure rash;
ARVIRAGUS:
    Thou hast finish'd joy and moan:

subscribe to, agree to. 19. EXORCISER *conjurer, raiser of spirits.* 21. GHOST UNLAID *a ghost which has not, through the power of an appropriate ritual, been prevented from walking the earth.*

This and the two following songs are sung by Autolycus and serve to introduce us to his lighthearted roguery in which is embodied the joy of everything that fulfills its own nature, and it thus stands in the play, along with grace, as a renewing power. Shakespeare's comedy is not to be restricted to the confines of doctrine. Autolycus is named for the maternal grandfather of Ulysses, the son of Hermes who was the god of luck, the patron of traders and thieves (Autolycus is both), and in parts of Greece, the god of fertility. The earliest known setting of "When daffodils" is by William Boyce (1710–1779). There is a modern setting by Roger Quilter (1877–1953). "But shall I go" was set to music by John Frederick Lampe (1703–1751). An anonymous setting of this song and the Boyce setting of "When daffodils" are reprinted in Caulfield.

2. DOXY *a woman available to any man.* 4. THE . . . PALE *The red blood reigns in place of the pale blood of winter.* 5. SHEET *the sheet that Autolycus will steal when (see the following poem, line 2) "The pale moon shines by night."* 7. SET . . . EDGE *1623 Folio: set an edge to.* PUGGING *thieving.* 11. AUNTS *doxies.*

BOTH:

All lovers young, all lovers must
Consign to thee and come to dust.

GUIDERIUS:

No exorciser harm thee!

ARVIRAGUS:

20   Nor no witchcraft charm thee!

GUIDERIUS:

Ghost unlaid forbear thee!

ARVIRAGUS:

Nothing ill come near thee!

BOTH:

Quiet consummation have,
And renowned be thy grave.

Act IV, scene 2, lines 258–281

THE WINTER'S TALE

When daffodils begin to peer,
    With heigh! the doxy o'er the dale,
Why then comes in the sweet o' the year,
    For the red blood reigns in the winter's pale.

5   The white sheet bleaching on the hedge,
    With heigh! the sweet birds, O, how they sing!
Doth set my pugging tooth an edge,
    For a quart of ale is a dish for a king.

The lark that tirra-lirra chants,
10   With heigh! with heigh! the thrush and the jay,
Are summer songs for me and my aunts,
    While we lie tumbling in the hay.

Act IV, scene 3, lines 1–12

1. THREE-PILE *a costly velvet.* *8*. SOW-SKIN BUDGET *pig-skin bag.* *9–10*. *If put in the stocks he will assert that he is a trader and not a thief.*

Shakespeare doubtless took these verses from a pop-ular song. They are found with only minor differences as the first stanza of a three-stanza song in An Antidote against Melancholy; Made up in Pills, 1661. The traditional tune for them is variously entitled "Hanskin," "Eighty-eight," and "Jog on." It is re-produced in Chappell.

2. HENT *clear, pass over.*

Autolycus, peddling his wares, "sings 'em over as they were gods and goddesses." The earliest known musical setting is by John Wilson (1595–1673) and was published in his Cheerful Ayres or Ballads, 1660.

1. LAWN *fine linen.* *2*. CYPRESS *crepe, a kind of cloth originally imported from Cyprus.* *3*. DAMASK *mingled red and white.* *5*. BUGLE BRACELET *bracelet of black-glass beads.* *7*. QUOIFS *caps.* STOMACHERS *ornamental coverings for the breast.* *9*. POKING STICKS *devices for setting pleats.*

I have served Prince Florizel and in my time wore three-pile, but now I am out of service:

But shall I go mourn for that, my dear?
The pale moon shines by night;
5 And when I wander here and there,
I then do most go right.

If tinkers may have leave to live
And bear the sow-skin budget,
Then my account I well may give,
10 And in the stocks avouch it.

Act IV, scene 3, lines 13–22

Jog on, jog on the footpath way,
And merrily hent the stile-a:
A merry heart goes all the day,
Your sad tires in a mile-a.

Act IV, scene 3, lines 132–135

Lawn as white as driven snow;
Cypress black as e'er was crow;
Gloves as sweet as damask roses;
Masks for faces and for noses;
5 Bugle bracelet, necklace amber,
Perfume for a lady's chamber;
Golden quoifs and stomachers
For my lads to give their dears;
Pins, and poking sticks of steel,
10 What maids lack from head to heel:
Come buy of me, come; come buy, come buy;
Buy, lads, or else your lasses cry:
Come buy!

Act IV, scene 4, lines 220–232

This is an instance of the three-part song popular
with the people of Shakespeare's time. Autolycus tells
Dorcus and Mopsa: "This is a merry ballad . . . and
goes to the tune of 'Two maids wooing a man':
there's scarce a maid westward but she sings it. . . ."
What is perhaps the original setting by Robert Johnson (fl. 1626) is published in Shakespeare Survey, 9.

The earliest known musical setting is by William
Boyce (1710–1779).

AUTOLYCUS:
Get you hence, for I must go
Where it fits not you to know.

DORCAS:
Whither?

MOPSA:
O, whither?

DORCAS:
5   Whither?

MOPSA:
It becomes thy oath full well
Thou to me thy secrets tell.

DORCAS:
Me too: let me go thither.

MOPSA:
Or thou go'st to the grange or mill.

DORCAS:
10 If to either, thou dost ill.

AUTOLYCUS:
Neither.

DORCAS:
What, neither?

AUTOLYCUS:
Neither.

DORCAS:
Thou hast sworn my love to be.

MOPSA:
15 Thou hast sworn it more to me:
Then whither go'st? say whither?

Act IV, scene 4, lines 303–314

Will you buy any tape,
Or lace for your cape,

5. TOYS *ornaments.* 8. MEDDLER *intruder into all things.* 9. UTTER *put on sale.*

Ariel's song, the first in the play, draws Ferdinand into the presence of Miranda. John Banister's (1630–1679) musical setting of these lines, composed for an adaptation of The Tempest *by John Dryden and Sir William Davenant in 1667, is the earliest known. A better-known setting by Henry Purcell (1659–1695), composed for* The Fairy Queen, *Elkanah Settle's adaptation of* A Midsummer Night's Dream *into which the song was inserted, is to be found in Caulfield. There is also a setting by Roger Quilter (1877–1953).*

3. KISS'D *Some dances began with a formal kiss by the partners.* 4. WHIST *an interjection requesting silence, that is, the storm with which the play began is past.* 5. FEATLY *adroitly.* 6–7. BEAR THE BURTHEN *1623 Folio. "The burthen bear" of many modern editions is an emendation by Alexander Pope (1688–1744), following Dryden.* 8. BURTHEN *refrain.*

Ariel sings to Ferdinand of the death and transformation of his father, Alonzo. This is suggestive of the regeneration Alonzo is to undergo in the course of the play. A musical setting for this song, probably the original one, was composed by Robert Johnson (d. 1634). It was harmonized for three voices by John Wilson and published in his Cheerful Ayres or Ballads, *1660. There are other settings by Henry Pur-*

1. FADOM *fathom.*

My dainty duck, my dear-a?
　　　　Any silk, any thread,
　　　　Any toys for your head,
Of the new'st and fin'st wear-a?
　　　　Come to the pedlar;
　　　　Money's a meddler
That doth utter all men's ware-a.

Act IV, scene 4, lines 322–330

Come unto these yellow sands,
　　　　And then take hands:
Curtsied when you have and kiss'd
　　　　The wild waves whist:
Foot it featly here and there,
　　　　And sweet sprites bear
The burthen. Hark, hark!
　　BURTHEN DISPERSEDLY: Bowgh, wawgh!
　　The watch dogs bark.
　　BURTHEN DISPERSEDLY: Bowgh, wawgh!
　　Hark, hark! I hear
The strain of strutting Chanticleer
　　Cry cock-a-diddle-dow.

Act I, scene 2, lines 375–386

Full fadom five thy father lies,
　　　　Of his bones are coral made:
Those are pearls that were his eyes;
　　　　Nothing of him that doth fade
But doth suffer a sea-change

cell (1659–1695), Roger Quilter (1877–1953), and Igor Stravinsky (b. 1882).

8. BURTHEN *refrain, undersong.*

Ariel's song warns Gonzalo of the plot of Sebastian and Antonio against his life. The earliest known music by Dr. T. A. Arne (1710–1788) is reprinted in Caulfield.

It was Shakespeare's custom to have the persons in his plays do something revelatory of their characters on their first entrance. This is our introduction to the bibulous and unprincipled sailor Stephano, who does his share in keeping the romance of The Tempest *anchored in reality. Perhaps the only musical setting for "The master, the swabber" is the anonymous one reprinted in Caulfield.*

6. MALL *an old abbreviation of Mary.* 11. TAILOR *The literary tradition held that tailors were unmanly. "It takes nine tailors to make a man" was a proverb known to Shakespeare.*

Into something rich and strange:
Sea nymphs hourly ring his knell:
    BURTHEN: Ding, dong.
Hark, now I hear them—ding-dong bell.

Act I, scene 2, lines 396–404

While you here do snoring lie,
Open-ey'd conspiracy
    His time doth take.
If of life you keep a care,
5 Shake off slumber and beware:
    Awake, Awake!

Act II, scene 1, lines 300–305

    I shall no more to sea, to sea,
      Here shall I die ashore—

This is a very scurvy tune to sing at a man's funeral; well, here's my
comfort.

(Drinks.)

    The master, the swabber, the boatswain, and I,
5   The gunner and his mate,
    Lov'd Mall, Meg, and Marian, and Margery,
      But none of us car'd for Kate;
      For she had a tongue with a tang,
      Would cry to a sailor, Go hang!
10 She lov'd not the savour of tar nor of pitch,
    Yet a tailor might scratch her where'er she did itch:
      Then to sea, boys, and let her go hang!

This is a scurvy tune too; but here's my comfort.

(Drinks.)
Act II, scene 2, lines 44–57

Caliban is now the willing "subject" of Stephano and Trinculo and all three of them drink and celebrate, as he thinks, his release from the domination of Prospero. The earliest known musical setting by John Christopher Smith (*1712–1795*), written for his operatic version of The Tempest, *is reprinted in Caulfield.*

2. FIRING *firewood.* 4. TRENCHERING *trenchers, plates.*

Henry Purcell's (*1659–1695*) setting of these lines as a round is reprinted in Caulfield.

1. SCOUT *deride. An emendation by Nicholas Rowe (*1674–1718*). 1623 Folio: cout.*

At Prospero's behest, Juno, the goddess of motherhood and the patroness of those who endure the pains of labor, and Ceres, the goddess of plenitude and marriage (*in art she is shown bearing a cornucopia*), appear to bless the betrothal of Ferdinand and Miranda. The original music has not survived. The lines have been set as a duet for soprano and contralto with chorus by Sir Arthur Sullivan (*1842–1900*).

1. MARRIAGE, BLESSING *The "marriage-blessing" of most modern editions is an unwarranted emendation deriving from Lewis Theobald (*1688–1744*). 5.* FOISON *harvest.*

Ariel, about to be released from servitude, sings of his freedom. The musical setting by Robert Johnson (*d. 1634*) was harmonized for three voices by John

No more dams I'll make for fish,
      Nor fetch in firing
            At requiring,
Nor scrape trenchering, nor wash dish;
      'Ban, 'Ban, Ca—Caliban
Has a new master—Get a new man.

Act II, scene 2, lines 184–189

Flout 'em and scout 'em
And scout 'em and flout 'em!
      Thought is free.

Act III, scene 2, lines 130–132

JUNO:
Honour, riches, marriage, blessing,
Long continuance, and increasing,
Hourly joys be still upon you!
Juno sings her blessings on you.
CERES:
Earth's increase, foison plenty,
Barns and garners never empty,
Vines with clust'ring bunches growing,
Plants with goodly burthen bowing;
Spring come to you at the farthest
In the very end of harvest!
Scarcity and want shall shun you,
Ceres' blessing so is on you.

Act IV, scene 1, lines 106–117

Where the bee sucks, there suck I:
      In a cowslip's bell I lie;
There I couch when owls do cry.

Wilson and published in his Cheerful Ayres or Ballads, *1660. It was probably written for the original production of the play. Henry Purcell (1659–1695), Dr. T. A. Arne (1710–1778), and Roger Quilter (1877–1953) have also set the song to music.*

It is not clear why Prospero, the speaker of the epilogue, should refer to the play as "my project" or ask to be released from his bands, or bonds. Shakespeare elsewhere uses "band" for "bond," and "bonds" is clearly the meaning here. But Shakespeare, as a member of the King's Company, was under bond, and if he acted the role of Prospero in the court performance of the play at about the time of his retirement, the reference and the request are clear and references to Prospero's magic may, at times in the play, be taken to indicate Shakespeare's art. But the temptation to allegorize the play with any thoroughness must be resisted.

It is maintained by some scholars that Henry VIII *is a collaboration by Shakespeare and John Fletcher*

1. ORPHEUS *The son of Apollo, patron of artists, and Calliope, muse of epic poetry, was the greatest singer and musician of classical myth.*

On the bat's back I do fly
         After summer merrily:
Merrily, merrily shall I live now
Under the blossom that hangs on the bough.

Act V, scene 1, lines 88–94

Now my charms are all o'erthrown,
And what strength I have's mine own,
Which is most faint: now 'tis true
I must be here confin'd by you,
Or sent to Naples. Let me not,
Since I have my dukedom got,
And pardon'd the deceiver, dwell
In this bare island by your spell;
But release me from my bands
With the help of your good hands:
Gentle breath of yours my sails
Must fill, or else my project fails,
Which was to please. Now I want
Spirits to enforce, art to enchant;
And my ending is despair
Unless I be reliev'd by prayer,
Which pierces so that it assaults
Mercy itself and frees all faults.
As you from crimes would pardon'd be,
Let your indulgence set me free.

Epilogue

KING HENRY THE EIGHTH

Orpheus with his lute made trees
And the mountain tops that freeze

(*1579–1625*) *and that the song may be Fletcher's.
Certainly there is nothing in it Fletcher could not
have written, but the play was printed as Shakespeare's in the 1623 Folio and passed for his until the
mid-nineteenth century; it may be entirely Shakespeare's. The song has been popular with English
composers since it was first set to music by Dr. T. A.
Arne* (*1710–1778*). *There are settings by Sir Arthur
Sullivan* (*1842–1900*) *and Roger Quilter* (*1877–
1953*).

*The Two Noble Kinsmen was first published in 1634
with the names of Shakespeare and John Fletcher
(1579–1625) on the title page. The wedding song is
found in a scene thought to be by Shakespeare, but
it could have been written by either of the collabora-
tors.*

1. BEING GONE *having been removed.* 5. QUAINT *pretty,
pleasant.* 7. VER *spring.* 11. DEATHBEDS *graves.* BLOWING
blooming. 12. TRIM *in prime condition.*

Bow themselves when he did sing:
To his music plants and flowers
5   Ever sprung, as sun and showers
There had made a lasting spring.

Everything that heard him play,
Even the billows of the sea,
Hung their heads, and then lay by:
10 In sweet music is such art
Killing care and grief of heart
Fall asleep, or hearing, die.

Act III, scene 1, lines 3–14

THE TWO NOBLE KINSMEN

Roses, their sharp spines being gone,
Not royal in their smells alone,
But in their hue;
Maiden pinks, of odour faint,
5   Daisies smell-less, yet most quaint,
And sweet thyme true;

Primrose, first-born child of Ver,
Merry springtime's harbinger,
With her bells dim;
10 Oxlips in their cradles growing,
Marigolds on deathbeds blowing,
Larks'-heels trim;

All dear Nature's children sweet,
Lie fore bride and bridegroom's feet,
15 Blessing their sense!   (*Strew flowers.*)

18. IS *1634 Quarto. The "Be" of some editions is an unwarranted emendation by Thomas Seward (1708–1790). 19. SLAND'ROUS because the cuckoo's call indicates a cuckold. 20. CHOUGH HOAR Seward's emendation. 1634 Quarto: clough hee. A chough is a bird of the crow family with red legs and glossy black plumage. 21. PIE magpie.*

Not an angel of the air,
Bird melodious or bird fair,
    Is absent hence!

The crow, the sland'rous cuckoo, nor
20 The boding raven, nor chough hoar,
    Nor chatt'ring pie
May on our bridehouse perch or sing,
Or with them any discord bring,
    But from it fly!

Act I, scene 1, lines 1–24

Shakespeare is buried at Stratford-on-Avon in the Church of the Holy Trinity on the north side of the chancel. Above his tomb is carved the epitaph which, according to tradition, he wrote himself. His admirers have sometimes doubted that England's greatest poet could have written these doggerel lines but there is little need to question his authorship. According to the custom of his time, the right of burial within the church could be claimed for people prominent in the parish, and as the centuries passed, the bones of the forgotten dead were dug up and thrown into the charnel house to make room for the newly deceased. The charnel house, since torn down, was an adjunct of the church. Its upper story served as the rector's study and the bones themselves as a memento mori. *It is just such a disinterment which takes place in* Hamlet *before the burial of Ophelia. Shakespeare had reason to fear that his remains might be treated in the same way. Long after his death the bones of his daughter Susanna were dug up and thrown into the charnel house to make room for someone then prominent in the parish named Watt. But Shakespeare's grave has never been disturbed, and we may believe that in the earlier years before his grave became a shrine the epitaph was instrumental in preserving it from desecration.*

Good friend, for Jesus' sake forbear
To dig the dust enclosed here;
Blest be the man that spares these stones,
And curst be he that moves my bones.

THE PASSIONATE PILGRIM

The fourth, sixth, ninth, and eleventh poems in The Passionate Pilgrim *are on the Venus and Adonis story and may be by Bartholomew Griffin. One of them, poem 11, appears in his* Fidessa, 1596, *but it is possible that he took it from Shakespeare. The poems strongly resemble each other, and when read together, have a certain unity. They are simpler than Shakespeare's characteristic poems. There is, for instance, none of the ambivalence that we find in Shakespeare's presentation of Venus' charms in* Venus and Adonis, *and the jokes are uncomplicated by the play of wit.*

1. CYTHEREA *another name for Venus.* 6. SHOW'D *as in poem 9.* 8. STILL *always.* 9. WANT CONCEIT *lack understanding.* 10. FIGUR'D *indicated by gesture rather than by word.* 13. TOWARD *eager.* 14. FROWARD *unwilling to comply.*

The poem is based on the story of Salmacis and Hermaphroditus, a favorite of the Elizabethan poets. It is told by Ovid in Metamorphoses, Book 4, lines 285–388. *This poem and the fourth, ninth, and eleventh comprise a group. See comment on poem 4.*

3. CYTHEREA *Venus.* 4. TARRIANCE *tarrying, waiting in expectation.* 5. OSIER *willow.* 6. SPLEEN *fire, impetuosity.* 12. WISTLY *attentively.* 13. BOUNC'D IN WHEREAS *leapt in suddenly from where.* 14. FLOOD *stream.*

FOUR

Sweet Cytherea, sitting by a brook
With young Adonis, lovely, fresh, and green,
Did court the lad with many a lovely look,
Such looks as none could look but beauty's queen:
5 She told him stories to delight his ears;
She show'd him favours to allure his eye;
To win his heart she touch'd him here and there—
Touches so soft still conquer chastity.
But whether unripe years did want conceit,
10 Or he refus'd to take her figur'd proffer,
The tender nibbler would not touch the bait,
But smile and jest at every gentle offer.
      Then fell she on her back, fair queen, and toward;
      He rose and ran away; ah, fool too froward!

SIX

Scarce had the sun dri'd up the dewy morn,
And scarce the herd gone to the hedge for shade,
When Cytherea, all in love forlorn,
A longing tarriance for Adonis made
5 Under an osier growing by a brook,
A brook where Adon us'd to cool his spleen.
Hot was the day; she hotter that did look
For his approach that often there had been.
Anon he comes, and throws his mantle by,
10 And stood stark naked on the brook's green brim.
The sun look'd on the world with glorious eye,
Yet not so wistly as this queen on him.
      He, spying her, bounc'd in whereas he stood.
      "O Jove," quoth she, "why was not I a flood?"

There is a manuscript copy of this poem, signed "W. S.," in the Folger Shakespeare Library, but it once belonged to John Payne Collier (1789–1883), whose accomplishments included forgery. Still, the ascription has a certain plausibility. Although the lady conforms to the Elizabethan ideal of beauty, her character is that of the Dark Lady of the sonnets.

5. DAMASK *mingled red and white, rose color.* 10. DREADING *being solicitous about.* STILL *always.* 15. FRAM'D *molded, fashioned.* FOIL'D *undid.* 16. A-TURN-ING *See poem 15, line 4.* 17. *Which of the two was she, a lover or a lecher?*

The poem appeared in Richard Barnfield's Poems: In diuers humors, *added to* The Encomion of Lady Pecunia, *1598, and was assigned to Shakespeare by William Jaggard in the year following. Scholarship of the past century has agreed to Barnfield's claim, although earlier scholars, without much confidence, claimed it for Shakespeare. The motivation for this is understandable; the poem pays homage to Spenser, and in it the interest in music, implicit throughout Shakespeare's works, is made explicit. The concluding phrase recalls the last line of Shakespeare's Sonnet 74.*

5. DOWLAND *John Dowland, famous lutanist and composer (1563?–1626?). He was lutanist to Charles I, 1625.* 7. SPENSER *Edmund Spenser (1552?–1599).* DEEP CONCEIT *profound imagination and understanding.*

SEVEN

Fair is my love, but not so fair as fickle;
Mild as a dove, but neither true nor trusty;
Brighter than glass, and yet, as glass is, brittle;
Softer than wax, and yet as iron rusty:
5   A lily pale, with damask dye to grace her;
       None fairer, nor none falser to deface her.

Her lips to mine how often hath she join'd,
Between each kiss her oaths of true love swearing!
How many tales to please me hath she coin'd,
10   Dreading my love, the loss whereof still fearing!
       Yet, in the midst of all her pure protestings,
       Her faith, her oaths, her tears, and all were jestings.

She burnt with love, as straw with fire flameth;
She burnt out love, as soon as straw outburneth;
15   She fram'd the love, and yet she foil'd the framing;
She bade love last, and yet she fell a-turning.
       Was this a lover, or a lecher whether?
       Bad in the best, though excellent in neither.

EIGHT

If music and sweet poetry agree,
As they must needs, the sister and the brother,
Then must the love be great 'twixt thee and me,
Because thou lov'st the one, and I the other;
5   Dowland to thee is dear, whose heavenly touch
Upon the lute doth ravish human sense;
Spenser to me, whose deep conceit is such
As, passing all conceit, needs no defence.

If music and sweet poetry agree

10. PHOEBUS *another name for Apollo, the god of light, medicine, poetry, and music.* *12.* HIMSELF *Phoebus.* *13.* ONE GOD *Phoebus.* *14.* ONE KNIGHT *We do not know who the knight was. Scholars have plausibly supposed him to be Sir George Carey, K. G., to whom Dowland dedicated his first book of airs (1597) and to whose wife Spenser dedicated* Muiopotmos, *1590.*

Presumably a second line, rhyming with "wild," is missing from the poem, dropped most probably by the printer. With such a line, the poem, like the other three on the Venus and Adonis story, would be a regular Shakespearean sonnet.

7. SILLY *here used as a term of pity.* *8.* PASS *enter, go across.* *10.* BRAKES *thicket.* *11.* RUTH *pity.*

The similarity of this to the thirteenth poem suggests that the same writer wrote both. He seems not to have been Shakespeare, but there is no evidence for ascribing them to anyone else.

1, 2. VADED *"Vade" is often synonymous with "fade," but Elizabethan poets sometimes used the two words in conjunction, implying an alternative meaning for "vade." If "vade" is taken to be derived from the Latin* vado, *it would mean "to go, go hastily, depart."* *3.* ORIENT PEARL *a kind of pearl characterized by its translucency.* TOO TIMELY *too soon.*

Thou lov'st to hear the sweet melodious sound
That Phœbus' lute, the queen of music, makes;
And I in deep delight am chiefly drown'd
When as himself to singing he betakes.
    One god is god of both, as poets feign;
    One knight loves both, and both in thee remain.

NINE

Fair was the morn when the fair queen of love,
Paler for sorrow than her milk-white dove,
For Adon's sake, a youngster proud and wild,
Her stand she takes upon a steep-up hill.
Anon Adonis comes with horn and hounds;
She, silly queen, with more than love's good will,
Forbade the boy he should not pass those grounds.
"Once," quoth she, "did I see a fair sweet youth
Here in these brakes deep wounded with a boar,
Deep in the thigh, a spectacle of ruth:
See in my thigh," quoth she, "here was the sore."
    She show'd hers; he saw more wounds than one,
    And blushing fled and left her all alone.

TEN

Sweet rose, fair flower, untimely pluck'd, soon vaded,
Pluck'd in the bud and vaded in the spring;
Bright orient pearl, alack, too timely shaded;
Fair creature, kill'd too soon by death's sharp sting,
    Like a green plum that hangs upon a tree,
    And falls, through wind, before the fall should be.

8, 10. FOR WHY *because.*

*The fourth, sixth, ninth, and eleventh poems com-
prise a group on the Venus and Adonis story. See
comment on poem 4.*

1. YOUNG *supplied by some editors from a manuscript
copy of the poem in the Folger Shakespeare Library.
The 1599 Octavo reads: "Venus, with Adonis. . . ."
3-4.* MARS . . . HIM *As Mars approached Venus sexually, so she approaches Adonis.* 11. FETCHED *drew. 13.*
AT THIS BAY *a hunting term for the point in the chase
at which the prey is cornered. 14.* CLIP *embrace.*

*This poem, with four additional stanzas apparently
by another hand and certainly in another manner,
appeared in Thomas Deloney's* Garden of Good Will
*in 1631, thirty-one years after Deloney's death. It is
possible that the poem appeared in earlier editions
of the* Garden *which have not survived. Jaggard
attributed the poem to Shakespeare in 1599, but some
of his attributions are not credible. On the basis of
our present knowledge it is not possible to prove or
disprove Shakespeare's authorship.*

2. PLEASANCE *joy, merriment. 4.* BRAVE *handsome.*

I weep for thee, and yet no cause I have,
For why thou lefts me nothing in thy will;
And yet thou lefts me more than I did crave,
10   For why I craved nothing of thee still.
          O yes, dear friend, I pardon crave of thee;
          Thy discontent thou didst bequeath to me.

ELEVEN

Venus, with young Adonis sitting by her
Under a myrtle shade, began to woo him;
She told the youngling how god Mars did try her,
And as he fell to her, she fell to him.
5   "Even thus," quoth she, "the warlike god embrac'd me;"
And then she clipp'd Adonis in her arms;
"Even thus," quoth she, "the warlike god unlac'd me,"
As if the boy should use like loving charms;
"Even thus," quoth she, "he seized on my lips,"
10   And with her lips on his did act the seizure;
And as she fetched breath, away he skips,
And would not take her meaning nor her pleasure.
          Ah, that I had my lady at this bay,
          To kiss and clip me till I run away!

TWELVE

Crabb'd age and youth cannot live together:
Youth is full of pleasance, age is full of care;
Youth like summer morn, age like winter weather;
Youth like summer brave, age like winter bare;
5   Youth is full of sport, age's breath is short;

11. DEFY *despise, renounce.* *12.* STAYS *tarries.*

The similarity of this poem to the tenth suggests that
they are by the same hand, but whether the hand was
or was not Shakespeare's is not known. There is no
evidence for ascribing it to anyone else.

2. VADETH *goes away. See note to poem 10, lines 1
and 2. 4.* PRESENTLY *in a short time. 7.* SELD *seldom.
10.* REDRESS *repair. 12.* PHYSIC *medicine in general.*

It is difficult to think that any gifted poet, let alone
Shakespeare, wrote this unrelievidly commonplace
composition. It was ascribed to Shakespeare by Jaggard, and no other writer claims it. The last three
stanzas are sometimes printed as a separate poem.

1. BE *let neither be. 3.* DAFF'D ME *turned me away to.*
CABIN *any small inclosed space, a room. 4.* DESCANT ON
sing about, compose variations on. DOUBTS *apprehensions.*

Youth is nimble, age is lame;
Youth is hot and bold, age is weak and cold;
Youth is wild, and age is tame.
  Age, I do abhor thee; youth, I do adore thee.
10   O, my love, my love is young!
   Age, I do defy thee. O sweet shepherd hie thee,
    For methinks thou stays too long.

THIRTEEN

Beauty is but a vain and doubtful good,
A shining gloss that vadeth suddenly,
A flower that dies when first it gins to bud,
A brittle glass that's broken presently;
5   A doubtful good, a gloss, a glass, a flower,
  Lost, vaded, broken, dead within an hour.

And as goods lost are seld or never found,
As vaded gloss no rubbing will refresh,
As flowers dead lie wither'd on the ground,
10 As broken glass no cement can redress;
  So beauty blemish'd once, for ever lost,
  In spite of physic, painting, pain, and cost.

FOURTEEN

Good night, good rest; ah, neither be my share!
She bade good night that kept my rest away,
And daff'd me to a cabin hang'd with care
To descant on the doubts of my decay.

8. NILL *will not, a contraction of "ne will."*
CONSTER *surmise.* WHETHER *which.* 11. SHADOWS *representations of reality rather than the thing itself. See* The Rape of Lucrece, *line 1457, note.* 12. AS *such as.* PELF *riches.* 14 CHARGE THE WATCH *charge the watchman to announce dawn.* 15. CITE *urge.* 17. PHILOMELA *See note, page 184.* MARK *listen.* 18. LAYS *songs.* 21. PACK'D *packed off, sent away.* 24. FOR WHY *because.* 27. A MOON *Emendation by George Steevens (1736–1800). The 1599 Octavo: an houre—presumably a compositor's confusion with the line above.* 30. SHORT *shorten.* LENGTH *lengthen.*

"Farewell," quoth she, "and come again tomorrow."
Fare well I could not, for I supp'd with sorrow.

Yet at my parting sweetly did she smile,
In scorn of friendship, nill I conster whether.
'T may be she joy'd to jest at my exile;
'T may be again, to make me wander thither:
    "Wander"—a word for shadows like myself
    As take the pain but cannot pluck the pelf.

Lord, how mine eyes throw gazes to the east!
My heart doth charge the watch; the morning rise
Doth cite each moving sense from idle rest,
Not daring trust the office of mine eyes.
    While Philomela sits and sings, I sit and mark
    And wish her lays were tuned like the lark;

For she doth welcome daylight with her ditty
And drives away dark dreaming night;
The night so pack'd, I post unto my pretty;
Heart hath his hope, and eyes their wished sight;
    Sorrow chang'd to solace and solace mix'd with
      sorrow
    For why she sigh'd and bade me come tomorrow.

Were I with her, the night would post too soon,
But now are minutes added to the hours;
To spite me now, each minute seems a moon;
Yet not for me, shine sun to succour flowers!
    Pack night, peep day; good day, of night now
      borrow:
    Short, night, to-night; and length thyself to-morrow.

Although the individuality of scholars prevents unanimity on any opinion involving the judgment, the agreement on refusing to ascribe this poem to Shakespeare is impressive. On the other hand, Quiller-Couch properly calls it "a gay little song," but the manner of its gaiety is unlike anything else in Shakespeare. The poetic tradition of the rivalry between the military and the learned goes back to the Middle Ages.

2. MASTER *the learned man of line 15, probably the girl's tutor.* 7. SPITE *vexation.* 8. SILLY *unsophisticated, simple.* 9. MORE MICKLE *more great, the greater.* 10. USED *put into practice.* 13. ART *letters, learning.*

The author of this poem is unknown. The attempts to ascribe it to Richard Barnfield have been shown to be without value. It was published in 1597 in a quarto collection of madrigals by Thomas Weelkes, Madrigals To 3. 4. 5. and 6. voyces. *Weelkes, organist and composer (dates unknown), claims the music but not the words. Presumably Jaggard lifted it from him. The compiler of* England's Helicon, 1600, *in which it appears, lifted it from* The Passionate Pilgrim. *If it is, incredibly, by Shakespeare, it is the only worthless thing he ever wrote. All three stanzas were set as madrigals for three voices by Weelkes.*

2. SPEED *flourish.* 3. DEFYING *renouncing.* 4. RENYING *Emendation by Edmund Malone (1741–1812), who explains that it is from the French* renier, *to forswear. Schmidt's* Shakespeare-Lexicon *explains it as "to disown, to become a renegade." The word does not occur elsewhere in Shakespeare or in works attributed to him. The 1599 Octavo reading, "nenying," does not seem to mean anything. The meaning of a word is established by its context, and when a nonce word occurs in a jejune context, a meaning cannot be confidently assigned to it.*

FIFTEEN

It was a lording's daughter, the fairest one of three
That liked of her master, as well as well might be,
Till looking on an Englishman, the fairest that eye could
see,
    Her fancy fell a-turning.

5   Long was the combat doubtful, that love with love did
fight
To leave the master loveless or kill the gallant knight;
To put in practise either, alas it was a spite
    Unto the silly damsel.

But one must be refused, more mickle was the pain,
10   That nothing could be used to turn them both to gain;
For of the two the trusty knight was wounded with
disdain;
    Alas she could not help it.

Thus art with arms contending was victor of the day,
Which by a gift of learning did bear the maid away;
15   Then lullaby, the learned man hath got the lady gay,
    For now my song is ended.

SEVENTEEN

My flocks feed not, my ewes breed not,
My rams speed not, all is amiss;
Love is dying, faith's defying,
Heart's renying, causer of this.
5   All my merry jigs are quite forgot,

9. SILLY *perhaps harmless, witless.* CROSS *reversal of fortune.* 16. SPEEDING *fortune.* 17. NO DEAL *perhaps not at all.* 18. WETHER'S BELL *the bell of the bellwether, a castrated ram which leads the flock.* 19. CURTAIL *variant of "curtal," having a docked tail.* 21. PROCURES *manages.* 26. DYE *color.* 28. BACK *Weelkes' Madrigals. 1599 Octavo: blacke.* 35. CORYDON *traditional name for a shepherd in pastoral poetry.*

All my lady's love is lost, God wot.
Where her faith was firmly fix'd in love,
There a nay is plac'd without remove.
    One silly cross wrought all my loss.
10   O frowning Fortune, cursed fickle dame,
    For now I see inconstancy
    More in women than in men remain.

In black mourn I, all fears scorn I,
Love hath forlorn me, living in thrall;
15 Heart is bleeding, all help needing;
O cruel speeding, fraughted with gall.
My shepherd's pipe can sound no deal,
My wether's bell rings doleful knell,
My curtail dog that wont to have play'd,
20 Plays not at all but seems afraid.
    My sighs so deep procures to weep
    In howling wise to see my doleful plight.
    How sighs resound through heartless ground,
    Like a thousand vanquish'd men in bloody fight!

25 Clear wells spring not, sweet birds sing not,
Green plants bring not forth their dye;
Herds stand weeping, flocks all sleeping,
Nymphs back peeping fearfully.
All our pleasure known to us poor swains,
30 All our merry meetings on the plains,
All our evening sport from us is fled,
All our love is lost, for Love is dead.
    Farewell sweet love! Thy like ne'er was
    For a sweet content, the cause of all my woe.
35   Poor Corydon must live alone;
    Other help for him I see that there is none.

Some scholars, finding a certain merit in this poem and having no reason to ascribe it to another writer, have accepted it as Shakespeare's. John Masefield finds that the poem has "a smack of" Shakespeare's "mind about it" and that it might be his earliest work. But Shakespeare was not the only English poet who thought of the true born Englishman as a forthright fellow. It seems better to say that the authorship of this poem is unknown. The fifth and sixth stanzas of this poem, as printed here, sometimes appear as the third and fourth.

2. STALL'D *a hunting term meaning "got within range."* 4. FANCY, PARTIAL MIGHT *love, a power incapable of objective judgment.* 8. FILED *studied.* 10. HALT *a physical fault, with a pun on the obsolete meaning, to be deceptive, false, or shifty.* 13. BROWS *eyebrows.* 20. BAN *curse.* 27. DESERT *deserving.*

EIGHTEEN

When as thine eye hath chose the dame
And stall'd the deer that thou shouldst strike,
Let reason rule things worthy blame,
As well as fancy, partial might;
    Take counsel of some wiser head,
    Neither too young nor yet unwed.

And when thou com'st thy tale to tell,
Smooth not thy tongue with filed talk,
Lest she some subtle practise smell—
A cripple soon can find a halt;
    But plainly say thou lov'st her well,
    And set thy person forth to sell.

What though her frowning brows be bent,
Her cloudy looks will calm ere night,
And then too late she will repent
That thus dissembled her delight,
    And twice desire, ere it be day,
    That which with scorn she put away.

What though she strive to try her strength,
And ban and brawl and say thee nay,
Her feeble force will yield at length,
When craft hath taught her thus to say:
    "Had women been so strong as men,
    In faith, you had not had it then."

And to her will frame all thy ways.
Spare not to spend, and chiefly there
Where thy desert may merit praise
By ringing in thy lady's ear.

PROFFER *attempt to do.* 39. TOYS *whims, fancies.* 40.
TREADS *the term used for the mating of birds and
fowl.* 43. STILL *always.* 44. TO SAINT *to play the saint.*
45. HEAVEN *It is a commonplace for the love poet to
speak of love's fulfillment as heaven.* BY HOLY THEN!
*This unique oath was perhaps intended to justify it-
self by indecent suggestion. The passage has troubled
the commentators. Kittredge, whose text reads "be
holy then," taking the "be" from a manuscript copy
in the Folger Shakespeare Library, explains:* "There
is the emphatic Elizabethan *there, which the editors
seem to ignore:* 'In them *(i.e. in your attempts to
achieve bliss by loving and serving* them) *there is no
heaven. Don't try, therefore, to be holy in love. Take
your pleasure, and when your feminine contemporaries are too old to be agreeable mistresses—and
you are, therefore, past the age of love—then be a
saint (not Love's, but God's saint).'* " 54. BEWRAY'D
laid bare.

*This poem, the first part expanded to six stanzas and
the second to five, appeared in* England's Helicon,

The strongest castle, tow'r, and town,
30   The golden bullet beats it down.

Serve always with assured trust
And in thy suit be humble-true;
Unless thy lady prove unjust,
Press never thou to choose a new.
35   When time shall serve, be thou not slack
            To proffer, though she put thee back.

The wiles and guiles that women work,
Dissembled with an outward show,
The tricks and toys that in them lurk,
40   The cock that treads them shall not know.
            Have you not heard it said full oft,
            A woman's nay doth stand for naught?

Think women still to strive with men
To sin, and never for to saint.
45   There is no heaven by holy then!
When time with age shall them attaint.
            Were kisses all the joys in bed,
            One woman would another wed.

But soft! enough!—too much, I fear;
50   Lest that my mistress hear my song;
She will not stick to round me on th' ear,
To teach my tongue to be so long.
            Yet will she blush, here be it said,
            To hear her secrets so bewray'd.

NINETEEN

Live with me and be my love,
And we will all the pleasures prove

1600. The first part bore the title "The passionate Sheepheard to his loue" and was signed "Chr. Marlow"; the second part was entitled "The Nimphs reply to the Sheepheard" and was signed "Ignoto." In the Compleat Angler, *1653, Isaak Walton identified Ignoto as Sir Walter Raleigh and "The Nimphs reply" is now commonly accepted as his, although the lateness of its ascription to him makes it doubtful. The "reply," in, perhaps, willful ignorance of the pastoral tradition in which the first part is written, views the proposal realistically. The first part is now accepted as Marlowe's. A musical setting of the poem was published in William Corkine's* The Second Booke of Ayres, *1612.*

10. POSES *posies.* 11. KIRTLE *a gown or skirt. The following are the textual variants found in England's Helicon: 1.* LIVE *Come live. 3–4. That valleys, groves, hills and fields,/Woods or steepy mountain yields. 5.* THERE WILL WE *And we will. 6.* AND SEE *Seeing the. 7.* BY *to. 9.* THERE . . . BED *And I will make thee beds. 10.* WITH *And. 17.* THAT *all.*

This poem, along with the eighth, appeared in Richard Barnfield's Poems: In diuers humors, *added to his* Encomion of Lady Pecunia, *1598, and is doubtless his. Attempts to claim it for Shakespeare have been proved vain. The compiler of* England's Helicon, *1600, lifted the first twenty-six lines from* The Passionate Pilgrim, *and in order to round them off,*

That hills and valleys, dales and fields,
And all the craggy mountains yield.

5   There will we sit upon the rocks,
And see the shepherds feed their flocks,
By shallow rivers by whose falls
Melodious birds sing madrigals.

There will I make thee a bed of roses,
10   With a thousand fragrant poses,
A cap of flowers, and a kirtle
Embroider'd all with leaves of myrtle,

A belt of straw and ivy buds,
With coral clasps and amber studs;
15   And if these pleasures may thee move,
Then live with me and be my love.

Love's answer
If that the world and love were young,
And truth in every shepherd's tongue,
These pretty pleasures might me move
20   To live with thee and be thy love.

TWENTY

As it fell upon a day
In the merry month of May,
Sitting in a pleasant shade
Which a grove of myrtles made,
5   Beasts did leap and birds did sing,
Trees did grow and plants did spring;
Everything did banish moan,

added two lines of his own: "Even so, poor bird, like thee,/None alive will pity me." The lines sometimes appear without justification in reprintings of the poem.

10. UP-TILL up against. The legend is that the nightingale in her melancholy presses her breast against a thorn while she sings. In Oscar Wilde's "The Nightingale and the Rose," she presses against the thorn until it touches her heart and the white rose on the rose tree turns a beautiful red. In his Pseudodoxia Epidemica (Book 3, chapter 28) Sir Thomas Browne questions "Whether the Nightingale's setting with her breast against a thorn, be any more than that she placeth some prickels on the outside of her nest, or roosteth in thorny and prickly places, where serpents may least approach her." 13–14. Now she would cry, "Fie, fie, fie!" and then, "Tereu, tereu!" 17. LIVELY lifelike, real. 21. SENSELESS lacking the senses. 22. BEARS England's Helicon and some modern editions read "beasts." 23. KING PANDION Philomela's father whose premature death was brought about by her suffering. 24. LAPP'D IN LEAD wrapped in a leaden winding sheet. 35. STORE OF CROWNS supply of money. 36. WANT lack. 40. Too bad that he is not a king.

Save the nightingale alone.
She, poor bird, as all forlorn,
Lean'd her breast up-till a thorn
And there sung the dolefull'st ditty,
That to hear it was great pity:
"Fie, fie, fie!" now would she cry;
"Tereu, tereu!" by-and-by;
That to hear her so complain
Scarce I could from tears refrain;
For her griefs, so lively shown,
Made me think upon mine own.
"Ah," thought I, "thou mourn'st in vain!
None takes pity on thy pain.
Senseless trees they cannot hear thee;
Ruthless bears they will not cheer thee.
King Pandion, he is dead;
All thy friends are lapp'd in lead;
All thy fellow birds do sing,
Careless of thy sorrowing.
Whilst as fickle Fortune smil'd,
Thou and I were both beguil'd."
Every one that flatters thee
Is no friend in misery.
Words are easy, like the wind;
Faithful friends are hard to find:
Every man will be thy friend
Whilst thou hast wherewith to spend;
But if store of crowns be scant,
No man will supply thy want.
If that one be prodigal,
Bountiful they will him call,
And with such-like flattering,
"Pity but he were a king."
If he be addict to vice,

Quickly him they will entice;
If to women he be bent,
They have at commandement;
45 But if Fortune once do frown,
Then farewell his great renown!
They that fawn'd on him before
Use his company no more.
He that is thy friend indeed,
50 He will help thee in thy need:
If thou sorrow, he will weep;
If thou wake, he cannot sleep:
Thus of every grief, in heart
He with thee doth bear a part.
55 These are certain signs to know
Faithful friend from flatt'ring foe.

THE PHOENIX AND THE TURTLE

1. LOUDEST LAY *loudest song. It is not necessary to think that Shakespeare intended any particular bird.* 2. SOLE *In* The Tempest, *Act III, scene 3, lines 22–24, Shakespeare writes "... in Arabia/There is one tree, the phoenix' throne; one phoenix/ At this hour reigning there." 3.* SAD *grave, serious.* 4. CHASTE WINGS *other birds summoned by the herald.* 5 HARBINGER *In* A Midsummer Night's Dream, *Act V, scene 1, lines 383–385, Shakespeare writes: "Whilst the screech owl, screeching loud,/Puts the wretch that lies in woe/In remembrance of a shroud." See page 195, lines 6–8.* 6. PRECURRER *forerunner.* 7. AUGUR *prophet.* 9. INTERDICT *be debarred.* 12. OBSEQUY *funeral rite; now common only in the plural.* 14. *who knows funeral music.* 15. DEATH-DIVINING SWAN *The swan's song proclaimed her imminent death.* 16. HIS *its, that is, requiem's.* RIGHT *right to appropriate music.* 17. TREBLE-DATED *"Date" is sometimes used by Shakespeare to mean "allotted time." Here the allotted time of the crow is multiple. Probably Shakespeare did not distinguish between the crow and the raven, both of which are members of the genus* Corvus. *The tradition of the raven's exceptional longevity goes back, at least, to Pliny* (A.D. 23–79). *18.* SABLE *black.* GENDER *progeny, race.* 19. *It was part of the natural history of Shakespeare's time that ravens conceived and laid their eggs at the bill.* 23. PHOENIX *The phoenix was a miraculous bird of extraordinary red-and-gold plumage which inhabited a paradise in Arabia where it sat on a tree reserved for it. There was only one phoenix alive at a time, and it lived some say 500 years, some a thousand or more. At the end of its life span, it built itself a nest of aromatic woods and spices, set fire to the nest, and was consumed in the flames. A new phoenix arose from the ashes, and its life cycle was repeated. The phoenix became the emblem of immortality, and was almost universally so regarded. It is to be noted that such is not the case with Shakespeare's poem.* TURTLE *turtledove.* 25. AS *that.* 27. *Two separate beings who were nonetheless one.* 28. *The concept of number was destroyed by the lovers' being at once both two and one.*

Let the bird of loudest lay,
On the sole Arabian tree,
Herald sad and trumpet be,
To whose sound chaste wings obey.

5   But thou shrieking harbinger,
Foul precurrer of the fiend,
Augur of the fever's end,
To this troop come thou not near.

From this session interdict
10   Every fowl of tyrant wing,
Save the eagle, feath'red king;
Keep the obsequy so strict.

Let the priest in surplice white,
That defunctive music can,
15   Be the death-divining swan,
Lest the requiem lack his right.

And thou treble-dated crow,
That thy sable gender mak'st,
With the breath thou giv'st and tak'st,
20   'Mongst our mourners shalt thou go.

Here the anthem doth commence:
Love and Constancy is dead;
Phoenix and the turtle fled
In a mutual flame from hence.

25   So they lov'd as love in twain
Had the essence but in one;
Two distincts, division none:
Number there in love was slain.

29. REMOTE *apart.* 30. DISTANCE *There was a distance between the hearts.* 32. *Except in them it would have been remarkable.* 34. HIS RIGHT *his due (see line 16). He had a right to her love by virtue of the love he gave her.* 35. SIGHT *eyes.* 36. MINE *source of riches with additional meanings of mien and self.* 37. PROPERTY *the concept of property, and propriety (Latin proprietas), appropriateness, the appropriateness of a being's attributes to itself.* 38. SELF *"Self" and "same" are here synonymous. The same not being the same destroys the concept of individuality.* 41. REASON *Reason is confounded by this unity in division.* 44. SIMPLE *A simple is a single ingredient in a compound. Here, the single ingredient is the compound.* 45. IT *reason.* 47. *Unity in division is beyond the comprehension of reason, but this is a phenomenon which love both creates and understands; love, therefore, has reason, or comprehension, that reason does not have.* 49. THRENE *lamentation.*

Hearts remote, yet not asunder;
30 Distance, and no space was seen
Twixt this turtle and his queen:
But in them it were a wonder.

So between them love did shine
That the turtle saw his right
35 Flaming in the phoenix' sight;
Either was the other's mine.

Property was thus appall'd,
That the self was not the same;
Single nature's double name
40 Neither two nor one was call'd.

Reason, in itself confounded,
Saw division grow together,
To themselves, yet either neither,
Simple were so well compounded

45 That it cried, "How true a twain
Seemeth this concordant one!
Love hath reason, Reason none,
If what parts can so remain."

Whereupon it made this threne
50 To the phoenix and the dove,
Co-supremes and stars of love,
As chorus to their tragic scene.

THRENOS

Beauty, Truth, and Rarity,
Grace in all simplicity,

55   Here enclos'd, in cinders lie.

      Death is now the phoenix nest,
      And the turtle's loyal breast
      To eternity doth rest,

      Leaving no posterity:
60   'Twas not their infirmity,
      It was married chastity.

      Truth may seem, but cannot be;
      Beauty brag, but 'tis not she;
      Truth and Beauty buried be.

65   To this urn let those repair
      That are either true or fair;
      For these dead birds sigh a prayer.

A LOVER'S COMPLAINT

From off a hill whose concave womb reworded
A plaintful story from a sist'ring vale,
My spirits t' attend this double voice accorded,
And down I laid to list the sad-tun'd tale;
5   Ere long espi'd a fickle maid full pale,
Tearing of papers, breaking rings atwain,
Storming her world with sorrow's wind and rain.

Upon her head a platted hive of straw,
Which fortifi'd her visage from the sun,
10 Whereon the thought might think sometime it saw
The carcass of a beauty spent and done.
Time had not scyth'd all that youth begun,
Nor youth all quit, but spite of heaven's fell rage,
Some beauty peep'd through lattice of sear'd age.

15 Oft did she heave her napkin to her eyne,
Which on it had conceited characters,
Laund'ring the silken figures in the brine
That season'd woe had pelleted in tears,
And often reading what contents it bears;
20 As often shrieking undistinguish'd woe
In clamours of all size, both high and low.

Sometimes her levell'd eyes their carriage ride,

1. REWORDED *echoed.*
2. SIST'RING VALE *neighboring vale of like description.*
3. ATTEND *listen to.*
5. ESPI'D *I espied. The poet has the un-Shakespearean habit of omitting the subjects of verbs.* FICKLE *unstable.*
7. WIND AND RAIN *sighs and tears.*
8. HIVE *hat. The usage is rare and probably is intended to suggest the shape of the hat.*
9. FORTIFI'D *protected.*
10. THOUGHT *mind.* SOMETIME *sometimes.*
11. DONE *departed. See* Venus and Adonis, *line 197.*
14. SEAR'D AGE *This is an exaggeration characteristic of Shakespeare. The lady is in her late youth. See Sonnet 62, line 10 for the poet's description of himself when he was approximately thirty.*
15. NAPKIN *handkerchief.* EYNE *eyes.*
16. CONCEITED CHARACTERS *imaginative figures.*
18. PELLETED *made into drops like small balls.*
20. UNDISTINGUISH'D WOE *inarticulate cries of woe.*
22–23. The image

As they did batt'ry to the spheres intend;
Sometime diverted their poor balls are tied
To th' orbed earth; sometimes they do extend
Their view right on; anon their gazes lend
To every place at once, and nowhere fix'd,
The mind and sight distractedly commix'd.

Her hair, nor loose nor tied in formal plat,
Proclaim'd in her a careless hand of pride,
For some, untuck'd, descended her sheav'd hat,
Hanging her pale and pined cheek beside;
Some in her threaden fillet still did bide,
And true to bondage, would not break from thence,
Though slackly braided in loose negligence.

A thousand favours from a maund she drew
Of amber, crystal, and of beaded jet,
Which one by one she in a river threw,
Upon whose weeping margent she was set;
Like usury, applying wet to wet,
Or monarch's hands that lets not bounty fall
Where want cries some, but where excess begs all.

Of folded schedules had she many a one
Which she perus'd, sigh'd, tore, and gave the flood;

25

30

35

40

*expresses defiance.
Her eyes are
"levell'd" (aimed)
like a cannon
mounted on (rid-
ing) its carriage in
an assault ("bat-
tr'y") on the stars
("spheres").*
*29. NOR . . . NOR
neither . . . nor.*
PLAT plait.
*30. CARELESS HAND
OF PRIDE hand in-
different to pride.*
*31. DESCENDED de-
scended from.*
*SHEAV'D presumably
made of straw. The
word does not oc-
cur elsewhere in
the language.*
*33. FILLET band
tied around the
head.*
*36. FAVOURS pres-
ents, love tokens.*
MAUND basket.
*37. BEADED 1609
Quarto: bedded.*
39. MARGENT bank.
*40. USURY the prac-
tice of taking in-
terest on money,
adding money to
money.*
*42. CRIES SOME cries
out for some.*
*43. SCHEDULES
pieces of paper bear-
ing writing.*

45   Crack'd many a ring of posied gold and
        bone,
    Bidding them find their sepulchres in
        mud;
    Found yet moe letters sadly penn'd in
        blood,
    With sleided silk feat and affectedly
    Enswath'd and seal'd to curious secrecy.

50   These often bath'd she in her fluxive eyes,
    And often kiss'd, and often gan to tear;
    Cried, "O false blood, thou register of lies,
    What unapproved witness dost thou
        bear!
    Ink would have seem'd more black and
        damned here!"
55   This said, in top of rage the lines she
        rents,
    Big discontent so breaking their contents.

    A reverend man that graz'd his cattle
        nigh—
    Sometime a blusterer that the ruffle knew
    Of court, of city, and had let go by
60   The swiftest hours, observed as they
        flew—
    Towards this afflicted fancy fastly drew,
    And privileg'd by age, desires to know
    In brief the grounds and motives of her
        woe.

    So slides he down upon his grained bat,
65   And comely distant sits he by her side:
    When he again desires her, being sat,
    Her grievance with his hearing to divide:

45. POSIED *inscribed with mottoes or verses.*
47. MOE *more.*
48. SLEIDED *raw, not yet twisted into thread.* FEAT *neatly.* AFFECTEDLY *lovingly.*
49. CURIOUS *scrupulous.*
50. FLUXIVE *flowing.*
51. GAN TO TEAR *Emendation by Alexander Dyce (1798–1869); 1609 Quarto: gaue to teare.*
53. UNAPPROVED *not justified by proof.*
57. REVEREND *The word was used interchangeably with "reverent."*
58. SOMETIME *formerly.* RUFFLE *bustle, stir.*
61. FANCY *lovelorn lady.* FASTLY *near*
64. GRAINED BAT *staff showing the grain of the wood.*

If that from him there may be aught
    appli'd
Which may her suffering ecstasy assuage,
70 'Tis promis'd in the charity of age.

"Father," she says, "though in me you be-
    hold
The injury of many a blasting hour,
Let it not tell your judgment I am old;
Not age, but sorrow, over me hath power:
75 I might as yet have been a spreading
    flower,
Fresh to myself, if I had self-appli'd
Love to myself, and to no love beside.

"But woe is me! too early I attended
A youthful suit—it was to gain my
    grace—
80 Of one by nature's outwards so com-
    mended
That maidens' eyes stuck over all his face.
Love lack'd a dwelling and made him her
    place;
And when in his fair parts she did abide,
She was new lodg'd and newly deifi'd.

85 "His browny locks did hang in crooked
    curls,
And every light occasion of the wind
Upon his lips their silken parcels hurls.
What's sweet to do, to do will aptly find:
Each eye that saw him did enchant the
    mind;
90 For on his visage was in little drawn

69. ECSTASY *state of being beside one's self.*
78. ATTENDED *listened to.*
80. OF *Emendation by Thomas Tyr-whitt (1730–1786). 1609 Quarto: O.* NATURE'S OUTWARDS *natural outward appearance.*
86. OCCASION *movement, impact.*
88. *A way will easily be found to do a thing which is agreeable to do.*

What largeness thinks in Paradise was
    sawn.

"Small show of man was yet upon his chin;
    His phoenix down began but to appear,
    Like unshorn velvet, on that termless
      skin,
95   Whose bare out-bragg'd the web it seem'd
      to wear;
    Yet show'd his visage by that cost more
      dear;
    And nice affections wav'ring stood in
      doubt
    If best were as it was, or best without.

"His qualities were beauteous as his form,
100   For maiden-tongu'd he was, and thereof
      free;
    Yet, if men mov'd him, was he such a
      storm
    As oft 'twixt May and April is to see,
    When winds breathe sweet, unruly
      though they be.
    His rudeness so with his authoriz'd youth
105   Did livery falseness in a pride of truth.

"Well could he ride, and often men would
      say,
    'That horse his mettle from his rider
      takes;
    Proud of subjection, noble by the sway,
    What rounds, what bounds, what course,
      what stop he makes!'
110   And controversy hence a question takes,

91. SAWN *seen; or more probably, sown.*

93. PHOENIX *as incomparable as the phoenix.*

94. TERMLESS *timeless, untouched by time. For "term" in the sense of "period of time," see Sonnet 146, line 11.*

95. BARE *the cheeks under the young beard.*

WEB *beard.*

96. COST *both ornament and expense.*

DEAR *both precious and expensive.*

97. NICE AFFECTIONS *scrupulously accurate tastes.*

100. MAIDEN-TONGU'D *modest of speech.*

104. *his rudeness, justified by his youth, so.*

105. LIVERY *dress.*

108. NOBLE . . . SWAY *made noble by the young man's management of him.*

A LOVER'S COMPLAINT / 331

Whether the horse by him became his deed,

Or he his manage by th' well-doing steed.

"But quickly on this side the verdict went:

His real habitude gave life and grace

115 To appertainings and to ornament,

Accomplish'd in himself, not in his case;

All aids, themselves made fairer by their place,

Came for additions; yet their purpos'd trim

Piec'd not his grace but were all grac'd by him.

120 "So on the tip of his subduing tongue

All kind of arguments and question deep,

All replication prompt and reason strong,

For his advantage still did wake and sleep:

To make the weeper laugh, the laugher weep,

125 He had the dialect and different skill,

Catching all passions in his craft of will,

"That he did in the general bosom reign

Of young, of old; and sexes both enchanted,

To dwell with him in thoughts, or to remain

130 In personal duty, following where he haunted.

Consents bewitch'd, ere he desire, have granted,

111–112. whether the horse, through the rider's superb horsemanship, moved with perfection, or whether the perfection resulted from the horse's having been perfectly trained.

112. MANAGE the training and government of a horse.

114. REAL HABITUDE essential personality.

115. APPERTAININGS external attributes.

116. IN HIS CASE through circumstances.

118. CAME Emendation by George Sewell (1725); 1609 Quarto: Can. ADDITIONS enhancements. TRIM ornamentation.

119. PIEC'D comprised.

122. REPLICATION reply, repartee.

123. STILL always.

125. DIFFERENT diverse.

126. CRAFT OF WILL ability to influence and persuade.

127. GENERAL BOSOM hearts of the people.

130. WHERE HE HAUNTED the places he frequented.

And dialogu'd for him what he would say,
Ask'd their own wills and made their
   wills obey.

"Many there were that did his picture get,
135 To serve their eyes, and in it put their
   mind;
Like fools that in th' imagination set
The goodly objects which abroad they
   find
Of lands and mansions, theirs in thought
   assign'd,
And labouring in moe pleasures to bestow them
140 Than the true gouty landlord which doth
   owe them.

"So many have, that never touch'd his
   hand,
Sweetly suppos'd them mistress of his
   heart.
My woful self, that did in freedom stand
And was my own fee-simple, not in part,
145 What with his art in youth and youth in
   art,
Threw my affections in his charmed
   power,
Reserv'd the stalk and gave him all my
   flower.

"Yet did I not, as some my equals did,
Demand of him, nor being desir'd
   yielded;
150 Finding myself in honour so forbid,

132. DIALOGU'D
spoke both parts of
a conversation.
138. THEIRS . . . AS-
SIGN'D allotted to
themselves in
imagination.
139–140. And exert
themselves to em-
ploy the fancied
possessions more
pleasurably than the
arthritic landlord
who truly owns
them.
144. had complete,
not partial, power
over them.

With safest distance I mine honour
shielded.
Experience for me many bulwarks
builded
Of proofs new-bleeding, which remain'd
the foil
Of this false jewel, and his amorous spoil.

155 "But ah, who ever shunn'd by precedent
The destin'd ill she must herself assay?
Or forc'd examples, 'gainst her own con-
tent,
To put the by-past perils in her way?
Counsel may stop awhile what will not
stay;
160 For when we rage, advice is often seen
By blunting us to make our wits more
keen.

"Nor gives it satisfaction to our blood
That we must curb it upon others' proof;
To be forbod the sweets that seems so
good
165 For fear of harms that preach in our behoof.
O appetite, from judgment stand aloof!
The one a palate hath that needs will
taste,
Though Reason weep and cry 'It is thy
last.'

"For further I could say, 'This man's untrue,'

151. DISTANCE a
fencing term mean-
ing "cautious
restraint."
153. PROOFS
examples. FOIL the
thing against which
a jewel is placed to
set it off.
155. BY PRECEDENT
by learning from
example.
156. ASSAY undergo.
157. FORC'D seri-
ously considered.
159. STAY stand still.
160. RAGE are driv-
en by passion.
162. BLOOD passion.
163. PROOF experi-
ence.
164. FORBOD forbid-
den.
165. BEHOOF ad-
vantage.

170   And knew the patterns of his foul beguil-
             ing;
         Heard where his plants in others' or-
             chards grew;
         Saw how deceits were gilded in his smil-
             ing;
         Knew vows were ever brokers to defiling;
         Thought characters and words merely but
             art
175   And bastards of his foul adulterate heart.

         "And long upon these terms I held my city,
         Till thus he gan besiege me: 'Gentle maid,
         Have of my suff'ring youth some feeling
             pity
         And be not of my holy vows afraid;
180   That's to ye sworn to none was ever said,
         For feasts of love I have been call'd unto,
         Till now did ne'er invite nor never woo.

         " 'All my offences that abroad you see
         Are errors of the blood, none of the mind;
185   Love made them not; with acture they
             may be.
         Where neither party is nor true nor kind:
         They sought their shame that so their
             shame did find;
         And so much less of shame in me re-
             mains
         By how much of me their reproach con-
             tains.

190   " 'Among the many that mine eyes have
             seen,

170. PATTERNS
instances. BEGUIL-
ING seduction.
173. BROKERS pro-
curers.
174. CHARACTERS
letters. ART instru-
ments of craft.
182. WOO Manu-
script correction
made by Edward
Capell (1713–
1781) in his copy of
Bernard Lintott's
edition, 1709, and
followed by most
later editors. 1609
Quarto: vovv.
185. WITH . . . BE
They may exist in
act only.

Not one whose flame my heart so much as
    warm'd,
Or my affection put to th' smallest teen,
Or any of my leisures ever charm'd:
Harm have I done to them, but ne'er was
    harm'd;
195 Kept hearts in liveries, but mine own was
    free
And reign'd commanding in his mon-
    archy.

   " 'Look here what tributes wounded fancies
    sent me
Of pallid pearls and rubies red as blood,
Figuring that they their passions likewise
    lent me
200 Of grief and blushes, aptly understood
In bloodless white and the encrimson'd
    mood;
Effects of terror and dear modesty,
Encamp'd in hearts, but fighting out-
    wardly.

   " 'And, lo, behold these talents of their hair,
205 With twisted metal amorously em-
    pleach'd,
I have receiv'd from many a several fair,
Their kind acceptance weepingly be-
    seech'd,
With th' annexions of fair gems enrich'd,
And deep-brain'd sonnets that did am-
    plify
210 Each stone's dear nature, worth, and
    quality.

192. TEEN *pain*.
195. LIVERIES *servi-
tude. Livery is the
dress of a servant.*
196. HIS *its*.
197. FANCIES *mis-
tresses*.
200. UNDERSTOOD
symbolized.
204. TALENTS *cut-
tings of the lady's
hair made into
jewels by inter-
twining it with
precious metal*.
205. EMPLEACH'D
interwoven.
206. SEVERAL *dif-
ferent*.

" 'The diamond—why, 'twas beautiful and hard,
  Whereto his invis'd properties did tend;
  The deep-green em'rald, in whose fresh regard
  Weak sights their sickly radiance do a-mend;
215 The heaven-hu'd sapphire, and the opal blend
  With objects manifold: each several stone,
  With wit well blazon'd, smil'd or made some moan.

" 'Lo, all these trophies of affections hot,
  Of pensiv'd and subdu'd desires the tender,
220 Nature hath charg'd me that I hoard them not,
  But yield them up where I myself must render,
  That is, to you, my origin and ender;
  For these of force must your oblations be,
  Since I their altar, you enpatron me.

225 " 'O, then, advance of yours that phraseless hand
  Whose white weighs down the airy scale of praise;
  Take all these similes to your own command,
  Hallow'd with sighs that burning lungs did raise;
  What me, your minister, for you obeys,

230   Works under you; and to your audit
        comes
    Their distract parcels in combined sums.

    " 'Lo, this device was sent me from a nun,
    Or sister sanctifi'd, of holiest note,
    Which late her noble suit in court did
        shun,
235   Whose rarest havings made the blossoms
        dote;
    For she was sought by spirits of richest
        coat,
    But kept cold distance, and did thence re-
        move
    To spend her living in eternal love.

    " 'But O my sweet, what labour is't to leave
240   The thing we have not, mast'ring what
        not strives,
    Paling the place which did no form re-
        ceive,
    Playing patient sports in unconstrained
        gyves?
    She that her fame so to herself contrives,
    The scars of battle scapeth by the flight
245   And makes her absence valiant, not her
        might.

    " 'O pardon me, in that my boast is true:
    The accident which brought me to her eye
    Upon the moment did her force subdue,
    And now she would the caged cloister fly:
250   Religious love put out religion's eye:

YOU *Whatever obeys me, your minister, instead of obeying you directly, works under you.*

234. SUIT *suitors.*

235. HAVINGS *endowments, possessions.* BLOSSOMS *young men of the court.*

236. COAT *attire.* See The Rape of Lucrece, *line 205.*

241. PALING *Emendation by Edmund Malone (1741–1812). 1609 Quarto: Playing— an obvious corruption, the compositor having caught "Playing" from the line below and substituted it for the word or phrase in the text. The emended line means "enclosing the heart that had never received the impression of love."*

242. UNCONSTRAINED *offering no constraint.*

243. *She who keeps her fame to herself, that is, avoids fame or reputation.*

250. RELIGIOUS LOVE *Love is here regarded as holy in itself. See Sonnet 31, line 6.*

Not to be tempted, would she be enur'd,
And now, to tempt, all liberty procur'd.

  " 'How mighty then you are, O hear me tell!
    The broken bosoms that to me belong
255   Have emptied all their fountains in my
       well,
    And mine I pour your ocean all among:
    I strong o'er them, and you o'er me being
       strong,
    Must for your victory us all congest,
    As compound love to physic your cold
       breast.

260 " 'My parts had pow'r to charm a sacred nun,
    Who, disciplin'd, ay, dieted in grace,
    Believ'd her eyes when they t' assail be-
       gun,
    All vows and consecrations giving place:
    O most potential love! vow, bond, nor
       space
265   In thee hath neither sting, knot, nor con-
       fine,
    For thou art all, and all things else are
       thine.

  " 'When thou impressest, what are precepts
      worth
    Of stale example? When thou wilt in-
      flame,
    How coldly those impediments stand
      forth
270   Of wealth, of filial fear, law, kindred,
      fame!

251. ENUR'D *inured, hardened. Many editors emend to immur'd.*
252. PROCUR'D *1609 Quarto: procure.*
258. CONGEST *receive, gather together.*
259. TO PHYSIC *to cure.*
260. NUN *Capell manuscript. See line 182, note. 1609 Quarto: Sunne.*
264. POTENTIAL *powerful.*
267. IMPRESSEST *compel into service.*

Love's arms are peace, 'gainst rule, 'gainst
sense, 'gainst shame;
And sweetens, in the suff'ring pangs it
bears,
The aloes of all forces, shocks, and fears.

" 'Now all these hearts that do on mine depend,
275   Feeling it break, with bleeding groans
they pine;
And supplicant their sighs to you extend,
To leave the batt'ry that you make 'gainst
mine,
Lending soft audience to my sweet design,
And credent soul to that strong bonded
oath
280   That shall prefer and undertake my troth.'

"This said, his wat'ry eyes he did dismount,
Whose sights till then were levell'd on
my face;
Each cheek a river running from a fount
With brinish current downward flow'd
apace:
285   O how the channel to the stream gave
grace!
Who glaz'd with crystal gate the glowing
roses
That flame through water which their
hue incloses.

"O father, what a hell of witchcraft lies
In the small orb of one particular tear!
290   But with the inundation of the eyes

273. ALOES *juice derived from aloe leaves. Aloes was a symbol of bitterness.*
276. SUPPLICANT *beseechingly.*
277. BATT'RY *assault.*
278. AUDIENCE *hearing.*
279. CREDENT *believing.*
280. PREFER *present.* UNDERTAKE *guarantee.*
281. DISMOUNT *lower.*
286. GATE *A gate is any natural, narrow passage through which water flows. Here the streams of crystal tears glaze the rosy cheeks over which they flow. The word is capable of various interpretations, but the one given is Shakespearean. See* Hamlet, *Act I, scene 5, line 67, "The natural gates and alleys of the body."*
287. HUE *See Sonnet 26, line 7, note.*

What rocky heart to water will not wear?
What breast so cold that is not warmed
    here?
O cleft effect! cold modesty, hot wrath,
Both fire from hence and chill extincture
    hath.

295 "For, lo, his passion, but an art of craft,
Even there resolv'd my reason into tears;
There my white stole of chastity I daff'd,
Shook off my sober guards and civil fears;
Appear to him as he to me appears,
300 All melting; though our drops this dif-
    f'rence bore—
His poison'd me, and mine did him re-
    store.

"In him a plenitude of subtle matter,
Applied to cautels, all strange forms re-
    ceives,
Of burning blushes, or of weeping water,
305 Or swooning paleness; and he takes and
    leaves,
In either's aptness, as it best deceives,
To blush at speeches rank, to weep at
    woes,
Or to turn white and swoon at tragic
    shows;

"That not a heart which in his level came
310 Could scape the hail of his all-hurting
    aim,
Showing fair nature is both kind and
    tame;

293. CLEFT *divided.*
297. DAFF'D *put off.*
The modern "doff"
is an elision of "do
off."
298. CIVIL *proper,*
decorous.
303. CAUTELS *de-*
ceits.
305. SWOONING *Ca-*
pell manuscript. See
line 182, note.
1609 Quarto:
sounding.
308. SWOON *Capell*
manuscript. See line
182, note. 1609
Quarto: sound.
309. LEVEL *line of*
fire.

And veil'd in them, did win whom he
    would maim:
Against the thing he sought he would
    exclaim:
When he most burn'd in heart-wish'd
    luxury,
315   He preach'd pure maid and prais'd cold
    chastity.

"Thus merely with the garment of a grace,
    The naked and concealed fiend he
      cover'd;
    That th' unexperient gave the tempter
      place,
    Which like a cherubin above them
      hover'd.
320   Who, young and simple, would not be so
    lover'd?
    Ay me! I fell; and yet do question make
    What I should do again for such a sake.

"O, that infected moisture of his eye,
    O, that false fire which in his cheek so
      glow'd,
325   O, that forc'd thunder from his heart did
    fly,
    O, that sad breath his spongy lungs
      bestow'd,
    O, all that borrow'd motion seeming
      ow'd,
    Would yet again betray the fore-betray'd
    And new pervert a reconciled maid!"

312. THEM *The
"strange forms" of
line 303.*
314. LUXURY *lech-
ery.*
316. GRACE *heavenly
virtue.*
318. UNEXPERIENT
inexperienced.
GAVE ... PLACE *gave
a place to the
tempter, received
him.*
323. INFECTED *in-
fectious.*
327. BORROW'D *put
on, pretended.*
OW'D *owned.*

VENUS AND ADONIS

VILIA MIRETUR VULGUS MIHI FLAVUS APOLLO
POCULA CASTALIA PLENA MINISTRET AQUA.
Ovid, Amores *1. 15. 11. 35–36*

Let base-conceited wits admire vain things:
Fair Phoebus lead me to the Muses' springs.
MARLOWE'S TRANSLATION, *& Ovid's Elegies.*

5. BURTHEN *burden.*

9. GRAVER LABOUR *The graver labor was to be* The Rape of Lucrece, *published the following year.*

9–10. THE FIRST HEIR OF MY INVENTION *Shakespeare had already written some plays, but this was to be his first excursion into the world of polite letters.*

12. EAR *plough.*

TO THE
RIGHT HONOURABLE HENRY WRIOTHESLEY,
EARL OF SOUTHAMPTON,
AND BARON OF TITCHFIELD.

Right Honourable,

    I know not how I shall offend in dedi-
cating my unpolish'd lines to your Lordship, nor how the world will censure me
for choosing so strong a prop to support
5   so weak a burthen; only, if your Honour
seem but pleased, I account myself highly
praised, and vow to take advantage of all
idle hours till I have honoured you with
some graver labour. But if the first heir of
10   my invention prove deformed, I shall be
sorry it had so noble a godfather, and
never after ear so barren a land, for fear it
yield me still so bad a harvest. I leave it
to your honourable survey, and your
15   Honour to your heart's content; which I
wish may always answer your own wish
and the world's hopeful expectation.

      Your Honour's in all duty,
        WILLIAM SHAKESPEARE.

Even as the sun with purple-colour'd face
Had ta'en his last leave of the weeping
  morn,
Rose-cheek'd Adonis hied him to the
  chase;
Hunting he lov'd, but love he laugh'd to
  scorn:
    Sick-thoughted Venus makes amain
    unto him
    And like a bold-fac'd suitor gins to
    woo him.

"Thrice fairer than myself," thus she
  began,
"The field's chief flower, sweet above compare,
Stain to all nymphs, more lovely than a
  man,
More white and red than doves or roses
  are;
    Nature that made thee, with herself
    at strife,
    Saith that the world hath ending
    with thy life.

"Vouchsafe, thou wonder, to alight thy
  steed
And rein his proud head to the saddle-
  bow;
If thou wilt deign this favour, for thy
  meed
A thousand honey secrets shalt thou
  know:

1. PURPLE-COLOUR'D
*In the poetic diction
of the time, "pur-
ple" was used for
any rich color but
most often for red.*
5. SICK-THOUGHTED
sick with love.
AMAIN *swiftly.*
9. STAIN *by eclipsing
them.*
15. MEED *reward.*

Here come and sit, where never
serpent hisses,
And being set, I'll smother thee with
kisses,
"And yet not cloy thy lips with loath'd
satiety,
20   But rather famish them amid their plenty,
Making them red and pale with fresh
variety;
Ten kisses short as one, one long as
twenty:
A summer's day will seem an hour
but short,
Being wasted in such time-beguiling
sport."

25   With this she seizeth on his sweating
palm,
The precedent of pith and livelihood,
And trembling in her passion, calls it
balm,
Earth's sovereign salve to do a gooddess
good:
Being so enrag'd, desire doth lend
her force
30   Courageously to pluck him from his
horse.

Over one arm the lusty courser's rein,
Under her other was the tender boy,
Who blush'd and pouted in a dull disdain,
With leaden appetite, unapt to toy;
35   She red and hot as coals of glowing
fire,

26. PRECEDENT *sign.*
PITH *strength, force.*
LIVELIHOOD *spirit,*
animation.

He red for shame, but frosty in
    desire.

The studded bridle on a ragged bough
Nimbly she fastens. (O, how quick is
    love!)
The steed is stalled up, and even now
40   To tie the rider she begins to prove:
      Backward she push'd him, as she
        would be thrust,
      And govern'd him in strength,
        though not in lust.

So soon was she along as he was down,
Each leaning on their elbows and their
    hips:
45   Now doth she stroke his cheek, now doth
    he frown,
And gins to chide, but soon she stops his
    lips;
      And kissing speaks, with lustful
        language broken,
      "If thou wilt chide, thy lips shall
        never open."

He burns with bashful shame; she with
    her tears
50   Doth quench the maiden burning of his
    cheeks;
Then with her windy sighs and golden
    hairs
To fan and blow them dry again she
    seeks:

40. PROVE *try*.
43. ALONG *at full
length on the
ground.*

He saith she is immodest, blames her
    miss;
What follows more she murthers
    with a kiss.

55   Even as an empty eagle, sharp by fast,
Tires with her beak on feathers, flesh,
    and bone,
Shaking her wings, devouring all in
    haste,
Till either gorge be stuff'd or prey be
    gone;
    Even so she kiss'd his brow, his
      cheek, his chin,
60   And where she ends she doth anew
      begin.

Forc'd to content, but never to obey,
Panting he lies and breatheth in her face;
She feedeth on the steam as on a prey
And calls it heavenly moisture, air of
    grace,
65   Wishing her cheeks were gardens
      full of flowers,
      So they were dew'd with such distill-
      ing showers.

Look how a bird lies tangled in a net,
So fast'ned in her arms Adonis lies;
Pure shame and aw'd resistance made
    him fret,
70   Which bred more beauty in his angry
    eyes:
      Rain added to a river that is rank

53. MISS *misbe-
havior.*
55. SHARP BY FAST
*appetite sharpened
by fasting.*
56. TIRES *tears.*
61. CONTENT *accept
the situation.*
67. LOOK HOW *just
as. See line 815.*
71. RANK *at the full.*

Perforce will force it overflow the
bank.

Still she entreats, and prettily entreats,
For to a pretty ear she tunes her tale;
75   Still is he sullen, still he low'rs and frets,
'Twixt crimson shame and anger ashy-
pale;
    Being red, she loves him best; and
    being white,
    Her best is better'd with a more de-
    light.

Look how he can, she cannot choose but
love;
80   And by her fair immortal hand she swears
From his soft bosom never to remove
Till he take truce with her contending
tears,
    Which long have rain'd, making her
    cheeks all wet;
    And one sweet kiss shall pay this
    comptless debt.

85   Upon this promise did he raise his chin,
Like a divedapper peering through a
wave,
Who being look'd on, ducks as quickly
in;
So offers he to give what she did crave;
    But when her lips were ready for his
    pay,
90   He winks and turns his lips another
way.

78. MORE *greater.*
84. COMPTLESS
*countless, beyond
reckoning.*
86. DIVEDAPPER *a
species of grebe, a
little water bird
whose habits Shake-
speare accurately de-
scribes.*
90. WINKS *shuts his
eyes.*

Never did passenger in summer's heat
More thirst for drink than she for this
    good turn.
Her help she sees, but help she cannot
    get;
She bathes in water, yet her fire must
    burn:
95   "O, pity," gan she cry, "flint-hearted
        boy!
        'Tis but a kiss I beg; why art thou
        coy?

"I have been woo'd, as I entreat thee now,
Even by the stern and direful god of war,
Whose sinewy neck in battle ne'er did
    bow,
100 Who conquers where he comes in every
        jar;
        Yet hath he been my captive and my
        slave
        And begg'd for that which thou un-
        ask'd shalt have.

"Over my altars hath he hung his lance,
His batt'red shield, his uncontrolled crest,
105 And for my sake hath learn'd to sport and
        dance,
        To toy, to wanton, dally, smile, and jest,
        Scorning his churlish drum and
        ensign red,
        Making my arms his field, his tent
        my bed.

98. GOD OF WAR
Mars.
100. JAR *encounter.*
107. CHURLISH
rough, brutal.

"Thus he that overrul'd I oversway'd,
110   Leading him prisoner in a red rose chain:
Strong-temper'd steel his stronger
    strength obey'd,
Yet was he servile to my coy disdain.
        O, be not proud, nor brag not of thy
            might,
        For mast'ring her that foil'd the god
            of fight.

115   "Touch but my lips with those fair lips of
        thine—
Though mine be not so fair, yet are they
    red—
The kiss shall be thine own as well as
    mine:
What see'st thou in the ground? Hold up
    thy head;
        Look in mine eyeballs; there thy
            beauty lies;
120   Then why not lips on lips, since eyes
            in eyes?

"Art thou asham'd to kiss? Then wink
    again,
And I will wink; so shall the day seem
    night;
Love keeps his revels where there are but
    twain;
Be bold to play, our sport is not in sight:
125   These blue-vein'd violets whereon
            we lean

121. WINK close
your eyes.

Never can blab, nor know not what
we mean.

"The tender spring upon thy tempting lip
Shows thee unripe, yet mayst thou well
be tasted:
Make use of time, let not advantage slip;
130 Beauty within itself should not be wasted:
Fair flowers that are not gath'red in
their prime
Rot and consume themselves in little
time.

"Were I hard-favour'd, foul, or wrinkled-
old,
Ill-nurtur'd, crooked, churlish, harsh in
voice,
135 O'erworn, despised, rheumatic, and cold,
Thick-sighted, barren, lean and lacking
juice,
Then mightst thou pause, for then I
were not for thee;
But having no defects, why do'st
abhor me?

"Thou canst not see one wrinkle in my
brow;
140 Mine eyes are grey and bright and quick
in turning;
My beauty as the spring doth yearly grow,
My flesh is soft and plump, my marrow
burning;

127. SPRING *young growth.*
136. JUICE *the fluid of animal bodies.*
140. GREY *blue-gray.* See line 482.

My smooth moist hand, were it with
thy hand felt,
Would in thy palm dissolve or seem
to melt.

145 "Bid me discourse, I will enchant thine ear,
Or like a fairy trip upon the green,
Or like a nymph with long dishevell'd
hair
Dance on the sands, and yet no footing
seen:
Love is a spirit all compact of fire,
150 Not gross to sink, but light, and will
aspire.

"Witness this primrose bank whereon I lie;
These forceless flowers like sturdy trees
support me;
Two strengthless doves will draw me
through the sky
From morn till night, even where I list to
sport me:
155 Is love so light, sweet boy, and may
it be
That thou shouldst think it heavy
unto thee?

"Is thine own heart to thine own face
affected?
Can thy right hand seize love upon thy
left?
Then woo thyself, be of thyself rejected,

143. MOIST HAND
*taken as indicative
of passion. See lines
25–26.*
149. COMPACT *composed.*
150. ASPIRE *rise,
tower.*
157. TO . . . AFFECTED *in love with
thine own face.*

160   Steal thine own freedom, and complain
       on theft:
         Narcissus so himself himself forsook,
         And died to kiss his shadow in the
           brook.

    "Torches are made to light, jewels to wear,
      Dainties to taste, fresh beauty for the use,
165   Herbs for their smell, and sappy plants to
       bear;
      Things growing to themselves are
       growth's abuse:
         Seeds spring from seeds and beauty
           breedeth beauty;
         Thou wast begot; to get it is thy
           duty.

    "Upon the earth's increase why shouldst
       thou feed
170   Unless the earth with thy increase be fed?
      By law of nature thou art bound to breed,
      That thine may live when thou thyself
       art dead;
         And so, in spite of death, thou dost
           survive,
         In that thy likeness still is left alive."

175   By this, the lovesick queen began to
       sweat,
      For where they lay the shadow had for-
       sook them,
      And Titan, tired in the midday heat,

160. ON of.
161. NARCISSUS the beautiful youth who disdained the nymphs because he loved himself. He fell in love with his own image reflected in a pool. See The Rape of Lucrece, lines 265–266. The early sonnets suggest that the young man does not marry because he is narcissistic. See Sonnet 3, line 8.
165. SAPPY full of vital fluid.
169–172. See the arguments urging the young man to marry and have children in Sonnets 1–17.
177. TITAN the sun. TIRED possibly "attired," though more probably Shakespeare attributes to the sun the weariness it inflicts on man.

With burning eye did hotly overlook
  them,
    Wishing Adonis had his team to
      guide,
180   So he were like him and by Venus'
      side.

And now Adonis with a lazy spright,
And with a heavy, dark, disliking eye,
His low'ring brows o'erwhelming his fair
  sight,
Like misty vapours when they blot the
  sky,
185   Souring his cheeks, cries, "Fie, no
      more of love!
    The sun doth burn my face; I must
      remove."

"Ay me," quoth Venus, "young, and so unkind!
What bare excuses mak'st thou to be
  gone!
I'll sigh celestial breath, whose gentle
  wind
190 Shall cool the heat of this descending sun:
    I'll make a shadow for thee of my
      hairs;
    If they burn too, I'll quench them
      with my tears.

"The sun that shines from heaven shines
  but warm,

And, lo, I lie between that sun and thee:

195 The heat I have from thence doth little
harm,

Thine eye darts forth the fire that burneth
me,

And were I not immortal, life were
done

Between this heavenly and earthly
sun.

"Art thou obdurate, flinty, hard as steel?

200 Nay, more than flint, for stone at rain relenteth:

Art thou a woman's son, and canst not
feel

What 'tis to love, how want of love tor-
menteth?

O, had thy mother borne so hard a
mind,

She had not brought forth thee, but
died unkind!

205 "What am I that thou shouldst contemn
me this?

Or what great danger dwells upon my
suit?

What were thy lips the worse for one
poor kiss?

Speak, fair; but speak fair words, or else
be mute:

Give me one kiss, I'll give it thee
again,

210 And one for int'rest, if thou wilt have
twain.

200. RELENTETH
grows less hard.
201. A WOMAN'S SON
*See Sonnet 41, lines
7–9.*
204. UNKIND *unnat-
ural.*
205. CONTEMN
despise. THIS *like
this.*
208. FAIR *fair one.*

"Fie, liveless picture, cold and senseless
  stone,
Well-painted idol, image dull and dead,
Statue contenting but the eye alone,
Thing like a man, but of no woman bred:
215   Thou art no man, though of a man's
           complexion,
         For men will kiss even by their own
           direction."

This said, impatience chokes her pleading tongue,
And swelling passion doth provoke a
  pause;
Red cheeks and fiery eyes blaze forth her
  wrong;
220 Being judge in love, she cannot right her
    cause:
         And now she weeps, and now she
           fain would speak,
         And now her sobs do her intend-
           ments break.

Sometime she shakes her head, and then
  his hand;
Now gazeth she on him, now on the
  ground;
225 Sometime her arms infold him like a
    band:
She would, he will not in her arms be
  bound;
         And when from thence he struggles
           to be gone,
         She locks her lily fingers one in one.

211. LIVELESS PIC-
TURE *lifeless picture,
image of a man.*
215. COMPLEXION
*outward appear-
ance.*
216. DIRECTION *voli-
tion.*
220. RIGHT *do jus-
tice to.*
222. INTENDMENTS
intentions to speak.
BREAK *interrupt.*

"Fondling," she saith, "since I have hemm'd thee here

230 Within the circuit of this ivory pale,
I'll be a park, and thou shalt be my deer;
Feed where thou wilt, on mountain or in dale;
Graze on my lips; and if those hills be dry,
Stray lower, where the pleasant fountains lie.

235 "Within this limit is relief enough,
Sweet bottom-grass, and high delightful plain,
Round rising hillocks, brakes obscure and rough,
To shelter thee from tempest and from rain:
Then be my deer, since I am such a park,
240 No dog shall rouse thee, though a thousand bark."

At this Adonis smiles as in disdain,
That in each cheek appears a pretty dimple:
Love made those hollows, if himself were slain,
He might be buried in a tomb so simple,
245 Foreknowing well, if there he came to lie,
Why, there Love liv'd, and there he could not die.

229. FONDLING *presumably a term of address, although it may describe Venus's actions. The word does not occur elsewhere in Shakespeare.*
240. ROUSE *drive an animal from its lair.*
243. IF HIMSELF *so that if he himself.*

These lovely caves, these round enchant-
    ing pits,
Open'd their mouths to swallow Venus'
    liking.
Being mad before, how doth she now for
    wits?
250   Struck dead at first, what needs a second
    striking?
      Poor queen of love, in thine own
      law forlorn,
      To love a cheek that smiles at thee
      in scorn!

Now which way shall she turn? what
    shall she say?
Her words are done, her woes the more
    increasing;
255   The time is spent, her object will away
And from her twining arms doth urge
    releasing.
      "Pity," she cries, "some favour, some
      remorse!"
      Away he springs, and hasteth to his
      horse.

But, lo, from forth a copse that neigh-
    bours by,
260   A breeding jennet, lusty, young, and
    proud,
Adonis' trampling courser doth espy,
And forth she rushes, snorts and neighs
    aloud:

248. LIKING *desire.*
260. PROUD *full of
vigor. "In pride"
means "in heat"*

The strong-neck'd steed, being tied
   unto a tree,
Breaketh his rein, and to her straight
   goes he.

265 Imperiously he leaps, he neighs, he
      bounds,
And now his woven girths he breaks
   asunder;
The bearing earth with his hard hoof he
   wounds,
Whose hollow womb resounds like
   heaven's thunder;
      The iron bit he crusheth 'tween his
         teeth,
270   Controlling what he was controlled
         with.

His ears up-prick'd; his braided hanging
   mane
Upon his compass'd crest now stand on
   end;
His nostrils drink the air, and forth
   again,
As from a furnace, vapours doth he send;
275   His eye, which scornfully glisters
         like fire,
         Shows his hot courage and his high
            desire.

Sometime he trots, as if he told the steps,
With gentle majesty and modest pride;
Anon he rears upright, curvets, and leaps,

277. TOLD *counted*.
279. CURVETS
bounds.

280 As who should say, "Lo, thus my strength is tried,
　　And this I do to captivate the eye
　　Of the fair breeder that is standing by."

What recketh he his rider's angry stir,
His flattering "Holla" or his "Stand, I say"?
285 What cares he now for curb or pricking spur,
For rich caparisons or trappings gay?
　　He sees his love, and nothing else he sees,
　　For nothing else with his proud sight agrees.

Look when a painter would surpass the life
290 In limning out a well-proportion'd steed,
His art with nature's workmanship at strife,
As if the dead the living should exceed;
　　So did this horse excel a common one
　　In shape, in courage, colour, pace, and bone.

295 Round-hoof'd, short-jointed, fetlocks shag and long,
Broad breast, full eye, small head, and nostril wide,
High crest, short ears, straight legs and passing strong,

286. CAPARISONS *covering laid over the saddle.*
289. LOOK WHEN *whenever.*
290. LIMNING OUT *portraying.*
295. FETLOCKS *the part of a horse's leg at the joint next to the foot; it is marked by a tuft of hair.*
297. CREST *the ridge of a horse's neck.*

Thin mane, thick tail, broad buttock,
  tender hide:
    Look what a horse should have he
      did not lack,
    Save a proud rider on so proud a
      back.

Sometime he scuds far off, and there he
  stares;
Anon he starts at stirring of a feather;
To bid the wind a base he now prepares,
And whe'r he run or fly they know not
  whether,
    For through his mane and tail the
      high wind sings,
    Fanning the hairs, who wave like
      feath'red wings.

He looks upon his love and neighs unto
  her;
She answers him, as if she knew his mind:
Being proud, as females are, to see him
  woo her,
She puts on outward strangeness, seems
  unkind,
    Spurns at his love and scorns the
      heat he feels,
    Beating his kind embracements with
      her heels.

Then like a melancholy malcontent,
He vails his tail, that, like a falling
  plume,

300

305

310

299. LOOK WHAT
whatever.
301. SCUDS *runs
swiftly.*
303. BID THE WIND
A BASE *outrun the
wind. Base, some-
times called prison
base, was a game in
which players ran
for the bases.
American children
call it prisoner's
base.*
304. WHE'R
whether.
314. VAILS *lets fall.*

315 Cool shadow to his melting buttock lent;
He stamps, and bites the poor flies in his
fume.
His love, perceiving how he is
enrag'd,
Grew kinder, and his fury was
assuag'd.

His testy master goeth about to take him,
320 When, lo, the unback'd breeder, full of
fear,
Jealous of catching, swiftly doth forsake
him,
With her the horse, and left Adonis there:
As they were mad, unto the wood
they hie them,
Outstripping crows that strive to
overfly them.

325 All swol'n with chafing, down Adonis
sits,
Banning his boist'rous and unruly beast:
And now the happy season once more fits
That lovesick Love by pleading may be
blest;
For lovers say the heart hath treble
wrong
330 When it is barr'd the aidance of the
tongue.

316. FUME *rage.*
321. JEALOUS *fear-
ful.*
322. WITH HER THE
HORSE *the horse
went with her.*
326. BANNING *curs-
ing.*

An oven that is stopp'd, or river stay'd,
Burneth more hotly, swelleth with more
rage;

So of concealed sorrow may be said:
Free vent of words love's fire doth assuage,
    But when the heart's attorney once is
    mute,
    The client breaks, as desperate in his
    suit.

He sees her coming and begins to glow,
Even as a dying coal revives with wind,
And with his bonnet hides his angry
  brow,
Looks on the dull earth with disturbed
  mind,
    Taking no notice that she is so nigh,
    For all askance he holds her in his
    eye.

O what a sight it was, wistly to view
How she came stealing to the wayward
  boy!
To note the fighting conflict of her hue,
How white and red each other did de-
  stroy!
    But now her cheek was pale, and by
    and by
    It flash'd forth fire, as lightning from
    the sky.

Now was she just before him as he sat,
And like a lowly lover down she kneels;
With one fair hand she heaveth up his
  hat,

335

340

345

350

343. WISTLY *atten-tively.*
344. WAYWARD *ca-pricious and obstin-ate.*
347. BY AND BY *presently.*

Her other tender hand his fair cheek
    feels:
        His tend'rer cheek receives her soft
            hand's print
        As apt as new-fall'n snow takes any
            dint.

355   O what a war of looks was then between
        them!
    Her eyes petitioners to his eyes suing,
    His eyes saw her eyes as they had not seen
        them;
    Her eyes woo'd still, his eyes disdain'd the
        wooing;
        And all this dumb play had his acts
            made plain
360   With tears, chorus-like her eyes did
            rain.

Full gently now she takes him by the
    hand,
    A lily prison'd in a jail of snow,
    Or ivory in an alablaster band;
    So white a friend engirts so white a foe:
365   This beauteous combat, wilful and
            unwilling,
        Show'd like two silver doves that sit
            a-billing.

Once more the engine of her thoughts be-
    gan:
    "O fairest mover on this mortal round,
    Would thou wert as I am, and I a man,

354. DINT *impression.*
359. HIS *its.*
367. ENGINE OF
HER THOUGHTS
tongue.

My heart all whole as thine, thy heart my
    wound;
      For one sweet look thy help I would
        assure thee,
      Though nothing but my body's bane
        would cure thee."

"Give me my hand," saith he; "why dost
    thou feel it?"
"Give me my heart," saith she, "and thou
    shalt have it;
O, give it me, lest thy hard heart do steel
    it,
And being steel'd, soft sighs can never
    grave it:
      Then love's deep groans I never shall
        regard,
      Because Adonis' heart hath made
        mine hard."

"For shame," he cries, "let go, and let me
    go;
My day's delight is past, my horse is gone,
And 'tis your fault I am bereft him so:
I pray you hence, and leave me here
    alone;
      For all my mind, my thought, my
        busy care,
      Is how to get my palfrey from the
        mare."

Thus she replies: "Thy palfrey, as he
    should,
Welcomes the warm approach of sweet
    desire:

370

375

380

385

372. MY BODY'S
BANE *the destruc-
tion of my body.*
376. STEEL'D *hard-
ened, with a pun on
"steal."* GRAVE *to
cut slightly, as in
engraving.*

Affection is the coal that must be cool'd;
Else, suffer'd, it will set the heart on fire:
    The sea hath bounds, but deep desire
    hath none;
390   Therefore no marvel though thy
    horse be gone.

"How like a jade he stood, tied to a tree,
Servilely master'd with a leathern rein!
But when he saw his love, his youth's fair
    fee,
He held such petty bondage in disdain,
395   Throwing the base thong from his
    bending crest,
    Enfranchising his mouth, his back,
    his breast.

"Who sees his true-love in her naked bed,
Teaching the sheets a whiter hue than
    white,
But, when his glutton eye so full hath fed,
400 His other agents aim at like delight?
    Who is so faint that dares not be so
    bold
    To touch the fire, the weather being
    cold?

"Let me excuse thy courser, gentle boy;
And learn of him, I heartily beseech thee,
405 To take advantage on presented joy;
Though I were dumb, yet his proceedings
    teach thee:
    O, learn to love; the lesson is but
    plain,

387. AFFECTION *passion.*
388. SUFFER'D *borne.*
391. JADE *term of contempt for a worthless horse.*
393. FEE *reward.*
396. ENFRANCHISING *setting free.*
403. COURSER *a fast horse, a runner.*
405. ON *of.*

And once made perfect, never lost
    again."

"I know not love," quoth he, "nor will not
    know it,
410   Unless it be a boar, and then I chase it;
'Tis much to borrow, and I will not owe
    it;
My love to love is love but to disgrace it;
    For I have heard it is a life in death,
    That laughs, and weeps, and all but
       with a breath.

415   "Who wears a garment shapeless and un-
    finish'd?
Who plucks the bud before one leaf put
    forth?
If springing things be any jot diminish'd,
They wither in their prime, prove noth-
    ing worth:
    The colt that's back'd and burthen'd
      being young
420   Loseth his pride and never waxeth
      strong.

"You hurt my hand with wringing; let us
    part,
And leave this idle theme, this bootless
    chat:
Remove your siege from my unyielding
    heart;
To love's alarms it will not ope the gate:
425   Dismiss your vows, your feigned
      tears, your flatt'ry;

412. *My attitude to-
ward love is only a
desire to discredit it.*
417. SPRINGING
growing.
422. BOOTLESS *fruit-
less, useless.*

For where a heart is hard they make
    no batt'ry."

"What! canst thou talk?" quoth she, "hast
    thou a tongue?
O, would thou hadst not, or I had no
    hearing!
Thy mermaid's voice hath done me
    double wrong;
430   I had my load before, now press'd with
    bearing:
        Melodious discord, heavenly tune
          harsh sounding,
        Ear's deep-sweet music, and heart's
          deep-sore wounding.

"Had I no eyes but ears, my ears would love
That inward beauty and invisible;
435   Or were I deaf, thy outward parts would
    move
Each part in me that were but sensible:
        Though neither eyes nor ears, to hear
          nor see,
        Yet should I be in love by touching
          thee.

"Say that the sense of feeling were bereft
    me,
440   And that I could not see, nor hear, nor
    touch,
And nothing but the very smell were left
    me,
Yet would my love to thee be still as
    much;

426. BATTR'Y *assault,
and by extension, a
successful assault.*
429. MERMAID'S
*commonly used for
sirens.*
430. *The meaning is
that Venus had born
a burden before and
that Adonis has
now added to it. He
had previously re-
jected her, but now
(lines 409–426) he
rejects love itself.*
437. THOUGH
NEITHER *though I
had neither.*

For from the stillitory of thy face ex-
celling
Comes breath perfum'd that breed-
eth love by smelling.

445 "But, O, what banquet wert thou to the
taste,
Being nurse and feeder of the other four!
Would they not wish the feast might ever
last
And bid Suspicion double-lock the door,
Lest Jealousy, that sour unwelcome
guest,
450 Should by his stealing in disturb the
feast?"

Once more the ruby-colour'd portal
open'd
Which to his speech did honey passage
yield;
Like a red morn, that ever yet betoken'd
Wrack to the seaman, tempest to the field,
455 Sorrow to shepherds, woe unto the
birds,
Gusts and foul flaws to herdmen and
to herds.

This ill presage advisedly she marketh:
Even as the wind is hush'd before it raineth,
Or as the wolf doth grin before he bark-
eth,
460 Or as the berry breaks before it staineth,

443. STILLITORY *de-
vice used for distill-
ing, alembic. Here
the word is disyllab-
ic.*
454. WRACK *ship-
wreck.*
456. FLAWS *blasts.*
459. GRIN *snarl,
show its teeth.*
460. STAINETH *dis-
colors.*

Or like the deadly bullet of a gun,
His meaning struck her ere his words
begun;

And at his look she flatly falleth down,
For looks kill love, and love by looks re-
viveth;
465 A smile recures the wounding of a frown:
But blessed bankrout that by love so
thriveth!
The silly boy, believing she is dead,
Claps her pale cheek till clapping
makes it red,

And all amaz'd brake off his late intent,
470 For sharply he did think to reprehend her,
Which cunning love did wittily prevent:
Fair fall the wit that can so well defend
her!
For on the grass she lies as she were
slain
Till his breath breatheth life in her
again.

475 He wrings her nose, he strikes her on the
cheeks,
He bends her fingers, holds her pulses
hard,
He chafes her lips; a thousand ways he
seeks
To mend the hurt that his unkindness
marr'd:

463. FLATLY FALL-
ETH DOWN *falls flat
on the ground.*
465. RECURES *cures,
heals.*
466. BANKROUT
bankrupt.
467. SILLY *simple,
innocent.*
470. DID THINK *had
thought.*
472. FAIR FALL THE
WIT *may the wit
prosper.*
478. MARR'D *in-
jured.*

He kisses her; and she, by her good
    will,
480   Will never rise, so he will kiss her
    still.

The night of sorrow now is turn'd to day:
Her two blue windows faintly she up-
    heaveth,
Like the fair sun when in his fresh array
He cheers the morn and all the earth re-
    lieveth;
485   And as the bright sun glorifies the
    sky,
    So is her face illumin'd with her eye,

Whose beams upon his hairless face are
    fix'd,
As if from thence they borrow'd all their
    shine.
Were never four such lamps together
    mix'd,
490   Had not his clouded with his brow's re-
    pine;
    But hers, which through the crystal
    tears gave light,
    Shone like the moon in water seen by
    night.

"O, where am I?" quoth she, "in earth or
    heaven,
Or in the ocean drench'd, or in the fire?
495   What hour is this? or morn or weary
    even?
Do I delight to die, or life desire?

480. so *so that.*
482. BLUE WINDOWS
eyes.
484. RELIEVETH
*brightens, relieves
from distress.*
490. REPINE *vexa-
tion.*
494. DRENCH'D
drowned.
495. OR . . . OR
either . . . or.

But now I liv'd, and life was death's
    annoy;
But now I died, and death was lively
    joy.

"O, thou didst kill me; kill me once again:
500   Thy eyes' shrowd tutor, that hard heart of
    thine,
Hath taught them scornful tricks, and
    such disdain
That they have mur'dred this poor heart
    of mine;
    And these mine eyes, true leaders to
    their queen,
    But for thy piteous lips no more had
    seen.

505   "Long may they kiss each other, for this
    cure!
O, never let their crimson liveries wear!
And as they last, their verdure still en-
    dure,
To drive infection from the dangerous
    year!
    That the stargazers, having writ on
    death,
510   May say the plague is banish'd by thy
    breath.

"Pure lips, sweet seals in my soft lips im-
    printed,
What bargains may I make, still to be
    sealing?
To sell myself I can be well contented,

497. ANNOY *grief.*
498. LIVELY *lifelike.*
500. SHROWD
shrewd.
503. LEADERS *those
who show the way.*
504. PITEOUS *piti-
ful.*
506. LIVERIES *garb;
here, the flower of
youth. See Sonnet 2,
line 3.* WEAR *wear
out.*
507. VERDURE *fresh-
ness and vigor of
youth.*
508. DANGEROUS
YEAR *1593, the date
of the publication of
this poem, was a
year of the plague.*
509. STARGAZERS
*astrologers. See "the
sad augurs," Sonnet
107, line 6.* WRIT ON
DEATH *predicted
death in their horo-
scopes.*
512. STILL *always.*
SEALING *kissing.
Kisses were "seals of
love" (see page
249).*

So thou wilt buy, and pay, and use good
 dealing;
515   Which purchase if thou make, for
          fear of slips,
          Set thy seal manual on my wax-red
          lips.

"A thousand kisses buys my heart from
 me;
And pay them at thy leisure, one by one:
What is ten hundred touches unto thee?
520 Are they not quickly told and quickly
 gone?
          Say for nonpayment that the debt
          should double,
          Is twenty hundred kisses such a
          trouble?"

"Fair queen," quoth he, "if any love you
 owe me,
Measure my strangeness with my unripe
 years:
525 Before I know myself, seek not to know
 me;
No fisher but the ungrown fry forbears:
          The mellow plum doth fall, the
          green sticks fast,
          Or being early pluck'd is sour to
          taste.

"Look, the world's comforter, with weary
 gait,

516. SEAL MANUAL
*signet ring, used
metaphorically for
his lips.*
520. TOLD *counted.*
524. STRANGENESS
shyness.
526. FRY *little fishes.*
529. WORLD'S COM-
FORTER *the sun.*

530 His day's hot task hath ended in the west;
The owl, night's herald, shrieks; 'tis very
late;
The sheep are gone to fold, birds to their
nest,
And coal-black clouds that shadow
heaven's light
Do summon us to part and bid good
night.

535 "Now let me say 'Good night,' and so say
you;
If you will say so, you shall have a kiss."
"Good night," quoth she; and, ere he says
"Adieu,"
The honey fee of parting tend'red is:
Her arms do lend his neck a sweet
embrace;
540 Incorporate then they seem; face
grows to face,

Till breathless he disjoin'd, and backward drew
The heavenly moisture, that sweet coral
mouth,
Whose precious taste her thirsty lips well
knew,
Whereon they surfeit, yet complain on
drouth:
545 He with her plenty press'd, she faint
with dearth,
Their lips together glu'd, fall to the
earth.

540. INCORPORATE
made one body.
544. ON *of.*
545. PRESS'D
crushed, oppressed.

Now quick desire hath caught the yield-
  ing prey,
And glutton-like she feeds, yet never
  filleth;
Her lips are conquerors, his lips obey,
Paying what ransom the insulter willeth;
    Whose vulture thought doth pitch
      the price so high
    That she will draw his lips' rich
      treasure dry.

And having felt the sweetness of the spoil,
With blindfold fury she begins to forage;
Her face doth reek and smoke, her blood
  doth boil,
And careless lust stirs up a desperate cour-
  age,
    Planting oblivion, beating reason
      back,
    Forgetting shame's pure blush and
      honour's wrack.

Hot, faint, and weary with her hard embracing,
Like a wild bird being tam'd with too
  much handling,
Or as the fleet-foot roe that's tir'd with
  chasing,
Or like the froward infant still'd with
  dandling,
    He now obeys and now no more re-
      sisteth,
    While she takes all she can, not all
      she listeth.

550. INSULTER *an
exultant enemy.*
556. CARELESS *heed-
less.*
558. WRACK *destruc-
tion, as in the phrase
"wrack and ruin."*
562. FROWARD *in-
tractable.*
564. LISTETH *pleases.*

565 What wax so frozen but dissolves with
    temp'ring
And yields at last to every light impres-
    sion?
Things out of hope are compass'd oft with
    vent'ring,
Chiefly in love, whose leave exceeds com-
    mission:
     Affection faints not like a pale-fac'd
      coward,
570   But then woos best when most his
      choice is froward.

When he did frown, O, had she then gave
    over,
Such nectar from his lips she had not
    suck'd.
Foul words and frowns must not repel a
    lover;
What though the rose have prickles, yet
    'tis pluck'd:
575   Were beauty under twenty locks kept
      fast,
     Yet love breaks through and picks
      them all at last.

For pity now she can no more detain him;
The poor fool prays her that he may de-
    part:
She is resolv'd no longer to restrain him;
580 Bids him farewell, and look well to her
    heart,
     The which, by Cupid's bow she doth
      protest,

565. TEMP'RING *Sealing wax was "tempered" between the fingers to make it malleable.*
567. VENT'RING *venturing.*
568. LEAVE EXCEEDS COMMISSION *liberty goes beyond what was granted.*
569. AFFECTION *passion.*
570. FROWARD *unwilling to comply.*
578. POOR FOOL *an expression of tenderness.*

He carries thence incaged in his
breast.

"Sweet boy," she says, "this night I'll waste
in sorrow,
For my sick heart commands mine eyes to
watch.
585   Tell me, love's master, shall we meet to-
morrow?
Say, shall we? shall we? wilt thou make
the match?"
      He tells her no; to-morrow he in-
tends
      To hunt the boar with certain of his
friends.

"The boar!" quoth she: whereat a sudden
pale,
590   Like lawn being spread upon the blushing
rose,
Usurps her cheek; she trembles at his
tale,
And on his neck her yoking arms she
throws;
      She sinketh down, still hanging by
his neck,
      He on her belly falls, she on her
back.

595   Now is she in the very lists of love,
Her champion mounted for the hot en-
counter:
All is imaginary she doth prove,

590. LAWN *a fine
linen.*
595. LISTS *enclosed
grounds on which
combats were
fought. The analogy
between love and
battle is a common-
place of Elizabethan
poetry.*
597. PROVE *learn
from experience.*

He will not manage her, although he
    mount her;
        That worse than Tantalus' is her an-
            noy,
600   To clip Elysium and to lack her joy.

Even so poor birds, deceiv'd with painted
    grapes,
Do surfeit by the eye and pine the maw;
Even so she languisheth in her mishaps
As those poor birds that helpless berries
    saw.
605   The warm effects which she in him
            finds missing
        She seeks to kindle with continual
            kissing.

But all in vain; good queen, it will not be:
She hath assay'd as much as may be
    prov'd;
Her pleading hath deserv'd a greater fee:
610   She's Love, she loves, and yet she is not
    lov'd.
        "Fie, fie!" he says, "you crush me; let
            me go;
        You have no reason to withhold me
            so."

"Thou hadst been gone," quoth she, "sweet
    boy, ere this,
But that thou told'st me thou wouldst
    hunt the boar.
615   O, be advis'd: thou know'st not what it is

598. MANAGE *a term in horsemanship meaning to put a horse through its paces. See* A Lover's Complaint, *line 112.*
599. THAT *so that.* TANTALUS' *Tantalus was punished in Hades by being inflicted with a great thirst and placed up to his chin in water which receded whenever he tried to drink.*
600. CLIP *embrace.*
602. PINE THE MAW *starve the stomach. The phrase was used in connection with animals.*
604. HELPLESS *of no help because they could not be eaten.*
605. EFFECTS *consequences. See* The Rape of Lucrece, *line 251.*
608. ASSAY'D *attempted.* PROV'D *realized.*

With javelin's point a churlish swine to
gore,
　　Whose tushes never sheath'd he
　　whetteth still,
　　Like to a mortal butcher bent to kill.

"On his bow-back he hath a battle set
620　Of bristly pikes that ever threat his foes;
His eyes like glowworms shine when he
doth fret;
His snout digs sepulchres where'er he
goes;
　　Being mov'd, he strikes whate'er is
　　in his way,
　　And whom he strikes his crooked
　　tushes slay.

625　"His brawny sides, with hairy bristles
arm'd,
Are better proof than thy spear's point
can enter;
His short thick neck cannot be easily
harm'd;
Being ireful, on the lion he will venter:
　　The thorny brambles and embracing
　　bushes,
630　　As fearful of him, part, through
　　whom he rushes.

"Alas, he naught esteems that face of thine,
To which Love's eyes pays tributary
gazes;
Nor thy soft hands, sweet lips, and crystal
eyne,

617. TUSHES *tusks*.
WHETTETH *sharpens
by rubbing.* STILL
always.
618. MORTAL
deadly.
619. BOW-BACK
*back arched like a
bow.* BATTLE *army
battalion.*
624. TUSHES *tusks.*
626. PROOF *tested
and found strong,
like armor.*
628. VENTER
venture.
630. FEARFUL OF *in
fear of.*
632. TRIBUTARY *See
line 1045, note.*
633. EYNE *eyes.*

Whose full perfection all the world amazes;
But having thee at vantage (wondrous dread!)
Would root these beauties as he roots the mead.

635

"O let him keep his loathsome cabin still;
Beauty hath naught to do with such foul fiends:
Come not within his danger by thy will;
They that thrive well take counsel of their friends.
When thou didst name the boar, not to dissemble,
I fear'd thy fortune, and my joints did tremble.

640

"Didst thou not mark my face? was it not white?
Saw'st thou not signs of fear lurk in mine eye?
Grew I not faint? and fell I not downright?
Within my bosom, whereon thou dost lie,
My boding heart pants, beats, and takes no rest,
But, like an earthquake, shakes thee on my breast.

645

"For where Love reigns, disturbing Jealousy
Doth call himself Affection's sentinel,

650

636. ROOT *uproot.*
MEAD *land covered with grass.*
637. KEEP *keep to occupy.* CABIN *widely used in Shakespeare's time to mean a small humble dwelling.*
639. WITHIN HIS DANGER *into his power.*

Gives false alarms, suggesteth mutiny,
And in a peaceful hour doth cry 'Kill,
    kill!'
        Distemp'ring gentle Love in his de-
        sire,
        As air and water do abate the fire.

655 "Tis sour informer, this bate-breeding spy,
This canker that eats up Love's tender
    spring,
This carry-tale, dissentious Jealousy,
That sometime true news, sometime false
    doth bring,
        Knocks at my heart, and whispers in
        mine ear
660   That if I love thee, I thy death should
        fear:

"And more than so, presenteth to mine eye
The picture of an angry chafing boar,
Under whose sharp fangs on his back
    doth lie
An image like thyself, all stain'd with
    gore;
665   Whose blood upon the fresh flowers
        being shed
        Doth make them droop with grief
        and hang the head.

"What should I do, seeing thee so indeed,
That tremble at th' imagination?
The thought of it doth make my faint
    heart bleed,
670 And fear doth teach it divination:

653. DISTEMP'RING
disordering; dilut-
ing, and therefore
decreasing.
655. BATE-BREEDING
creating strife.
656. CANKER a
worm that preys
upon blossoms.
SPRING the bud of
growing love.

I prophesy thy death, my living sor-
    row,
If thou encounter with the boar to-
    morrow.

"But if thou needs wilt hunt, be rul'd by
    me;
Uncouple at the timorous flying hare,
675   Or at the fox which lives by subtlety,
Or at the roe which no encounter dare:
    Pursue these fearful creatures o'er
        the downs,
    And on thy well-breath'd horse keep
        with thy hounds.

"And when thou hast on foot the purblind
    hare,
680   Mark the poor wretch, to over-shut his
    troubles,
How he outruns the wind, and with what
    care
He cranks and crosses with a thousand
    doubles:
    The many musits through the which
        he goes
    Are like a labyrinth to amaze his
        foes.

685   "Sometime he runs among a flock of sheep,
To make the cunning hounds mistake
    their smell,
And sometime where earth-delving conies
    keep,
To stop the loud pursuers in their yell;

677. FEARFUL *full of fear, timid.*
678. WELL-BREATH'D *in good wind, therefore in good condition.*
679. PURBLIND *half-blind, shortsighted. It was thought that the hare's sight was weak because its eyelids were too short to cover the eyes.*
680. OVER-SHUT *get rid of.*
682. CRANKS *turns suddenly.*
683. MUSITS *hole or short tunnel in fence, hedge, or wall.*
685. SOMETIME *sometimes.*
687. CONIES *a species of European rabbit.*

And sometime sorteth with a herd of
    deer:
690   Danger deviseth shifts; wit waits on
    fear;

"For there his smell with others being
    mingled,
The hot scent-snuffing hounds are driven
    to doubt,
Ceasing their clamorous cry till they have
    singled
With much ado the cold fault cleanly out;
695   Then do they spend their mouths:
    echo replies,
    As if another chase were in the skies.

"By this, poor Wat, far off upon a hill,
Stands on his hinder legs with list'ning
    ear,
To hearken if his foes pursue him still:
700   Anon their loud alarums he doth hear,
       And now his grief may be compared
    well
       To one sore sick that hears the pass-
    ing-bell.

"Then shalt thou see the dew-bedabbled
    wretch
Turn, and return, indenting with the way;
705   Each envious brier his weary legs doth
    scratch,
Each shadow makes him stop, each mur-
    mur stay;

694. FAULT *scent.*
695. SPEND *expend,
put to use.*
697. WAT *the pro-
verbial name for a
rabbit in the six-
teenth and seven-
teenth centuries.*
702. PASSING-BELL
*the bell that tolls at
the hour of death.*
704. INDENTING
. . . WAY *following
a zigzag course.*

For misery is trodden on by many,
And being low, never reliev'd by
any.

"Lie quietly and hear a little more;
710   Nay, do not struggle, for thou shalt not
rise:
To make thee hate the hunting of the
boar,
Unlike myself thou hear'st me moralize,
Applying this to that, and so to so;
For love can comment upon every
woe.

715   "Where did I leave?" "No matter where,"
quoth he;
"Leave me, and then the story aptly ends:
The night is spent." "Why, what of that?"
quoth she.
"I am," quoth he, "expected of my friends;
And now 'tis dark, and going I shall
fall."
720   "In night," quoth she, "desire sees
best of all.

"But if thou fall, O, then imagine this:
The earth, in love with thee, thy footing
trips,
And all is but to rob thee of a kiss.
Rich preys make true men thieves; so do
thy lips
725   Make modest Dian cloudy and forlorn,

712. UNLIKE MY-
SELF *Venus did not
normally moralize.*
724. TRUE *honest.*
725. DIAN *goddess
of chastity and the
hunt, Cynthia. See
Hecate, note, page
194.* CLOUDY *ill-
tempered, sullen.*

VENUS AND ADONIS / 387

Lest she should steal a kiss and die
forsworn.

"Now of this dark night I perceive the
reason:
Cynthia for shame obscures her silver
shine,
Till forging Nature be condemn'd of
treason
730 For stealing moulds from heaven that
were divine;
Wherein she fram'd thee, in high
heaven's despite,
To shame the sun by day, and her by
night.

"And therefore hath she brib'd the Destinies
To cross the curious workmanship of Nature,
735 To mingle beauty with infirmities
And pure perfection with impure defeature,
Making it subject to the tyranny
Of mad mischances and much misery;

"As burning fevers, agues pale and faint,
740 Life-poisoning pestilence, and frenzies
wood,
The marrow-eating sickness whose attaint
Disorder breeds by heating of the blood,

726. FORSWORN hav-
ing violated a
pledge, that is, her
oath of chastity.
728–732. Cynthia,
the moon, shamed,
as is the sun, by the
beauty of Adonis,
obscures her light
until Nature shall
be convicted of the
crime of stealing
from heaven the
mold after which
Adonis was formed,
for he is the Pla-
tonic idea of beauty,
of which things on
earth should be only
pale reflections.
733. DESTINIES the
Fates. Clotho held
the distaff; Lachesis
spun the thread of
life; Atropos cut it
off.
736. DEFEATURE dis-
figurement.
739. AGUES sick-
nesses characterized
by chills and fever.
740. WOOD mad.
741. MARROW-EAT-
ING SICKNESS the
"incurable bone-
ache," Troilus and
Cressida, Act V,
scene 1, line 25;
syphilis. ATTAINT
infection.

Surfeits, imposthumes, grief, and
    damn'd despair
Swear Nature's death for framing
    thee so fair.

745   "And not the least of all these maladies
    But in one minute's fight brings beauty
        under:
    Both favour, savour, hue, and qualities,
    Whereat th' impartial gazer late did won·
        der,
            Are on the sudden wasted, thaw'd,
                and done,
750   As mountain snow melts with the
                midday sun.

    "Therefore, despite of fruitless chastity,
    Love-lacking vestals, and self-loving
        nuns,
    That on the earth would breed a scarcity
    And barren dearth of daughters and of
        sons,
755   Be prodigal: the lamp that burns by
                night
                Dries up his oil to lend the world his
                light.

    "What is thy body but a swallowing grave,
    Seeming to bury that posterity
    Which by the rights of time thou needs
        must have
760   If thou destroy them not in dark obscur·
        ity?

743. SURFEITS *sick-*
nesses resulting
from overindul-
gence.
747. FAVOUR *fea-*
tures, countenance,
figure. HUE *com-*
plexion. See Sonnet
20, line 7, note.
760. *The falsity of*
the posterity-ob-
scurity rhyme has
been much com-
mented upon, but
like rhymes, and
worse, may be
found throughout
Elizabethan poetry.
The line is an
alexandrine.

If so, the world will hold thee in dis-
     dain,
Sith in thy pride so fair a hope is
     slain.

"So in thyself thyself art made away;
     A mischief worse than civil home-bred
          strife,
765 Or theirs whose desperate hands them-
          selves do slay,
     Or butcher sire that reaves his son of life.
          Foul cank'ring rust the hidden treas-
               ure frets,
          But gold that's put to use more gold
               begets."

"Nay then," quoth Adon, "you will fall
     again
770 Into your idle over-handled theme:
     The kiss I gave you is bestow'd in vain,
     And all in vain you strive against the
          stream;
          For, by this black-fac'd night, desire's
               foul nurse,
          Your treatise makes me like you
               worse and worse.

775 "If love have lent you twenty thousand
          tongues,
     And every tongue more moving than your
          own,
     Bewitching like the wanton mermaid's
          songs,

762. SITH since.
766. REAVES de-
prives; from
"bereaves."
768. PUT TO USE
lent at interest.
774. TREATISE dis-
course.
777. MERMAID'S
siren's.

Yet from mine ear the tempting tune is
	blown;
    For know, my heart stands armed in
		mine ear
780   And will not let a false sound enter
		there,

"Lest the deceiving harmony should run
Into the quiet closure of my breast;
And then my little heart were quite un-
	done,
In his bedchamber to be barr'd of rest.
785   No, lady, no; my heart longs not to
		groan,
    But soundly sleeps while now it
		sleeps alone.

"What have you urg'd that I cannot re-
	prove?
The path is smooth that leadeth on to
	danger:
I hate not love, but your device in love,
790 That lends embracements unto every
		stranger.
    You do it for increase: O strange ex-
		cuse,
    When reason is the bawd to lust's
		abuse!

"Call it not love, for Love to heaven is fled
Since sweating Lust on earth usurp'd his
	name;
795 Under whose simple semblance he hath
		fed

782. CLOSURE en-
closure.
784. HIS its.
787. REPROVE re-
fute.
789. DEVICE be-
havior.
791. INCREASE
progeny.
792. BAWD procurer.

Upon fresh beauty, blotting it with
blame;
    Which the hot tyrant stains and soon
    bereaves,
    As caterpillars do the tender leaves.

"Love comforteth like sunshine after rain,
800 But Lust's effect is tempest after sun;
Love's gentle spring doth always fresh remain,
Lust's winter comes ere summer half be
done;
    Love surfeits not, Lust like a glutton
    dies;
    Love is all truth, Lust full of forged
    lies.

805 "More I could tell, but more I dare not say;
The text is old, the orator too green:
Therefore in sadness now I will away;
My face is full of shame, my heart of teen;
    Mine ears, that to your wanton talk
    attended,
810   Do burn themselves for having so
    offended.

With this he breaketh from the sweet
embrace
Of those fair arms which bound him to
her breast
And homeward through the dark lawnd
runs apace;
Leaves Love upon her back, deeply distress'd.

797. BEREAVES
plunders.
806. GREEN *young.*
807. IN SADNESS *in
all seriousness.*
808. TEEN *vexation.*
813. LAWND *an
open space in a
forest.*

815   Look how a bright star shooteth from
                the sky,
             So glides he in the night from Venus'
                eye,

         Which after him she darts, as one on
             shore
         Gazing upon a late-embarked friend
         Till the wild waves will have him seen no
             more,
820   Whose ridges with the meeting clouds
             contend:
             So did the merciless and pitchy night
             Fold in the object that did feed her
                sight.

         Whereat amaz'd, as one that unaware
         Hath dropp'd a precious jewel in the
             flood,
825   Or stonish'd as night-wand'rers often are,
         Their light blown out in some mistrustful
             wood;
             Even so confounded in the dark she
                lay,
             Having lost the fair discovery of her
                way.

         And now she beats her heart, whereat it
             groans,
830   That all the neighbour caves, as seeming
             troubled,
         Make verbal repetition of her moans;
         Passion on passion deeply is redoubled:

*815. LOOK HOW
just as. See line 67.
825. STONISH'D con-
founded, thunder-
struck. NIGHT-
WAND'RERS travelers
on foot at night.
826. MISTRUSTFUL
arousing suspicion
and apprehension.
832. PASSION violent
lamentation.*

"Ay me!" she cries, and twenty times,
        "Woe, woe!"
    And twenty echoes twenty times cry
        so.

835 She, marking them, begins a wailing note,
    And sings extemporally a woeful ditty;
    How love makes young men thrall, and
        old men dote;
    How love is wise in folly, foolish-witty:
        Her heavy anthem still concludes in
            woe,
840   And still the choir of echoes answer
                so.

    Her song was tedious and outwore the
        night,
    For lovers' hours are long, though seem-
        ing short:
    If pleas'd themselves, others, they think,
        delight
    In such-like circumstance, with such-like
        sport:
845   Their copious stories, oftentimes be-
                gun,
            End without audience, and are never
                done.

    For who hath she to spend the night
        withal
    But idle sounds resembling parasits,
    Like shrill-tongued tapsters answering
        every call,

838. FOOLISH-WITTY
foolish in wisdom,
sophomoric.
848. PARASITS para-
sites, fawning flat-
terers.
849–850. The lines
recall the "Anon,
anon" passage in
Henry IV, Part I,
Act II, scene 4.

850   Soothing the humour of fantastic wits?
            She says " 'Tis so:" they answer all
            " 'Tis so;"
            And would say after her if she said
            "No."

       Lo, here the gentle lark, weary of rest,
       From his moist cabinet mounts up on high
855   And wakes the morning, from whose sil-
            ver breast
       The sun ariseth in his majesty;
            Who doth the world so gloriously
            behold
            That cedar tops and hills seem burn-
            ish'd gold.

       Venus salutes him with this fair good-
            morrow:
860   "O thou clear god, and patron of all light,
       From whom each lamp and shining star
            doth borrow
       The beauteous influence that makes him
            bright,
            There lives a son that suck'd an
            earthly mother
            May lend thee light, as thou dost
            lend to other."

865   This said, she hasteth to a myrtle grove,
       Musing the morning is so much o'erworn
       And yet she hears no tidings of her love:
       She hearkens for his hounds and for his
            horn:

850. FANTASTIC WITS
capricious patrons.
Folio designates
Lucio in Measure
for Measure as "a
fantastique."
853–858. The musi-
cal setting of these
lines for coloratura
soprano and flute
obbligato by Sir
Henry Bishop, 1819,
was popular for
more than a cen-
tury.
854. CABINET nest.
858. Compare Son-
net 33, lines 1–4.
864. OTHER others.

Anon she hears them chant it lustily,
870   And all in haste she coasteth to the
          cry;

And as she runs, the bushes in the way
Some catch her by the neck, some kiss her
     face,
Some twine about her thigh to make her
     stay:
She wildly breaketh from their strict em-
     brace,
875   Like a milch doe whose swelling
               dugs do ache,
               Hasting to feed her fawn hid in some
               brake.

By this she hears the hounds are at a bay;
Whereat she starts, like one that spies an
     adder
Wreath'd up in fatal folds just in his way,
880   The fear whereof doth make him shake
          and shudder;
               Even so the timorous yelping of the
               hounds
               Appals her senses and her spirit con-
               founds.

For now she knows it is no gentle chase,
But the blunt boar, rough bear, or lion
     proud,
885   Because the cry remaineth in one place,
Where fearfully the dogs exclaim aloud;
          Finding their enemy to be so curst,

870. COASTETH
hastens.
874. STRICT *close.*
875. MILCH *fresh,
giving milk.*
876. BRAKE *thicket.*
877. AT A BAY *the
point in a chase
when the game is
driven to extremity
and turns against its
pursuers.*
887. CURST *vicious,
savage.*

They all strain court'sy who shall
cope him first.

This dismal cry rings sadly in her ear,
890 Through which it enters to surprise her
heart,
Who, overcome by doubt and bloodless
fear,
With cold-pale weakness numbs each
feeling part;
    Like soldiers when their captain once
    doth yield,
    They basely fly and dare not stay the
    field.

895 Thus stands she in a trembling ecstasy;
Till cheering up her senses all dismay'd,
She tells them 'tis a causeless fantasy,
And childish error that they are afraid;
    Bids them leave quaking, bids them
    fear no more:
900   And with that word she spied the
    hunted boar,

Whose frothy mouth, bepainted all with
red,
Like milk and blood being mingled both
togither,
A second fear through all her sinews
spread,
Which madly hurries her she knows not
whither:
905   This way she runs, and now she will
    no further,

888. STRAIN
COURT'SY *A man
who hesitated to
advance into danger
before someone took
the lead was sarcas-
tically said to strain
courtesy.* COPE *en-
counter, attack.*
891. WHO *which.*
895. ECSTASY *uncon-
trollable excitement.*

But back retires to rate the boar for
murther.

A thousand spleens bear her a thousand
ways;
She treads the path that she untreads
again;
Her more than haste is mated with delays,
910 Like the proceedings of a drunken brain,
Full of respects, yet naught at all
respecting;
In hand with all things, naught at
all effecting.

Here kennell'd in a brake she finds a
hound
And asks the weary caitiff for his master;
915 And there another licking of his wound,
'Gainst venom'd sores the only sovereign
plaster;
And here she meets another sadly
scowling,
To whom she speaks, and he replies
with howling.

When he hath ceas'd his ill-resounding
noise,
920 Another flap-mouth'd mourner, black and
grim,
Against the welkin volleys out his voice;
Another and another answer him,
Clapping their proud tails to the
ground below,

906. RATE *berate*.
907. SPLEENS
impulses.
909. MATED
checked,
frustrated.
911. RESPECTS *considerations*.
RESPECTING *considering*.
912. IN HAND WITH
busied with.
913. BRAKE *thicket*.
914. CAITIFF
wretch.
916. SOVEREIGN *efficacious*.
921. WELKIN *sky*.

Shaking their scratch'd ears, bleeding as they go.

925 Look how the world's poor people are
amaz'd
At apparitions, signs, and prodigies,
Whereon with fearful eyes they long have
gaz'd,
Infusing them with dreadful prophecies;
So she at these sad signs draws up her
breath
930 And sighing it again, exclaims on
Death.

"Hard-favour'd tyrant, ugly, meagre, lean,
Hateful divorce of love, (thus chides she
Death)
Grim-grinning ghost, earth's worm, what
dost thou mean
To stifle beauty and to steal his breath
935 Who when he liv'd, his breath and
beauty set
Gloss on the rose, smell to the violet?

"If he be dead—O no, it cannot be,
Seeing his beauty, thou shouldst strike
at it;
O yes, it may; thou hast no eyes to see,
940 But hatefully at randon dost thou hit;
Thy mark is feeble age, but thy false
dart
Mistakes that aim and cleaves an
infant's heart.

925–928. The
world's pitiful
people attribute to
apparitions, signs,
and prodigies the
power to prophesy.
925. LOOK HOW just
as. See line 67.
928. THEM the ap-
paritions, etc.
930. EXCLAIMS ON
upbraids.
933. WORM serpent.
940. RANDON
random.

"Hadst thou but bid beware, then he had
    spoke,
And hearing him, thy power had lost his
    power.
945 The Destinies will curse thee for this
    stroke;
They bid thee crop a weed, thou pluck'st
    a flower:
        Love's golden arrow at him should
            have fled,
        And not Death's ebon dart, to strike
            him dead.

"Dost thou drink tears, that thou provok'st
    such weeping?
950 What may a heavy groan advantage thee?
Why hast thou cast into eternal sleeping
Those eyes that taught all other eyes to
    see?
        Now Nature cares not for thy mortal
            vigour,
        Since her best work is ruin'd with
            thy rigour."

955 Here overcome, as one full of despair,
She vail'd her eyelids, who, like sluices,
    stopp'd
The crystal tide that from her two cheeks
    fair
In the sweet channel of her bosom
    dropp'd;
        But through the floodgates breaks
            the silver rain

944. HIS *its.*
948. EBON *black,
like ebony.*
956. VAIL'D *low-
ered* WHO *which.*

960   And with his strong course opens
       them again.

O, how her eyes and tears did lend and
    borrow!
Her eyes seen in the tears, tears in her
    eye;
Both crystals, where they view'd each
    other's sorrow,
Sorrow that friendly sighs sought still to
    dry;
965   But like a stormy day, now wind,
       now rain,
       Sighs dry her cheeks, tears make
       them wet again.

Variable passions throng her constant
    woe,
As striving who should best become her
    grief;
All entertain'd, each passion labours so
970 That every present sorrow seemeth chief,
       But none is best; then join they all
       together,
       Like many clouds consulting for foul
       weather.

By this, far off she hears some huntsman
    hallow;
A nurse's song ne'er pleas'd her babe so
    well:
975 The dire imagination she did follow
This sound of hope doth labour to expel;

975. IMAGINATION
*the things she had
imagined.*

For now reviving joy bids her re-
joice
And flatters her it is Adonis' voice.

Whereat her tears began to turn their
tide,
980 Being prison'd in her eye like pearls in
glass;
Yet sometimes falls an orient drop
beside,
Which her cheek melts, as scorning it
should pass
    To wash the foul face of the sluttish
ground,
    Who is but drunken when she
seemeth drown'd.

985 O hard-believing love, how strange it
seems
Not to believe, and yet too credulous!
Thy weal and woe are both of them
extremes;
Despair and hope makes thee ridiculous:
    The one doth flatter thee in thoughts
unlikely,
990   In likely thoughts the other kills thee
quickly.

Now she unweaves the web that she hath
wrought;
Adonis lives, and Death is not to blame;
It was not she that call'd him all to
naught:

981. ORIENT *bright.
Certain pearls were
called "orient" be-
cause of their rela-
tive transparency.*
983. SLUTTISH *un-
clean. See Sonnet
55, line 4.*
984. DRUNKEN *In*
Richard III, *Act IV,
scene 4, line 30, the
earth is "made
drunk with in-
nocent blood."*
993. ALL TO
NAUGHT *good for
nothing.*

Now she adds honours to his hateful
   name;
995   She clepes him king of graves, and
       grave for kings,
      Imperious supreme of all mortal
       things.

"No, no," quoth she, "sweet Death, I did
   but jest;
Yet pardon me, I felt a kind of fear
When as I met the boar, that bloody beast
1000 Which knows no pity but is still severe;
      Then, gentle shadow (truth I must
       confess),
      I rail'd on thee, fearing my love's
       decesse.

" 'Tis not my fault: the boar provok'd my
   tongue;
Be wreak'd on him, invisible commander;
1005 'Tis he, foul creature, that hath done thee
   wrong;
I did but act, he's author of thy slander:
      Grief hath two tongues, and never
       woman yet
      Could rule them both without ten
       women's wit."

Thus hoping that Adonis is alive,
1010 Her rash suspect she doth extenuate;
And that his beauty may the better thrive,
With Death she humbly doth insinuate,
      Tell him of trophies, statues, tombs,
       and stories,

995. CLEPES *calls*.
996. IMPERIOUS
imperial, lordly.
1002. DECESSE
decease.
1010. SUSPECT *sus-
picion.*
1012. INSINUATE
*wheedles herself
into his favor.*

His victories, his triumphs, and his
   glories.

1015 "O Jove," quoth she, "how much a fool
   was I
To be of such a weak and silly mind
To wail his death who lives and must not
   die
Till mutual overthrow of mortal kind!
    For he being dead, with him is
    beauty slain,
1020   And beauty dead, black chaos comes
    again.

"Fie, fie, fond love, thou art as full of fear
As one with treasure laden hemm'd with
   thieves;
Trifles unwitnessed with eye or ear
Thy coward heart with false bethinking
   grieves."
1025   Even at this word she hears a merry
    horn,
    Whereat she leaps that was but late
    forlorn.

As falcons to the lure, away she flies;
The grass stoops not, she treads on it so
   light;
And in her haste unfortunately spies
1030 The foul boar's conquest on her fair delight;
    Which seen, her eyes, as murd'red
    with the view,

1026. LEAPS *leaps
for joy.*

Like stars asham'd of day, themselves
  withdrew;

Or as the snail, whose tender horns being
  hit,
Shrinks backward in his shelly cave with
  pain,
1035 And there all smooth'red up in shade
  doth sit,
Long after fearing to creep forth again;
    So at his bloody view her eyes are
    fled
      Into the deep-dark cabins of her
      head;

Where they resign their office and their
  light
1040 To the disposing of her troubled brain;
Who bids them still consort with ugly
  night
And never wound the heart with looks
  again;
    Who, like a king perplexed in his
    throne,
      By their suggestion gives a deadly
      groan,

1045 Whereat each tributary subject quakes;
As when the wind, imprison'd in the
  ground,
Struggling for passage, earth's founda-
  tion shakes,
Which with cold terror doth men's minds
  confound.

1038. CABINS *eye sockets.*
1043. PERPLEXED *bewildered.*
1045. TRIBUTARY *paying tribute.*
1046–1047. *The Elizabethans held to the belief of ancient times that earthquakes were caused by winds imprisoned in subterranean caverns.*

This mutiny each part doth so surprise
1050   That from their dark beds once more
leap her eyes,

And being open'd threw unwilling light
Upon the wide wound that the boar had
trench'd
In his soft flank, whose wonted lily white
With purple tears that his wound wept
was drench'd:
1055   No flow'r was nigh, no grass, herb,
leaf, or weed,
But stole his blood and seem'd with
him to bleed.

This solemn sympathy poor Venus
noteth;
Over one shoulder doth she hang her
head;
Dumbly she passions, franticly she
doteth;
1060   She thinks he could not die, he is not
dead;
Her voice is stopp'd, her joints forget
to bow,
Her eyes are mad that they have wept
till now.

Upon his hurt she looks so steadfastly
That her sight dazzling makes the wound
seem three;
1065   And then she reprehends her mangling
eye,

1059. PASSIONS
grieves, suffers.
DOTETH behaves ir-
rationally.
1062. She feels that
all previous oc-
casions of weeping
were as nothing
compared with this
one.
1064. SIGHT DAZ-
ZLING losing distinc-
tion of vision.

That makes more gashes where no breach
    should be:
        His face seems twain, each several
            limb is doubled;
        For oft the eye mistakes, the brain
            being troubled.

"My tongue cannot express my grief for
    one,
1070 And yet," quoth she, "behold two Adons
    dead!
    My sighs are blown away, my salt tears
    gone,
    Mine eyes are turn'd to fire, my heart to
    lead:
        Heavy heart's lead, melt at mine
            eyes' red fire!
        So shall I die by drops of hot desire.

1075 "Alas, poor world, what treasure has thou
    lost!
    What face remains alive that's worth the
    viewing?
    Whose tongue is music now? what canst
    thou boast
    Of things long since, or any thing
    ensuing?
        The flowers are sweet, their colours
            fresh and trim;
1080   But true-sweet beauty liv'd and di'd
            with him.

"Bonnet nor veil henceforth no creature
    wear!

Nor sun nor wind will ever strive to kiss
you:
Having no fair to lose, you need not fear;
The sun doth scorn you, and the wind
doth hiss you:
1085   But when Adonis liv'd, sun and
sharp air
Lurk'd like two thieves, to rob him
of his fair;

"And therefore would he put his bonnet
on,
Under whose brim the gaudy sun would
peep;
The wind would blow it off, and, being
gone,
1090   Play with his locks; then would Adonis
weep;
And straight, in pity of his tender
years,
They both would strive who first
should dry his tears.

"To see his face the lion walk'd along
Behind some hedge, because he would
not fear him;
1095   To recreate himself when he hath song,
The tiger would be tame, and gently hear
him;
If he had spoke, the wolf would
leave his prey
And never fright the silly lamb that
day.

1083. FAIR *beauty*.
1086. FAIR *beauty*.
1088. GAUDY *showy,
full of splendor,
festive.*
1094. FEAR *frighten*.
1095. WHEN . . .
SONG *when Adonis
was singing. Shake-
speare used the
form "song" for
the sake of the
rhyme.*
1098. SILLY *in-
nocent.*

"When he beheld his shadow in the brook,
1100 The fishes spread on it their golden gills;
When he was by, the birds such pleasure took
That some would sing, some other in their bills
Would bring him mulberries and ripe-red cherries;
He fed them with his sight, they him with berries.

1105 "But this foul, grim, and urchin-snouted boar,
Whose downward eye still looketh for a grave,
Ne'er saw the beauteous livery that he wore;
Witness the entertainment that he gave:
If he did see his face, why then I know
1110 He thought to kiss him, and hath kill'd him so.

" 'Tis true, 'tis true; thus was Adonis slain:
He ran upon the boar with his sharp spear,
Who did not whet his teeth at him again,
But by a kiss thought to persuade him there;
1115 And nuzzling in his flank, the loving swine
Sheath'd unaware the tusk in his soft groin.

1101. BY *close by.*
1105. URCHIN-SNOUTED *with armed snout. The urchin, now known as the hedgehog, is a small European mammal with sharp spines on its back.*
1106. DOWNWARD *directed to the ground.*
1114. THERE *to stay there.*

VENUS AND ADONIS / 409

"Had I been tooth'd like him, I must con-
    fess,
With kissing him I should have kill'd him
    first;
But he is dead, and never did he bless
My youth with his; the more am I ac-
    curst."
        With this, she falleth in the place
            she stood
        And stains her face with his con-
            gealed blood.

She looks upon his lips, and they are pale;
She takes him by the hand, and that is
    cold;
She whispers in his ears a heavy tale,
As if they heard the woful words she
    told;
        She lifts the coffer-lids that close his
            eyes,
        Where, lo, two lamps burnt out in
            darkness lies;

Two glasses, where herself herself be-
    held
A thousand times, and now no more
    reflect;
Their virtue lost wherein they late ex-
    cell'd,
And every beauty robb'd of his effect:
        "Wonder of time," quoth she, "this is
            my spite,
        That, thou being dead, the day
            should yet be light.

1135   "Since thou art dead, lo, here I prophesy
       Sorrow on love hereafter shall attend:
       It shall be waited on with jealousy,
       Find sweet beginning but unsavoury end;
          Ne'er settled equally, but high or
             low,
1140   That all love's pleasure shall not
             match his woe.

    "It shall be fickle, false, and full of fraud,
       Bud, and be blasted, in a breathing while,
       The bottom poison, and the top o'er-
         straw'd
       With sweets that shall the truest sight
         beguile:
1145   The strongest body shall it make
             most weak,
           Strike the wise dumb, and teach the
             fool to speak.

    "It shall be sparing and too full of riot,
       Teaching decrepit age to tread the
         measures;
       The staring ruffian shall it keep in quiet,
1150   Pluck down the rich, enrich the poor with
         treasures;
           It shall be raging mad and silly mild,
           Make the young old, the old become
             a child.

    "It shall suspect where is no cause of fear;
       It shall not fear where it should most
         mistrust;
1155   It shall be merciful and too severe,

1140. HIS *love's.*
1148. TREAD THE
MEASURES *dance.*
1149. STARING *look-*
ing with boldness,
brazen.
1151. SILLY *harm-*
less, innocent.

Resembling well his pale cheeks and the blood
Which in round drops upon their whiteness stood.

1 *Flos Adonis flore rubro.*
Adonis with red floures.

And most deceiving when it seems most
    just;
      Perverse it shall be where it shows
        most toward,
      Put fear to valour, courage to the
        coward.

"It shall be cause of war and dire events,
1160 And set dissension 'twixt the son and sire,
Subject and servile to all discontents,
As dry combustious matter is to fire:
      Sith in his prime death doth my love
        destroy,
      They that love best their loves shall
        not enjoy."

1165 By this, the boy that by her side lay kill'd
Was melted like a vapour from her sight,
And in his blood, that on the ground lay
    spill'd,
A purple flower sprung up, check'red
    with white,
      Resembling well his pale cheeks and
        the blood
1170   Which in round drops upon their
        whiteness stood.

She bows her head the new-sprung flower
    to smell,
Comparing it to her Adonis' breath,
And says within her bosom it shall dwell,
Since he himself is reft from her by death;

1157. TOWARD *willing, ready to do.*
1163. SITH *since.*

1175 She crops the stalk, and in the breach
    appears
  Green-dropping sap, which she com-
    pares to tears.

  "Poor flow'r," quoth she, "this was thy
    father's guise—
  Sweet issue of a more sweet-smelling
    sire—
  For every little grief to wet his eyes:
1180 To grow unto himself was his desire,
    And so 'tis thine; but know, it is as
     good
    To wither in my breast as in his
     blood.

  "Here was thy father's bed, here in my
    breast;
  Thou art the next of blood, and 'tis thy
    right:
1185 Lo, in this hollow cradle take thy rest;
  My throbbing heart shall rock thee day
    and night:
    There shall not be one minute in an
     hour
    Wherein I will not kiss my sweet
     love's flow'r."

  Thus weary of the world, away she hies
1190 And yokes her silver doves, by whose
    swift aid
  Their mistress, mounted, through the
    empty skies

1177. GUISE *custom, practice.*

In her light chariot quickly is convey'd,
  Holding their course to Paphos,
  where their queen
Means to immure herself and not be
  seen.

1193. PAPHOS *The place in Cyprus where, according to the legend, Venus first emerged from the sea.*

THE RAPE OF LUCRECE

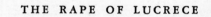

2. PAMPHLET *poem*. WITHOUT BEGINNING *The poem begins in the middle of the action.* MOIETY *small part.*

TO THE
RIGHT HONOURABLE HENRY WRIOTHESLEY,
EARL OF SOUTHAMPTON, AND BARON OF TITCHFIELD.

The love I dedicate to your Lordship is without end; whereof this pamphlet without beginning is but a superfluous moiety. The warrant I have of your honourable disposition, not the worth of my untutor'd lines, makes it assured of acceptance. What I have done is yours; what I have to do is yours; being part in all I have, devoted yours. Were my worth greater, my duty would show greater; meantime, as it is, it is bound to your Lordship, to whom I wish long life still length'ned with all happiness.

Your Lordship's in all duty,
WILLIAM SHAKESPEARE.

The argument to The Rape of Lucrece *and the dedications to it and to* Venus and Adonis *are Shakespeare's only surviving nondramatic prose compositions. His authorship of the argument has been questioned, chiefly because of certain discrepancies between it and the poem. The argument, for instance, says that after the departure of Tarquin Lucrece despatched two messengers, one to her father at Rome and another to her husband at Ardea, whereas the poem tells of only one. But there is no textual reason for doubting his authorship, and given Shakespeare's recurrent impatience with detail, the discrepancies are hardly conclusive. Most scholars are content to allow him the argument. His poem begins in the middle of the action, and he has provided an argument recounting the events in their chronological order and providing some not strictly germane to his purpose as poet.*

1. LUCIUS TARQUINIUS *the last legendary king of Rome.* 3. REQUIRING *requesting.* 20. COLLATIUM *more properly called Collatia.* 24. JUNIUS BRUTUS *According to Livy (*Ab Urbe Condita, *Book I, section 58), Lucius Junius Brutus was the man with whom Collatine happened to be returning to Rome when they encountered the messenger from Lucrece.* 25. PUBLIUS VALERIUS *According to Livy, Valerius was the friend whom Lucretius brought with him. He is not mentioned by name in the poem.*

THE ARGUMENT.

Lucius Tarquinius (for his excessive pride surnamed Superbus), after he had caused his own father-in-law Servius Tullius to be cruelly murd'red, and, contrary to the Roman laws and customs, not requiring or staying for the people's suffrages, had possessed himself of the king-
5 dom, went, accompanied with his sons and other noblemen of Rome, to besiege Ardea; during which siege the principal men of the army meeting one evening at the tent of Sextus Tarquinius, the King's son, in their discourses after supper every one commended the virtues of his own wife; among whom Collatinus extolled the incomparable chastity
10 of his wife Lucretia. In that pleasant humour they all posted to Rome; and intending by their secret and sudden arrival to make trial of that which every one had before avouched, only Collatinus finds his wife (though it were late in the night) spinning amongst her maids; the other ladies were all found dancing and revelling, or in several disports.
15 Whereupon the noblemen yielded Collatinus the victory, and his wife the fame. At that time Sextus Tarquinius being inflamed with Lucrece' beauty, yet smothering his passions for the present, departed with the rest back to the camp; from whence he shortly after privily withdrew himself, and was (according to his estate) royally entertained and
20 lodged by Lucrece at Collatium. The same night he treacherously stealeth into her chamber, violently ravish'd her, and early in the morning speedeth away. Lucrece, in this lamentable plight, hastily dispatcheth messengers, one to Rome for her father, another to the camp for Collatine. They came, the one accompanied with Junius Brutus, the other
25 with Publius Valerius; and finding Lucrece attired in mourning habit, demanded the cause of her sorrow. She, first taking an oath of them for her revenge, revealed the actor and whole manner of his dealing, and withal suddenly stabbed herself. Which done, with one consent they all vowed to root out the whole hated family of the Tarquins; and bearing the
30 dead body to Rome, Brutus acquainted the people with the doer and manner of the vile deed, with a bitter invective against the tyranny of the King; wherewith the people were so moved that with one consent and a general acclamation the Tarquins were all exiled, and the state government changed from kings to consuls.

From the besieg'd Ardea all in post,
Borne by the trustless wings of false
    desire,
Lust-breathed Tarquin leaves the Roman
    host
And to Collatium bears the lightless fire
Which, in pale embers hid, lurks to aspire
      And girdle with embracing flames
      the waist
      Of Collatine's fair love, Lucrece the
      chaste.

Haply that name of "chaste" unhap'ly set
This bateless edge on his keen appetite;
When Collatine unwisely did not let
To praise the clear unmatched red and
    white
Which triumph'd in that sky of his de-
    light,
      Where mortal stars, as bright as
      heaven's beauties,
      With pure aspects did him peculiar
      duties.

For he the night before, in Tarquin's
    tent,
Unlock'd the treasure of his happy state;
What priceless wealth the heavens had
    him lent
In the possession of his beauteous mate;
Reck'ning his fortune at such high proud
    rate
      That kings might be espoused to
      more fame,

1. ALL IN POST *in all haste.*
5. ASPIRE *ascend.*
8. HAPLY *perhaps.*
UNHAP'LY *unhappily.*
9. BATELESS *not to be blunted.*
10. LET *hesitate.*
13. MORTAL STARS *Lucrece's eyes.*
14. ASPECTS *the relative positions of the stars or planets.* PECULIAR *private.*

But king nor peer to such a peerless
    dame.

O happiness enjoy'd but of a few,
And if possess'd, as soon decay'd and done
As is the morning's silver-melting dew
Against the golden splendour of the sun!
An expir'd date, cancell'd ere well begun:
    Honour and beauty, in the owner's
      arms,
    Are weakly fortress'd from a world
      of harms.

Beauty itself doth of itself persuade
The eyes of men without an orator;
What needeth then apologies be made
To set forth that which is so singular?
Or why is Collatine the publisher
    Of that rich jewel he should keep
      unknown
    From thievish ears, because it is his
      own?

Perchance his boast of Lucrece' sov'-
    reignty
Suggested this proud issue of a king,
For by our ears our hearts oft tainted be;
Perchance that envy of so rich a thing
Braving compare, disdainfully did sting
    His high-pitch'd thoughts that
      meaner men should vaunt
    That golden hap which their supe-
      riors want.

23. DONE *lost, con-
sumed, as in* Venus
and Adonis, *line
749.*
32. SINGULAR
unique.
33. PUBLISHER *pro-
claimer, one who
makes known.*
37. SUGGESTED
tempted.
40. BRAVING
defying.
42. HAP *fortune.*
WANT *lack.*

But some untimely thought did instigate
His all too timeless speed, if none of
    those:
45   His honour, his affairs, his friends, his
    state,
Neglected all, with swift intent he goes
To quench the coal which in his liver
    glows.
    O rash false heat, wrapp'd in re-
        pentant cold,
    Thy hasty spring still blasts and ne'er
        grows old!

50   When at Collatium this false lord arriv'd,
    Well was he welcom'd by the Roman
        dame,
    Within whose face Beauty and Virtue
        striv'd
    Which of them both should underprop
        her fame:
    When Virtue bragg'd, Beauty would
        blush for shame;
55   When Beauty boasted blushes, in
            despite
            Virtue would stain that o'er with
                silver white.

    But Beauty, in that white entituled,
    From Venus' doves doth challenge that
        fair field:
    Then Virtue claims from Beauty Beauty's
        red,

47. LIVER *thought
to be the seat of the
passions.*
49. STILL *always.*
BLASTS *withers.*
52–70. *The general
meaning is as fol-
lows: Beauty and
virtue are at strife
to determine for
which of them
Venus should be
most celebrated. In
this contest, the
bragging of virtue
made beauty blush,
and her blushing
made her red more
apparent; then, in
defiance of beauty,
virtue covered over
the blush with
white. Beauty re-
taliated by laying a
claim to white, the
color of the doves
which draw Venus
through the air.
Virtue then lay a
claim to red, be-
cause that is the
color she gave to the
cheeks of man in
the golden age.
Each argues that her
claim to the other's
color goes back to
the infancy of the
world. Each has
such sovereignty
that each at times
assumes the place
of the other.*
55. DESPITE *defiance
of.*
57. IN . . . ENTI-
TULED *entitled to
that white.*
58. CHALLENGE
claim.

60 Which Virtue gave the golden age to gild
Their silver cheeks, and call'd it then
their shield,
    Teaching them thus to use it in the
    fight,
    When shame assail'd, the red should
    fence the white.

This heraldry in Lucrece' face was seen,
65 Argu'd by Beauty's red and Virtue's
white:
Of either's colour was the other queen,
Proving from world's minority their
right:
Yet their ambition makes them still to
fight;
    The sovereignty of either being so
    great
70 That oft they interchange each
    other's seat.

This silent war of lilies and of roses
Which Tarquin view'd in her fair face's
field,
In their pure ranks his traitor eye en-
closes;
Where lest between them both it should
be kill'd.
75 The coward captive vanquished doth
yield
    To those two armies that would let
    him go
    Rather than triumph in so false a foe.

60. THE GOLDEN AGE
The poets of the Renaissance liked to write of a golden age, the period of man's innocence, since lost. At this time, according to Spenser (The Faerie Queene, Pro-logue, Book 5), all men loved virtue, no fraud was found in them, no one was afraid of force, war was unknown, uni-versal peace reigned among men and ani-mals, all things grew freely out of the ground, and jus-tice reigned su-preme. TO GILD *to color.*
63. FENCE *defend.*
67. *each arguing that her claim dates from the time when the world was young.*

Now thinks he that her husband's shallow tongue,
The niggard prodigal that prais'd her so,
80 In that high task hath done her beauty
wrong,
Which far exceeds his barren skill to
show:
Therefore that praise which Collatine
doth owe
  Enchanted Tarquin answers with
  surmise,
  In silent wonder of still-gazing eyes.

85 This earthly saint, adored by this devil,
Little suspecteth the false worshipper;
For unstain'd thoughts do seldom dream
on evil;
Birds never lim'd no secret bushes fear:
So guiltless she securely gives good cheer
90   And reverend welcome to her
    princely guest,
      Whose inward ill no outward harm
      express'd;

For that he colour'd with his high estate,
Hiding base sin in pleats of majesty;
That nothing in him seem'd inordinate,
95 Save sometime too much wonder of his
eye,
Which, having all, all could not satisfy;
    But, poorly rich, so wanteth in his
    store
      That, cloy'd with much, he pineth
      still for more.

*83. SURMISE amaze-
ment.
87. UNSTAIN'D pure.
88. LIM'D caught
with birdlime, a
sticky substance put
on the twigs of trees
to catch birds.
89. SECURELY with
no apprehensions.
90. REVEREND rever-
ent. Shakespeare
used the two forms
interchangeably.
92. COLOUR'D gave
a different appear-
ance to.
93. PLEATS folds,
like those in a royal
robe.
97. STORE abun-
dance.*

But she, that never cop'd with stranger
eyes,

100 Could pick no meaning from their parling
looks,
Nor read the subtle shining secrecies
Writ in the glassy margents of such
books:
She touch'd no unknown baits, nor fear'd
no hooks;
Nor could she moralize his wanton
sight,

105 More than his eyes were open'd to
the light.

He stories to her ears her husband's
fame,
Won in the fields of fruitful Italy;
And decks with praises Collatine's high
name,
Made glorious by his manly chivalry

110 With bruised arms and wreaths of victory:
Her joy with heav'd-up hand she
doth express,
And wordless so greets heaven for
his success.

Far from the purpose of his coming
thither
He makes excuses for his being there:

115 No cloudy show of stormy blust'ring
weather
Doth yet in his fair welkin once appear,
Till sable Night, mother of dread and
fear,

99. COP'D WITH *en-
countered.*
100. PARLING *speak-
ing.*
102. MARGENTS
*margins, explana-
tory matter printed
in the margins of
pages.*
104. MORALIZE *inter-
pret, assess the
meaning of.*
105. THAN *than that.*
111. HEAV'D-UP *up-
lifted.*
113. FROM *different
from.*
116. WELKIN *sky.*

Upon the world dim darkness doth
display
And in her vaulty prison stows the
day.

120 For then is Tarquin brought unto his bed,
Intending weariness with heavy sprite;
For after supper long he questioned
With modest Lucrece, and wore out the
night:
Now leaden slumber with live's strength
doth fight,
125 And every one to rest themselves be-
take,
Save thieves and cares and troubl'd
minds that wake.

As one of which doth Tarquin lie revolv-
ing
The sundry dangers of his will's obtain-
ing
Yet ever to obtain his will resolving,
130 Though weak-built hopes persuade him
to abstaining:
Despair to gain doth traffic oft for gaining,
And when great treasure is the meed
propos'd,
Though death be adjunct, there's no
death suppos'd.

Those that much covet are with gain so
fond
135 For what they have not, that which they
possess,

*118. DISPLAY spread out.
121. INTENDING pretending. SPRITE spirit.
122. QUESTIONED talked.
124. LIVE's life's.
129. WILL both volition and desire.
130. WEAK-BUILT having little basis.
132. MEED reward.
133. ADJUNCT a consequence.
134. FOND eager.
135. FOR Emendation suggested by Edward Capell (1713–1781). 1594 Quarto: That.*

They scatter and unloose it from their
bond,
And so, by hoping more, they have but
less;
Or, gaining more, the profit of excess
Is but to surfeit, and such griefs
sustain
140　That they prove bankrout in this
poor rich gain.

The aim of all is but to nurse the life
With honour, wealth, and ease in waning
age;
And in this aim there is such thwarting
strife
That one for all, or all for one we gage;
145　As life for honour in fell battle's rage;
Honour for wealth; and oft that
wealth doth cost
The death of all, and all together
lost;

So that in vent'ring ill we leave to be
The things we are for that which we
expect;
150　And this ambitious foul infirmity,
In having much, torments us with defect
Of that we have: so then we do neglect
The thing we have, and, all for want
of wit,
Make something nothing by aug-
menting it.

155　Such hazard now must doting Tarquin
make,

138. EXCESS *having
more than enough.*
140. BANKROUT
bankrupt.
144. GAGE *pledge,
risk.*
145. FELL *fierce,
savage.*
148. VENT'RING *ven-
turing, risking.*
LEAVE *cease.*
151. DEFECT *ab-
sence of, loss.*

Pawning his honour to obtain his lust;
And for himself himself he must forsake:
Then where is truth, if there be no self-
    trust?
When shall he think to find a stranger
    just
160   When he himself himself confounds,
            betrays
        To sland'rous tongues and wretched
            hateful days?

Now stole upon the time the dead of
    night,
When heavy sleep had clos'd up mortal
    eyes:
No comfortable star did lend his light,
165 No noise but owls' and wolves' death-
    boding cries;
Now serves the season that they may
    surprise
        The silly lambs: pure thoughts are
            dead and still,
        While lust and murder wakes to
            stain and kill.

And now this lustful lord leapt from his
    bed,
170 Throwing his mantle rudely o'er his arm;
Is madly toss'd between desire and dread;
Th' one sweetly flatters, th' other feareth
    harm;
But honest fear, bewitch'd with lust's foul
    charm,
        Doth too too oft betake him to retire,

157. *See* Venus and
Adonis, *line 161.*
164. COMFORTABLE
comforting.
167. SILLY *innocent,*
harmless.

THE RAPE OF LUCRECE / 431

175   Beaten away by brainsick rude de-
                sire,

        His falchion on a flint he softly smiteth,
        That from the cold stone sparks of fire
            do fly;
        Whereat a waxen torch forthwith he
            lighteth,
        Which must be lodestar to his lustful eye;
180   And to the flame thus speaks advisedly:
                "As from this cold flint I enforc'd this
                    fire,
                So Lucrece must I force to my desire."

        Here pale with fear he doth premeditate
        The dangers of his loathsome enterprise,
185   And in his inward mind he doth debate
        What following sorrow may on this arise;
        Then looking scornfully he doth despise
                His naked armour of still-slaugh-
                    ter'd lust
                And justly thus controls his thoughts
                    unjust:

190   "Fair torch, burn out thy light, and lend it
            not
        To darken her whose light excelleth
            thine:
        And die, unhallow'd thoughts, before you
            blot
        With your uncleanness that which is
            divine:
        Offer pure incense to so pure a shrine:
195   Let fair humanity abhor the deed

176. FALCHION curved sword.
179. LODESTAR star by which one guides a course.
180. ADVISEDLY deliberately.
188. NAKED unarmed, as in "naked as I am, I will assault thee" (Othello, Act V, scene 2, line 258). Tarquin's armor is without protective power; it is only lust. STILL-SLAUGHTER'D *always slaughtered, always coming to nothing. The crime his lust motivates "will bear an ever-during blame" (line 224).*

That spots and stains love's modest
  snow-white weed.

"O shame to knighthood and to shining
  arms!
O foul dishonour to my household's
  grave!
O impious act including all foul harms!
A martial man to be soft fancy's slave!
True valour still a true respect should
  have;
        Then my digression is so vile, so
          base,
        That it will live engraven in my face.

"Yea, though I die, the scandal will survive
And be an eyesore in my golden coat;
Some loathsome dash the herald will con-
  trive
To cipher me how fondly I did dote;
That my posterity, sham'd with the note,
        Shall curse my bones and hold it for
          no sin
        To wish that I their father had not
          been.

"What win I if I gain the thing I seek?
A dream, a breath, a froth of fleeting joy.
Who buys a minute's mirth to wail a
  week,
Or sells eternity to get a toy?
For one sweet grape who will the vine
  destroy?

196. WEED garment.
198. HOUSEHOLD'S
GRAVE the grave of
his ancestors.
200. FANCY'S love's.
The usage survives
in "fancy free."
201. STILL always.
202. DIGRESSION de-
viation from the
good, transgression.
205. GOLDEN COAT
coat of arms.
206. DASH mark of
infamy. HERALD the
officer who controls
heraldic devices.
207. CIPHER express.
FONDLY foolishly.
DOTE give in to pas-
sion.
208. NOTE mark of
disgrace.
212. DREAM unreal
joy, illusion. See
Sonnet 129, line 12.

Or what fond beggar, but to touch
the crown,
Would with the sceptre straight be
stroken down?

"If Collatinus dream of my intent,
Will he not wake, and in a desp'rate rage
220 Post hither this vile purpose to prevent—
This siege that hath engirt his marriage,
This blur to youth, this sorrow to the sage,
This dying virtue, this surviving
shame,
Whose crime will bear an ever-dur-
ing blame?

225 "O what excuse can my invention make
When thou shalt charge me with so black
a deed?
Will not my tongue be mute, my frail
joints shake,
Mine eyes forgo their light, my false heart
bleed?
The guilt being great, the fear doth still
exceed;
230 And extreme fear can neither fight
nor fly,
But coward-like with trembling terror die.

"Had Collatinus kill'd my son or sire,
Or lain in ambush to betray my life,
Or were he not my dear friend, this desire
235 Might have excuse to work upon his wife,

216. FOND *foolish*.
221. ENGIRT *sur-
rounded in order to
attack*.
226. THOU *Collatine*.
229. DOTH STILL
EXCEED *is always
greater*.

As in revenge or quittal of such strife:
>   But as he is my kinsman, my dear
>   friend,
>   The shame and fault finds no excuse
>   nor end.

"Shameful it is; ay, if the fact be known:
240 Hateful it is; there is no hate in loving:
I'll beg her love; but she is not her own:
The worst is but denial and reproving:
My will is strong, past reason's weak re-
moving;
>   Who fears a sentence or an old man's
>   saw
245 >   Shall by a painted cloth be kept in
>   awe."

Thus graceless holds he disputation
'Tween frozen conscience and hot-burning will,
And with good thoughts makes dispensation,
Urging the worser sense for vantage still;
250 Which in a moment doth confound and
kill
>   All pure effects, and doth so far pro-
>   ceed
>   That what is vile shows like a virtu-
>   ous deed.

Quoth he, "She took me kindly by the
hand
And gaz'd for tidings in my eager eyes,

236. QUITTAL *re-quital.*
243. WILL *desire.*
244. SENTENCE *maxim, axiom.*
245. PAINTED CLOTH *cloth painted in imitation of tapestry. The design of such cloths often included moral maxims.*
248. GOOD . . . DISPENSATION *exempts himself from the demands of righteous thinking.*
249. FOR . . . STILL *always for his advantage.*
251. EFFECTS *consequences of good thoughts. See* Venus and Adonis, *line 605.*

255   Fearing some hard news from the warlike
           band
       Where her beloved Collatinus lies.
       O, how her fear did make her colour rise!
           First red as roses that on lawn we lay,
           Then white as lawn, the roses took
             away.

260   "And how her hand, in my hand being
           lock'd,
       Forc'd it to tremble with her loyal fear!
       Which struck her sad, and then it faster
           rock'd
       Until her husband's welfare she did hear;
       Whereat she smiled with so sweet a cheer
265   That had Narcissus seen her as she
             stood,
          Self-love had never drown'd him in
             the flood.

       "Why hunt I then for colour or excuses?
       All orators are dumb when beauty plead-
           eth;
       Poor wretches have remorse in poor
           abuses;
270   Love thrives not in the heart that shadows
           dreadeth:
       Affection is my captain, and he leadeth;
          And when his gaudy banner is dis-
             play'd,
          The coward fights and will not be
             dismay'd.

       "Then, childish fear avaunt! debating die!
275   Respect and reason wait on wrinkled age!

255. HARD NEWS *bad tidings.*
258–259. *See* Venus and Adonis, *lines 589–591.*
262. *The trembling of Tarquin's hand suggested to her that he was the bearer of bad news.*
265. NARCISSUS *See* Venus and Adonis, *lines 161–162, note.*
267. COLOUR *pretext, as in line 476.*
269. *Remorse is appropriate to lesser men engaged in lesser wrongs.*
270. SHADOWS *things having only the appearance of reality.*
271. AFFECTION *passion.*
272. GAUDY *showy, florid.*
275. RESPECT *prudence.*

My heart shall never countermand mine
  eye:
Sad pause and deep regard beseems the
  sage;
My part is youth, and beats these from the
  stage:
 Desire my pilot is, beauty my prize;
280 Then who fears sinking where such
  treasure lies?"

As corn o'ergrown by weeds, so heedful
  fear
Is almost chok'd by unresisted lust.
Away he steals with open list'ning ear,
Full of foul hope and full of fond mistrust;
285 Both which, as servitors to the unjust,
  So cross him with their opposite persuasion
  That now he vows a league, and now
   invasion.

Within his thought her heavenly image
  sits,
And in the selfsame seat sits Collatine:
290 That eye which looks on her confounds
 his wits;
That eye which him beholds, as more
  divine,
Unto a view so false will not incline;
  But with a pure appeal seeks to the
   heart,
  Which once corrupted takes the
   worser part;

276. COUNTERMAND
oppose, contradict.
277. SAD *serious.*
281. CORN *such
plants as barley,
wheat, and rye; not
maize, as in Amer-
ica.*
284. FOND *not very
deep.*
287. LEAGUE *peace,
friendship.*

295 And therein heartens up his servile
powers,
Who, flatt'red by their leader's jocund
show,
Stuff up his lust, as minutes fill up hours;
And as their captain, so their pride doth
grow,
Paying more slavish tribute than they
owe.
300 By reprobate desire thus madly led,
The Roman lord marcheth to Lucrece' bed.

The locks between her chamber and his
will,
Each one by him enforc'd retires his ward;
But as they open, they all rate his ill,
305 Which drives the creeping thief to some
regard:
The threshold grates the door to have him
heard;
Night-wand'ring weasels shriek to
see him there;
They fright him, yet he still pursues
his fear.

As each unwilling portal yields him way,
310 Through little vents and crannies of the
place
The wind wars with his torch to make
him stay,
And blows the smoke of it into his face,
Extinguishing his conduct in this case;

295. SERVILE POWERS
the "mortal instru-
ments" of Julius
Caesar, *Act II, scene
1, line 66, where
they are opposed to
"the genius" of the
mind and spirit.
They are the "cor-
poral agents" of the
mind.*
296. JOCUND *lively,
brisk.*
303. RETIRES *with-
draws.* WARD *that
part of a lock which
opposes an obstacle
to a key not having
a corresponding
notch.*
304. RATE HIS ILL
*condemn his evil in-
tentions by their
creaking.*
306. GRATES . . .
HEARD *makes a grat-
ing noise against the
door to warn of Tar-
quin's approach.*
307. WEASELS *There
was thought to be a
species of weasel
which lived in
houses and always
lay at night in a dif-
ferent lair.*
308. HIS FEAR *the
cause of his fear.*
313. CONDUCT *that
which conducts him,
shows him the way.*

But his hot heart, which fond desire
    doth scorch,
Puffs forth another wind that fires
    the torch;

And being lighted, by the light he spies
Lucretia's glove, wherein her needle
    sticks:
He takes it from the rushes where it lies,
And griping it, the needle his finger
    pricks,
As who should say "This glove to wanton
    tricks
        Is not inur'd. Return again in haste;
        Thou see'st our mistress' ornaments
            are chaste."

But all these poor forbiddings could not
    stay him;
He in the worst sense consters their de-
    nial:
The doors, the wind, the glove, that did
    delay him,
He takes for accidental things of trial;
Or as those bars which stop the hourly
    dial,
        Who with a ling'ring stay his course
            doth let
        Till every minute pays the hour his
            debt.

"So, so," quoth he, "these lets attend the
    time,

315

320

325

330

319. NEEDLE *here*
monosyllabic.
324. CONSTERS *con-*
strues, interprets.
326. ACCIDENTAL . . .
TRIAL *chance annoy-*
ances unrelated to
his plans. It is
characteristic of
Shakespeare's vil-
lains not to believe
in portents.
328. LET *hinder.*
330. LETS *hin-*
drances.

Like little frosts that sometime threat the
  spring
To add a more rejoicing to the prime
And give the sneaped birds more cause to
  sing.
Pain pays the income of each precious
  thing;
  Huge rocks, high winds, strong
    pirates, shelves and sands,
  The merchant fears ere rich at home
    he lands."

Now is he come unto the chamber door
That shuts him from the heaven of his
  thought,
Which with a yielding latch, and with no
  more,
Hath barr'd him from the blessed thing he
  sought.
So from himself impiety hath wrought
  That for his prey to pray he doth
    begin,
  As if the heavens should counte-
    nance his sin.

But in the midst of his unfruitful prayer,
Having solicited th' eternal power
That his foul thoughts might compass his
  fair fair,
And they would stand auspicious to the
  hour,
Even there he starts: quoth he, "I must de-
  flow'r:

335

340

345

332. PRIME *spring
of the year.*
333. SNEAPED
*chilled, nipped by
cold.*
341. *Impiety has
warped him so far
from himself.*
346. FAIR FAIR *fair
beauty.*

The powers to whom I pray abhor
    this fact;

350 How can they then assist me in the
    act?

"Then Love and Fortune be my gods, my
    guide!
My will is back'd with resolution:
Thoughts are but dreams till their effects
    be tried;
The blackest sin is clear'd with absolu-
    tion;
355 Against love's fire fear's frost hath disso-
    lution.
        The eye of heaven is out, and misty
            night
        Covers the shame that follows sweet
            delight."

This said, his guilty hand pluck'd up the
    latch,
And with his knee the door he opens wide.
360 The dove sleeps fast that this night owl
    will catch:
Thus treason works ere traitors be espi'd.
Who sees the lurking serpent steps aside;
        But she, sound sleeping, fearing no
            such thing,
        Lies at the mercy of his mortal sting.

365 Into the chamber wickedly he stalks
And gazeth on her yet unstained bed.
The curtains being close, about he walks,   352. WILL *desire*.
Rolling his greedy eyeballs in his head: 353. THEIR EFFECTS
                                                BE TRIED *They are
                                                put into action.*

By their high treason is his heart misled,

370   Which gives the watchword to his
    hand full soon
    To draw the cloud that hides the
    silver moon.

Look as the fair and fiery-pointed sun,

Rushing from forth a cloud, bereaves our
sight,

Even so, the curtain drawn, his eyes begun

375 To wink, being blinded with a greater
light;

Whether it is that she reflects so bright

    That dazzleth them, or else some
    shame supposed;

    But blind they are, and keep them-
    selves enclosed.

O, had they in that darksome prison died,

380 Then had they seen the period of their ill;

Then Collatine again, by Lucrece' side,

In his clear bed might have reposed still;

But they must ope, this blessed league to
kill,

    And holy-thoughted Lucrece to their
    sight

385   Must sell her joy, her life, her world's
    delight.

Her lily hand her rosy cheek lies under,

Coz'ning the pillow of a lawful kiss;

Who, therefore angry, seems to part in
sunder,

Swelling on either side to want his bliss;

371. CLOUD *bed curtain.* MOON *Lucrece, because she is as chaste as Diana, goddess of the moon.*
372. LOOK *just.*
373. BEREAVES *impairs.*
375. WINK *close.*
377. DAZZLETH *See* Venus and Adonis, *line 1064.*
380. PERIOD *end.*
387. COZ'NING *cheating.* KISS *the touch of her hand. See* Sonnet 128, *line 6.*
388. WHO *which, that is, the pillow.*

390 Between whose hills her head entombed
 is;
  Where like a virtuous monument she
   lies,
  To be admir'd of lewd unhallow'd
   eyes.

Without the bed her other fair hand was,
On the green coverlet; whose perfect
 white
395 Show'd like an April daisy on the grass,
With pearly sweat resembling dew of
 night.
Her eyes, like marigolds, had sheath'd
 their light,
  And canopied in darkness sweetly
   lay
  Till they might open to adorn the
   day.

400 Her hair like golden threads play'd with
 her breath—
O modest wantons, wantons modesty!
Showing life's triumph in the map of
 death,
And death's dim look in life's mortality:
Each in her sleep themselves so beautify
405   As if between them twain there were
   no strife,
  But that life liv'd in death, and death
   in life.

Her breasts like ivory globes circled with
 blue,

402. MAP *picture.*
See line 1712 and
Sonnet 68, line 1.

THE RAPE OF LUCRECE / 443

A pair of maiden worlds unconquered,
Save of their lord no bearing yoke they
knew,
410 And him by oath they truly honoured:
These worlds in Tarquin new ambition
bred,
Who like a foul usurper went about
From this fair throne to heave the
owner out.

What could he see but mightily he noted?
415 What did he note but strongly he desired?
What he beheld, on that he firmly doted,
And in his will his wilful eye he tired.
With more than admiration he admired
Her azure veins, her alablaster skin,
420 Her coral lips, her snow-white
dimpled chin.

As the grim lion fawneth o'er his prey,
Sharp hunger by the conquest satisfi'd,
So o'er this sleeping soul doth Tarquin
stay,
His rage of lust by gazing qualifi'd;
425 Slack'd, not suppress'd; for, standing by
her side,
His eye, which late this mutiny re-
strains,
Unto a greater uproar tempts his
veins;

And they, like straggling slaves for pil-
lage fighting,

417. WILL *desire.*
418. ADMIRATION
wonder.
421. FAWNETH *re-
gards with anticipa-
tory pleasure.*

Obdurate vassals fell exploits effecting,
430 In bloody death and ravishment delight-
ing,
Nor children's tears nor mothers' groans
respecting,
Swell in their pride, the onset still expect-
ing:
Anon his beating heart, alarum striking,
Gives the hot charge and bids them
do their liking.

435 His drumming heart cheers up his burning eye,
His eye commends the leading to his hand,
His hand, as proud of such a dignity,
Smoking with pride, march'd on to make
his stand
On her bare breast, the heart of all her
land;
440 Whose ranks of blue veins, as his
hand did scale,
Left their round turrets destitute and
pale;

They, must'ring to the quiet cabinet
Where their dear governess and lady lies,
Do tell her she is dreadfully beset
445 And fright her with confusion of their
cries:
She, much amaz'd, breaks ope her lock'd-
up eyes,
Who, peeping forth this tumult to
behold,

429. FELL *fierce,
savage.*
432. PRIDE *Here the
word suggests pas-
sion. "In pride" was
Shakespeare's
phrase for "in heat,"
said of female ani-
mals. There is also
the suggestion of
"proud flesh," flesh
inflamed and swol-
len. See Sonnet 151,
lines 7–12.*
433. ALARUM *a call
to attack in battle.*
436. COMMENDS
commits.
442. CABINET *the
chest.*
443. GOVERNESS AND
LADY *both the heart,
which governs the
movement of the
blood, and the lady
herself.*

Imagine her as one in dead of night,
From forth dull sleep by dreadful fancy waking

Are by his flaming torch dimm'd and
    controll'd.

Imagine her as one in dead of night,
450 From forth dull sleep by dreadful fancy
    waking,
That thinks she hath beheld some ghastly
    sprite,
Whose grim aspect sets every joint a-
    shaking;
What terror 'tis! but she, in worser tak-
    ing,
    From sleep disturbed, heedfully doth
      view
455   The sight which makes supposed ter-
      ror true.

Wrapp'd and confounded in a thousand
    fears,
Like to a new-kill'd bird she trembling
    lies;
She dares not look; yet, winking, there
    appears
Quick-shifting antics ugly in her eyes:
460 Such shadows are the weak brain's for-
    geries,
    Who, angry that the eyes fly from
      their lights,
    In darkness daunts them with more
      dreadful sights.

His hand, that yet remains upon her
    breast
    (Rude ram, to batter such an ivory wall!)

453. TAKING *plight.*
454. HEEDFULLY
with deliberation.
458. WINKING *clos-
ing her eyes.*
459. ANTICS *gro-
tesque apparitions.*
460. SHADOWS *prod-
ucts of the imagina-
tion.*

465   May feel her heart (poor citizen!) dis-
      tress'd,
  Wounding itself to death, rise up and fall,
  Beating her bulk, that his hand shakes
      withal.
      This moves in him more rage and
          lesser pity,
      To make the breach and enter this
          sweet city.

470   First like a trumpet doth his tongue begin
  To sound a parley to his heartless foe;
  Who o'er the white sheet peers her whiter
      chin,
  The reason of this rash alarm to know,
  Which he by dumb demeanour seeks to
      show;
475   But she with vehement prayers urg-
          eth still
      Under what colour he commits this
          ill.

  Thus he replies: "The colour in thy face,
  That even for anger makes the lily pale
  And the red rose blush at her own dis-
      grace,
480   Shall plead for me and tell my loving tale:
  Under that colour am I come to scale
      Thy never-conquer'd fort: the fault
          is thine,
      For those thine eyes betray thee unto
          mine.

  "Thus I forestall thee, if thou mean to
      chide:

467. BULK body, the walls of the chest.
468. RAGE extreme passion.
471. HEARTLESS without heart, frightened.
472. PEERS lets appear.
474. DUMB DEMEANOUR gesture without words.
476. UNDER WHAT COLOUR under what appearance if right, for what specious reason.
479. DISGRACE lack of beauty as compared to Lucrece.

485 Thy beauty hath ensnar'd thee to this
　　　night,
　　Where thou with patience must my will
　　　abide;
　　My will, that marks thee for my earth's
　　　delight,
　　Which I to conquer sought with all my
　　　might;
　　　　But as reproof and reason beat it
　　　　dead,
490　　By thy bright beauty was it newly
　　　　bred.

　　"I see what crosses my attempt will bring;
　　I know what thorns the growing rose de-
　　　fends;
　　I think the honey guarded with a sting;
　　All this beforehand counsel compre-
　　　hends:
495　But Will is deaf and hears no heedful
　　　friends;
　　　　Only he hath an eye to gaze on
　　　　Beauty,
　　　　And dotes on what he looks, 'gainst
　　　　law or duty.

　　"I have debated even in my soul
　　What wrong, what shame, what sorrow I
　　　shall breed;
500　But nothing can affection's course control
　　Or stop the headlong fury of his speed.
　　I know repentant tears ensue the deed,
　　　　Reproach, disdain, and deadly en-
　　　　mity;

486, 487. WILL *de-
sire.*
*496. His eyes look
only on beauty.*
497. LOOKS *looks at.*
500. AFFECTION'S
passion's.

Yet strive I to embrace mine infamy."

505   This said, he shakes aloft his Roman
blade,
Which, like a falcon tow'ring in the skies,
Coucheth the fowl below with his wings'
shade,
Whose crooked beak threats if he mount
he dies:
So under his insulting falchion lies
510   Harmless Lucretia, marking what he
tells
With trembling fear, as fowl hear
falcons' bells.

"Lucrece," quoth he, "this night I must en-
joy thee:
If thou deny, then force must work my
way,
For in thy bed I purpose to destroy thee;
515   That done, some worthless slave of thine
I'll slay,
To kill thine honour with thy live's decay;
And in thy dead arms do I mean to
place him,
Swearing I slew him, seeing thee em-
brace him.

"So thy surviving husband shall remain
520   The scornful mark of every open eye;
Thy kinsmen hang their heads at this disdain,

507. COUCHETH
makes to lie close.
508. WHOSE the
falcon's.
509. INSULTING FAL-
CHION triumphing
curved sword.
516. LIVE's life's.

Thy issue blurr'd with nameless bastardy;
And thou, the author of their obloquy,
        Shalt have thy trespass cited up in
            rhymes
525   And sung by children in succeeding
            times.

"But if thou yield, I rest thy secret friend:
The fault unknown is as a thought un-
            acted;
A little harm done to a great good end
For lawful policy remains enacted.
530   The poisonous simple sometime is com-
            pacted
        In a pure compound; being so ap-
            pli'd,
        His venom in effect is purifi'd.

"Then, for thy husband and thy children's
            sake,
Tender my suit, bequeath not to their lot
535   The shame that from them no device can
            take,
The blemish that will never be forgot;
Worse than a slavish wipe or birth-hour's
            blot;
        For marks descri'd in men's nativity
        Are nature's faults, not their own in-
            famy."

540   Here with a cockatrice' dead-killing eye
He rouseth up himself and makes a pause;
While she, the picture of pure piety,

527–532. If a guilty act remains unknown, it is as though it had never taken place; a guilty act done prudently to serve a good end remains an act, but, it is implied, the act is in effect pure, like the poisonous ingredient in a wholesome medicine.
529. ENACTED set down, recorded.
530. SIMPLE a single ingredient in a compound, especially in medicine. COMPACTED compounded.
534. TENDER regard with favor.
537. SLAVISH WIPE the brand on a slave. BIRTH-HOUR'S BLOT a heraldic device which is the mark of illegitimacy, the bar sinister; less probably, a birthmark.
540. COCKATRICE' an imaginary creature which could kill with a look.

Like a white hind under the gripe's sharp
claws,
Pleads, in a wilderness where are no laws,
545   To the rough beast that knows no
gentle right
Nor aught obeys but his foul appetite.

But when a black-fac'd cloud the world
doth threat,
In his dim mist th' aspiring mountains
hiding,
From earth's dark womb some gentle gust
doth get,
550   Which blows these pitchy vapours from
their biding,
Hind'ring their present fall by this divid-
ing;
So his unhallow'd haste her words
delays,
And moody Pluto winks while Orpheus plays.

Yet, foul night-waking cat, he doth but
dally,
555   While in his hold-fast foot the weak
mouse panteth:
Her sad behaviour feeds his vulture folly,
A swallowing gulf that even in plenty
wanteth;
His ear her prayers admits, but his heart
granteth
No penetrable entrance to her plain-
ing:

543. HIND the fe-
male of the red
deer.
GRIPE's griffin, a
fabled animal, half
lion, half eagle; per-
haps a vulture.
548. ASPIRING tower-
ing.
549. GET go.
551. FALL falling as
rain.
553. PLUTO . . .
PLAYS Pluto, god of
the underworld,
closes his eyes while
Orpheus, who as a
mortal should have
been forbidden en-
trance to Hades,
plays his music and
leads Eurydice back
toward the world.
557. WANTETH
hungers.

560   Tears harden lust, though marble
          wear with raining.

       Her pity-pleading eyes are sadly fix'd
       In the remorseless wrinkles of his face;
       Her modest eloquence with sighs is mix'd,
       Which to her oratory adds more grace.
565   She puts the period often from his place,
              And midst the sentence so her accent
                breaks
              That twice she doth begin ere once
                she speaks.

       She conjures him by high almighty Jove,
       By knighthood, gentry, and sweet friend-
          ship's oath,
570   By her untimely tears, her husband's love,
       By holy human law and common troth,
       By heaven and earth, and all the power of
          both,
              That to his borrow'd bed he make
                retire
              And stoop to honour, not to foul de-
                sire.

575   Quoth she: "Reward not hospitality
       With such black payment as thou hast
          pretended;
       Mud not the fountain that gave drink to
          thee;
       Mar not the thing that cannot be a-
          mended;
       End thy ill aim before thy shoot be ended;

562. WRINKLES *frowns.*
565–566. *She hesitates before speaking and pauses in the midst of sentences.*
568. JOVE *Jove and Jupiter were Roman names for Zeus, the son of Cronus and Rhea and the supreme power of the gods.*
576. PRETENDED *intended.*
579. SHOOT *act of shooting.*

580   He is no woodman that doth bend
               his bow
            To strike a poor unseasonable doe.

      "My husband is thy friend; for his sake
            spare me:
         Thyself art mighty; for thine own sake
            leave me:
         Myself a weakling; do not then ensnare
            me:
585   Thou look'st not like deceit; do not de-
            ceive me.
         My sighs like whirlwinds labour hence to
            heave thee:
               If ever man were mov'd with
                  woman's moans,
               Be moved with my tears, my sighs,
                  my groans;

      "All which together, like a troubled
            ocean,
590   Beat at thy rocky and wrack-threat'ning
            heart,
         To soften it with their continual motion;
         For stones dissolv'd to water do convert.
         O, if no harder than a stone thou art,
               Melt at my tears and be compassion-
                  ate!
595   Soft pity enters at an iron gate.

      "In Tarquin's likeness I did entertain thee:
         Hast thou put on his shape to do him
            shame?
         To all the host of heaven I complain me,

590. WRACK-
THREAT'NING
threatening ruin.

Thou wrong'st his honour, wound'st his
    princely name.
600 Thou are not what thou seem'st; and if
    the same,
        Thou seem'st not what thou art, a
        god, a king;
        For kings like gods should govern
        everything.

"How will thy shame be seeded in thine
    age
When thus thy vices bud before thy
    spring!
605 If in thy hope thou dar'st do such outrage,
What dar'st thou not when once thou art
    a king?
O, be rememb'red, no outrageous thing
        From vassal actors can be wip'd
        away;
        Then kings' misdeeds cannot be hid
        in clay.

610 "This deed will make thee only lov'd for
    fear;
But happy monarchs still are fear'd for
    love:
With foul offenders thou perforce must
    bear
When they in thee the like offences prove:
If but for fear of this, thy will remove;
615   For princes are the glass, the school,
        the book,
        Where subjects' eyes do learn, do
        read, do look.

603. SEEDED *full-grown*.
608. ACTORS *doers*.
611. STILL *always*.
614. IF BUT FOR *if only for*. WILL *desire and determination*.

456 / THE RAPE OF LUCRECE

"And wilt thou be the school where Lust
shall learn?
Must he in thee read lectures of such
shame?
Wilt thou be glass wherein it shall discern
620 Authority for sin, warrant for blame,
To privilege dishonour in thy name?
    Thou back'st reproach against long-
    living laud
    And mak'st fair reputation but a
    bawd.

"Hast thou command? by him that gave it
thee,
625 From a pure heart command thy rebel
will:
Draw not thy sword to guard iniquity,
For it was lent thee all that brood to kill.
Thy princely office how canst thou fulfil,
    When, pattern'd by thy fault, foul
    Sin may say
630   He learn'd to sin and thou didst
    teach the way?

"Think but how vile a spectacle it were
To view thy present trespass in another.
Men's faults do seldom to themselves appear;
Their own transgressions partially they
smother:
635 This guilt would seem death-worthy in
thy brother.
    O, how are they wrapp'd in with in-
    famies

619. GLASS *the look-
ing glass.*
623. BAWD *procurer.*

That from their own misdeeds
askaunce their eyes!

"To thee, to thee, my heav'd-up hands appeal,
Not to seducing lust, thy rash relier:
640   I sue for exil'd majesty's repeal;
Let him return, and flatt'ring thoughts retire:
His true respect will prison false desire
    And wipe the dim mist from thy doting eyne,
    That thou shalt see thy state and pity mine."

645   "Have done," quoth he, "my uncontrolled tide
Turns not, but swells the higher by this let.
Small lights are soon blown out; huge fires abide
And with the wind in greater fury fret:
The petty streams that pay a daily debt
650   To their salt sovereign with their fresh falls' haste
    Add to his flow, but alter not his taste."

"Thou art," quoth she, "a sea, a sovereign king;
And, lo, there falls into thy boundless flood
Black lust, dishonour, shame, misgoverning,

637. ASKAUNCE *turn.*
638. HEAV'D-UP *uplifted.*
639. THY RASH RELIER *lust.* Lust relies *rashly on the passion which motivates it, even though, as here, Tarquin is aware of the consequences.*
643. EYNE *eyes.*
646. LET *hindrance.*

655 Who seek to stain the ocean of thy blood.
If all these petty ills shall change thy
good,
Thy sea within a puddle's womb is
hears'd,
And not the puddle in thy sea dispers'd.

"So shall these slaves be king, and thou
their slave;
660 Thou nobly base, they basely dignifi'd;
Thou their fair life, and they thy fouler
grave;
Thou loathed in their shame, they in thy
pride:
The lesser thing should not the greater
hide;
The cedar stoops not to the base
shrub's foot,
665 But low shrubs wither at the cedar's
root.

"So let thy thoughts, low vassals to thy
state"—
"No more," quoth he; "by heaven, I will
not hear thee!
Yield to my love; if not, enforced hate,
Instead of love's coy touch, shall rudely
tear thee:
670 That done, despitefully I mean to bear
thee
Unto the base bed of some rascal
groom,

657. HEARS'D con-
fined, enclosed in a
coffin.
669. COY tender.

To be thy partner in this shameful
doom."

This said, he sets his foot upon the light,
For light and lust are deadly enemies;
675 Shame folded up in blind concealing
night,
When most unseen, then most doth tyran-
nize.
The wolf hath seiz'd his prey; the poor
lamb cries,
    Till with her own white fleece her
    voice controll'd
    Entombs her outcry in her lips' sweet
    fold;

680 For with the nightly linen that she wears
He pens her piteous clamours in her head,
Cooling his hot face in the chastest tears
That ever modest eyes with sorrow shed.
O, that prone lust should stain so pure a
bed!
685   The spots whereof could weeping
    purify,
    Her tears should drop on them per-
    petually.

But she hath lost a dearer thing than life,
And he hath won what he would lose
again:
This forced league doth force a further
strife;
690 This momentary joy breeds months of
pain;

678. WHITE FLEECE
*bedclothes. See line
680.*
684. PRONE *eager.*
685. *if weeping
could purify the
spots of lust.*

This hot desire converts to cold disdain:
　　Pure Chastity is rifled of her store,
　　And Lust, the thief, far poorer than
　　　　before.

Look as the full-fed hound or gorged
　　　hawk,
695　Unapt for tender smell or speedy flight,
Make slow pursuit, or altogether balk
The prey wherein by nature they delight,
So surfeit-taking Tarquin fares this
　　　night:
　　His taste delicious, in digestion sour-
　　　　ing,
700　Devours his will, that liv'd by foul
　　　　devouring.

O, deeper sin than bottomless conceit
Can comprehend in still imagination!
Drunken Desire must vomit his receipt
Ere he can see his own abomination.
705　While Lust is in his pride, no exclamation
　　Can curb his heat or rein his rash
　　　desire
　　Till, like a jade, Self-will himself
　　　doth tire.

And then with lank and lean discolour'd
　　　cheek,
With heavy eye, knit brow, and strength-
　　　less pace,
710　Feeble Desire, all recreant, poor, and
　　　meek,
Like to a bankrout beggar wails his case:

696. BALK *neglect to*
pursue.
700. WILL *desire.*
701. BOTTOMLESS
fathomless. CONCEIT
understanding and
imagination func-
tioning together.
703. HIS RECEIPT
what it has re-
ceived.
705. IN HIS PRIDE *in*
his full power. See
line 342. EXCLAMA-
TION *exhortation.*
707. JADE *a term of*
extreme contempt.
710. RECREANT *re-*
tracting its errors.
711. BANKROUT *pen-*
niless.

The flesh being proud, Desire doth fight
with Grace,
For there it revels, and when that decays,
The guilty rebel for remission prays.

715 So fares it with this fault-full lord of
Rome,
Who this accomplishment so hotly chas'd;
For now against himself he sounds this
doom
That through the length of times he
stands disgrac'd:
Besides, his soul's fair temple is defac'd,
720 To whose weak ruins muster troops
of cares
To ask the spotted princess how she
fares.

She says her subjects with foul insurrection
Have batter'd down her consecrated wall,
And by their mortal fault brought in subjection
725 Her immortality and made her thrall
To living death and pain perpetual;
Which in her prescience she controlled still,
But her foresight could not forestall
their will.

Ev'n in this thought through the dark
night he stealeth,
730 A captive victor that hath lost in gain;

713. THERE in its
pride.
716. ACCOMPLISH-
MENT action, de-
sired end.
718. LENGTH OF
TIMES all time to
come.
719. FAIR TEMPLE
body. See lines
1170–1173.
721. PRINCESS Tar-
quin's soul.
722–726. Compare
Sonnet 146.

Bearing away the wound that nothing
　　healeth,
The scar that will despite of cure remain;
Leaving his spoil perplex'd in greater
　　pain.
　　　　She bears the load of lust he left be-
　　　　　hind,
735　　　And he the burthen of a guilty mind.

He like a thievish dog creeps sadly thence;
She like a wearied lamb lies panting
　　there;
He scowls, and hates himself for his
　　offence;
She desperate with her nails her flesh
　　doth tear;
740　He faintly flies, sweating with guilty fear;
　　　　She stays, exclaiming on the direful
　　　　　night;
　　　　He runs, and chides his vanish'd
　　　　　loath'd delight.

He thence departs a heavy convertite;
She there remains a hopeless castaway;
745　He in his speed looks for the morning
　　light;
She prays she never may behold the day,
"For day," quoth she, "night's scapes doth
　　open lay,
　　　　And my true eyes have never prac-
　　　　　tis'd how
　　　　To cloak offences with a cunning
　　　　　brow.

733. PERPLEX'D
bewildered.
743. CONVERTITE
convert.
747. SCAPES trans-
gressions.

750   "They think not but that every eye can see
    The same disgrace which they themselves
      behold;
    And therefore would they still in dark-
      ness be,
    To have their unseen sin remain untold;
    For they their guilt with weeping will
      unfold
755   And grave, like water that doth eat
        in steel,
        Upon my cheeks what helpless
          shame I feel."

    Here she exclaims against repose and rest
    And bids her eyes hereafter still be blind.
    She wakes her heart by beating on her
      breast
760   And bids it leap from thence, where it
      may find
    Some purer chest to close so pure a mind.
      Frantic with grief thus breathes she
        forth her spite
      Against the unseen secrecy of night:

    "O comfort-killing Night, image of hell!
765   Dim register and notary of shame!
    Black stage for tragedies and murthers
      fell!
    Vast sin-concealing chaos! nurse of
      blame!
    Blind muffled bawd! dark harbour for
      defame!
      Grim cave of death! whisp'ring con-
        spirator

755. GRAVE *engrave*.
WATER *acid*.
758. STILL *always*.
761. CLOSE *enclose*.
768. BAWD *procurer*.
DEFAME *disgrace*.

464 / THE RAPE OF LUCRECE

770   With close-tongu'd treason and the
                ravisher!

"O hateful, vaporous, and foggy Night!
    Since thou art guilty of my cureless crime,
    Muster thy mists to meet the Eastern light,
    Make war against proportion'd course of
        time;
775   Or if thou wilt permit the sun to climb
        His wonted height, yet ere he go to
          bed,
        Knit poisonous clouds about his
          golden head.

"With rotten damps ravish the morning
        air;
    Let their exhal'd unwholesome breaths
        make sick
780   The life of purity, the supreme fair,
    Ere he arrive his weary noontide prick;
    And let thy musty vapours march so thick
        That in their smoky ranks his
          smoth'red light
        May set at noon and make per-
          petual night.

785   "Were Tarquin Night, as he is but Night's
        child,
    The silver-shining queen he would dis-
        tain;
    Her twinkling handmaids too, by him
        defil'd,
    Through Night's black bosom should not
        peep again:

774. PROPORTION'D
orderly.
780. SUPREME FAIR
the sun.
781. ARRIVE *arrive
at.* NOONTIDE PRICK
*the mark of noon on
the dial, the center
of the sky.*
786. SILVER-SHINING
QUEEN *the moon.*
DISTAIN *defile.*
787. HANDMAIDS *the
stars.*

So should I have copartners in my pain;
790   And fellowship in woe doth woe
         assuage,
            As palmers' chat makes short their
            pilgrimage;

"Where now I have no one to blush with
   me,
To cross their arms and hang their heads
   with mine,
To mask their brows and hide their infamy;
795   But I alone, alone must sit and pine,
Seasoning the earth with show'rs of silver
   brine,
      Mingling my talk with tears, my
      grief with groans,
      Poor wasting monuments of lasting
      moans.

"O Night, thou furnace of foul reeking
   smoke,
800   Let not the jealous Day behold that face
Which underneath thy black all-hiding
   cloak
Immodestly lies martyr'd with disgrace!
Keep still possession of thy gloomy place
      That all the faults which in thy reign
      are made
805   May likewise be sepulcher'd in thy
      shade!

"Make me not object to the telltale Day!

791. PALMERS' pil-
grims or crusaders
who returned from
the Holy Land bear-
ing crosses or
branches of palm.

The light will show, character'd in my
brow,
The story of sweet chastity's decay,
The impious breach of holy wedlock
vow:
810   Yea, the illiterate, that know not how
To cipher what is writ in learned
books,
Will quote my loathsome trespass in
my looks.

"The nurse, to still her child, will tell my
story
And fright her crying babe with Tarquin's name;
815   The orator, to deck his oratory,
Will couple my reproach to Tarquin's
shame;
Feast-finding minstrels, tuning my defame,
Will tie the hearers to attend each
line,
How Tarquin wronged me, I Collatine.

820   "Let my good name, that senseless reputation,
For Collatine's dear love be kept un-
spotted;
If that be made a theme for disputation,
The branches of another root are rotted,
And undeserv'd reproach to him allotted
825   That is as clear from this attaint of
mine

807. CHARACTER'D
lettered.
811. CIPHER deci-
pher, read.
812. QUOTE observe.
817. FEAST-FINDING
searching for feasts
at which to per-
form. TUNING sing-
ing songs about.
DEFAME disgrace.
818. TIE . . . ATTEND
command the atten-
tion of the hearers
to.
820. SENSELESS exist-
ing beyond the
realm of the senses.
Cassio regards his
reputation as "the
immortal part of
myself" (Othello,
Act II, scene 3, line
264).
823. BRANCHES OF
ANOTHER ROOT
branches of Colla-
tine's family tree.
825. ATTAINT taint,
disgrace.

As I ere was pure to Collatine.

"O unseen shame! invisible disgrace!
    O unfelt sore! crest-wounding private
    scar!
Reproach is stamp'd in Collatinus' face,
And Tarquin's eye may read the mot afar,
How he in peace is wounded, not in war.
        Alas, how many bear such shameful
        blows
            Which not themselves, but he that
            gives them knows!

"If, Collatine, thine honour lay in me,
From me by strong assault it is bereft;
My honey lost, and I, a drone-like bee,
Have no perfection of my summer left,
But robb'd and ransack'd by injurious
    theft:
        In thy weak hive a wand'ring wasp
        hath crept
            And suck'd the honey which thy
            chaste bee kept.

"Yet am I guilty of thy honour's wrack;
Yet for thy honour did I entertain him;
Coming from thee, I could not put him
    back,
For it had been dishonour to disdain him:
Besides, of weariness he did complain
    him,
        And talk'd of virtue: O unlook'd-for
        evil

828. CREST-WOUND-
ING *wounding to the
top, to the crest, to
the helmet; defiling
the family crest; dis-
gracing nobility.*
830. MOT *motto.*
835. BEREFT *taken
away.*
836. DRONE-LIKE
BEE *The drones are
the males of the hive
and are destroyed
by the workers
when the commun-
ity no longer needs
them.*
841. WRACK *ruin.*
842. YET *even
though.*

When virtue is profan'd in such a
    devil!

"Why should the worm intrude the maiden
    bud?
Or hateful cuckoos hatch in sparrows'
    nests?
850 Or toads infect fair founts with venom
    mud?
Or tyrant folly lurk in gentle breasts?
Or kings be breakers of their own be-
    hests?
        But no perfection is so absolute
        That some impurity doth not pollute.

855 "The aged man that coffers up his gold
Is plagu'd with cramps and gouts and
    painful fits,
And scarce hath eyes his treasure to be-
    hold,
But like still-pining Tantalus he sits
And useless barns the harvest of his wits,
860   Having no other pleasure of his gain
        But torment that it cannot cure his
        pain.

"So then he hath it when he cannot use it,
And leaves it to be mast'red by his young,
Who in their pride do presently abuse it;
865 Their father was too weak, and they too
    strong,
To hold their cursed-blessed fortune
    long:

The sweets we wish for turn to
    loathed sours
Even in the moment that we call
    them ours.

"Unruly blasts wait on the tender spring;
870   Unwholesome weeds take root with pre-
    cious flow'rs;
The adder hisses where the sweet birds
    sing;
What virtue breeds iniquity devours:
We have no good that we can say is ours
    But ill-annexed Opportunity
875   Or kills his life or else his quality.

"O Opportunity, thy guilt is great!
'Tis thou that execut'st the traitor's
    treason;
Thou sets the wolf where he the lamb
    may get;
Whoever plots the sin, thou point'st the
    season;
880   'Tis thou that spurn'st at right, at law, at
    reason;
        And in thy shady cell, where none
        may spy him,
        Sits Sin, to seize the souls that
        wander by him.

"Thou makest the vestal violate her oath;
Thou blowest the fire when temperance is
    thaw'd;
885   Thou smother'st honesty, thou murth'rest
    troth,

874. ILL-ANNEXED
closely connected
with evil things.
The phrase does not
occur elsewhere in
Shakespeare.
875. OR . . . OR.
either . . . or.
QUALITY nature,
character.
879. POINT'ST ap-
points.
883. VESTAL priest-
ess at the Temple of
Vesta in Rome. Ves-
tals were sworn to
remain chaste and
serve the goddess
for thirty years.

Thou foul abettor! thou notorious bawd!
Thou plantest scandal and displacest
laud:
    Thou ravisher, thou traitor, thou
    false thief!
    Thy honey turns to gall, thy joy to
    grief.

890 "Thy secret pleasure turns to open shame,
Thy private feasting to a public fast,
Thy smoothing titles to a ragged name,
Thy sug'red tongue to bitter wormwood
taste:
Thy violent vanities can never last.
895   How comes it then, vile Opportunity,
    Being so bad, such numbers seek for
    thee?

"When wilt thou be the humble sup-
pliant's friend
And bring him where his suit may be
obtain'd?
When wilt thou sort an hour great strifes
to end,
900 Or free that soul which wretchedness
hath chain'd?
Give physic to the sick, ease to the pain'd?
    The poor, lame, blind, halt, creep,
    cry out for thee;
    But they ne'er meet with Op-
    portunity.

"The patient dies while the physician
sleeps;

886. ABETTOR *insti-gator*. BAWD *pro-curer*.
887. LAUD *praise*.
892. SMOOTHING *flattering*. RAGGED *beggarly, wretched*.
899. SORT *choose*.
901. PHYSIC *medi-cine*.

905 The orphan pines while the oppressor
feeds;
Justice is feasting while the widow
weeps;
Advice is sporting while infection breeds:
Thou grant'st no time for charitable
deeds:
Wrath, envy, treason, rape, and
murther's rages,
910 Thy heinous hours wait on them as
their pages.

"When Truth and Virtue have to do with
thee,
A thousand crosses keep them from thy
aid:
They buy thy help, but Sin ne'er gives a
fee;
He gratis comes, and thou art well apaid
915 As well to hear as grant what he hath
said.
My Collatine would else have come
to me
When Tarquin did, but he was
stay'd by thee.

"Guilty thou art of murther and of theft,
Guilty of perjury and subornation,
920 Guilty of treason, forgery, and shift,
Guilty of incest, that abomination;
An accessary by thine inclination
To all sins past and all that are to
come,

907. ADVICE *knowledge, or more particularly, medical knowledge, and by extension those who have such knowledge, that is, men in authority, government.* INFECTION *the plague.* BREEDS *spreads. The line is generally taken to mean that the neglectful authorities amuse themselves while the plague spreads, but the meaning may be less particular.*
912. CROSSES *hindrances.*
914. APAID *pleased.*
919. SUBORNATION *inducing someone to do a bad or criminal act.*
920. SHIFT *contriving, swindling.*

From the creation to the general
doom.

925 "Misshapen Time, copesmate of ugly
Night,
Swift subtle post, carrier of grisly care,
Eater of youth, false slave to false delight,
Base watch of woes, sin's packhorse,
virtue's snare;
Thou nursest all, and murth'rest all that
are:
930   O, hear me then, injurious, shifting
Time!
          Be guilty of my death, since of my
crime.

"Why hath thy servant Opportunity
Betray'd the hours thou gav'st me to re-
pose,
Cancell'd my fortunes and enchained me
935 To endless date of never-ending woes?
Time's office is to fine the hate of foes,
          To eat up errors by opinion bred,
          Not spend the dowry of a lawful bed.

"Time's glory is to calm contending kings,
940 To unmask falsehood and bring truth to
light,
To stamp the seal of time in aged things,
To wake the morn and sentinel the night,
To wrong the wronger till he render
right,
          To ruinate proud buildings with thy
hours

925. COPESMATE
companion.
926. SUBTLE *moving
imperceptibly.*
935. DATE *appointed
time.*
936. FINE *end.*
942. SENTINEL
guard.
944–945. *Compare
Sonnet 55.*

945   And smear with dust their glitt'ring
            golden tow'rs,

"To fill with wormholes stately monu-
     ments,
To feed oblivion with decay of things,
To blot old books and alter their con-
     tents,
To pluck the quills from ancient ravens'
     wings,
950 To dry the old oak's sap and cherish
     springs,
     . To spoil antiquities of hammer'd
       steel
     And turn the giddy round of For-
       tune's wheel,

"To show the beldame daughters of her
     daughter,
To make the child a man, the man a child,
955 To slay the tiger that doth live by
     slaughter,
To tame the unicorn and lion wild,
To mock the subtle in themselves
     beguil'd,
     To cheer the ploughman with in-
       creaseful crops
     And waste huge stones with little
       waterdrops.

960 "Why work'st thou mischief in thy pil-
     grimage,
Unless thou couldst return to make
     amends?

949. *Although the longevity of the raven was legendary, even it is subject to time.*
950. CHERISH SPRINGS *renews the water of springs. Or "springs" may mean "young shoots," presumably of the oak.*
953. BELDAME *old woman, grandmother.*
956. UNICORN *The unicorn was said to be untamable after the age of two.*
958. INCREASEFUL *fruitful.*

One poor retiring minute in an age
Would purchase thee a thousand thousand friends,
Lending him wit that to bad debtors
lends:
965   O this dread night, wouldst thou one
hour come back,
I could prevent this storm and shun
thy wrack!

"Thou ceaseless lackey to Eternity,
With some mischance cross Tarquin in his
flight;
Devise extremes beyond extremity
970   To make him curse this cursed crimeful
night;
Let ghastly shadows his lewd eyes
affright,
And the dire thought of his committed evil
Shape every bush a hideous shapeless devil;

"Disturb his hours of rest with restless
trances,
975   Afflict him in his bed with bedrid groans;
Let there bechance him pitiful michances
To make him moan, but pity not his
moans;
Stone him with hard'ned hearts harder
than stones,
And let mild women to him lose their
mildness,

962. RETIRING com-
ing back again, re-
turning.
966. WRACK ruin.
967. Compare Son-
net 77, line 8.

Wilder to him than tigers in their wildness;

"Let him have time to tear his curled hair,
Let him have time against himself to rave,
Let him have time of Time's help to despair,
Let him have time to live a loathed slave,
985 Let him have time a beggar's orts to crave,
    And time to see one that by alms doth live
    Disdain to him disdained scraps to give;

"Let him have time to see his friends his foes
And merry fools to mock at him resort;
990 Let him have time to mark how slow time goes
In time of sorrow, and how swift and short
His time of folly and his time of sport;
    And ever let his unrecalling crime
    Have time to wail th' abusing of his time.

995 "O Time, thou tutor both to good and bad,
Teach me to curse him that thou taught'st this ill!
At his own shadow let the thief run mad,
Himself himself seek every hour to kill!
Such wretched hands such wretched blood should spill,

985. ORTS *scraps of food, refuse.*
993. UNRECALLING *past recall.*

For who so base would such an office
		have
	As sland'rous deathsman to so base
		a slave?

"The baser is he, coming from a king,
	To shame his hope with deeds degene-
		rate:
	The mightier man, the mightier is the
		thing
1005	That makes him honour'd or begets him
		hate;
	For greatest scandal waits on greatest
		state.
		The moon being clouded presently
			is miss'd,
		But little stars may hide them when
			they list.

"The crow may bathe his coal-black
		wings in mire
1010	And unperceiv'd fly with the filth away;
	But if the like the snow-white swan
		desire,
	The stain upon his silver down will stay.
	Poor grooms are sightless night, kings
		glorious day:
		Gnats are unnoted wheresoe'er they
			fly,
1015		But eagles gaz'd upon with every
			eye.

"Out, idle words, servants to shallow fools,
Unprofitable sounds, weak arbitrators!

1001. SLAND'ROUS
contemptible,
worthless.
1003. HOPE expecta-
tions, the things he
could hope for.
1013. GROOMS low
persons. SIGHTLESS
not visible.

Busy yourselves in skill-contending
    schools;
Debate where leisure serves with dull
    debaters;
1020 To trembling clients be you mediators:
      For me, I force not argument a straw,
      Since that my case is past the help
        of law.

"In vain I rail at Opportunity,
    At Time, at Tarquin, and uncheerful
    Night;
1025 In vain I cavil with mine infamy,
    In vain I spurn at my confirm'd despite:
    This helpless smoke of words doth me no
    right.
      The remedy indeed to do me good
      Is to let forth my foul defiled blood.

1030 "Poor hand, why quiver'st thou at this
    decree?
Honour thyself to rid me of this shame;
For if I die, my honour lives in thee,
But if I live, thou liv'st in my defame:
Since thou couldst not defend thy loyal
    dame
1035   And wast afeard to scratch her
      wicked foe,
      Kill both thyself and her for yield-
      ing so."

This said, from her betombled couch she
    starteth

1018. SKILL-CON-
TENDING SCHOOLS
*among scholars to
whom argument is
a show of skill
rather than a means
of eliciting truth.*
1021. FORCE *value.*
1027. HELPLESS *use-
less.* SMOKE *cloud,
mist.*
1037. BETOMBLED
*betumbled, disar-
ranged by tossing.*

To find some desp'rate instrument of
  death;
But this no slaughterhouse no tool im-
  parteth
1040 To make more vent for passage of her
  breath;
Which, thronging through her lips, so
  vanisheth
    As smoke from Ætna that in air
    consumes
    Or that which from discharged can-
    non fumes.

"In vain," quoth she, "I live, and seek in
  vain
1045 Some happy mean to end a hapless life.
I fear'd by Tarquin's falchion to be slain,
Yet for the selfsame purpose seek a knife:
But when I fear'd I was a loyal wife:
    So am I now: O no, that cannot be;
1050   Of that true type hath Tarquin rifled
    me.

"O, that is gone for which I sought to live,
And therefore now I need not fear to die.
To clear this spot by death, at least I give
A badge of fame to slander's livery,
1055 A dying life to living infamy:
    Poor helpless help, the treasure
    stol'n away,
    To burn the guiltless casket where it
    lay!

"Well, well, dear Collatine, thou shalt not
  know

1042. CONSUMES
consumes itself,
vanishes.
1045. HAPLESS un-
fortunate.
1046. FALCHION
curved sword.

The stained taste of violated troth;

1060 I will not wrong thy true affection so,
To flatter thee with an infringed oath;
This bastard graff shall never come to growth:
He shall not boast who did thy stock pollute
That thou art doting father of his fruit.

1065 "Nor shall he smile at thee in secret thought,
Nor laugh with his companions at thy state;
But thou shalt know thy int'rest was not bought
Basely with gold, but stol'n from forth thy gate.
For me, I am the mistress of my fate,
1070 And with my trespass never will dispense
Till life to death acquit my forc'd offence.

"I will not poison thee with my attaint
Nor fold my fault in cleanly-coin'd excuses;
My sable ground of sin I will not paint
1075 To hide the truth of this false night's abuses:
My tongue shall utter all; mine eyes, like sluices,
As from a mountain spring that feeds a dale,

1062. GRAFF *graft, a small shoot of a tree inserted into another tree of the same genus, although generally of another species, which will sustain and nourish it.*
1067. INT'REST *property.*
1070. DISPENSE *come to terms with, grant dispensation to, that is, to pardon.*
1072. ATTAINT *disgrace, taint.*
1074. SABLE *dark, black. "Sable" is the heraldic term for black. She will not paint out the "sable ground of sin" in her coat of arms.*

Shall gush pure streams to purge my
impure tale."

By this, lamenting Philomel had ended
1080   The well-tun'd warble of her nightly sorrow,
And solemn night with slow sad gait
descended
To ugly hell; when, lo, the blushing morrow
Lends light to all fair eyes that light will
borrow:
     But cloudy Lucrece shames herself to
see,
1085   And therefore still in night would
cloist'red be.

Revealing day through every cranny
spies
And seems to point her out where she sits
weeping;
To whom she sobbing speaks: "O eye of
eyes,
Why pry'st thou through my window?
leave thy peeping;
1090   Mock with thy tickling beams eyes that
are sleeping:
     Brand not my forehead with thy
piercing light,
     For day hath naught to do what's
done by night."

Thus cavils she with everything she sees:
True grief is fond and testy as a child,

1079. PHILOMEL
*The nightingale,
whose song for
Elizabethan poets
became the emblem
of melancholy and
suffering. See page
184.*
1083. BORROW *take,
accept, admit.*
1088. EYE OF EYES
the sun.
1092. DO *do with.*

1095   Who wayward once, his mood with
      naught agrees:
  Old woes, not infant sorrows, bear them
      mild;
  Continuance tames the one, the other wild
      Like an unpractis'd swimmer plung-
        ing still
      With too much labour drowns for
        want of skill.

1100   So she, deep drenched in a sea of care,
  Holds disputation with each thing she
      views
  And to herself all sorrow doth compare;
  No object but her passion's strength re-
      news,
  And as one shifts, another straight ensues:
1105   Sometime her grief is dumb and
        hath no words,
      Sometime 'tis mad and too much talk
        affords.

  The little birds that tune their morning's
      joy
  Make her moans mad with their sweet
      melody:
  For mirth doth search the bottom of
      annoy;
1110   Sad souls are slain in merry company;
  Grief best is pleas'd with grief's society;
      True sorrow then is feelingly suffic'd
      When with like semblance it is sym-
        pathiz'd.

1095. WAYWARD
capricious.
1098. STILL *always.*
1105. SOMETIME
sometimes.
1109. SEARCH *pene-
trate to and affect
the nature of.* AN-
NOY *grief.*
1112. SUFFIC'D *con-
tented.*
1113. SYMPATHIZ'D
*associated with, put
in relation with
something so that
both may suffer to-
gether.*

'Tis double death to drown in ken of
shore;

1115 He ten times pines that pines beholding
food;

To see the salve doth make the wound
ache more;

Great grief grieves most at that would do
it good;

Deep woes roll forward like a gentle
flood,

Who, being stopp'd, the bounding
banks o'erflows;

1120 Grief dallied with nor law nor limit
knows.

"You mocking birds," quoth she, "your
tunes entomb

Within your hollow-swelling feather'd
breasts,

And in my hearing be you mute and
dumb;

My restless discord loves no stops nor
rests;

1125 A woeful hostess brooks not merry guests:

Relish your nimble notes to pleasing
ears;

Distress likes dumps when time is
kept with tears.

"Come, Philomel, that sing'st of ravishment,

Make thy sad grove in my dishevell'd
hair:

1114. KEN *view,
sight.*
1120. NOR . . . NOR
neither . . . nor.
1127. DUMPS
*mournful strains in
music.*
1128. PHILOMEL
see line 1079, note.

1130 As the dank earth weeps at thy languish-
ment,
So I at each sad strain will strain a tear
And with deep groans the diapason bear;
For burthen-wise I'll hum on Tar-
quin still,
While thou on Tereus descants bet-
ter skill.

1135 "And whiles against a thorn thou bear'st
thy part,
To keep thy sharp woes waking, wretched
I,
To imitate thee well, against my heart
Will fix a sharp knife, to affright mine
eye;
Who, if it wink, shall thereon fall and
die.
1140 These means, as frets upon an instrument,
Shall tune our heart-strings to true
languishment.

"And for, poor bird, thou sing'st not in the
day,
As shaming any eye should thee behold,
Some dark deep desert, seated from the
way,
1145 That knows not parching heat nor freez-
ing cold,
Will we find out; and there we will unfold
To creatures stern sad tunes, to
change their kinds:

1132. DEEP . . .
BEAR *Lucrece's
groans will be the
diapason* (bass notes
harmoniously ac-
companying an-
other air) *to Philo-
mel's song.*
1133. BURTHEN-
WISE *The burthen,
or burden, was the
refrain of a song.
Sometimes, as here,
it was confused
with "bourdon,"
the bass accompani-
ment of a melody.
The confusion of
the terms was so
frequent that they
were often used
interchangeably.*
1134. TEREUS *See
line 1079, note, and*
The Passionate Pil-
grim, *poem 20,
line 10, note.*
DESCANTS *sings.*
BETTER SKILL *more
skillfully.*
1142. FOR *because.*
1144. DESERT *de-
serted or unin-
habited place.*
1147. KINDS *natures,
dispositions.*

Since men prove beasts, let beasts
bear gentle minds."

As the poor frighted deer that stands at
gaze,
1150 Wildly determining which way to fly,
Or one encompass'd with a winding maze
That cannot tread the way out readily,
So with herself is she in mutiny,
    To live or die which of the twain
        were better
1155   When life is sham'd and death re-
        proach's debtor.

"To kill myself," quoth she, "alack what
    were it
But with my body my poor soul's pol-
    lution?
They that lose half with greater patience
    bear it
Than they whose whole is swallowed in
    confusion.
1160 That mother tries a merciless conclusion
    Who, having two sweet babes, when
        death takes one,
        Will slay the other and be nurse to
        none.

"My body or my soul, which was the dearer
When the one pure, the other made
    divine?
1165 Whose love of either to myself was nearer
When both were kept for heaven and
    Collatine?

1149. STANDS AT
GAZE *stands in
bewilderment.*
1155. DEATH RE-
PROACH'S DEBTOR
*Her death is a debt
owed to the re-
proaches of her
conscience.*
*1156–1157. What
would killing my-
self be but to pol-
lute my soul?*
1160. CONCLUSION
experiment.

Ay me! the bark pil'd from the lofty pine,
 His leaves will wither and his sap
  decay;
 So must my soul, her bark being
  pil'd away.

1170 "Her house is sack'd, her quiet interrupted,
 Her mansion batter'd by the enemy;
 Her sacred temple spotted, spoil'd, cor-
  rupted,
 Grossly engirt with daring infamy:
 Then let it not be call'd impiety
1175   If in this blemish'd fort I make some
   hole
   Through which I may convey this
    troubled soul.

 "Yet die I will not till my Collatine
 Have heard the cause of my untimely
  death;
 That he may vow, in that sad hour of
  mine,
1180 Revenge on him that made me stop my
  breath.
 My stained blood to Tarquin I'll bequeath,
   Which, by him tainted, shall for him
    be spent
   And as his due writ in my testament.

 "My honour I'll bequeath unto the knife
1185 That wounds my body so dishonoured.
 'Tis honour to deprive dishonour'd life;
 The one will live, the other being dead:

1167. PIL'D *stripped off.*
1173. ENGIRT *en-compassed.*
1186. DEPRIVE *take away.*

So of shame's ashes shall my fame be bred,
 For in my death I murther shameful
  scorn;
1190 My shame so dead, mine honour is
  new born.

"Dear lord of that dear jewel I have lost,
What legacy shall I bequeath to thee?
My resolution, love, shall be thy boast
By whose example thou reveng'd mayst
 be.
1195 How Tarquin must be us'd, read it in me:
 Myself, thy friend, will kill myself,
  thy foe,
 And for my sake serve thou false
  Tarquin so.

"This brief abridgment of my will I make:
My soul and body to the skies and ground;
1200 My resolution, husband, do thou take;
Mine honour be the knife's that makes
 my wound;
My shame be his that did my fame confound;
 And all my fame that lives disbursed
  be
 To those that live and think no
  shame of me.

1205 "Thou, Collatine, shalt oversee this will;
How was I overseen that thou shalt see it!
My blood shall wash the slander of mine
 ill;

1202. FAME *reputation.*
1205. OVERSEE *Overseers of wills had no legal status; presumably they acted with the executors in an advisory capacity. Shakespeare appointed his daughter Susanna and her husband, Dr. John Hall, executors of his will. His friends, Thomas Russell and Francis Collins, were appointed overseers.*
1206. OVERSEEN *betrayed, deluded.*

My live's foul deed my life's fair end shall
    free it.
Faint not, faint heart, but stoutly say 'So
    be it:'
1210   Yield to my hand; my hand shall
        conquer thee:
    Thou dead, both die and both shall
        victors be."

This plot of death when sadly she had
    laid
And wip'd the brinish pearl from her
    bright eyes,
With untun'd tongue she hoarsely calls
    her maid,
1215 Whose swift obedience to her mistress
    hies;
For fleet-wing'd duty with thought's
    feathers flies.
    Poor Lucrece' cheeks unto her maid
        seem so
    As winter meads when sun doth melt
        their snow.

Her mistress she doth give demure good-
    morrow
1220 With soft slow tongue, true mark of
    modesty,
And sorts a sad look to her lady's sorrow,
For why her face wore sorrow's livery,
But durst not ask of her audaciously
    Why her two suns were cloud-
        eclipsed so,

1208. LIVE's *life's.*
1216. THOUGHT'S
FEATHERS *the wings
of thought. For the
speed of thought,
see Sonnet 44, lines
9–10.*
1221. SORTS *adapts.*
1222. FOR WHY *be-
cause.*
1224. SUNS *eyes.*

Nor why her fair cheeks overwash'd
with woe.

But as the earth doth weep, the sun being
set,
Each flower moist'ned like a melting eye,
Even so the maid with swelling drops gan
wet
Her circled eyne, enforc'd by sympathy
1230 Of those fair suns set in her mistress' sky,
Who in a salt-wav'd ocean quench
their light,
Which makes the maid weep like the
dewy night.

A pretty while these pretty creatures
stand,
Like ivory conduits coral cisterns filling:
1235 One justly weeps, the other takes in hand
No cause, but company, of her drops
spilling:
Their gentle sex to weep are often willing,
Grieving themselves to guess at
others' smarts,
And then they drown their eyes or
break their hearts.

1240 For men have marble, women waxen
minds,
And therefore are they form'd as marble
will:
The weak oppress'd, th' impression of
strange kinds

1229. EYNE *eyes.*
1231. WHO *which,
that is, Lucrece's
eyes.*
1235–1236. TAKES
. . . SPILLING *Has
no reason for her
tears except her as-
sociation with her
mistress.*
1242. KINDS *natures.*

Is form'd in them by force, by fraud, or
  skill:
Then call them not the authors of their
  ill,

1245
    No more than wax shall be ac-
    counted evil
    Wherein is stamp'd the semblance of
    a devil.

Their smoothness, like a goodly cham-
  pain plain,
Lays open all the little worms that creep;
In men, as in a rough-grown grove, remain

1250
Cave-keeping evils that obscurely sleep:
Through crystal walls each little mote
  will peep:
    Though men can cover crimes with
    bold stern looks,
    Poor women's faces are their own
    faults' books.

No man inveigh against the withered
  flow'r,

1255
But chide rough winter that the flow'r
  hath kill'd:
Not that devour'd, but that which doth
  devour,
Is worthy blame. O let it not be hild
Poor women's faults that they are so
  fulfill'd
    With men's abuses: those proud
    lords to blame

1247. SMOOTHNESS
gentleness. CHAM-
PAIN *open country.*
1248. LAYS OPEN
makes visible.
1253. FAULTS' BOOKS
publications of
faults.
1257. HILD *held;*
used for the sake
of the rhyme.
1258. FULFILL'D
made full.

Make weak-made women tenants to
            their shame.

      The precedent whereof in Lucrece view,
      Assail'd by night with circumstances
            strong
      Of present death, and shame that might
            ensue
      By that her death, to do her husband
            wrong:
1265 Such danger to resistance did belong
            That dying fear through all her body
                  spread;
            And who cannot abuse a body dead?

      By this, mild patience bid fair Lucrece
            speak
      To the poor counterfeit of her complain-
            ing:
1270 "My girl," quoth she, "on what occasion
            break
            Those tears from thee that down thy
                  cheeks are raining?
            If thou dost weep for grief of my sustain-
                  ing,
                  Know, gentle wench, it small avails
                        my mood:
                  If tears could help, mine own would
                        do me good.

1275 "But tell me, girl, when went"—and there
            she stay'd
            Till after a deep groan—"Tarquin from
                  hence?"

*1261. PRECEDENT
proof.
1264. THAT the fact
of.
1269. COUNTERFEIT
Lucrece's maid,
whose grief was
patterned after hers.
"Counterfeit" was
sometimes used for
"portrait."
1272. OF MY SUS-
TAINING for what I
suffer.*

"Madam, ere I was up," replied the maid,
"The more to blame my sluggard negli-
    gence:
Yet with the fault I thus far can dispense;
1280   Myself was stirring ere the break of
      day,
    And ere I rose was Tarquin gone
      away.

"But, lady, if your maid may be so bold,
She would request to know your heavi-
    ness."
"O, peace!" quoth Lucrece, "if it should
    be told,
1285The repetition cannot make it less,
For more it is than I can well express:
    And that deep torture may be call'd
      a hell
    When more is felt than one hath
      power to tell.

"Go get me hither paper, ink, and pen:
1290Yet save that labour, for I have them here.
What should I say? One of my husband's
    men
Bid thou be ready by and by to bear
A letter to my lord, my love, my dear;
    Bid him with speed prepare to carry
      it;
1295   The cause craves haste, and it will
      soon be writ."

Her maid is gone, and she prepares to
    write,

1292. BY AND BY
right away.

492 / THE RAPE OF LUCRECE

First hovering o'er the paper with her
   quill:
Conceit and grief an eager combat fight;
What wit sets down is blotted straight
   with will;
1300　This is too curious-good, this blunt and
   ill:
      Much like a press of people at a door,
      Throng her inventions, which shall
         go before.

At last she thus begins: "Thou worthy
   lord
Of that unworthy wife that greeteth thee,
1305　Health to thy person! Next vouchsafe t'
   afford
(If ever, love, thy Lucrece thou wilt see)
Some present speed to come and visit me.
      So I commend me from our house in
         grief:
      My woes are tedious, though my
         words are brief."

1310　Here folds she up the tenure of her woe,
Her certain sorrow writ uncertainly.
By this short schedule Collatine may
   know
Her grief, but not her grief's true quality:
She dares not thereof make discovery,
1315　 Lest he should hold it her own gross
         abuse
      Ere she with blood had stain'd her
         stain'd excuse.

1298. CONCEIT *the conception in her mind.*
1300. THIS . . . THIS *this on the one hand, that on the other.* CURIOUS-GOOD *skillfully and carefully done.*
1302. INVENTIONS *thoughts.*
1310. TENURE *a legal term meaning copy. The implication is that the copy is an exact transcription of the original.*
1312. SCHEDULE *letter.*
1316. HAD . . . EXCUSE *had disgraced her written statement.*

Besides, the life and feeling of her passion
She hoards, to spend when he is by to hear
her,
When sighs and groans and tears may
grace the fashion
1320 Of her disgrace, the better so to clear her
From that suspicion which the world
might bear her.
  To shun this blot, she would not
  blot the letter
  With words till action might become
  them better.

To see sad sights moves more than hear
them told,
1325 For then the eye interprets to the ear
The heavy motion that it doth behold,
When every part a part of woe doth bear.
'Tis but a part of sorrow that we hear:
  Deep sounds make lesser noise than
  shallow fords,
1330 And sorrow ebbs, being blown with
  wind of words.

Her letter now is seal'd, and on it writ,
"At Ardea to my lord with more than
haste."
The post attends, and she delivers it,
Charging the sour-fac'd groom to hie as
fast
1335 As lagging fowls before the Northern
blast:
  Speed more than speed but dull and
  slow she deems:
  Extremity still urgeth such extremes.

1317. PASSION suf-
fering.
1329. SOUNDS bodies
of water.
1334. SOUR-FAC'D
sad-faced.
1335. BEFORE
blown by.

The homely villain cursies to her low,
And blushing on her, with a steadfast
    eye

1340 Receives the scroll without or yea or
    no
And forth with bashful innocence doth
    hie.
But they whose guilt within their bosoms
    lie
        Imagine every eye beholds their
            blame,
        For Lucrece thought he blush'd to see
            her shame,

1345 When, seely groom! God wot, it was
    defect
Of spirit, life, and bold audacity.
Such harmless creatures have a true
    respect
To talk in deeds, while others saucily
Promise more speed but do it leisurely:

1350   Even so this pattern of the worn-out
            age
        Pawn'd honest looks, but laid no
            words to gage.

His kindled duty kindled her mistrust,
That two red fires in both their faces
    blaz'd;
She thought he blush'd as knowing Tar-
    quin's lust,

1355 And blushing with him, wistly on him
    gaz'd;

1338. HOMELY VIL-
LAIN simple servant.
CURSIES curtsie's.
"Curtsy" was used
for both men and
women.
1340. OR . . . OR
either . . . or.
1345. WHEN ex-
clamation of im-
patience. SEELY
simple, plain.
1347. RESPECT
motivation.
1350. THIS PATTERN
OF this man pat-
terned after. THE
WORN-OUT AGE the
golden age when
all men were
honest. See line 60,
note, and Sonnet
68, line 1.
1351. PAWN'D
pledged. TO GAGE to
bind him as by an
oath.
1355. WISTLY at-
tentively.

Her earnest eye did make him more
    amaz'd:
       The more she saw the blood his
          cheeks replenish,
       The more she thought he spied in her
          some blemish.

But long she thinks till he return again,
1360 And yet the duteous vassal scarce is gone.
The weary time she cannot entertain,
For now 'tis stale to sigh, to weep and
    groan:
So woe hath wearied woe, moan tired
    moan,
       That she her plaints a little while
          doth stay,
1365   Pausing for means to mourn some
          newer way.

At last she calls to mind where hangs a
    piece
Of skilful painting, made for Priam's
    Troy,
Before the which is drawn the power of
    Greece,
For Helen's rape the city to destroy,
1370 Threat'ning cloud-kissing Ilion with an-
    noy;
       Which the conceited painter drew so
          proud
       As heaven, it seem'd, to kiss the tur-
          rets bow'd.

A thousand lamentable objects there,
In scorn of nature, art gave liveless life:

1361. ENTERTAIN pass pleasantly.
1364. STAY stop.
1367. PRIAM'S TROY Priam was the king of Troy at the time of the Trojan War.
1368. DRAWN drawn up, assembled.
1369. HELEN'S RAPE the abduction of Helen of Troy.
1370. ILION Troy, a fortified town on the Asiatic shore of the Hellespont. The excavations of the German archaeologist Schliemann (1822–1890) uncovered nine settlements, one on top of the other, the earliest dating from the Stone Age. The sixth of these settlements is the Troy of legend. According to Greek legend, Dardanus, the son of Zeus, established Dardania, a district northeast of Troy, and hence the region is sometimes called Dardan. His grandson Tros, founded the district of the Troads from which the Trojans derive their name. The son of Tros, Ilus, founded the city of Troy and gave it the name Ilium or Ilon.
1371. CONCEITED imaginative.
1374. ART . . . LIFE Art gave life to the lifeless objects.

1375 Many a dry drop seem'd a weeping tear
Shed for the slaught'red husband by the
wife:
The red blood reek'd to show the painter's strife,
And dying eyes gleam'd forth their
ashy lights,
Like dying coals burnt out in tedious
nights.

1380 There might you see the labouring
pioneer
Begrim'd with sweat and smeared all
with dust;
And from the tow'rs of Troy there would
appear
The very eyes of men through loopholes
thrust,
Gazing upon the Greeks with little lust:
1385 Such sweet observance in this work
was had
That one might see those far-off eyes
look sad.

In great commanders grace and majesty
You might behold triumphing in their
faces,
In youth, quick bearing and dexterity;
1390 And here and there the painter interlaces
Pale cowards marching on with trembling paces,
Which heartless peasants did so well
resemble

1380. PIONEER sol-
dier whose work it
was to build roads,
fortifications, etc.
1384. LUST pleasure.
1392. HEARTLESS
without courage.

That one would swear he saw them
    quake and tremble.

In Ajax and Ulysses, O, what art
1395 Of physiognomy might one behold!
The face of either cipher'd either's heart;
Their face their manners most expressly
    told:
  In Ajax' eyes blunt rage and rigour roll'd,
    But the mild glance that sly Ulysses
    lent
1400   Show'd deep regard and smiling
    government.

There pleading might you see grave
    Nestor stand,
As 'twere encouraging the Greeks to fight,
Making such sober action with his hand
That it beguil'd attention, charm'd the
    sight:
1405 In speech it seem'd his beard all silver-
    white
      Wagg'd up and down, and from his
    lips did fly
      Thin winding breath which purl'd
    up to the sky.

About him were a press of gaping faces
Which seem'd to swallow up his sound
    advice,
1410 All jointly list'ning, but with several
    graces,
As if some mermaid did their ears entice,

1394. AJAX a leader of the Greek forces. He is depicted by Homer as stubborn to the point of stupidity. Shakespeare darkened the portrait (see Troilus and Cressida). ULYSSES Roman name for Odysseus, a brave Greek leader of great physical strength and wisdom and a fitting hero for Homer's Odyssey. 1396. EITHER CIPHER'D EITHER'S set forth their individual characters. 1400. REGARD wisdom. GOVERNMENT a knowledge of governing, including governing one's self. 1401. NESTOR an aged and honored Greek leader, whose name, in modern English, has come to mean a sage and serious counselor. 1407. PURL'D UP twirled upwards, as smoke in still air. 1410. SEVERAL distinct, different. 1411. MERMAID siren.

Some high, some low; the painter was so nice.

> The scalps of many, almost hid behind,
> To jump up higher seem'd, to mock the mind.

1415 Here one man's hand lean'd on another's head,
His nose being shadow'd by his neighbour's ear;
Here one, being throng'd, bears back, all boll'n and red;
Another, smother'd, seems to pelt and swear;
And in their rage such signs of rage they bear
1420 > As, but for loss of Nestor's golden words,
> It seem'd they would debate with angry swords.

For much imaginary work was there;
Conceit deceitful, so compact, so kind,
That for Achilles' image stood his spear
1425 Grip'd in an armed hand; himself behind
Was left unseen, save to the eye of mind:
> A hand, a foot, a face, a leg, a head
> Stood for the whole to be imagined.

And from the walls of strong-besieged Troy
1430 When their brave hope, bold Hector, march'd to field,

1412. NICE *precise.*
1413. BEHIND *behind other figures.*
1414. HIGHER *higher than the figures which almost concealed them.* TO MOCK THE MIND *to tease the mind of the observer by making him speculate on the identity or nature of the partly concealed figures.*
1417. THRONG'D *crushed in the crowd.* BOLL'N *swollen.*
1422–1428. *This is not a picture for the passive viewer. It demands his close attention and requires that he meet the artist on the artist's own terms.*
1422. IMAGINARY *imaginative.*
1423. CONCEIT *imaginative conception.* COMPACT *both compact and composed.* KIND *natural, always assuming the difference between nature and the artist's recreation of it.*
1424. ACHILLES' *Achilles, the chief warrior of the Greek forces, met Hector in combat and killed him.*
1430. HECTOR *the son of Priam and chief warrior of the Trojan forces.*

Stood many Troyan mothers, sharing joy
To see their youthful sons bright weapons
    wield;
And to their hope they such odd action
    yield
        That through their light joy seemed
            to appear,
1435   (Like bright things stain'd) a kind of
            heavy fear.

And from the strond of Dardan, where
    they fought,
To Simois' reedy banks the red blood ran,
Whose waves to imitate the battle sought
With swelling ridges; and their ranks
    began
1440 To break upon the galled shore, and than
        Retire again, till, meeting greater
            ranks,
            They join and shoot their foam at
                Simois' banks.

To this well-painted piece is Lucrece
    come,
To find a face where all distress is stell'd.
1445 Many she sees where cares have carved
    some,
But none where all distress and dolour
    dwell'd
Till she despairing Hecuba beheld
        Staring on Priam's wounds with her
            old eyes,
            Which bleeding under Pyrrhus'
                proud foot lies.

1433. HOPE *their hopes for their sons who were to go down in defeat.*
1436. STROND *strand.* DARDAN *See line 1370, note.*
1437. SIMOIS' *a river flowing from Mount Ida across the plains of Troy.*
1444. STELL'D *set forth. See Sonnet 24, line 1.*
1447. HECUBA *the wife of Priam, king of Troy. Her despair is the subject of the First Player's recitation,* Hamlet, *Act II, scene 2, lines 474–541.*
1449. PYRRHUS' *Greek warrior who slew Priam.*

1450   In her the painter had anatomiz'd
        Time's ruin, beauty's wrack, and grim
           care's reign;
        Her cheeks with chops and wrinkles were
           disguis'd;
        Of what she was no semblance did re-
           main:
        Her blue blood chang'd to black in every
           vein,
1455   Wanting the spring that those
           shrunk pipes had fed,
          Show'd life imprison'd in a body
           dead.

        On this sad shadow Lucrece spends her
           eyes
        And shapes her sorrow to the beldame's
           woes,
        Who nothing wants to answer her but
           cries
1460   And bitter words to ban her cruel foes:
        The painter was no god to lend her those;
          And therefore Lucrece swears he did
           her wrong
          To give her so much grief and not a
           tongue.

        "Poor instrument," quoth she, "without a
           sound,
1465   I'll tune thy woes with my lamenting
           tongue,
        And drop sweet balm in Priam's painted
           wound,

1450. ANATOMIZ'D *dissected for the purpose of examination. The painter has anatomized Hecuba and set forth his findings in her portrait.*
1451. WRACK *destruction.*
1452. CHOPS *cracks.*
1455. SPRING *fountain, source.*
1457. SHADOW *painted representation of reality.*
SPENDS *fixes.*
1458. BELDAME'S *old woman's.*
1459. WHO *Hecuba.* WANTS *lacks.*
1460. BAN *curse.*
1461. *The painter would have had to be a god to endow her with a voice.*

And rail on Pyrrhus that hath done him
wrong,
And with my tears quench Troy that
burns so long,
 And with my knife scratch out the
 angry eyes
1470 Of all the Greeks that are thine enemies.

"Show me the strumpet that began this
stir,
That with my nails her beauty I may
tear.
Thy heat of lust, fond Paris, did incur
This load of wrath that burning Troy
doth bear:
1475 Thy eye kindled the fire that burneth
here,
 And here in Troy, for trespass of
 thine eye,
 The sire, the son, the dame and
 daughter die.

"Why should the private pleasure of some
one
Become the public plague of many moe?
1480 Let sin, alone committed, light alone
Upon his head that hath transgressed so;
Let guiltless souls be freed from guilty
woe:
 For one's offence why should so
 many fall,
 To plague a private sin in general?

1471. STRUMPET
Helen.
1473. FOND *foolish.*
1478. ONE *individ-
ual.*
1479. MOE *more.*
1484. *to make the
sin of an individual
the plague of many.*

502 / THE RAPE OF LUCRECE

1485   "Lo, here weeps Hecuba, here Priam dies,
      Here manly Hector faints, here Troilus
        sounds,
      Here friend by friend in bloody channel
        lies,
      And friend to friend gives unadvised
        wounds,
      And one man's lust these many lives con-
        founds:
1490   Had doting Priam check'd his son's
          desire,
        Troy had been bright with fame and
          not with fire."

      Here feelingly she weeps Troy's painted
        woes;
      For sorrow, like a heavy hanging bell
      Once set on ringing, with his own weight
        goes;
1495   Then little strength rings out the doleful
        knell:
      So Lucrece, set awork, sad tales doth tell
        To pencil'd pensiveness and colour'd
          sorrow:
        She lends them words, and she their
          looks doth borrow.

      She throws her eyes about the painting
        round,
1500   And who she finds forlorn she doth la-
        ment.
      At last she sees a wretched image bound
      That piteous looks to Phrygian shepherds
        lent:

1486. SOUNDS *old spelling for "swounds" or "swoons."*
1487. CHANNEL *gutter, little canal.*
1488. UNADVISED *unintended, done in ignorance.*
1501. BOUND *His hands, Virgil tells us (The Aeneid, Book 2, line 57), were bound behind his back. The character of Sinon was drawn from the second book of* The Aeneid, *which Shakespeare, as is clear from his use of it, read in the original.*
1502. PHRYGIAN SHEPHERDS *shepherds on the plains of Troy which at that time was in the possession of the Phrygians, immigrants from the Balkans.* LENT *bestowed on. His dissimulation had aroused their pity.*

His face, though full of cares, yet show'd content;
    Onward to Troy with the blunt swains he goes,
1505   So mild that Patience seem'd to scorn his woes.

In him the painter labour'd with his skill
To hide deceit, and give the harmless show
An humble gait, calm looks, eyes wailing still,
A brow unbent that seem'd to welcome woe,
1510 Cheeks neither red nor pale, but mingled so
    That blushing red no guilty instance gave
    Nor ashy pale the fear that false hearts have;

But like a constant and confirmed devil
He entertain'd a show so seeming just,
1515 And therein so ensconc'd his secret evil
That jealousy itself could not mistrust
False creeping craft and perjury should thrust
    Into so bright a day such black-fac'd storms
    Or blot with hell-born sin such saint-like forms.

1520 The well-skill'd workman this mild image drew

1504. BLUNT *not sharp, imperceptive.*
1508. WAILING STILL *always mourning.*
1509. UNBENT *not frowning.*
1514. ENTERTAIN'D A SHOW *kept up an appearance.*
1516. JEALOUSY *suspicion.* MISTRUST *suspect.*

For perjur'd Sinon, whose enchanting story
The credulous old Priam after slew;
Whose words, like wildfire, burnt the shining glory
Of rich-built Ilion, that the skies were sorry,
1525   And little stars shot from their fix'd places,
     When their glass fell wherein they view'd their faces.

This picture she advisedly perus'd,
And chid the painter for his wondrous skill,
Saying some shape in Sinon's was abus'd;
1530 So fair a form lodg'd not a mind so ill:
And still on him she gaz'd, and gazing still
     Such signs of truth in his plain face she spied
     That she concludes the picture was belied.

"It cannot be," quoth she, "that so much guile"—
1535 She would have said "can lurk in such a look;"
But Tarquin's shape came in her mind the while
And from her tongue "can lurk" from "cannot" took:
"It cannot be" she in that sense forsook

And turn'd it thus: "It cannot be, I
    find,
1540   But such a face should bear a wicked
    mind;

"For even as subtill Sinon here is painted,
So sober-sad, so weary, and so mild,
As if with grief or travail he had fainted,
To me came Tarquin armed, so beguil'd
1545   With outward honesty, but yet defil'd
    With inward vice: as Priam him did
    cherish,
    So did I Tarquin; so my Troy did
    perish.

"Look, look, how listening Priam wets his
    eyes,
    To see those borrow'd tears that Sinon
    sheeds!
1550   Priam, why art thou old and yet not wise?
For every tear he falls a Troyan bleeds:
His eye drops fire, no water thence pro-
    ceeds;
    Those round clear pearls of his that
    move thy pity
    Are balls of quenchless fire to burn
    thy city.

1555   "Such devils steal effects from lightless
    hell;
For Sinon in his fire doth quake with cold,
And in that cold hot-burning fire doth
    dwell;
These contraries such unity do hold,

1549. SHEEDS *sheds;*
to rhyme with
"bleeds."
1551. FALLS *drops.*

Only to flatter fools and make them bold:
1560   So Priam's trust false Sinon's tears
              doth flatter,
          That he finds means to burn his Troy
              with water."

Here, all enrag'd, such passion her assails
That patience is quite beaten from her
    breast;
She tears the senseless Sinon with her
    nails,
1565 Comparing him to that unhappy guest
Whose deed hath made herself herself de-
    test:
       At last she smilingly with this gives
           o'er;
       "Fool, fool!" quoth she, "his wounds
           will not be sore."

Thus ebbs and flows the current of her
    sorrow,
1570 And time doth weary time with her com-
    plaining;
She looks for night, and then she longs
    for morrow,
And both she thinks too long with her re-
    maining:
Short time seems long in sorrow's sharp
    sustaining;
       Though woe be heavy, yet it seldom
           sleeps,
1575   And they that watch see time how
           slow it creeps;

1562. PASSION com-
motion of the mind.
1564. SENSELESS the
figure cannot, of
course, feel.

Which all this time hath overslipp'd her
    thought
That she with painted images hath spent,
Being from the feeling of her own grief
    brought
By deep surmise of others' detriment,
1580   Losing her woes in shows of discontent.
        It easeth some, though none it ever
          cur'd,
        To think their dolour others have
          endur'd.

But now the mindful messenger, come
    back,
Brings home his lord and other company;
1585   Who finds his Lucrece clad in mourning
    black;
And round about her tear-distained eye
Blue circles stream'd, like rainbows in the
    sky:
        These water-galls in her dim element
        Foretell new storms to those already
          spent.

1590   Which when her sad-beholding husband
    saw,
Amazedly in her sad face he stares:
Her eyes, though sod in tears, look'd red
    and raw,
Her lively colour kill'd with deadly cares.
He hath no power to ask her how she
    fares;
1595   Both stood, like old acquaintance in
        a trance,

1576–1577. *She had
not realized that the
figures with which
she had been spend-
ing all this time
were painted repre-
sentations of reality.*
1578–1579. *forget-
ting her own suffer-
ing by concentrat-
ing on that of
others.*
1579. SURMISE
thought.
1586. TEAR-DIS-
TAINED *tear-stained.
See line 786.*
1588. WATER-GALLS
*an appearance in
the sky resembling
imperfect rainbows
and presaging rain.*
ELEMENT *the nat-
ural habitation of
the spheres, hence
the areas around
Lucrece's eyes.*
1592. SOD *sodden.*
1593. LIVELY *life-
like.*

Met far from home, wond'ring each other's chance.

At last he takes her by the bloodless hand
And thus begins: "What uncouth ill event
Hath thee befall'n that thou dost trembling stand?
1600 Sweet love, what spite hath thy fair colour spent?
Why art thou thus attir'd in discontent?
  Unmask, dear dear, this moody heaviness
  And tell thy grief that we may give redress."

Three times with sighs she gives her sorrow fire
1605 Ere once she can discharge one word of woe:
At length address'd to answer his desire,
She modestly prepares to let them know
Her honour is ta'en prisoner by the foe,
  While Collatine and his consorted lords
1610 With sad attention long to hear her words.

And now this pale swan in her wat'ry nest
Begins the sad dirge of her certain ending:
"Few words," quoth she, "shall fit the trespass best

1596. CHANCE accident, the accidental meeting of old acquaintances.
1598. UNCOUTH unknown.
1601. DISCONTENT grief.
1604–1605. The image is that of firing a cannon by means of igniting the charge. The first three attempts did not produce a discharge.
1611. SWAN The swan was thought to sing before it died. (See The Phoenix and the Turtle, line 15.)

Where no excuse can give the fault
   amending:
In me moe woes than words are now depending,
      And my laments would be drawn out
         too long
      To tell them all with one poor tired
         tongue.

"Then be this all the task it hath to say:
Dear husband, in the interest of thy bed
A stranger came and on that pillow lay
Where thou wast wont to rest thy weary
   head;
And what wrong else may be imagined
      By foul enforcement might be done
         to me,
      From that, alas, thy Lucrece is not
         free.

"For in the dreadful dead of dark midnight
With shining falchion in my chamber
   came
A creeping creature with a flaming light
And softly cried, 'Awake, thou Roman
   dame,
And entertain my love; else lasting shame
      On thee and thine this night I will
         inflict,
      If thou my love's desire do con-
         tradict.

" 'For some hard-favour'd groom of thine,'
   quoth he,

1615. MOE *more.*
DEPENDING *im-
pending.*
1626. FALCHION
curved sword.
1632. HARD-
FAVOUR'D *ugly,
repulsive.*

'Unless thou yoke thy liking to my will,
I'll murther straight, and then I'll slaugh-
    ter thee
1635 And swear I found you where you did
    fulfil
The loathsome act of lust, and so did kill
    The lechers in their deed: this act
        will be
    My fame and thy perpetual infamy.'

"With this I did begin to start and cry;
1640 And then against my heart he set his
    sword,
Swearing, unless I took all patiently,
I should not live to speak another word;
So should my shame still rest upon record,
    And never be forgot in mighty Rome
1645   Th' adulterate death of Lucrece and
        her groom.

"Mine enemy was strong, my poor self
    weak,
And far the weaker with so strong a fear:
My bloody judge forbode my tongue to
    speak;
No rightful plea might plead for justice
    there:
1650 His scarlet lust came evidence to swear
    That my poor beauty had purloin'd
        his eyes;
    And when the judge is robb'd, the
        prisoner dies.

"O teach me how to make mine own ex-
    cuse!

1650. EVIDENCE
witness, one who
gives evidence.

Or, at the least, this refuge let me find:
Though my gross blood be stain'd with
    this abuse,
Immaculate and spotless is my mind;
That was not forc'd; that never was in-
    clin'd
    To accessary yieldings, but still pure
    Doth in her poison'd closet yet en-
        dure."

Lo, here, the hopeless merchant of this
    loss,
With head declin'd and voice damm'd up
    with woe,
With sad-set eyes and wretched arms
    across,
From lips new-waxen pale begins to blow
The grief away that stops his answer so:
    But wretched as he is, he strives in
        vain;
    What he breathes out his breath
        drinks up again.

As through an arch the violent roaring
    tide
Outruns the eye that doth behold his
    haste,
Yet in the eddy boundeth in his pride
Back to the strait that forc'd him on so
    fast,
In rage sent out, recall'd in rage being
    past:
    Even so his sighs, his sorrows, make
        a saw,

1655

1660

1665

1670

1658. ACCESSARY
YIELDINGS *yieldings
that would have
made me an ac-
cessary to the act.*
1659. CLOSET *body.*
1660. MERCHANT OF
THIS LOSS *owner
who suffered this
loss, that is, Col-
latine.*
1672. SAW *His sighs
and sorrows push
his griefs away and
draw them back
again like the
motion of a saw.*

To push grief on and back the same
　　grief draw.

Which speechless woe of his poor she at-
　　tendeth
1675　And his untimely frenzy thus awaketh:
"Dear lord, thy sorrow to my sorrow lend-
　　eth
Another power; no flood by raining slak-
　　eth.
My woe too sensible thy passion maketh
　　More feeling-painful: let it then suf-
　　fice
1680　To drown on woe, one pair of weep-
　　ing eyes:

"And for my sake when I might charm thee
　　so,
For she that was thy Lucrece, now attend
　　me.
Be suddenly revenged on my foe,
Thine, mine, his own: suppose thou dost
　　defend me
1685　From what is past: the help that thou shalt
　　lend me
　　Comes all too late, yet let the traitor
　　die,
　　For sparing justice feeds iniquity.

"But ere I name him, you fair lords,"
　　quoth she,
　　Speaking to those that came with Colla-
　　tine,
1690　"Shall plight your honourable faiths to me

1674. POOR *pitiable*
condition.
1680. ON WOE
Most editors print
"one woe," regard-
ing "on" as a mis-
print, but the words
were pronounced
alike, or very nearly
so, in Shakespeare's
time. He puns on
the words elsewhere,
and in this instance
he doubtless in-
tended to suggest
them both.
1684. DEFEND *pro-*
tect.
1687. SPARING *too*
merciful.

With swift pursuit to venge this wrong
    of mine;
For 'tis a meritorious fair design
        To chase injustice with revengeful
            arms:
        Knights by their oaths should right
            poor ladies' harms."

1695   At this request, with noble disposition
       Each present lord began to promise aid,
       As bound in knighthood to her imposi-
           tion,
       Longing to hear the hateful foe bewray'd.
       But she, that yet her sad task hath not
           said,
1700   The protestation stops. "O, speak,"
               quoth she,
           "How may this forced stain be wip'd
               from me?

       "What is the quality of my offence,
       Being constrain'd with dreadful circum-
           stance?
       May my pure mind with the foul act dis-
           pense,
1705   My low-declined honour to advance?
       May any terms acquit me from this
           chance?
           The poison'd fountain clears itself
               again,
           And why not I from this compelled
               stain?"

1697. IMPOSITION
injunction.
1698. BEWRAY'D
revealed.

With this they all at once began to say,
1710   Her body's stain her mind untainted
            clears;
While with a joyless smile she turns away
The face, that map which deep impres-
            sion bears
Of hard misfortune carv'd in it with tears.
            "No, no!" quoth she, "no dame here-
                  after living
1715   By my excuse shall claim excuse's
                  giving."

Here with a sigh as if her heart would
      break
She throws forth Tarquin's name: "He,
      he," she says,
But more than "he" her poor tongue
      could not speak,
Till after many accents and delays,
1720   Untimely breathings, sick and short as-
            says,
            She utters this: "He, he, fair lords,
                  'tis he
            That guides this hand to give this
                  wound to me."

Even here she sheathed in her harmless
      breast
A harmful knife, that thence her soul un-
      sheath'd:
1725   That blow did bail it from the deep un-
            rest
Of that polluted prison where it breath'd:

1719. ACCENTS *hesi-*
tations. See line 566.
1720. ASSAYS *at-*
tempts.

Her contrite sighs unto the clouds be-
    queath'd
        Her winged sprite, and through her
            wounds doth fly
        Live's lasting date from cancell'd
            destiny.

1730   Stone-still, astonish'd with this deadly
            deed,
    Stood Collatine and all his lordly crew,
    Till Lucrece' father, that beholds her
        bleed,
    Himself on her self-slaught'red body
        threw;
    And from the purple fountain Brutus
        drew
1735   The murd'rous knife, and as it left
            the place,
        Her blood, in poor revenge, held it
            in chase;

    And bubbling from her breast, it doth di-
        vide
    In two slow rivers, that the crimson
        blood
    Circles her body in on every side,
1740   Who, like a late-sack'd island, vastly
        stood
    Bare and unpeopled in this fearful flood.
        Some of her blood still pure and red
            remain'd,
        And some look'd black, and that
            false Tarquin stain'd.

1728. SPRITE *spirit,
soul.*
1729. *her life's al-
lotted period of
time, now can-
celed by destiny.*
1730. ASTONISH'D
astounded.
1734. BRUTUS *See
Argument, line 24,
note.*
1740. WHO *which.*
VASTLY *desolate,
devasted. Shake-
speare does not use
the word elsewhere.*

About the mourning and congealed face
1745 Of that black blood a wat'ry rigoll goes,
Which seems to weep upon the tainted
place;
And ever since, as pitying Lucrece' woes,
Corrupted blood some watery token
shows,
And blood untainted still doth red
abide,
1750 Blushing at that which is so putre-
fi'd.

"Daughter, dear daughter!" old Lucretius
cries,
"That life was mine which thou hast here
depriv'd.
If in the child the father's image lies,
Where shall I live now Lucrece is un-
liv'd?
1755 Thou wast not to this end from me de-
riv'd.
If children predecease progenitors,
We are their offspring, and they none
of ours.

"Poor broken glass, I often did behold
In thy sweet semblance my old age new
born;
1760 But now that fair fresh mirror, dim and
old,
Shows me a bare-bon'd death by time outworn:
O, from thy cheeks my image thou hast
torn

1744. FACE *surface*.
1745. RIGOLL *circle*.
1752. DEPRIV'D
taken away.
1758. GLASS *looking
glass. See Sonnet 3,
lines 9–10*

And shiver'd all the beauty of my
    glass,
That I no more can see what once I
    was.

1765 "O time, cease thou thy course and last no
    longer,
If they surcease to be that should survive.
Shall rotten death make conquest of the
    stronger
And leave the falt'ring feeble souls alive?
The old bees die, the young possess their
    hive:
1770   Then live, sweet Lucrece, live again
        and see
        Thy father die, and not thy father
        thee!"

By this, starts Collatine as from a dream
And bids Lucretius give his sorrow place;
And then in key-cold Lucrece' bleeding
    stream
1775 He falls, and bathes the pale fear in his
    face,
And counterfeits to die with her a space;
    Till manly shame bids him possess
        his breath
    And live to be revenged on her death.

The deep vexation of his inward soul
1780 Hath serv'd a dumb arrest upon his
    tongue;
Who, mad that sorrow should his use con-
    trol

1763. SHIVER'D
shattered.
1766. SURCEASE
cease.
1774. KEY-COLD
cold as a key, a
phrase used of dead
bodies.
1776. COUNTERFEITS
TO DIE *lies in a*
swoon.

Or keep him from heart-easing words so
long,
Begins to talk; but through his lips do
throng
  Weak words, so thick come in his
  poor heart's aid
1785 That no man could distinguish what
  he said.

Yet sometime "Tarquin" was pronounced
plain,
But through his teeth, as if the name he
tore.
This windy tempest, till it blow up rain,
Held back his sorrow's tide to make it
more;
1790 At last it rains, and busy winds give o'er:
  Then son and father weep with equal
  strife
  Who should weep most, for daughter or for wife.

The one doth call her his, the other his,
Yet neither may possess the claim they
lay.
1795 The father says "She's mine." "O, mine
 she is,"
Replies her husband: "do not take away
My sorrow's interest; let no mourner say
  He weeps for her, for she was only
  mine,
  And only must be wail'd by Collatine."

1784. THICK
rapidly.

1800 "O," quoth Lucretius, "I did give that life
Which she too early and too late hath
spill'd."
"Woe, woe," quoth Collatine, "she was my
wife;
I ow'd her, and 'tis mine that she hath
kill'd."
"My daughter" and "my wife" with clamours fill'd
1805 The dispers'd air, who, holding Lucrece' life,
Answer'd their cries, "my daughter"
and "my wife."

Brutus, who pluck'd the knife from Lu-
crece' side,
Seeing such emulation in their woe,
Began to clothe his wit in state and pride,
1810 Burying in Lucrece' wound his folly's
show.
He with the Romans was esteemed so
As seely jeering idiots are with kings,
For sportive words and uttering fool-
ish things:

But now he throws that shallow habit by
1815 Wherein deep policy did him disguise,
And arm'd his long-hid wits advisedly
To check the tears in Collatinus' eyes.
"Thou wronged lord of Rome," quoth he,
"arise:
Let my unsounded self, suppos'd a
fool,

1801. LATE
recently.
1803. I OW'D HER
I owned her, that
is, she was mine.
1805. DISPERS'D
boundless. LIFE
spirit.
1810. FOLLY'S SHOW
appearance of folly.
1812. SEELY pitiful.
1813. SPORTIVE
merry.
1819. UNSOUNDED
unfathomed,
hitherto un-
revealed.

1820   Now set thy long-experienc'd wit to
              school.

"Why, Collatine, is woe the cure for woe?
  Do wounds help wounds, or grief help
    grievous deeds?
  Is it revenge to give thyself a blow
  For his foul act by whom thy fair wife
    bleeds?
1825 Such childish humour from weak minds
    proceeds:
      Thy wretched wife mistook the mat-
        ter so,
      To slay herself, that should have
        slain her foe.

"Courageous Roman, do not steep thy heart
  In such relenting dew of lamentations,
1830 But kneel with me and help to bear thy
    part
  To rouse our Roman gods with invoca-
    tions
  That they will suffer these abominations,
      Since Rome herself in them doth
        stand disgrac'd,
      By our strong arms from forth her
        fair streets chas'd.

1835 "Now, by the Capitol that we adore,
  And by this chaste blood so unjustly
    stain'd,
  By heaven's fair sun that breeds the fat
    earth's store,

1821. WHY *exclama-
tion of impatience.*
1837. FAT *rich,
fertile.* STORE
abundance.

By all our country rights in Rome maintain'd,
And by chaste Lucrece' soul that late complain'd
1840   Her wrongs to us, and by this bloody
knife,
We will revenge the death of this
true wife!"

This said, he struck his hand upon his
breast
And kiss'd the fatal knife to end his vow,
And to his protestation urg'd the rest,
1845   Who, wond'ring at him, did his words
allow:
Then jointly to the ground their knees
they bow;
And that deep vow which Brutus
made before
He doth again repeat, and that they
swore.

When they had sworn to this advised
doom,
1850   They did conclude to bear dead Lucrece
thence,
To show her bleeding body thorough
Rome,
And so to publish Tarquin's foul offence;
Which being done with speedy diligence,
The Romans plausibly did give consent
1855   To Tarquin's everlasting banish-
ment.

1838. COUNTRY
RIGHTS *rights of
our country.*
1845. ALLOW *ap-
prove.*
1849. ADVISED
DOOM *considered
judgment.*
1854. PLAUSIBLY
approvingly.

INDEX OF NAMES AND TITLES

INDEX OF TITLES AND FIRST LINES

Those lips that Love's own hand did make 157

Those parts of thee that the world's eye doth view 77

Those pretty wrongs that liberty commits 47

Thou art as tyrannous, so as thou art 143

Thou blind fool, Love, what dost thou to mine eyes 149

Thou canst not hit it, hit it, hit it 173

Three merry men be we 228

Thus can my love excuse the slow offence 57

Thus dost thou hear the Nemean lion roar 173

Thus far with rough and all unable pen 211

Thus is his cheek the map of days outworn 75

Thy bosom is endeared with all hearts 37

Thy gift, thy tables, are within my brain 131

Thy glass will show thee how thy beauties wear 85

Time's glory is to calm contending kings 473

Tir'd with all these, for restful death I cry 73

'Tis better to be vile than vile esteemed 131

To me, fair friend, you never can be old 113

To shallow rivers, to whose falls 213

To-morrow is Saint Valentine's day 241

Two households both alike in dignity 195

Two loves I have of comfort and despair 155

Under the greewood tree 215

Unthrifty loveliness, why dost thou spend 7

Up and down, up and down 189

VENUS AND ADONIS 343

Venus with young Adonis sitting by her 297

Was it the proud full sail of his great verse 93

Was this fair face the cause, quoth she 245

Weary with toil I haste me to my bed 33

Wedding is great Juno's crown 227

Were't aught to me I bore the canopy 135

What is love? 'tis not hereafter 229

What is your substance, whereof are you made 59

What potions have I drunk of Siren tears 129

What shall he have that kill'd the deer 223

What thou seest when thou dost wake 187

What's in the brain that ink may character 117

When Arthur first in court 203

When as thine eye hath chose the dame 307

When daffodils began to peer 267

When daisies pied and violets blue 181

When forty winters shall besiege thy brow 5

When griping griefs the heart doth wound 199

When I consider everything that grows 19

When I do count the clock that tells the time 15

When I have seen by Time's fell hand defaced 71

When icicles hang by the wall 183

When in disgrace with fortune and men's eyes 35

When in the chronicle of wasted time 115

When most I wink, then do mine eyes best see 49